The Last of the MOHICANS

JAMES FENIMORE COOPER

MARVEL ILLUSTRATED: LAST OF THE MOHICANS. Contains material originally published in magazine form as MARVEL ILLUSTRATED: LAST OF THE MOHICANS #1-6. First printing 2008. ISBN# 978-0-7851-
444-3. Published by MARVEL PUBLISHING, INC., a subsidiary of MARVEL ENTERTAINMENT, INC. OFFICE OF PUBLICATION: 417 5th Avenue, New York, NY 10016. Copyright © 2008 Marvel Characters, Inc.
l rights reserved. $14.99 per copy in the U.S. and $15.75 in Canada (GST #R127032852); Canadian Agreement #40668537. All characters featured in this issue and the distinctive names and likenesses
ereof, and all related indicia are trademarks of Marvel Characters, Inc. No similarity between any of the names, characters, persons, and/or institutions in this magazine with those of any living or dead
erson or institution is intended, and any such similarity which may exist is purely coincidental. Printed in the U.S.A. ALAN FINE, CEO Marvel Toys & Publishing Divisions and CMO Marvel Characters,
c.; DAVID GABRIEL, SVP of Publishing Sales & Circulation; DAVID BOGART, SVP of Business Affairs & Talent Management; MICHAEL PASCIULLO, VP of Merchandising & Communications; JIM O'KEEFE,
° of Operations & Logistics; DAN CARR, Executive Director of Publishing Technology; JUSTIN F. GABRIE, Director of Editorial Operations; SUSAN CRESPI, Editorial Operations Manager; OMAR OTIEKU,
oduction Manager; STAN LEE, Chairman Emeritus. For information regarding advertising in Marvel Comics or on Marvel.com, please contact Mitch Dane, Advertising Director, at mdane@marvel.com.
r Marvel subscription inquiries, please call 800-217-9158.

9 8 7 6 5 4 3 2 1

The Last of the MOHICANS

Last of the Mohicans
Adapted from the novel by James Fenimore Cooper

Writer: Roy Thomas
Penciler: Steve Kurth
Inker: Cam Smith
Colorist: June Chung

The Deerslayer
Adapted from the novel by James Fenimore Cooper

Writer: Roy Thomas
Artist: Denis Medri

Letterer: VC's Joe Caramagna
Cover Artists: Jo Chen, Alex Maleev, Jelena Kevic-Djurdjevic,
David Mack & Gerald Parel
Consulting Editor: John Barber
Assistant Editor: Lauren Sankovitch
Associate Editor: Nicole Boose
Editor: Ralph Macchio

Special Thanks to Luca Malisan, Chris Allo & Steve Kurth's parents, James & Marcy.

Collection Editor: Mark D. Beazley
Assistant Editors: John Denning & Cory Levine
Editor, Special Projects: Jennifer Grünwald
Senior Editor, Special Projects: Jeff Youngquist
Senior Vice President of Sales: David Gabriel
Book Design: Dave Barry, Dayle Chesler & Spring Hoteling
Vice President of Creative: Tom Marvelli

Editor in Chief: Joe Quesada
Publisher: Dan Buckley

I felt that, so far as possible, Cooper's own words should be used, merely pared down and choosing amongst phrases. It might've been simpler to recast his descriptions and dialogue in my own words, with syllables and syntax chosen that were easiest on the modern eye and ear. One example, which will suffice for many instances:

When, in an early scene, Chingachgook inquires of his newly-arrived son Uncas if any of their Indian enemies are around, he asks, "Do the Maquas dare to leave the print of their moccasins in these woods?" ("Maquas" being one of several terms used in the books for the Iroquois, who fight on the side of the French.)

It might be tempting to render that in more modern phraseology: "Are there any Maquas [or merely "Indians"] nearby?" But the poetic mode of speech is as intricate a part of *Mohicans* as is the action itself.

So, I merely added two words to underscore the relationship between Chingachgook and Uncas, and kept the sentence as it flowed from Cooper's feathered pen: "My son...do the Iroquois dare to leave the print of their moccasins in these woods?"

Why the change from "Maquas" to "Iroquois"? I felt there were so many names used in the novel for the same Native American groups, even if they weren't all totally synonymous, that I should keep it down to just a few. After all, we already had "Iroquois," "Hurons" (a branch of the Iroquois), and "Mingos" (the Delaware tribe's disparaging term for their hereditary foes).

Repeat the operation a thousand times—excising and rearranging words and actions, sometimes with a surgeon's knife, often with a butcher's cleaver, to turn a 400-page novel into a 130-page *graphic novel*—and you have both the challenge (and, to me, the *fun*) of adapting *The Last of the Mohicans* for *Marvel Illustrated*.

As for the 31-page adaptation of part of Cooper's *The Deerslayer* which follows *Mohicans*:

I was asked, early on, if I'd like to spin a yarn of Hawkeye's youth at that approximate length. Naturally, it would've been a lark to make up stories about the fabled scout, who must've had many more exploits that Cooper told in the five novels that make up what are often called "The Leatherstocking Saga"...but I felt the tale that should be told first was how Natty Bumppo acquired the nickname "Hawkeye," the most famous of the several monickers by which he was called over the years. Although written years after *Mohicans*, *The Deerslayer* is chronologically the earliest part of the epic, and it was an honor—tricky, but still an honor—to to tell that story in truncated form, in conjunction with the skilled young artist Denis Medri.

Who knows? Perhaps one day *The Deerslayer*, too, will be adapted in full in such a volume... and *The Pathfinder*, and *The Pioneers*, and finally even *The Prairie*, in which Hawkeye meets his valiant end.

But no need to talk of endings here. This is, rather, a beginning...both in American literature, and in the annals of *Marvel Illustrated*.

Roy Thomas

Roy Thomas started his career in comics as a writer and editor working with Stan Lee in the early days of the Marvel Age of Comics, where he scripted key runs in The X-Men, The Avengers, Fantastic Four, Daredevil, Amazing Spider-Man, Thor, Sub-Mariner, Dr. Strange, *and others. During the 1970s he wrote the first ten years of Marvel's* Conan the Barbarian *and* Savage Sword of Conan *and launched such series as* The Invaders, The Defenders, Warlock, Iron Fist, *and the revived X-Men. In the 1980s he developed* All-Star Squadron, Infinity Inc., *et al., for DC, and co-scripted the sword-and-sorcery films* Fire and Ice *and* Conan the Destroyer. *Over the years he has won numerous awards, including the Alley, Shazam, Eagle, Alfred, and Eisner. Roy and his wife Dann currently live in rural South Carolina, amid a mirthful menagerie of birds and beasts.*

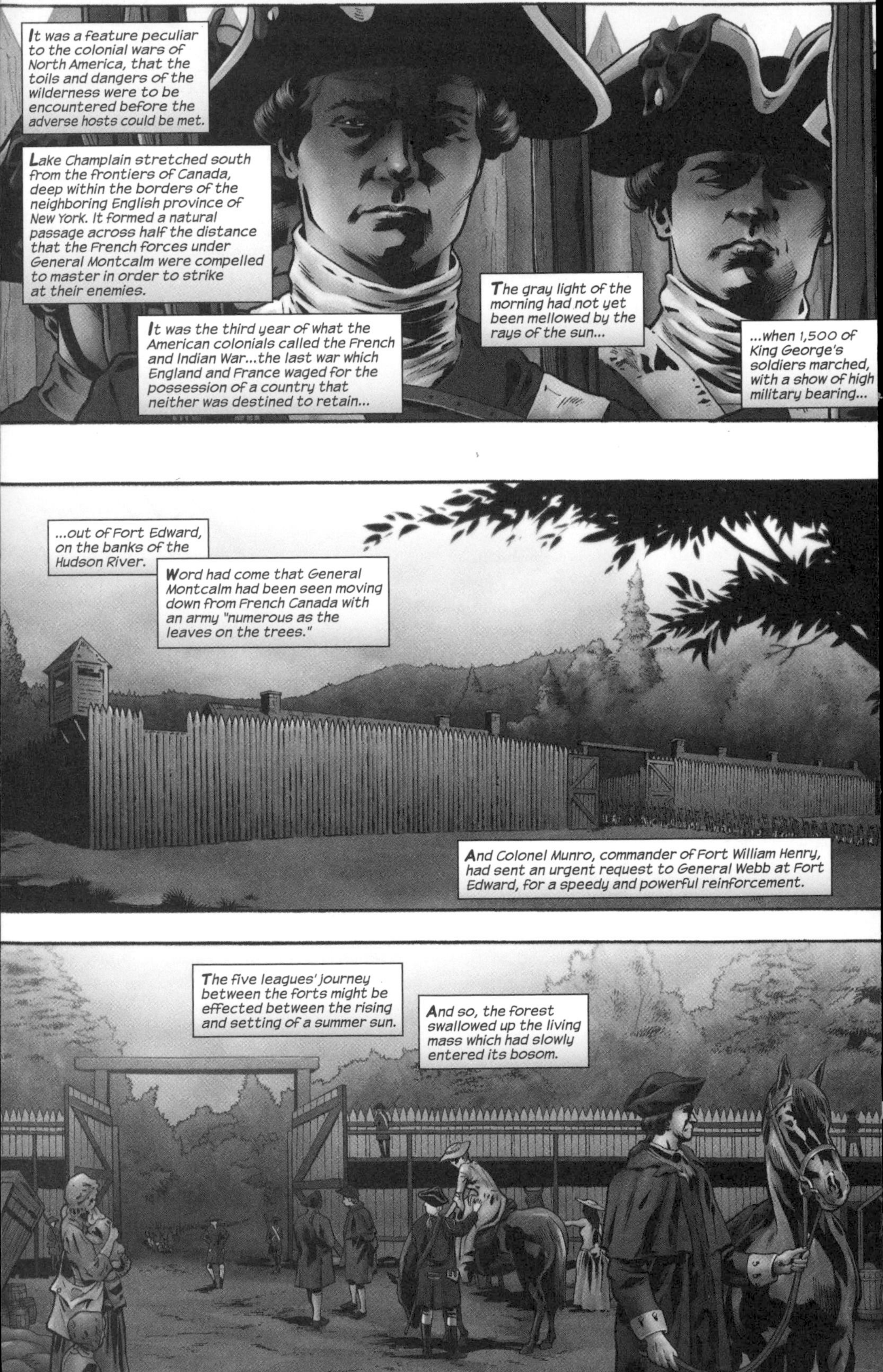
It was a feature peculiar to the colonial wars of North America, that the toils and dangers of the wilderness were to be encountered before the adverse hosts could be met.
Lake Champlain stretched south from the frontiers of Canada, deep within the borders of the neighboring English province of New York. It formed a natural passage across half the distance that the French forces under General Montcalm were compelled to master in order to strike at their enemies.
It was the third year of what the American colonials called the French and Indian War...the last war which England and France waged for the possession of a country that neither was destined to retain...
The gray light of the morning had not yet been mellowed by the rays of the sun...
...when 1,500 of King George's soldiers marched, with a show of high military bearing...
...out of Fort Edward, on the banks of the Hudson River.
Word had come that General Montcalm had been seen moving down from French Canada with an army "numerous as the leaves on the trees."
And Colonel Munro, commander of Fort William Henry, had sent an urgent request to General Webb at Fort Edward, for a speedy and powerful reinforcement.
The five leagues' journey between the forts might be effected between the rising and setting of a summer sun.
And so, the forest swallowed up the living mass which had slowly entered its bosom.

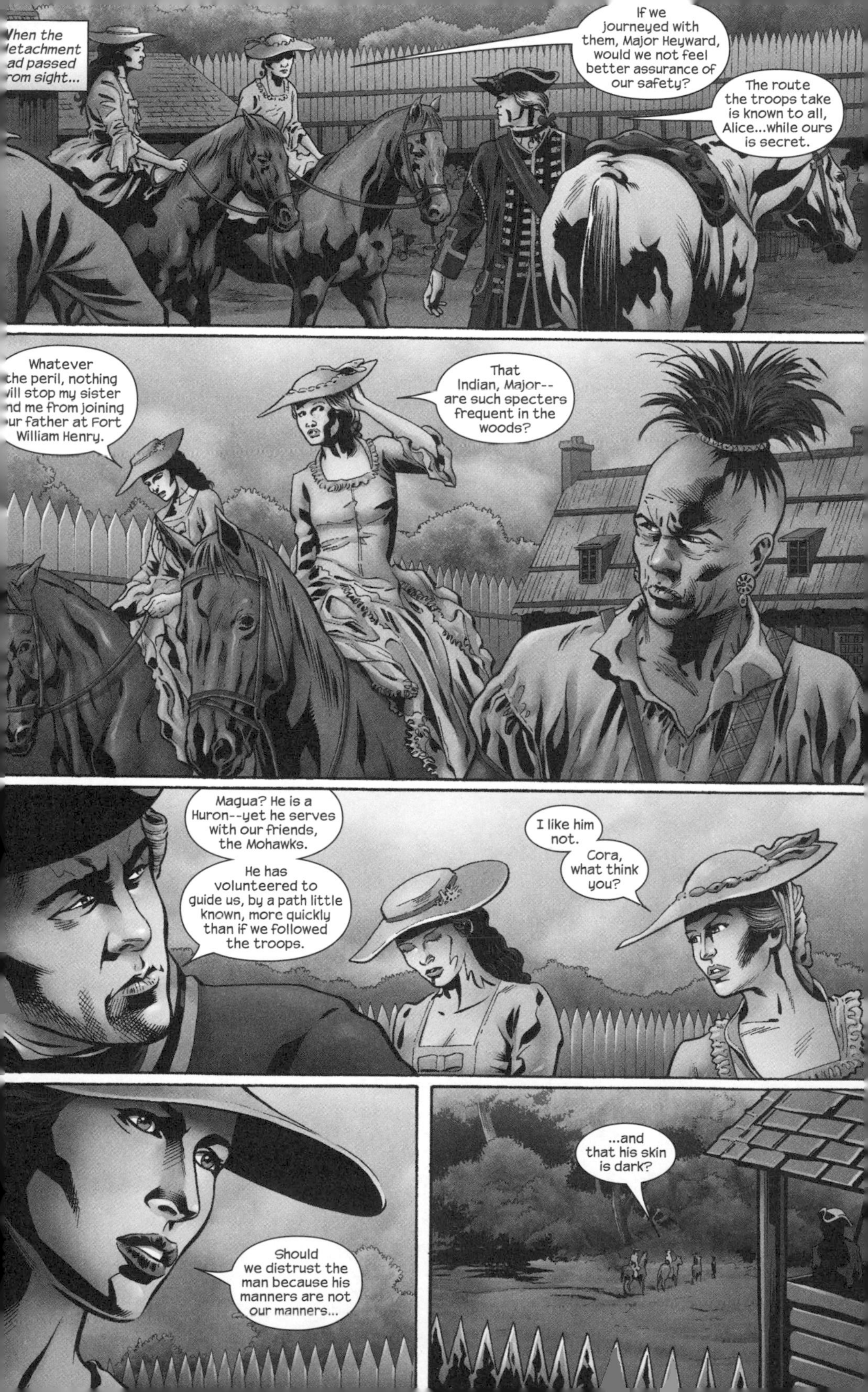
When the detachment had passed from sight...
If we journeyed with them, Major Heyward, would we not feel better assurance of our safety?
The route the troops take is known to all, Alice...while ours is secret.
Whatever the peril, nothing will stop my sister and me from joining our father at Fort William Henry.
That Indian, Major-- are such specters frequent in the woods?
Magua? He is a Huron--yet he serves with our friends, the Mohawks.
He has volunteered to guide us, by a path little known, more quickly than if we followed the troops.
I like him not.
Cora, what think you?
Should we distrust the man because his manners are not our manners...
...and that his skin is dark?

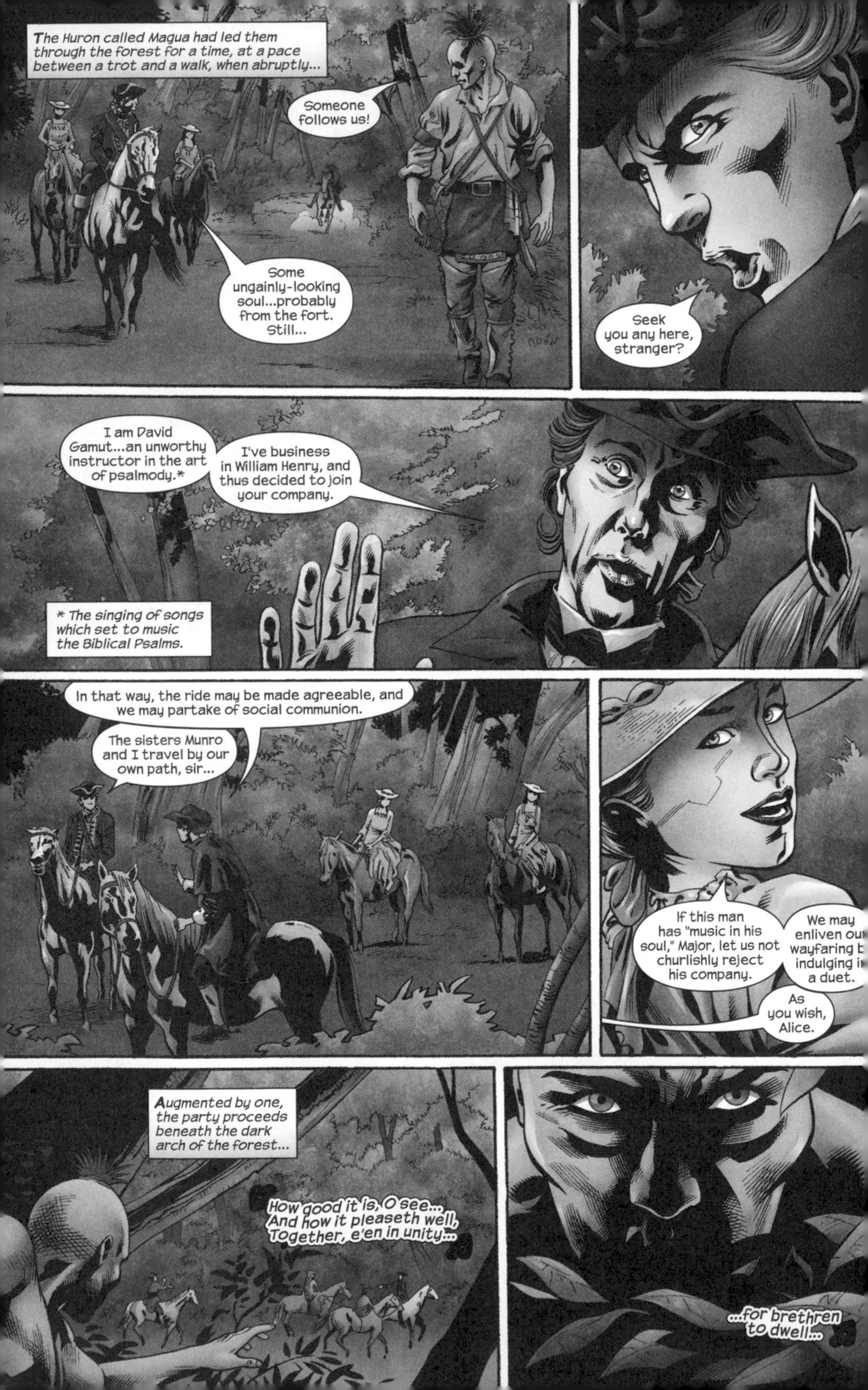

The Huron called Magua had led them through the forest for a time, at a pace between a trot and a walk, when abruptly...
Someone follows us!
Some ungainly-looking soul...probably from the fort. Still...
Seek you any here, stranger?
I am David Gamut...an unworthy instructor in the art of psalmody.*
I've business in William Henry, and thus decided to join your company.
* The singing of songs which set to music the Biblical Psalms.
In that way, the ride may be made agreeable, and we may partake of social communion.
The sisters Munro and I travel by our own path, sir...
If this man has "music in his soul," Major, let us not churlishly reject his company.
We may enliven ou wayfaring b indulging i a duet.
As you wish, Alice.
Augmented by one, the party proceeds beneath the dark arch of the forest...
How good it is, O see... And how it pleaseth well, Together, e'en in unity...
...for brethren to dwell...

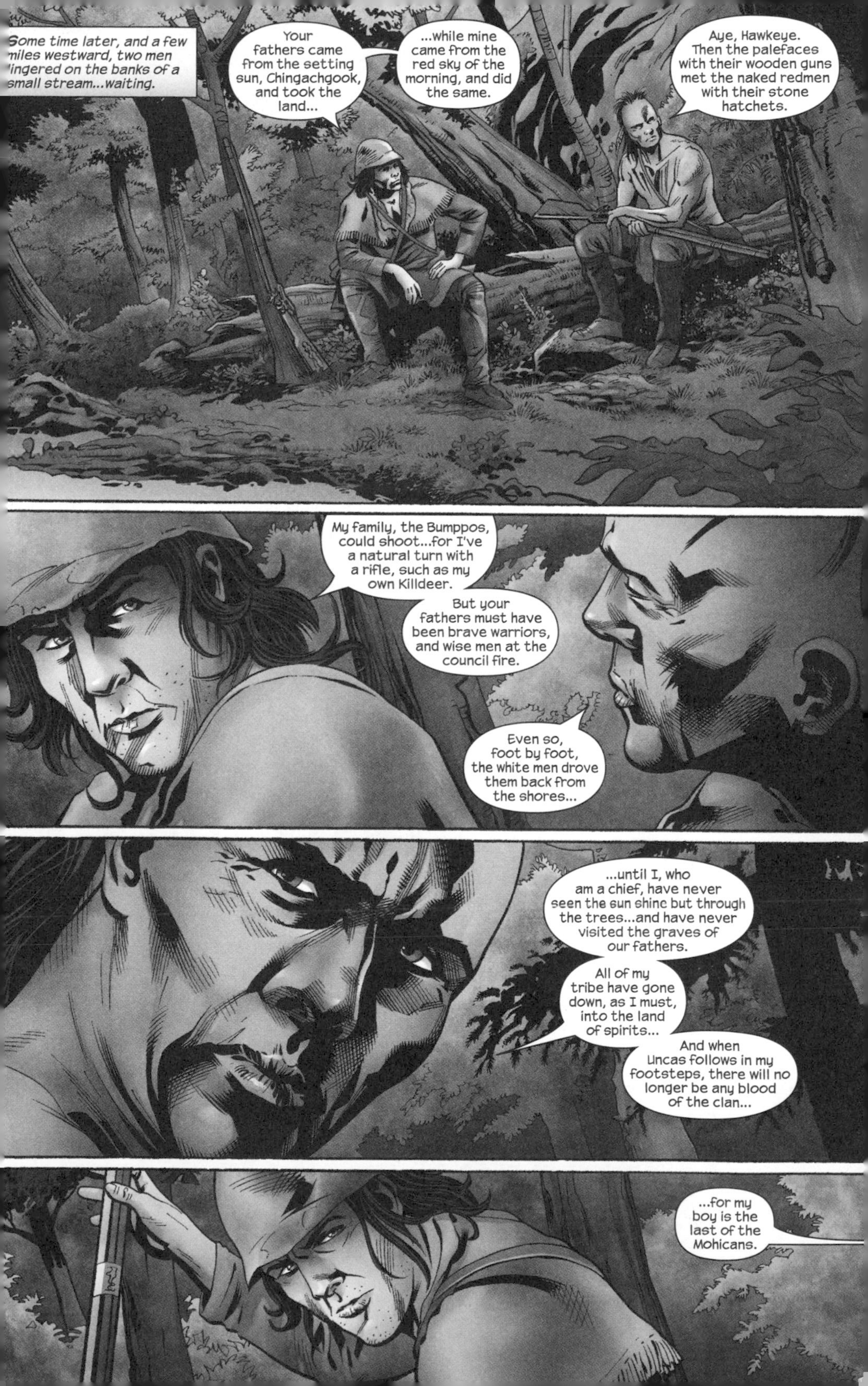
Some time later, and a few miles westward, two men lingered on the banks of a small stream...waiting.
Your fathers came from the setting sun, Chingachgook, and took the land...
...while mine came from the red sky of the morning, and did the same.
Aye, Hawkeye. Then the palefaces with their wooden guns met the naked redmen with their stone hatchets.
My family, the Bumppos, could shoot...for I've a natural turn with a rifle, such as my own Killdeer.
But your fathers must have been brave warriors, and wise men at the council fire.
Even so, foot by foot, the white men drove them back from the shores...
...until I, who am a chief, have never seen the sun shine but through the trees...and have never visited the graves of our fathers.
All of my tribe have gone down, as I must, into the land of spirits...
And when Uncas follows in my footsteps, there will no longer be any blood of the clan...
...for my boy is the last of the Mohicans.

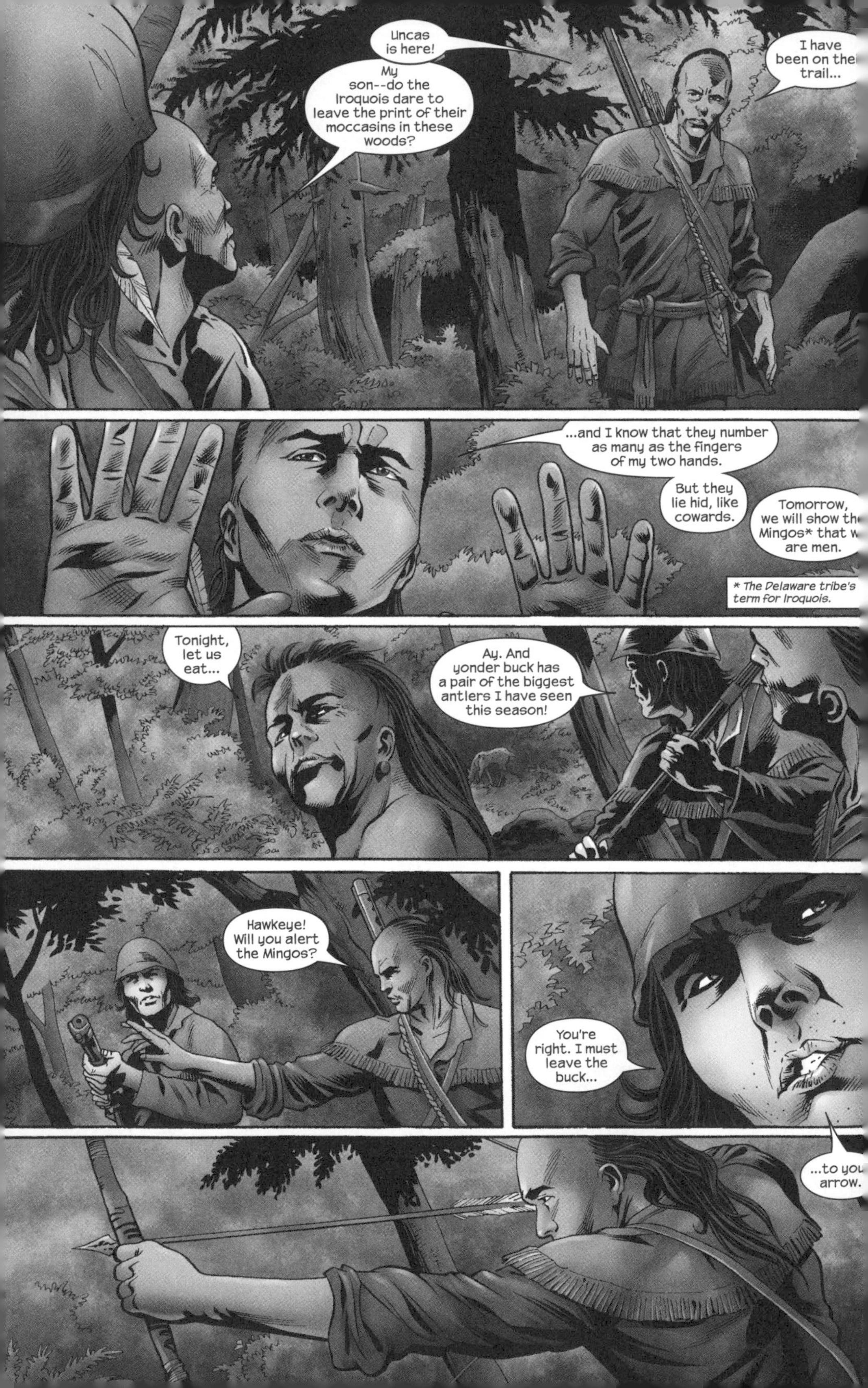
Uncas is here!
My son--do the Iroquois dare to leave the print of their moccasins in these woods?
I have been on the trail...
...and I know that they number as many as the fingers of my two hands.
But they lie hid, like cowards.
Tomorrow, we will show the Mingos* that we are men.
* The Delaware tribe's term for Iroquois.
Tonight, let us eat...
Ay. And yonder buck has a pair of the biggest antlers I have seen this season!
Hawkeye! Will you alert the Mingos?
You're right. I must leave the buck...
...to your arrow.

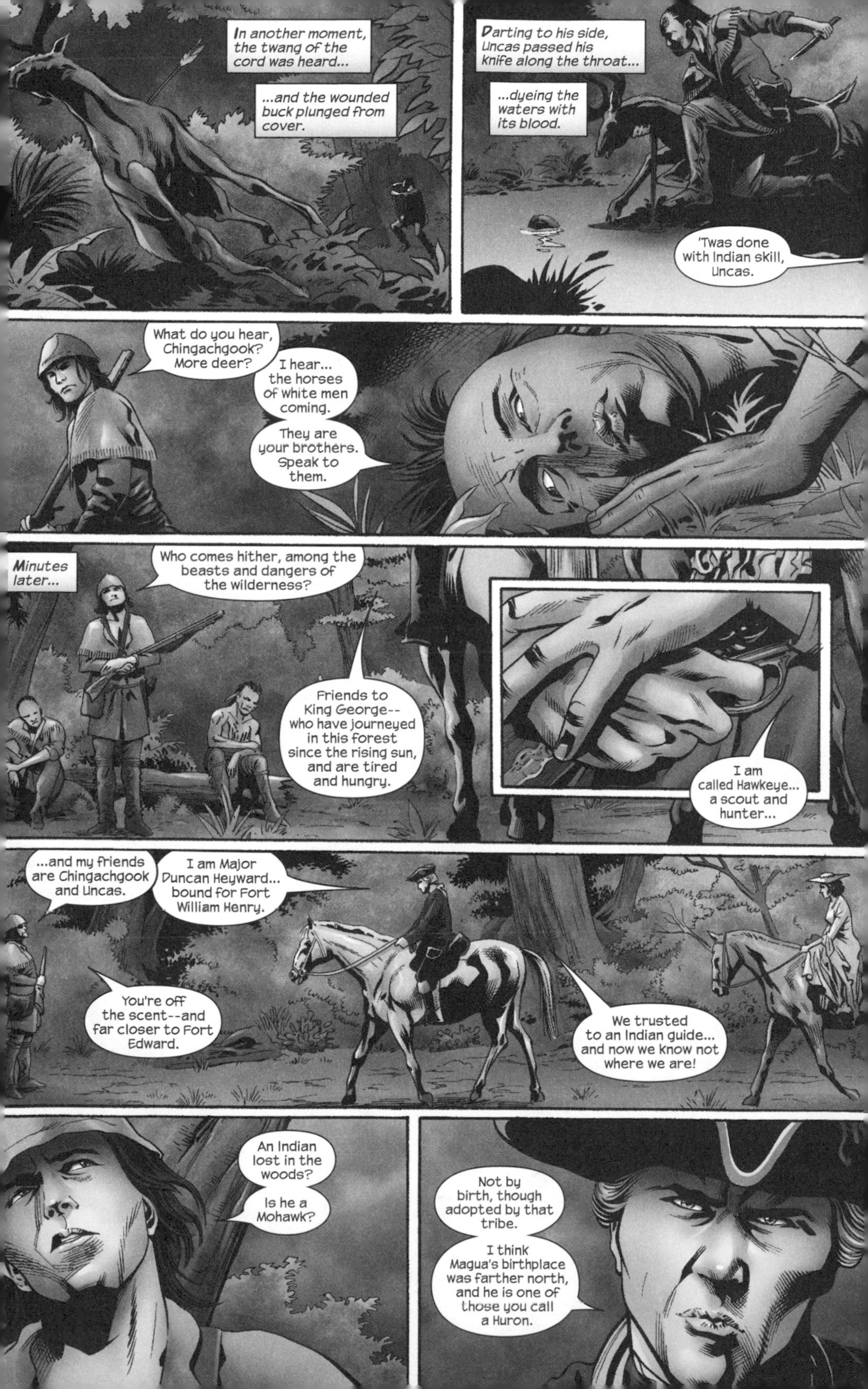
In another moment, the twang of the cord was heard...
...and the wounded buck plunged from cover.
Darting to his side, Uncas passed his knife along the throat...
...dyeing the waters with its blood.
'Twas done with Indian skill, Uncas.
What do you hear, Chingachgook? More deer?
I hear... the horses of white men coming.
They are your brothers. Speak to them.
Minutes later...
Who comes hither, among the beasts and dangers of the wilderness?
Friends to King George-- who have journeyed in this forest since the rising sun, and are tired and hungry.
I am called Hawkeye... a scout and hunter...
...and my friends are Chingachgook and Uncas.
I am Major Duncan Heyward... bound for Fort William Henry.
You're off the scent--and far closer to Fort Edward.
We trusted to an Indian guide... and now we know not where we are!
An Indian lost in the woods?
Is he a Mohawk?
Not by birth, though adopted by that tribe.
I think Magua's birthplace was farther north, and he is one of those you call a Huron.

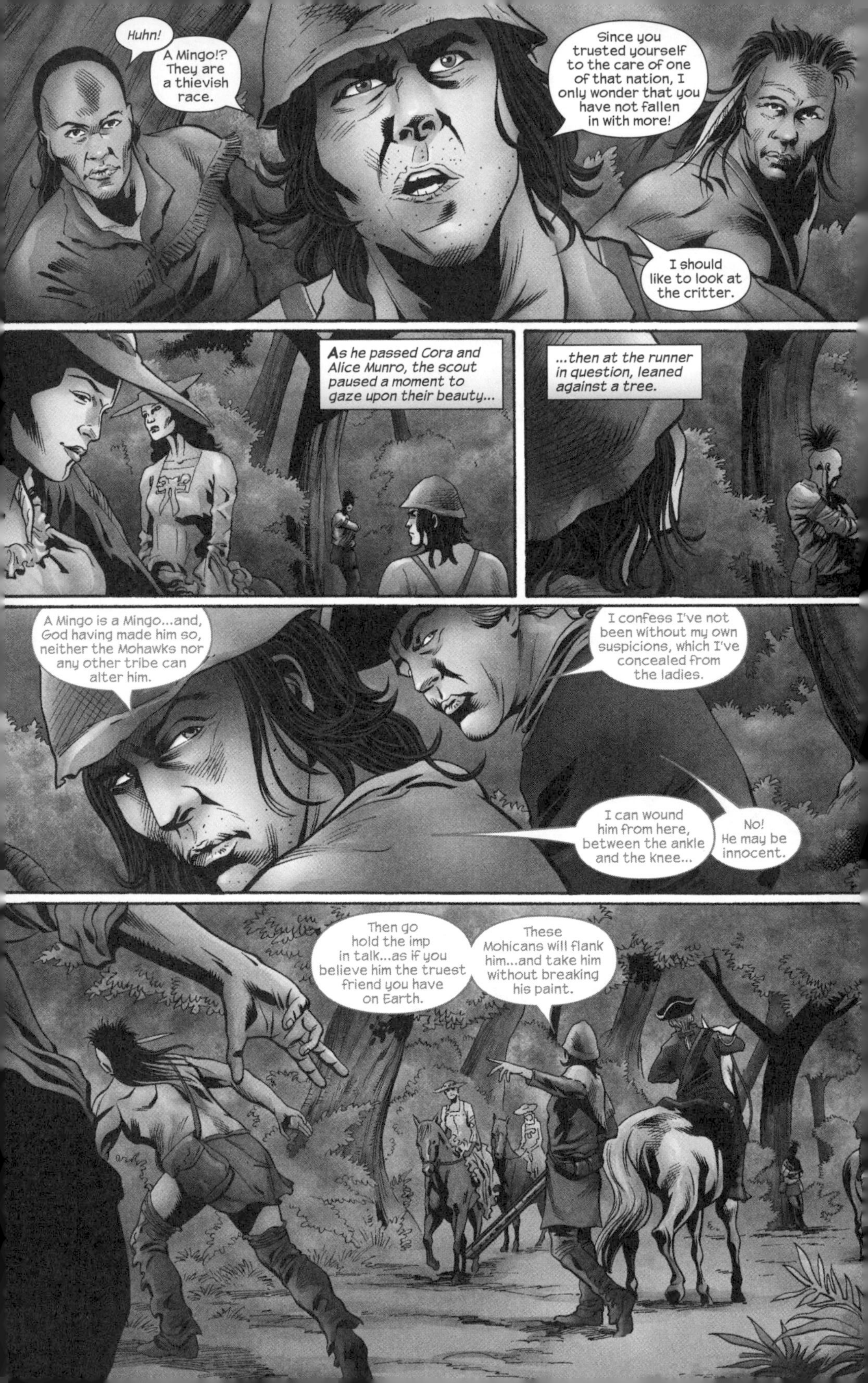
Huhn!
A Mingo!? They are a thievish race.
Since you trusted yourself to the care of one of that nation, I only wonder that you have not fallen in with more!
I should like to look at the critter.
As he passed Cora and Alice Munro, the scout paused a moment to gaze upon their beauty...
...then at the runner in question, leaned against a tree.
A Mingo is a Mingo...and, God having made him so, neither the Mohawks nor any other tribe can alter him.
I confess I've not been without my own suspicions, which I've concealed from the ladies.
I can wound him from here, between the ankle and the knee...
No! He may be innocent.
Then go hold the imp in talk...as if you believe him the truest friend you have on Earth.
These Mohicans will flank him...and take him without breaking his paint.

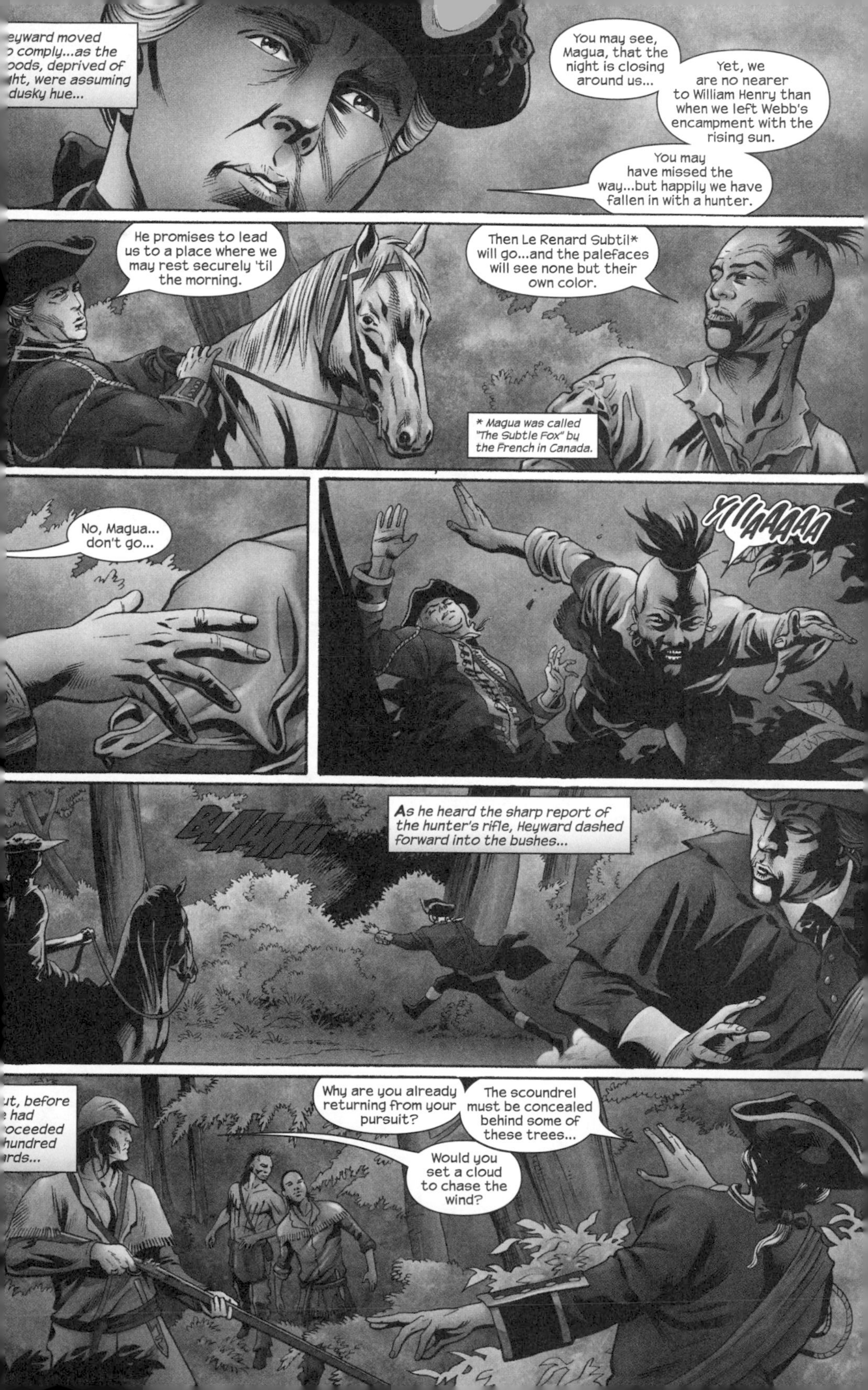
eyward moved
o comply...as the
oods, deprived of
ght, were assuming
dusky hue...
You may see, Magua, that the night is closing around us...
Yet, we are no nearer to William Henry than when we left Webb's encampment with the rising sun.
You may have missed the way...but happily we have fallen in with a hunter.
He promises to lead us to a place where we may rest securely 'til the morning.
Then Le Renard Subtil* will go...and the palefaces will see none but their own color.
* Magua was called "The Subtle Fox" by the French in Canada.
No, Magua... don't go...
YIIIAAAAA
BLAAAM
As he heard the sharp report of the hunter's rifle, Heyward dashed forward into the bushes...
ut, before
had
oceeded
hundred
rds...
Why are you already returning from your pursuit?
The scoundrel must be concealed behind some of these trees...
Would you set a cloud to chase the wind?

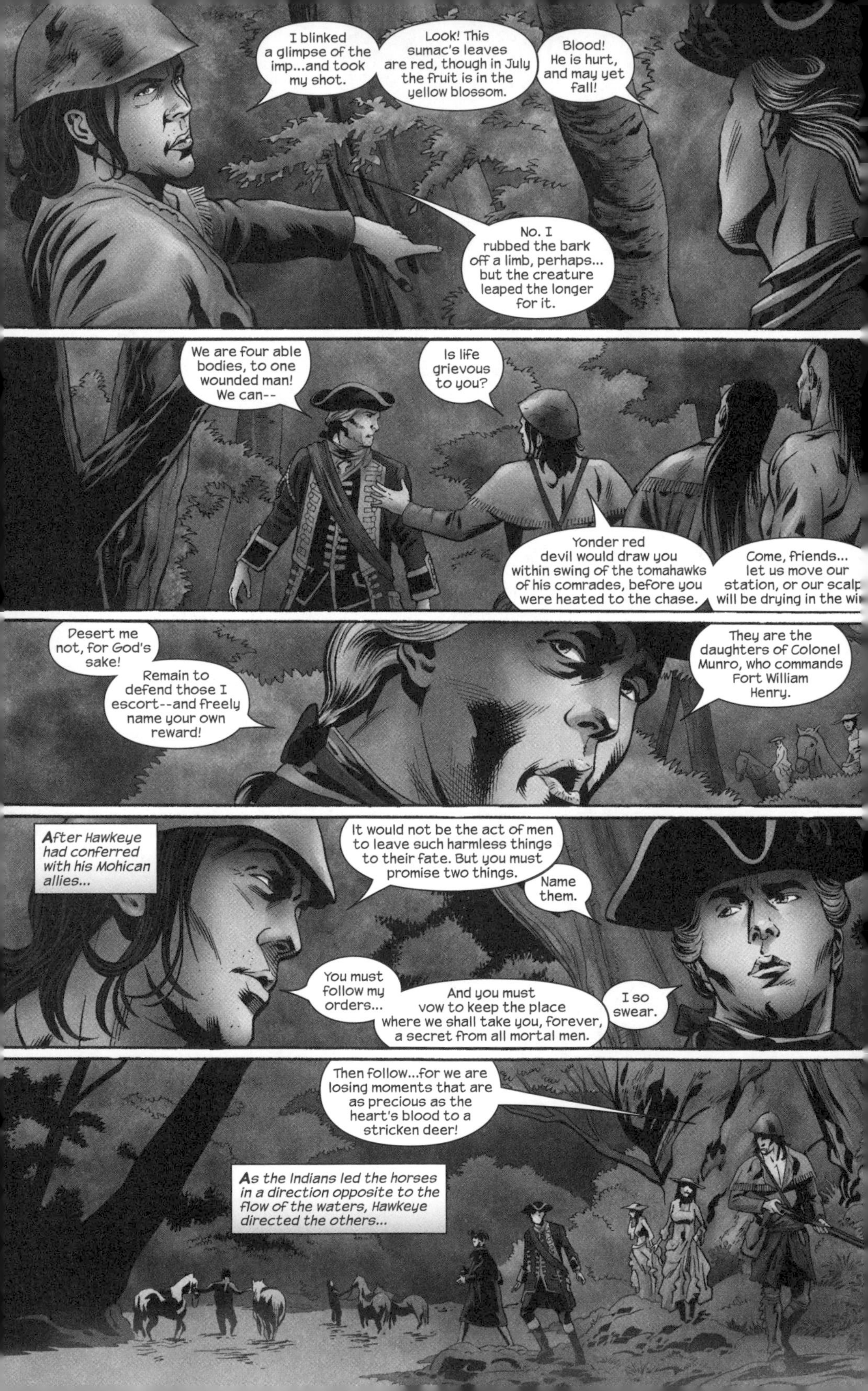
I blinked a glimpse of the imp...and took my shot.
Look! This sumac's leaves are red, though in July the fruit is in the yellow blossom.
Blood! He is hurt, and may yet fall!
No. I rubbed the bark off a limb, perhaps... but the creature leaped the longer for it.
We are four able bodies, to one wounded man! We can--
Is life grievous to you?
Yonder red devil would draw you within swing of the tomahawks of his comrades, before you were heated to the chase.
Come, friends... let us move our station, or our scalp will be drying in the wi
Desert me not, for God's sake!
Remain to defend those I escort--and freely name your own reward!
They are the daughters of Colonel Munro, who commands Fort William Henry.
After Hawkeye had conferred with his Mohican allies...
It would not be the act of men to leave such harmless things to their fate. But you must promise two things.
Name them.
You must follow my orders...
And you must vow to keep the place where we shall take you, forever, a secret from all mortal men.
I so swear.
Then follow...for we are losing moments that are as precious as the heart's blood to a stricken deer!
As the Indians led the horses in a direction opposite to the flow of the waters, Hawkeye directed the others...

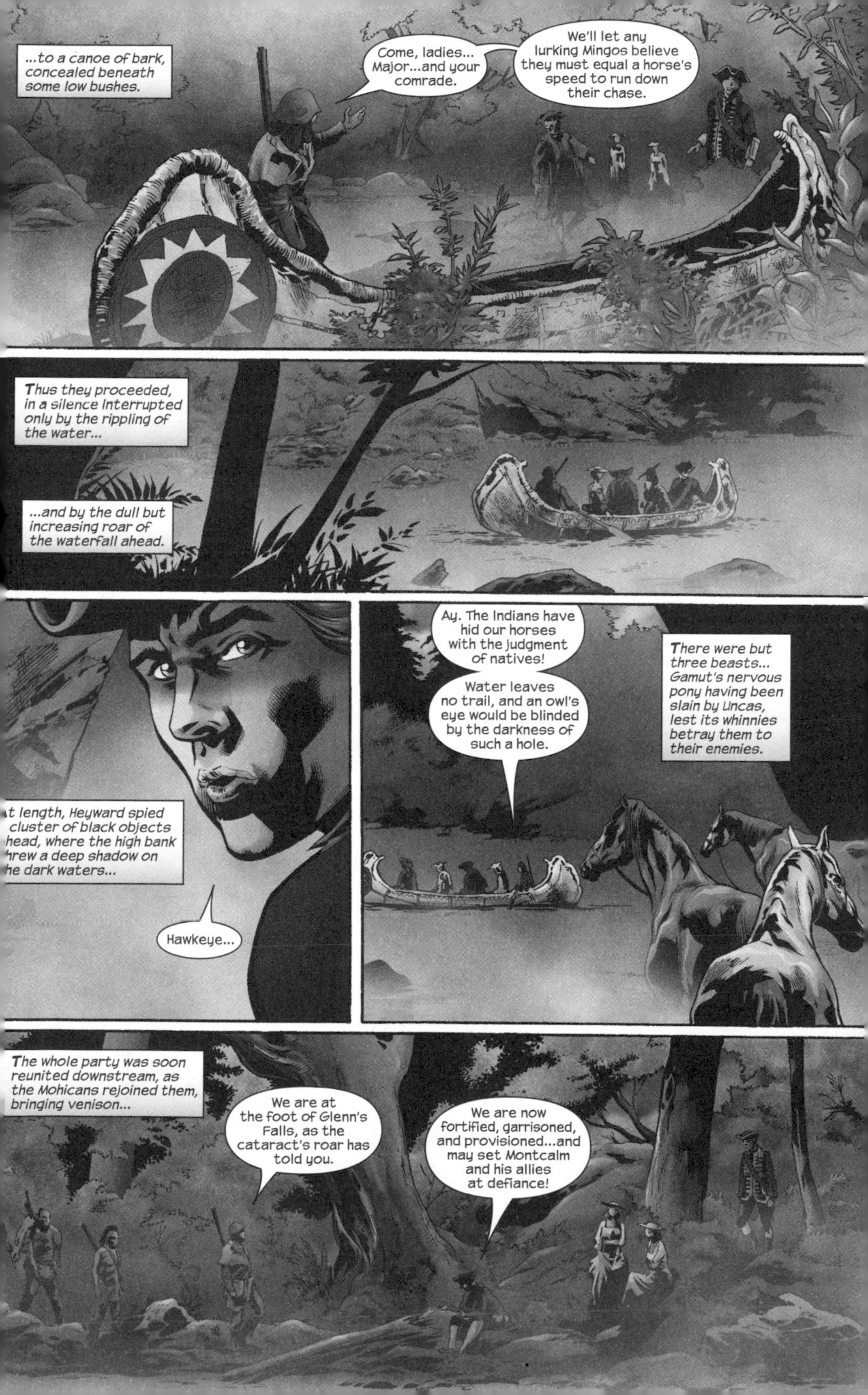

...to a canoe of bark, concealed beneath some low bushes.
Come, ladies... Major...and your comrade.
We'll let any lurking Mingos believe they must equal a horse's speed to run down their chase.
Thus they proceeded, in a silence interrupted only by the rippling of the water...
...and by the dull but increasing roar of the waterfall ahead.
t length, Heyward spied cluster of black objects head, where the high bank hrew a deep shadow on he dark waters...
Hawkeye...
Ay. The Indians have hid our horses with the judgment of natives!
Water leaves no trail, and an owl's eye would be blinded by the darkness of such a hole.
There were but three beasts... Gamut's nervous pony having been slain by Uncas, lest its whinnies betray them to their enemies.
The whole party was soon reunited downstream, as the Mohicans rejoined them, bringing venison...
We are at the foot of Glenn's Falls, as the cataract's roar has told you.
We are now fortified, garrisoned, and provisioned...and may set Montcalm and his allies at defiance!

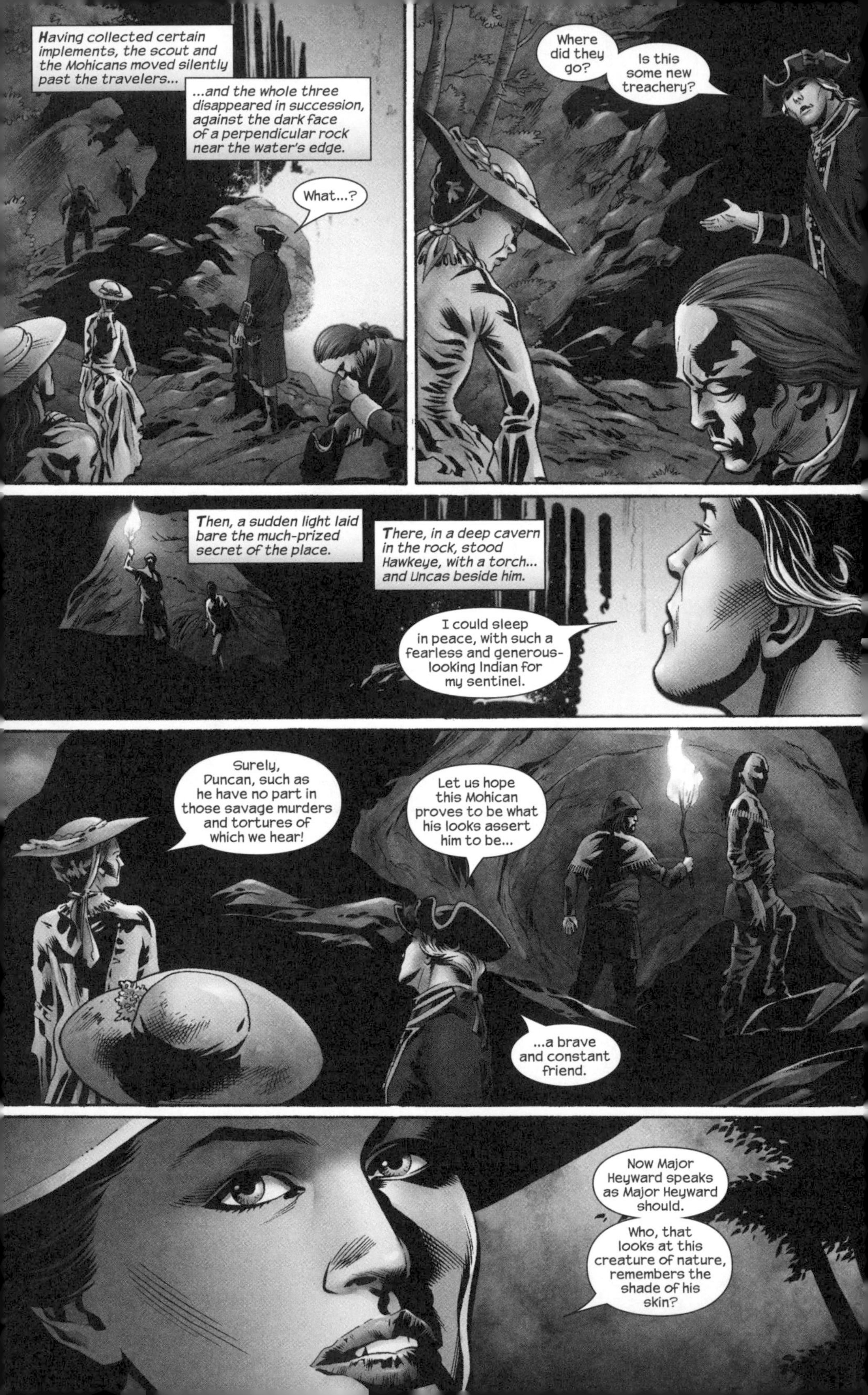
Having collected certain implements, the scout and the Mohicans moved silently past the travelers...
...and the whole three disappeared in succession, against the dark face of a perpendicular rock near the water's edge.
What...?
Where did they go?
Is this some new treachery?
Then, a sudden light laid bare the much-prized secret of the place.
There, in a deep cavern in the rock, stood Hawkeye, with a torch... and Uncas beside him.
I could sleep in peace, with such a fearless and generous-looking Indian for my sentinel.
Surely, Duncan, such as he have no part in those savage murders and tortures of which we hear!
Let us hope this Mohican proves to be what his looks assert him to be...
...a brave and constant friend.
Now Major Heyward speaks as Major Heyward should.
Who, that looks at this creature of nature, remembers the shade of his skin?

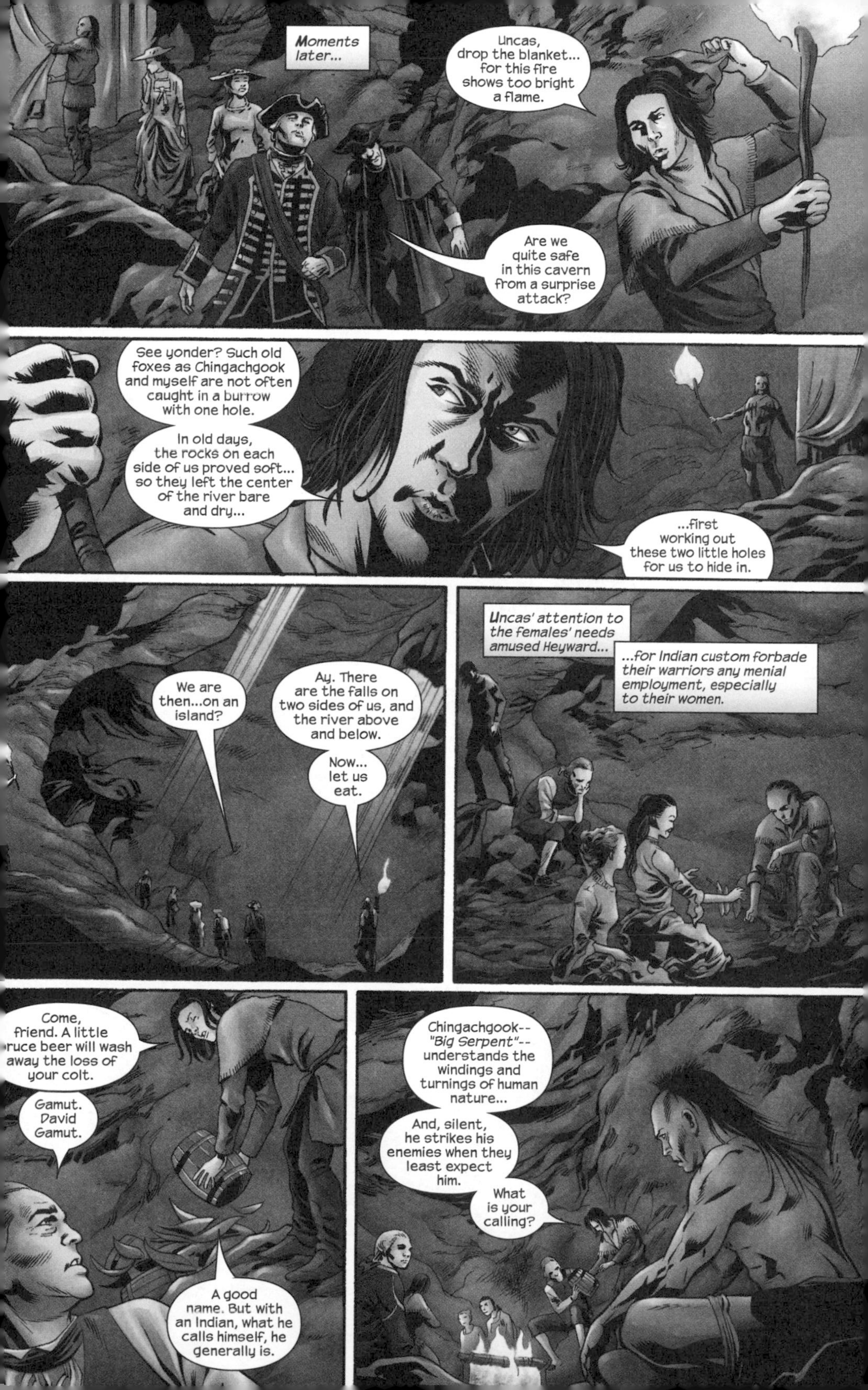
Moments later...
Uncas, drop the blanket... for this fire shows too bright a flame.
Are we quite safe in this cavern from a surprise attack?
See yonder? Such old foxes as Chingachgook and myself are not often caught in a burrow with one hole.
In old days, the rocks on each side of us proved soft... so they left the center of the river bare and dry...
...first working out these two little holes for us to hide in.
We are then...on an island?
Ay. There are the falls on two sides of us, and the river above and below.
Now... let us eat.
Uncas' attention to the females' needs amused Heyward...
...for Indian custom forbade their warriors any menial employment, especially to their women.
Come, friend. A little ruce beer will wash away the loss of your colt.
Gamut. David Gamut.
A good name. But with an Indian, what he calls himself, he generally is.
Chingachgook-- "Big Serpent"-- understands the windings and turnings of human nature...
And, silent, he strikes his enemies when they least expect him.
What is your calling?

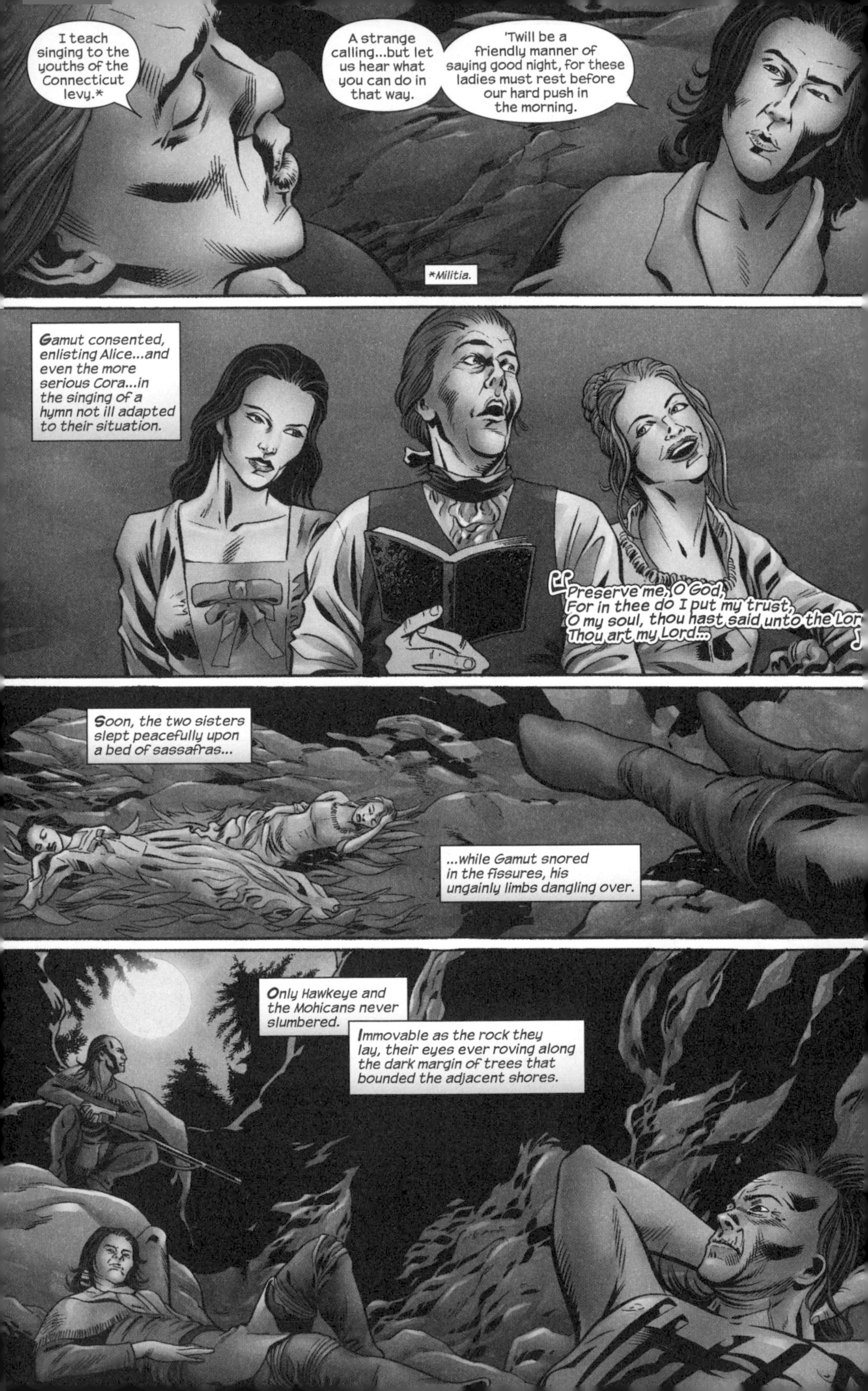
I teach singing to the youths of the Connecticut levy.*
A strange calling...but let us hear what you can do in that way.
'Twill be a friendly manner of saying good night, for these ladies must rest before our hard push in the morning.
*Militia.
Gamut consented, enlisting Alice...and even the more serious Cora...in the singing of a hymn not ill adapted to their situation.
Preserve me, O God,
For in thee do I put my trust,
O my soul, thou hast said unto the Lor
Thou art my Lord...
Soon, the two sisters slept peacefully upon a bed of sassafras...
...while Gamut snored in the fissures, his ungainly limbs dangling over.
Only Hawkeye and the Mohicans never slumbered.
Immovable as the rock they lay, their eyes ever roving along the dark margin of trees that bounded the adjacent shores.

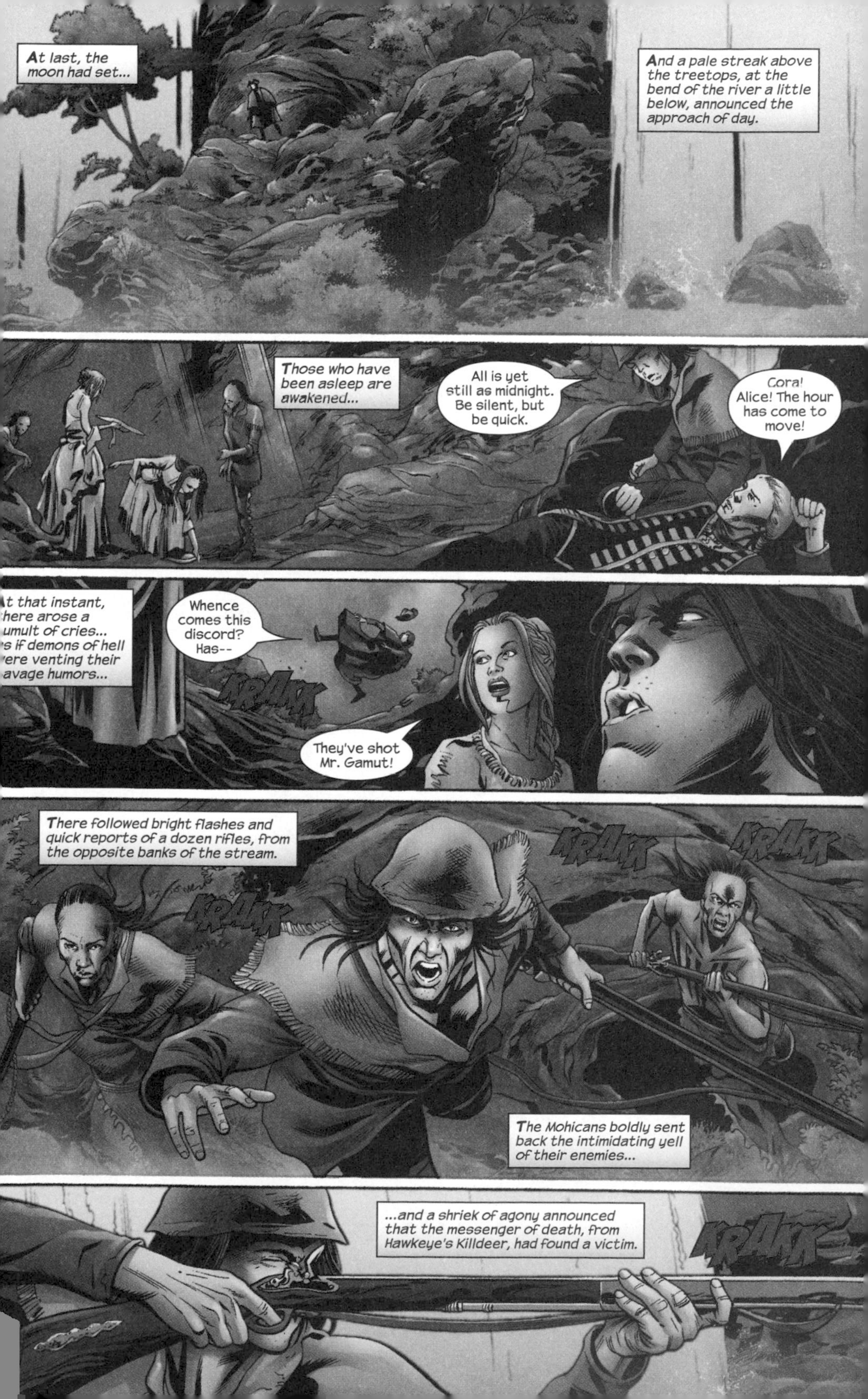
At last, the moon had set...
And a pale streak above the treetops, at the bend of the river a little below, announced the approach of day.
Those who have been asleep are awakened...
All is yet still as midnight. Be silent, but be quick.
Cora! Alice! The hour has come to move!
t that instant, here arose a umult of cries... s if demons of hell vere venting their avage humors...
Whence comes this discord? Has--
KRAKK
They've shot Mr. Gamut!
There followed bright flashes and quick reports of a dozen rifles, from the opposite banks of the stream.
KRAKK
KRAKK
KRAKK
The Mohicans boldly sent back the intimidating yell of their enemies...
...and a shriek of agony announced that the messenger of death, from Hawkeye's Killdeer, had found a victim.
KRAKK

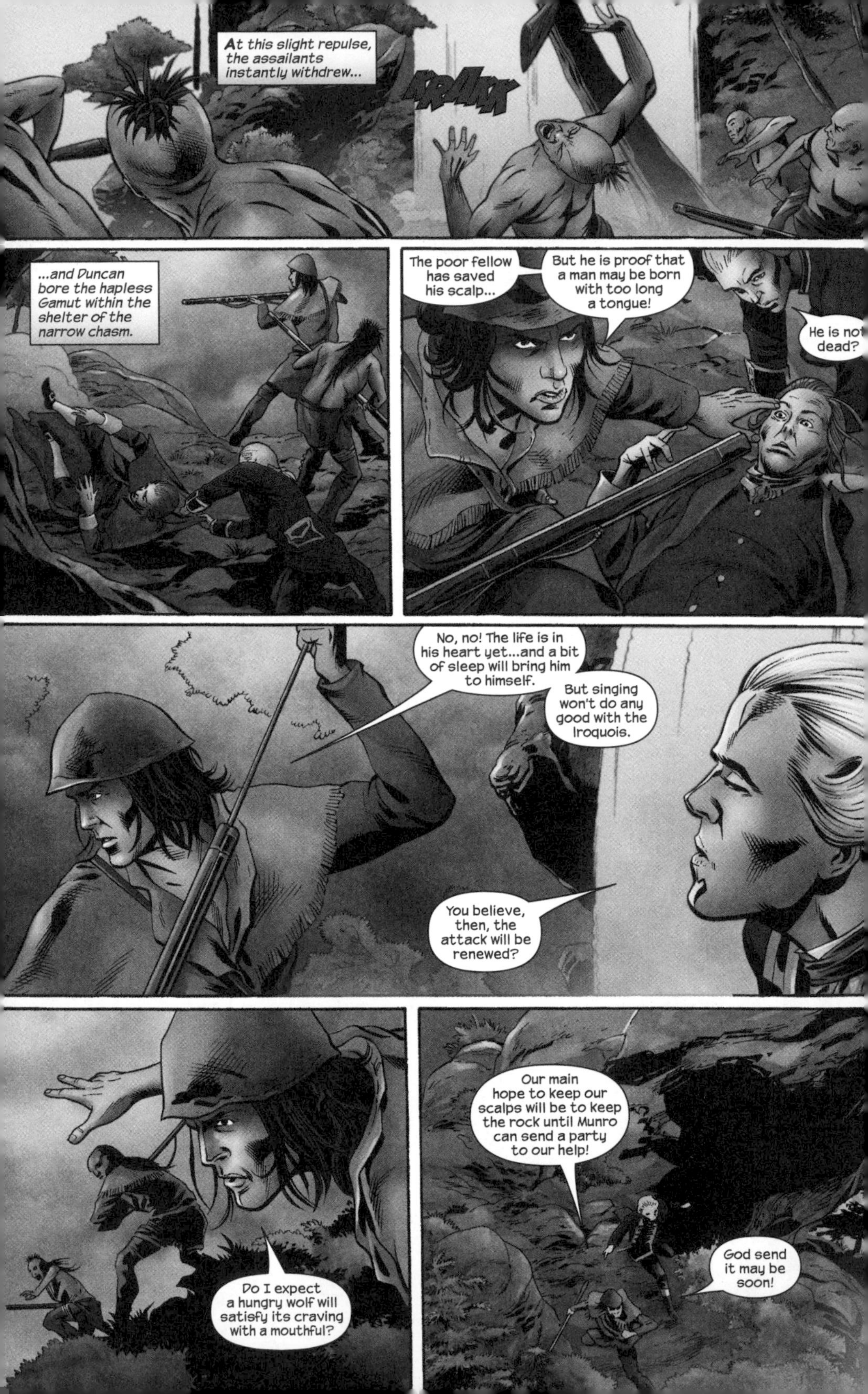
At this slight repulse, the assailants instantly withdrew...
KRAKK
...and Duncan bore the hapless Gamut within the shelter of the narrow chasm.
The poor fellow has saved his scalp...
But he is proof that a man may be born with too long a tongue!
He is not dead?
No, no! The life is in his heart yet...and a bit of sleep will bring him to himself.
But singing won't do any good with the Iroquois.
You believe, then, the attack will be renewed?
Do I expect a hungry wolf will satisfy its craving with a mouthful?
Our main hope to keep our scalps will be to keep the rock until Munro can send a party to our help!
God send it may be soon!

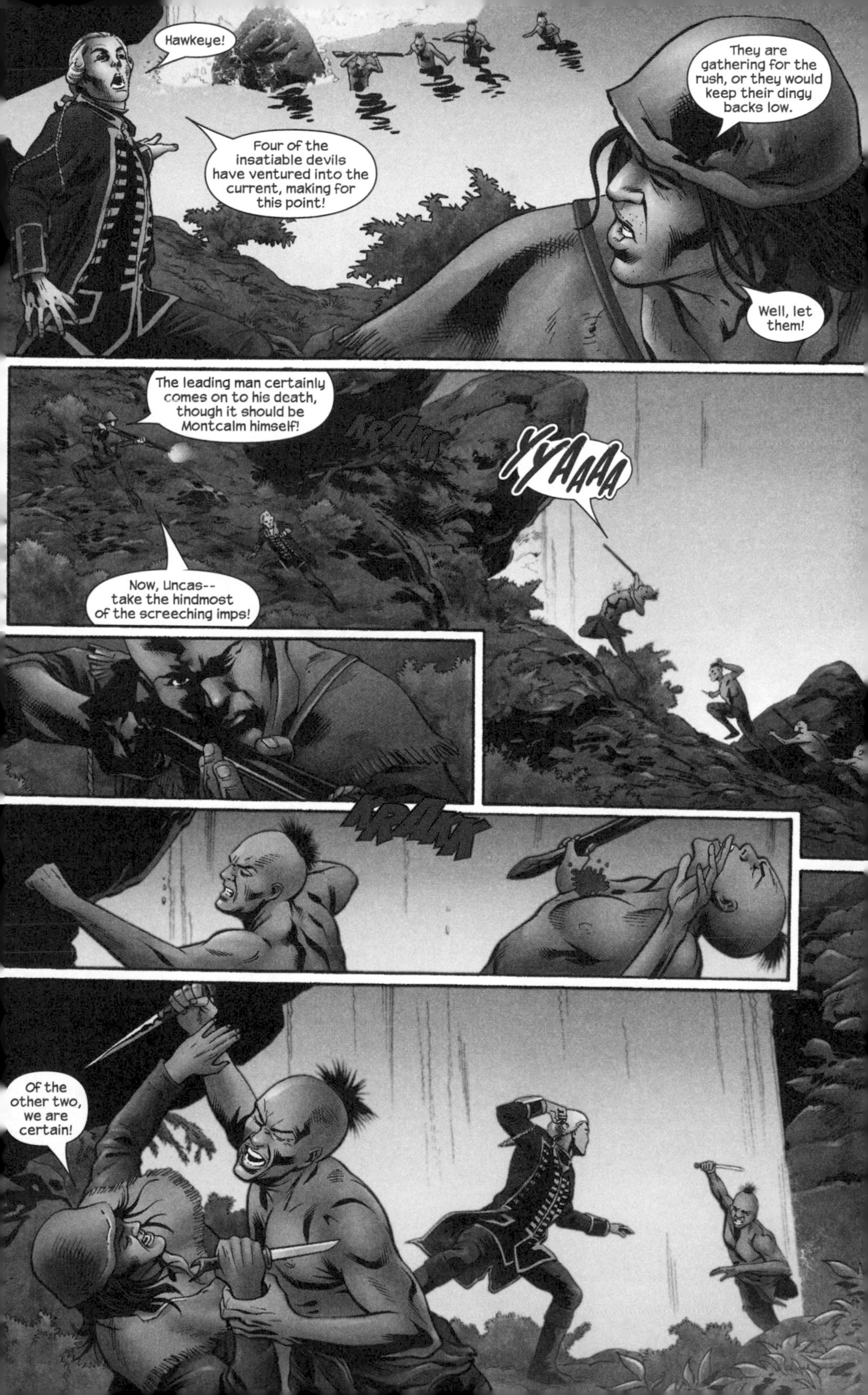
Hawkeye!
Four of the insatiable devils have ventured into the current, making for this point!
They are gathering for the rush, or they would keep their dingy backs low.
Well, let them!
The leading man certainly comes on to his death, though it should be Montcalm himself!
KRAKK
YYAAAA
Now, Uncas-- take the hindmost of the screeching imps!
KRAKK
Of the other two, we are certain!

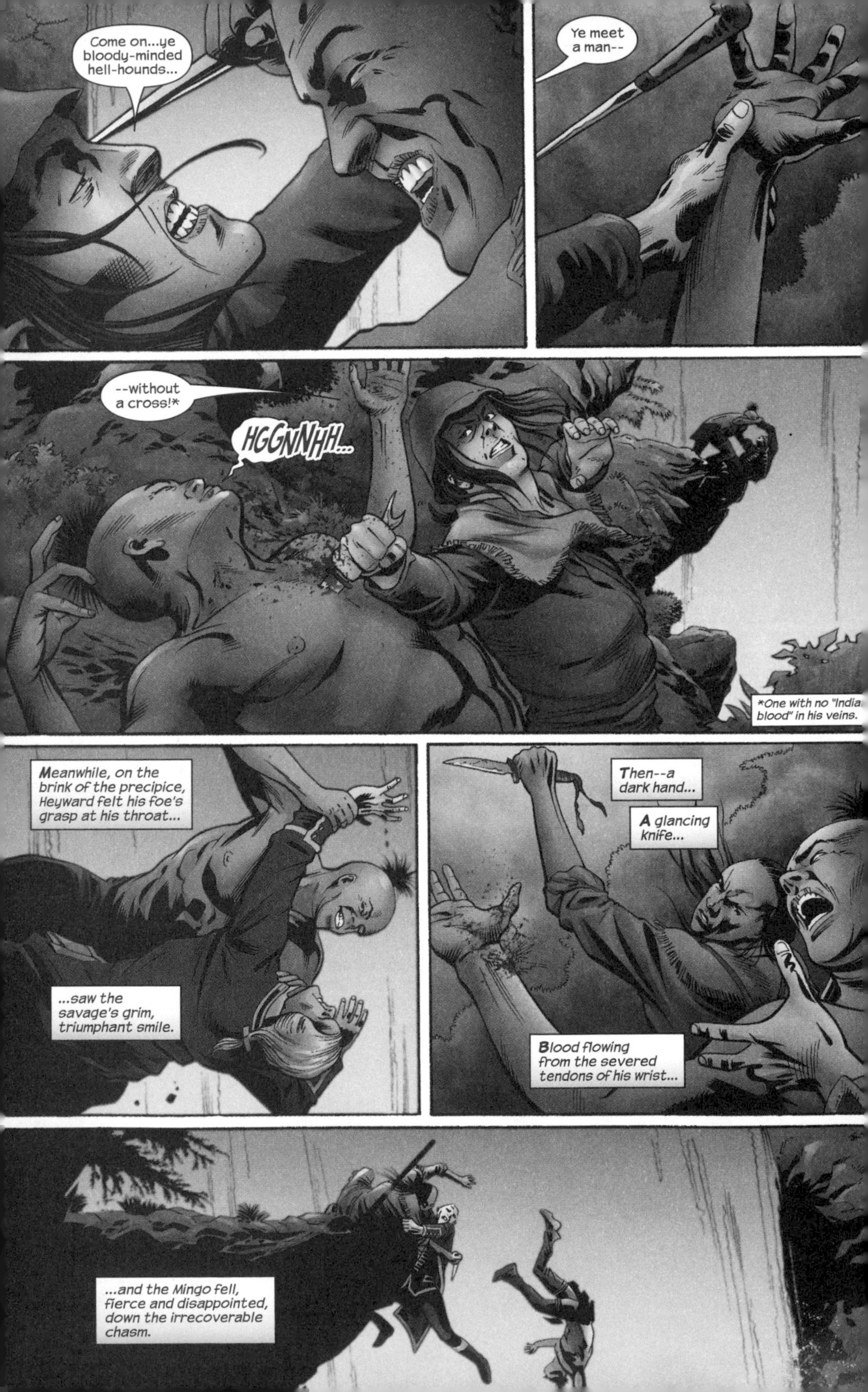
Come on...ye bloody-minded hell-hounds...
Ye meet a man--
--without a cross!*
HGGNNHH...
*One with no "India blood" in his veins.
Meanwhile, on the brink of the precipice, Heyward felt his foe's grasp at his throat...
...saw the savage's grim, triumphant smile.
Then--a dark hand...
A glancing knife...
Blood flowing from the severed tendons of his wrist...
...and the Mingo fell, fierce and disappointed, down the irrecoverable chasm.

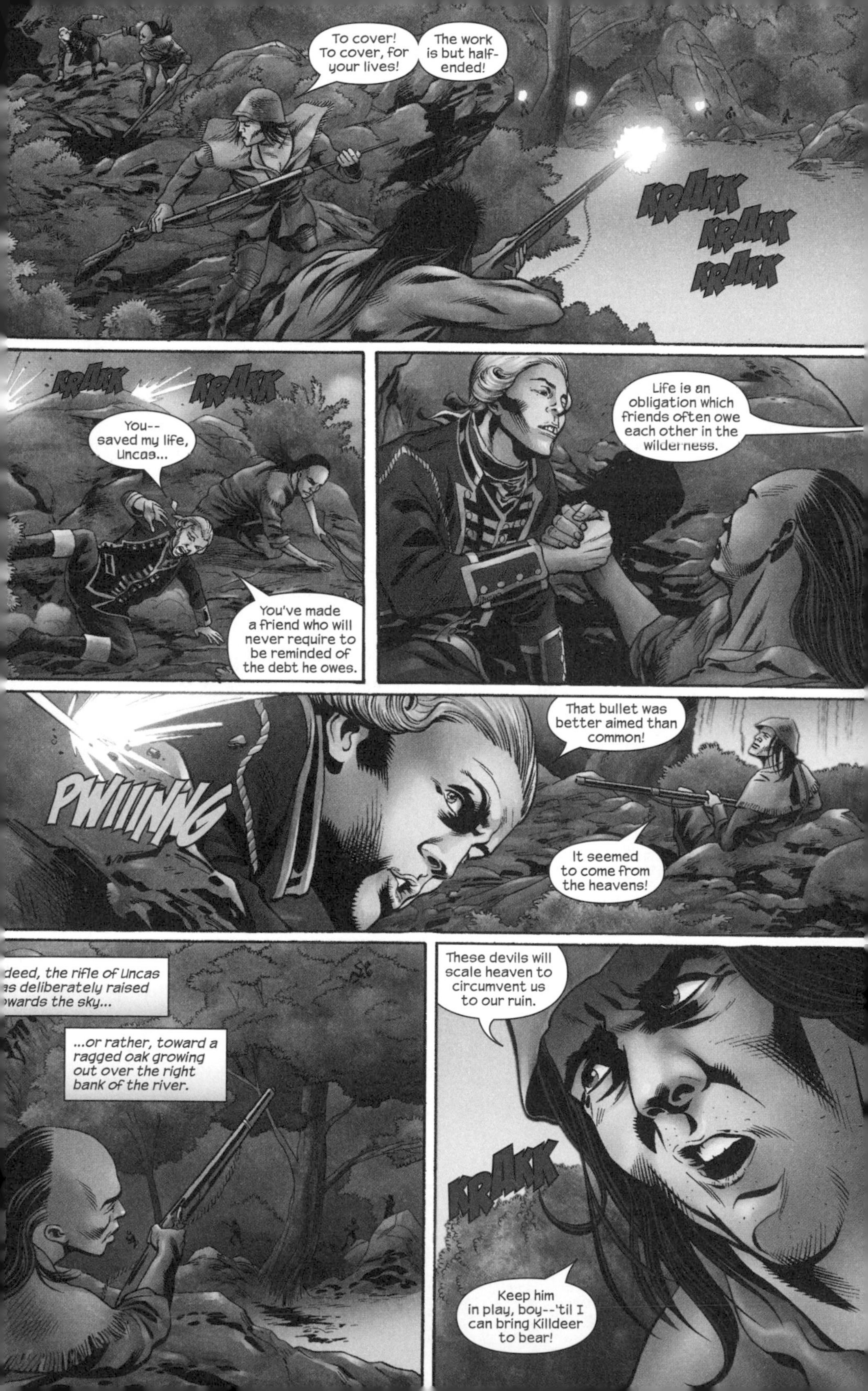
To cover! To cover, for your lives!
The work is but half-ended!
KRAKK KRAKK KRAKK
KRAKK KRAKK
You-- saved my life, Uncas...
You've made a friend who will never require to be reminded of the debt he owes.
Life is an obligation which friends often owe each other in the wilderness.
PWIIINNG
That bullet was better aimed than common!
It seemed to come from the heavens!
deed, the rifle of Uncas as deliberately raised owards the sky...
...or rather, toward a ragged oak growing out over the right bank of the river.
These devils will scale heaven to circumvent us to our ruin.
KRAKK
Keep him in play, boy--'til I can bring Killdeer to bear!

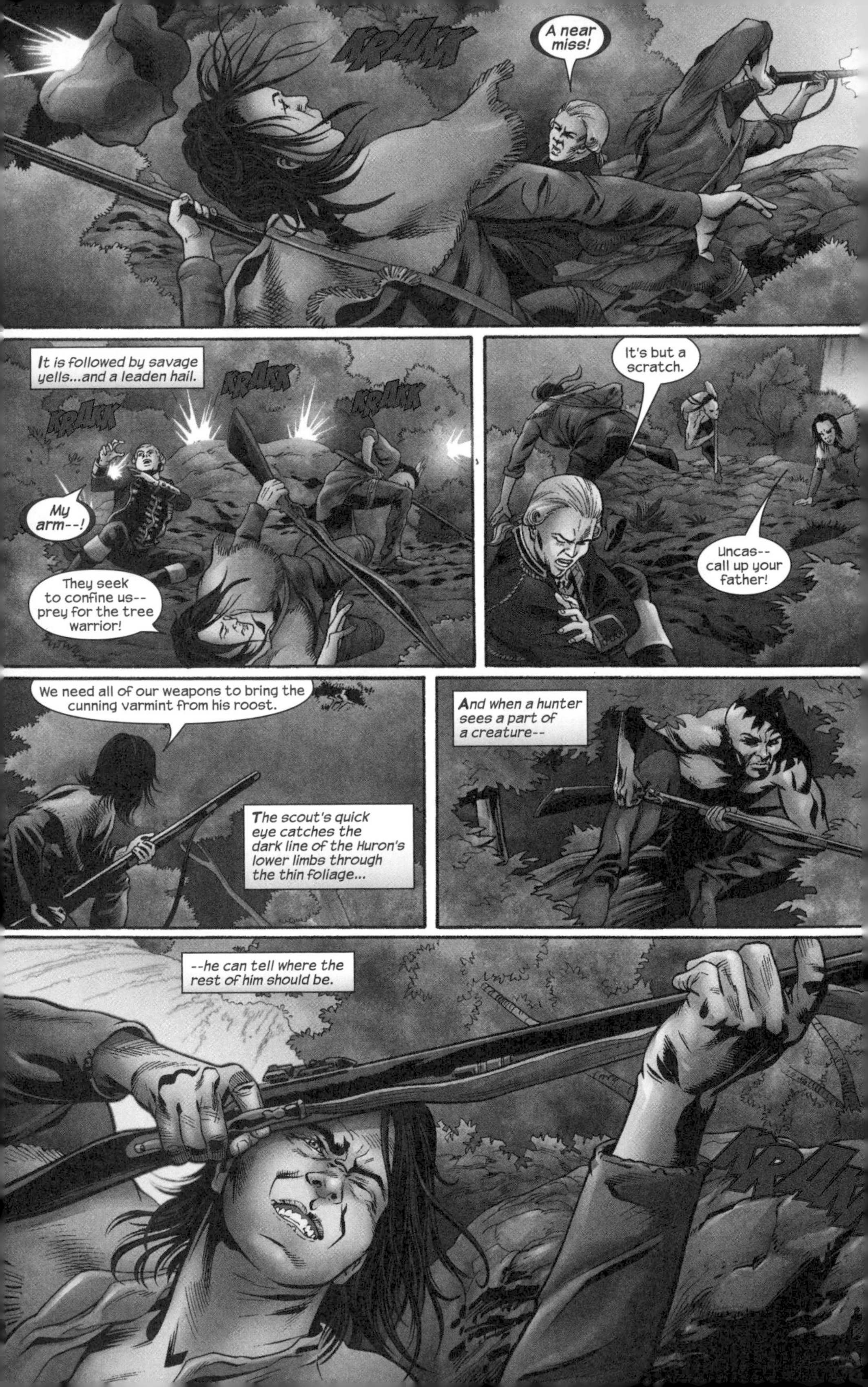
KRAKK
A near miss!
It is followed by savage yells...and a leaden hail.
KRAKK
KRAKK
KRAKK
My arm--!
They seek to confine us--prey for the tree warrior!
It's but a scratch.
Uncas--call up your father!
We need all of our weapons to bring the cunning varmint from his roost.
The scout's quick eye catches the dark line of the Huron's lower limbs through the thin foliage...
And when a hunter sees a part of a creature--
--he can tell where the rest of him should be.

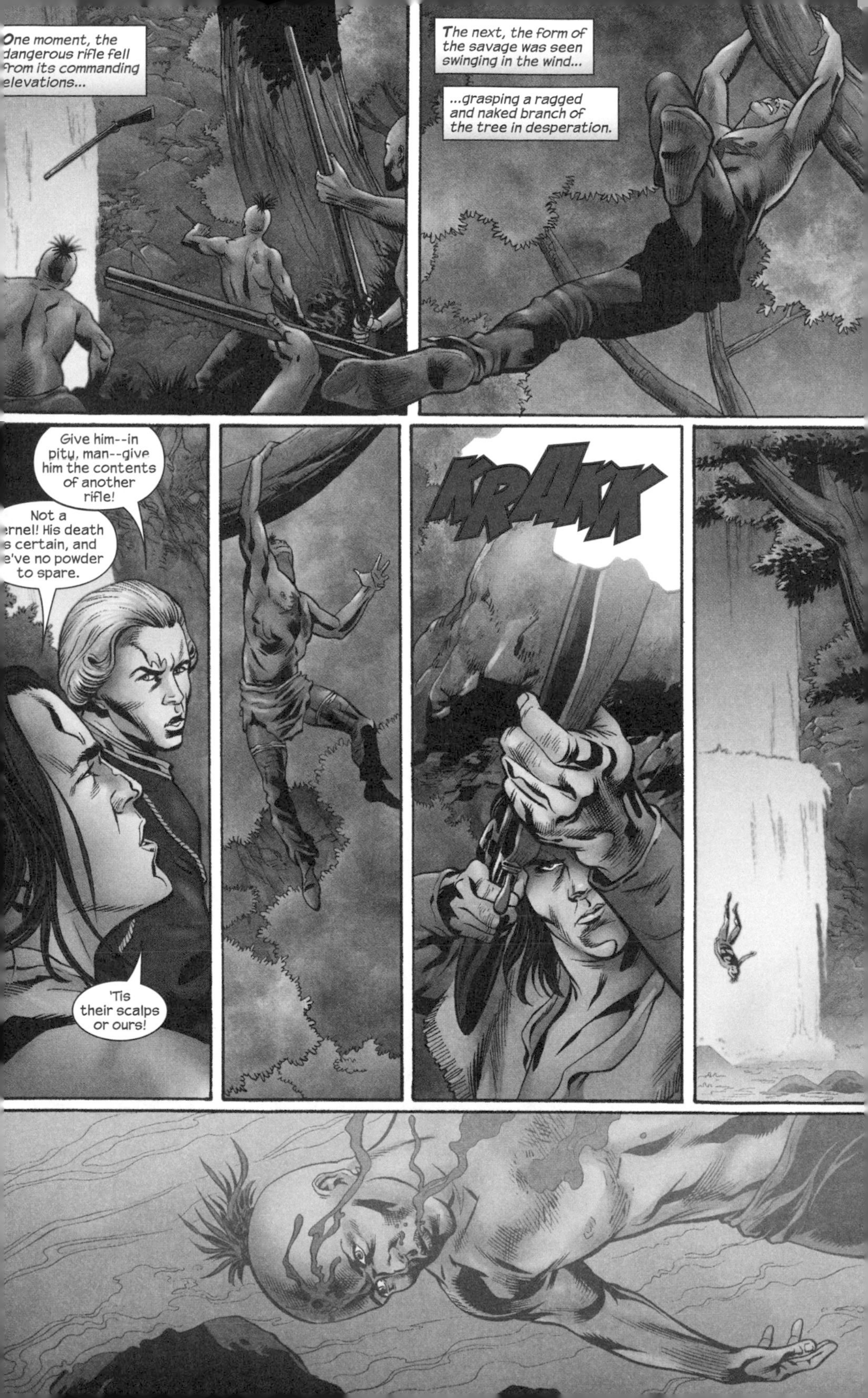
One moment, the dangerous rifle fell from its commanding elevations...
The next, the form of the savage was seen swinging in the wind...
...grasping a ragged and naked branch of the tree in desperation.
Give him--in pity, man--give him the contents of another rifle!
Not a ernel! His death s certain, and e've no powder to spare.
'Tis their scalps or ours!
KRAKK

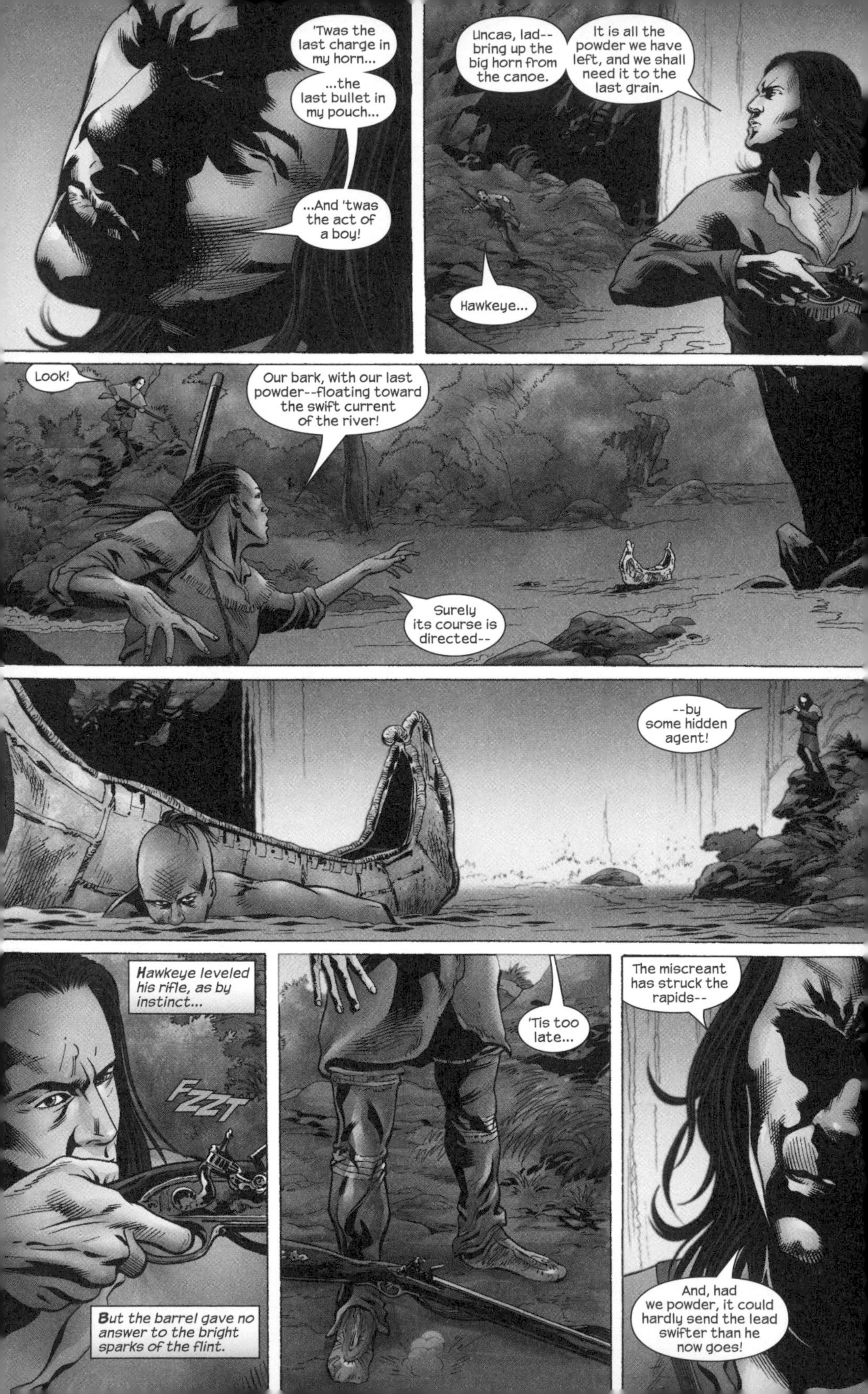
'Twas the last charge in my horn...
...the last bullet in my pouch...
...And 'twas the act of a boy!
Hawkeye...
Uncas, lad-- bring up the big horn from the canoe.
It is all the powder we have left, and we shall need it to the last grain.
Look!
Our bark, with our last powder--floating toward the swift current of the river!
Surely its course is directed--
--by some hidden agent!
Hawkeye leveled his rifle, as by instinct...
FZZT
But the barrel gave no answer to the bright sparks of the flint.
'Tis too late...
The miscreant has struck the rapids--
And, had we powder, it could hardly send the lead swifter than he now goes!

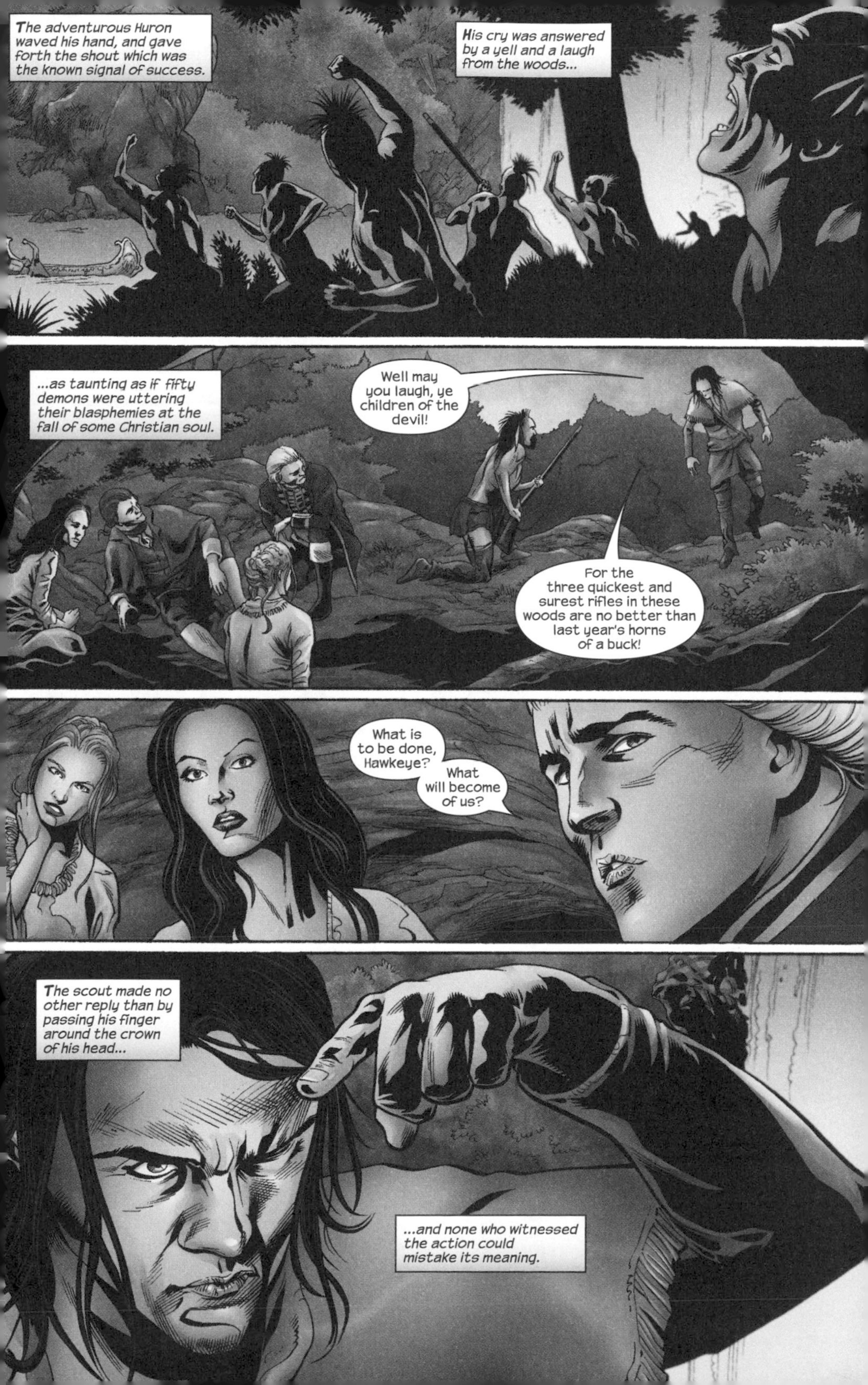
The adventurous Huron waved his hand, and gave forth the shout which was the known signal of success.
His cry was answered by a yell and a laugh from the woods...
...as taunting as if fifty demons were uttering their blasphemies at the fall of some Christian soul.
Well may you laugh, ye children of the devil!
For the three quickest and surest rifles in these woods are no better than last year's horns of a buck!
What is to be done, Hawkeye?
What will become of us?
The scout made no other reply than by passing his finger around the crown of his head...
...and none who witnessed the action could mistake its meaning.

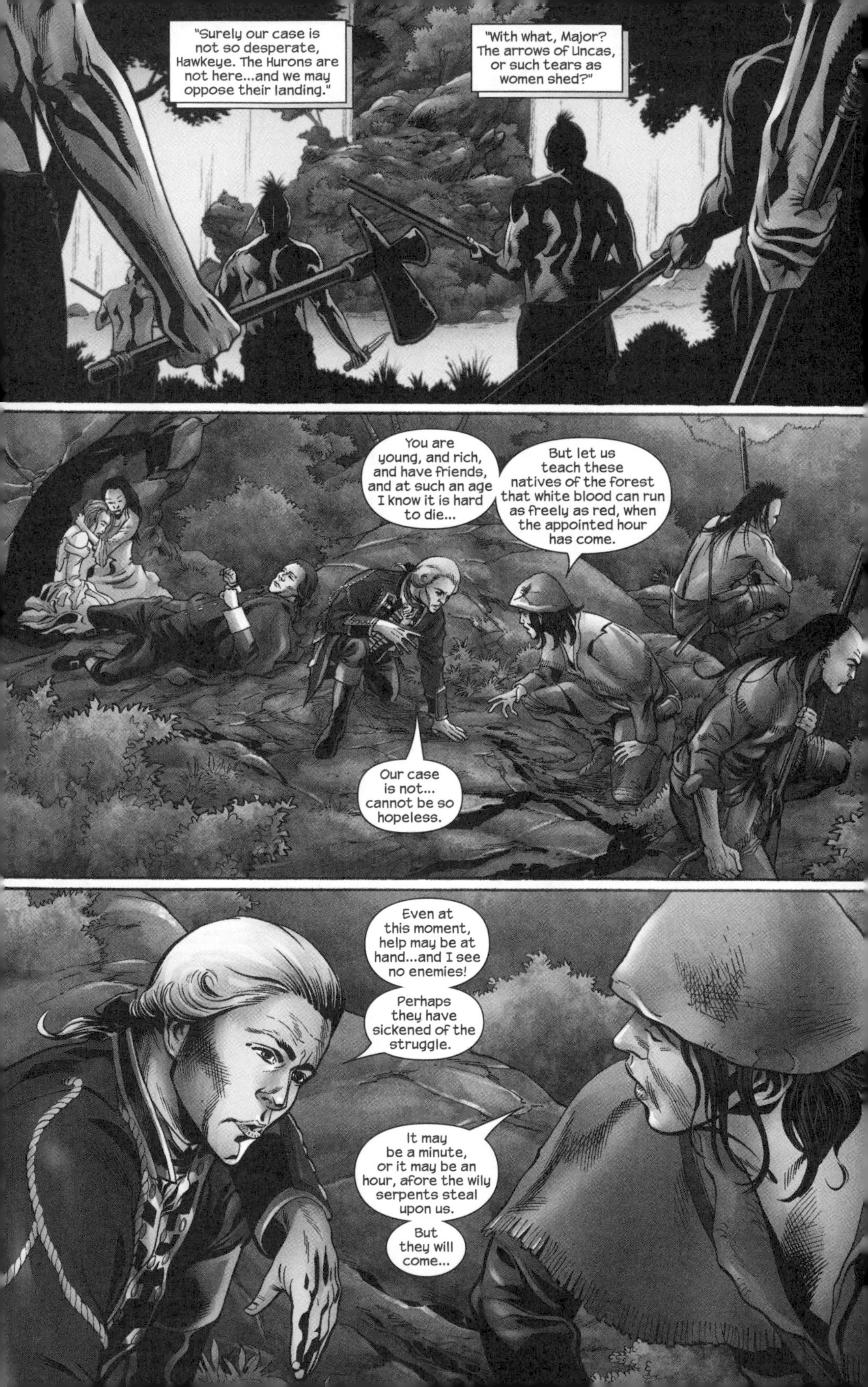
"Surely our case is not so desperate, Hawkeye. The Hurons are not here...and we may oppose their landing."
"With what, Major? The arrows of Uncas, or such tears as women shed?"
You are young, and rich, and have friends, and at such an age I know it is hard to die...
But let us teach these natives of the forest that white blood can run as freely as red, when the appointed hour has come.
Our case is not... cannot be so hopeless.
Even at this moment, help may be at hand...and I see no enemies!
Perhaps they have sickened of the struggle.
It may be a minute, or it may be an hour, afore the wily serpents steal upon us.
But they will come...

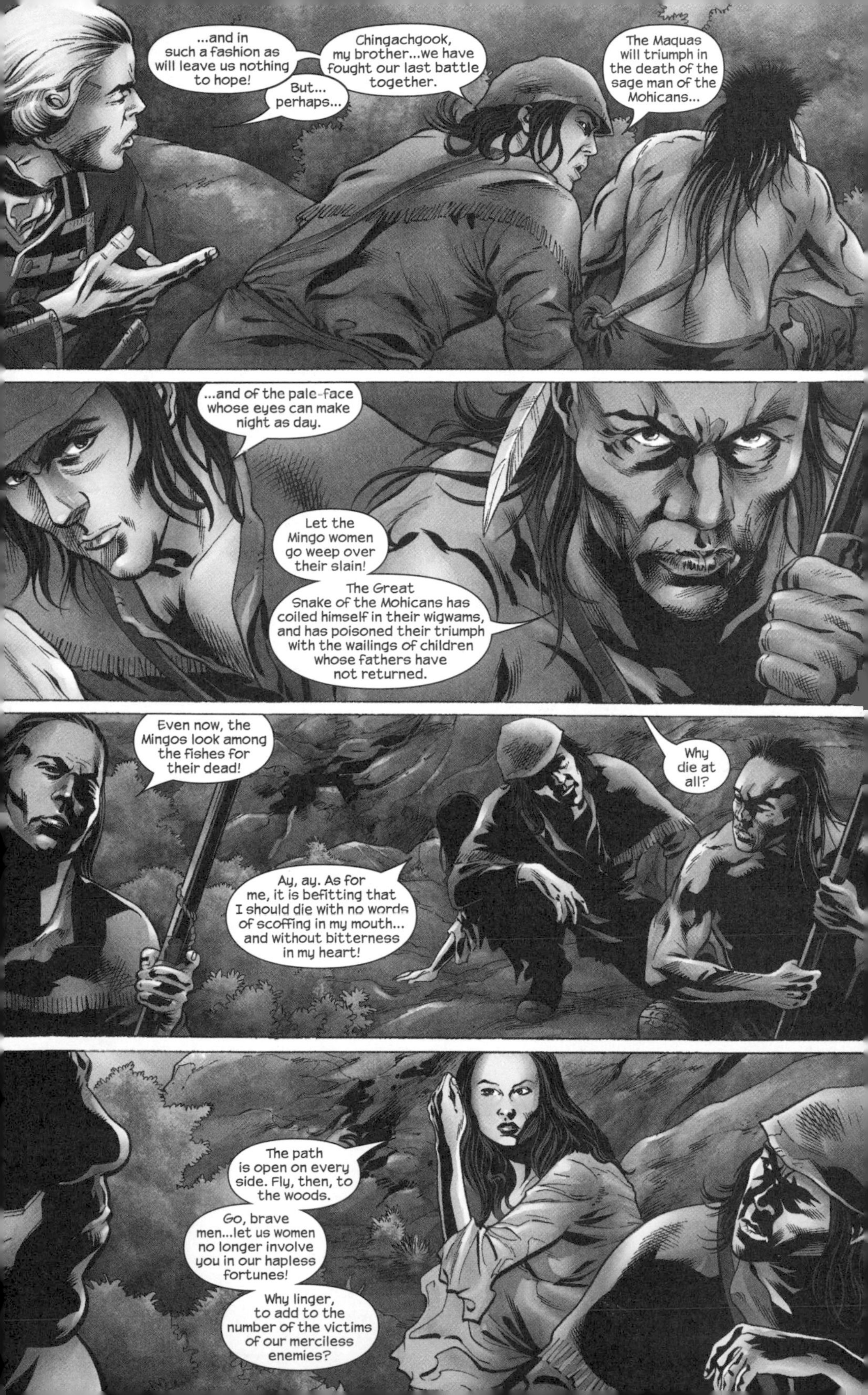
...and in such a fashion as will leave us nothing to hope!
But... perhaps...
Chingachgook, my brother...we have fought our last battle together.
The Maquas will triumph in the death of the sage man of the Mohicans...
...and of the pale-face whose eyes can make night as day.
Let the Mingo women go weep over their slain!
The Great Snake of the Mohicans has coiled himself in their wigwams, and has poisoned their triumph with the wailings of children whose fathers have not returned.
Even now, the Mingos look among the fishes for their dead!
Why die at all?
Ay, ay. As for me, it is befitting that I should die with no words of scoffing in my mouth... and without bitterness in my heart!
The path is open on every side. Fly, then, to the woods.
Go, brave men...let us women no longer involve you in our hapless fortunes!
Why linger, to add to the number of the victims of our merciless enemies?

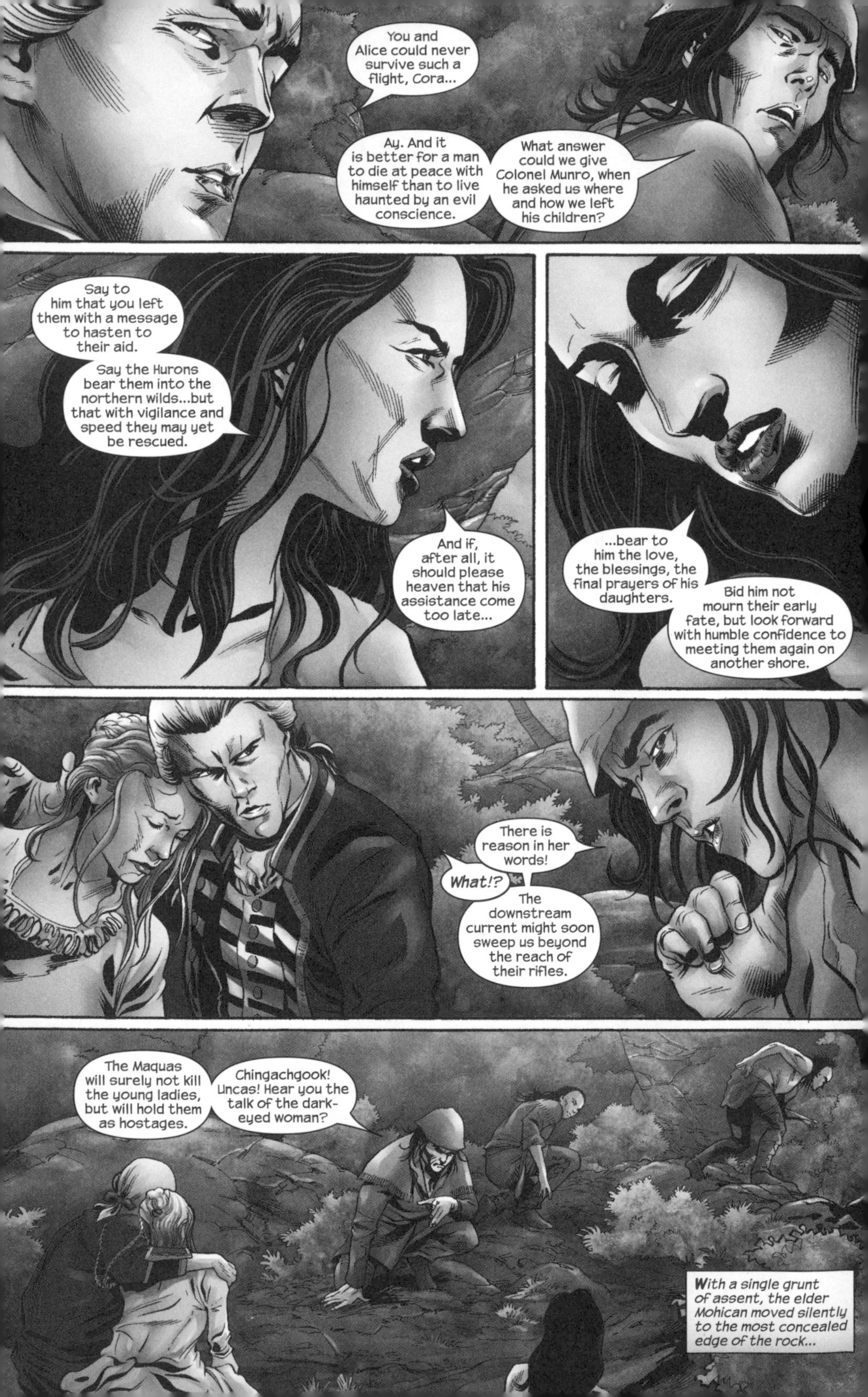

You and Alice could never survive such a flight, Cora...
Ay. And it is better for a man to die at peace with himself than to live haunted by an evil conscience.
What answer could we give Colonel Munro, when he asked us where and how we left his children?
Say to him that you left them with a message to hasten to their aid.
Say the Hurons bear them into the northern wilds...but that with vigilance and speed they may yet be rescued.
And if, after all, it should please heaven that his assistance come too late...
...bear to him the love, the blessings, the final prayers of his daughters.
Bid him not mourn their early fate, but look forward with humble confidence to meeting them again on another shore.
There is reason in her words!
What!?
The downstream current might soon sweep us beyond the reach of their rifles.
The Maquas will surely not kill the young ladies, but will hold them as hostages.
Chingachgook! Uncas! Hear you the talk of the dark-eyed woman?
With a single grunt of assent, the elder Mohican moved silently to the most concealed edge of the rock...

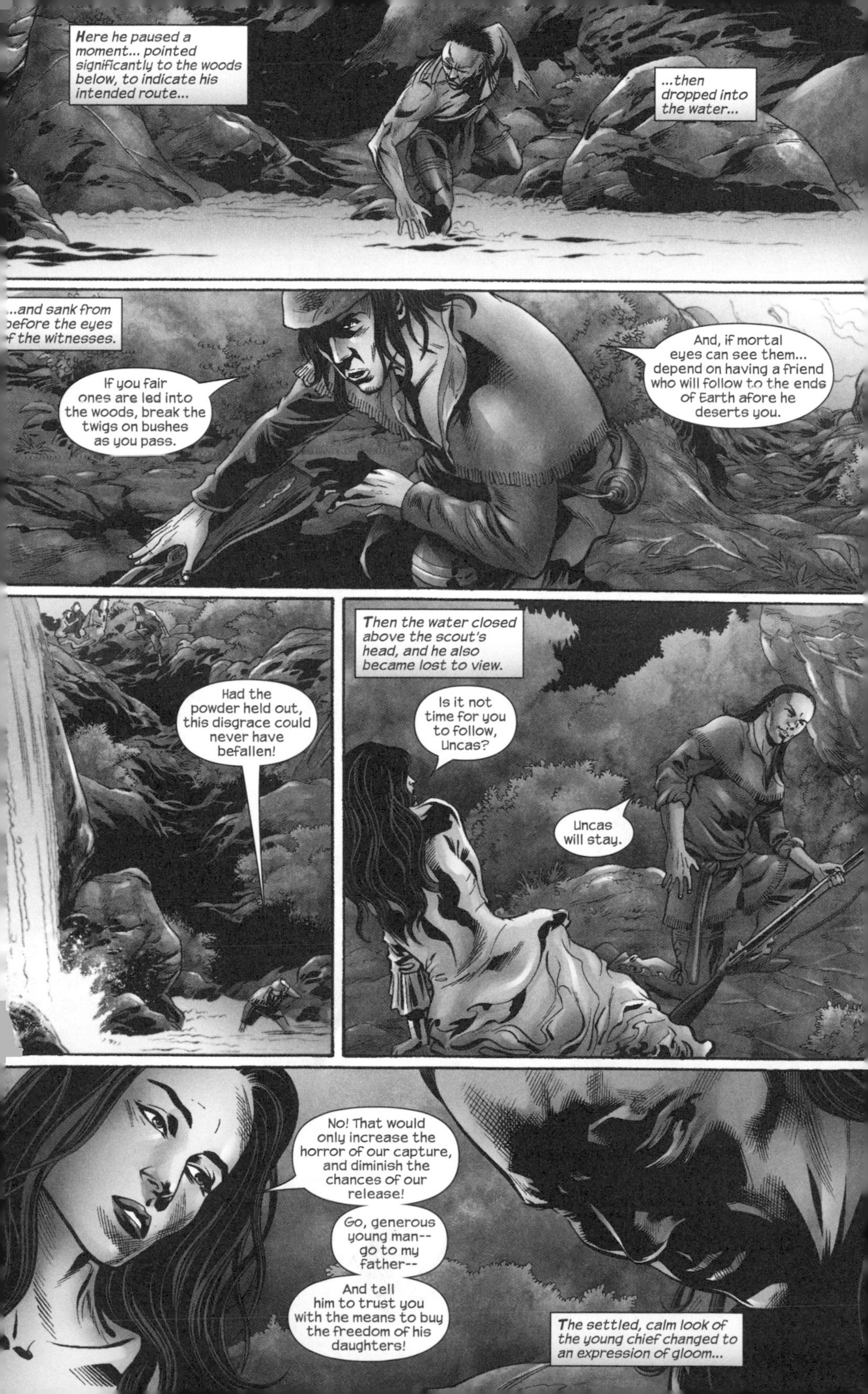
Here he paused a moment... pointed significantly to the woods below, to indicate his intended route...
...then dropped into the water...
...and sank from before the eyes of the witnesses.
If you fair ones are led into the woods, break the twigs on bushes as you pass.
And, if mortal eyes can see them... depend on having a friend who will follow to the ends of Earth afore he deserts you.
Had the powder held out, this disgrace could never have befallen!
Then the water closed above the scout's head, and he also became lost to view.
Is it not time for you to follow, Uncas?
Uncas will stay.
No! That would only increase the horror of our capture, and diminish the chances of our release!
Go, generous young man-- go to my father--
And tell him to trust you with the means to buy the freedom of his daughters!
The settled, calm look of the young chief changed to an expression of gloom...

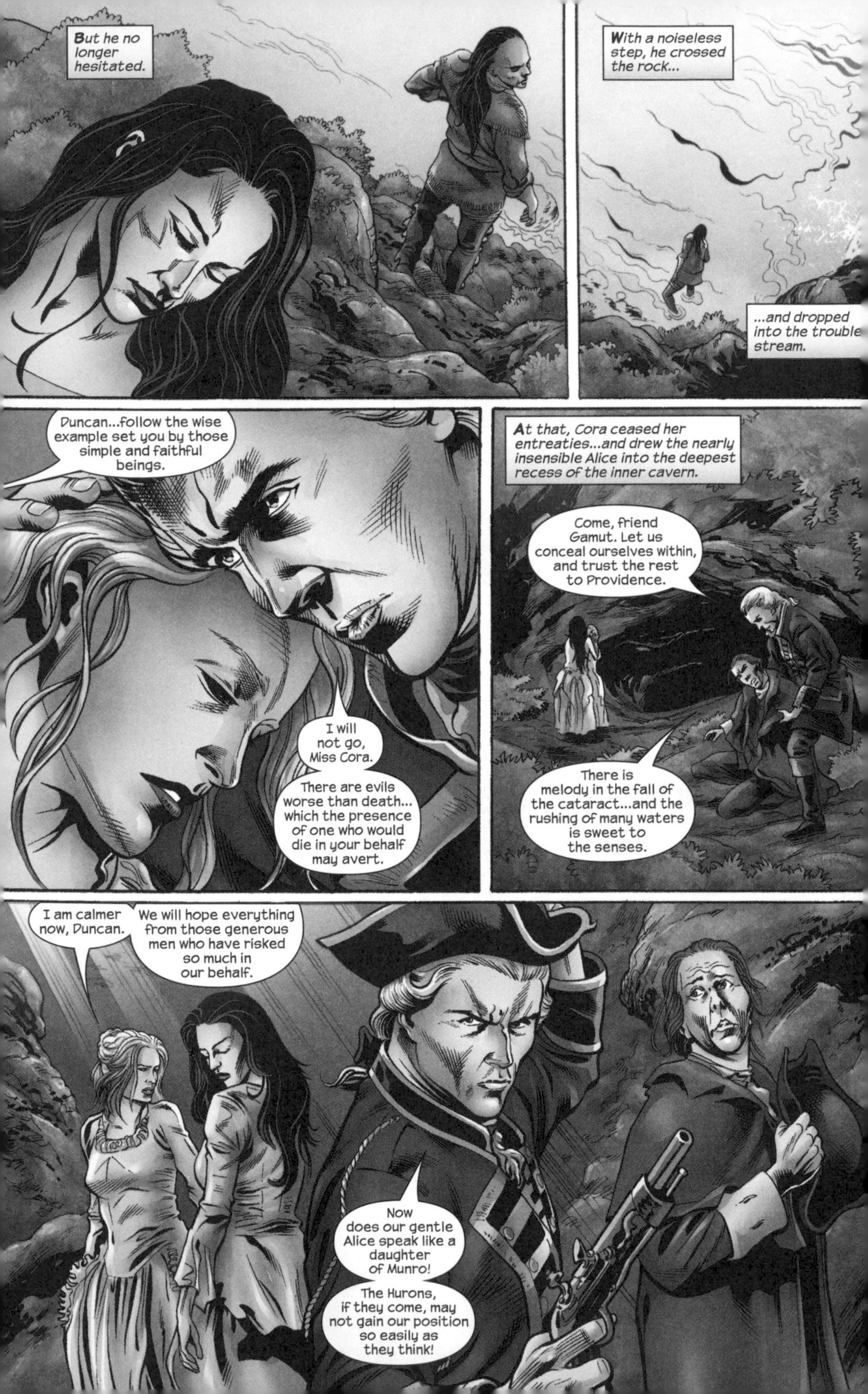

But he no longer hesitated.
With a noiseless step, he crossed the rock...
...and dropped into the trouble stream.
Duncan...follow the wise example set you by those simple and faithful beings.
I will not go, Miss Cora.
There are evils worse than death... which the presence of one who would die in your behalf may avert.
At that, Cora ceased her entreaties...and drew the nearly insensible Alice into the deepest recess of the inner cavern.
Come, friend Gamut. Let us conceal ourselves within, and trust the rest to Providence.
There is melody in the fall of the cataract...and the rushing of many waters is sweet to the senses.
I am calmer now, Duncan.
We will hope everything from those generous men who have risked so much in our behalf.
Now does our gentle Alice speak like a daughter of Munro!
The Hurons, if they come, may not gain our position so easily as they think!

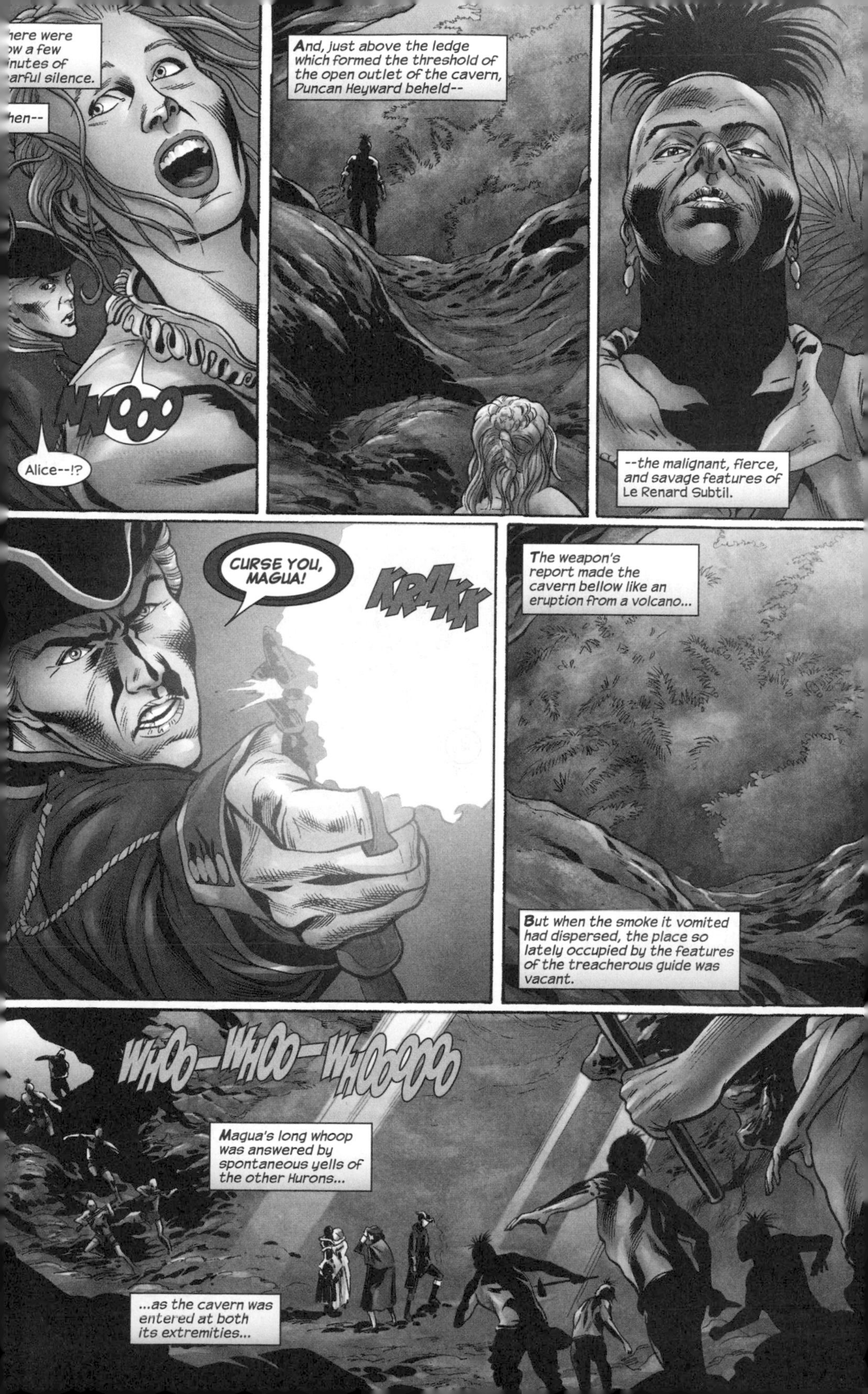
here were
ow a few
inutes of
earful silence.
hen--
NNOOOO
Alice--!?
And, just above the ledge which formed the threshold of the open outlet of the cavern, Duncan Heyward beheld--
--the malignant, fierce, and savage features of Le Renard Subtil.
CURSE YOU, MAGUA!
KRAKK
The weapon's report made the cavern bellow like an eruption from a volcano...
But when the smoke it vomited had dispersed, the place so lately occupied by the features of the treacherous guide was vacant.
WHOO-WHOO-WHOOOOO
Magua's long whoop was answered by spontaneous yells of the other Hurons...
...as the cavern was entered at both its extremities...

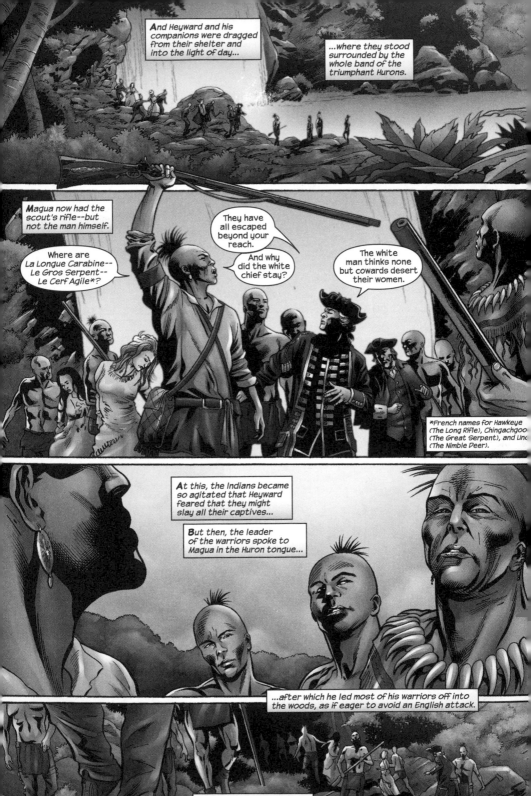

And Heyward and his companions were dragged from their shelter and into the light of day...

...where they stood surrounded by the whole band of the triumphant Hurons.

Magua now had the scout's rifle--but not the man himself.

Where are La Longue Carabine-- Le Gros Serpent-- Le Cerf Agile*?

They have all escaped beyond your reach.

And why did the white chief stay?

The white man thinks none but cowards desert their women.

*French names for Hawkeye (The Long Rifle), Chingachgook (The Great Serpent), and Unc (The Nimble Deer).

At this, the Indians became so agitated that Heyward feared that they might slay all their captives...

But then, the leader of the warriors spoke to Magua in the Huron tongue...

...after which he led most of his warriors off into the woods, as if eager to avoid an English attack.

The prisoners were left to proceed by a slower route, in the charge of Magua and five other savages.

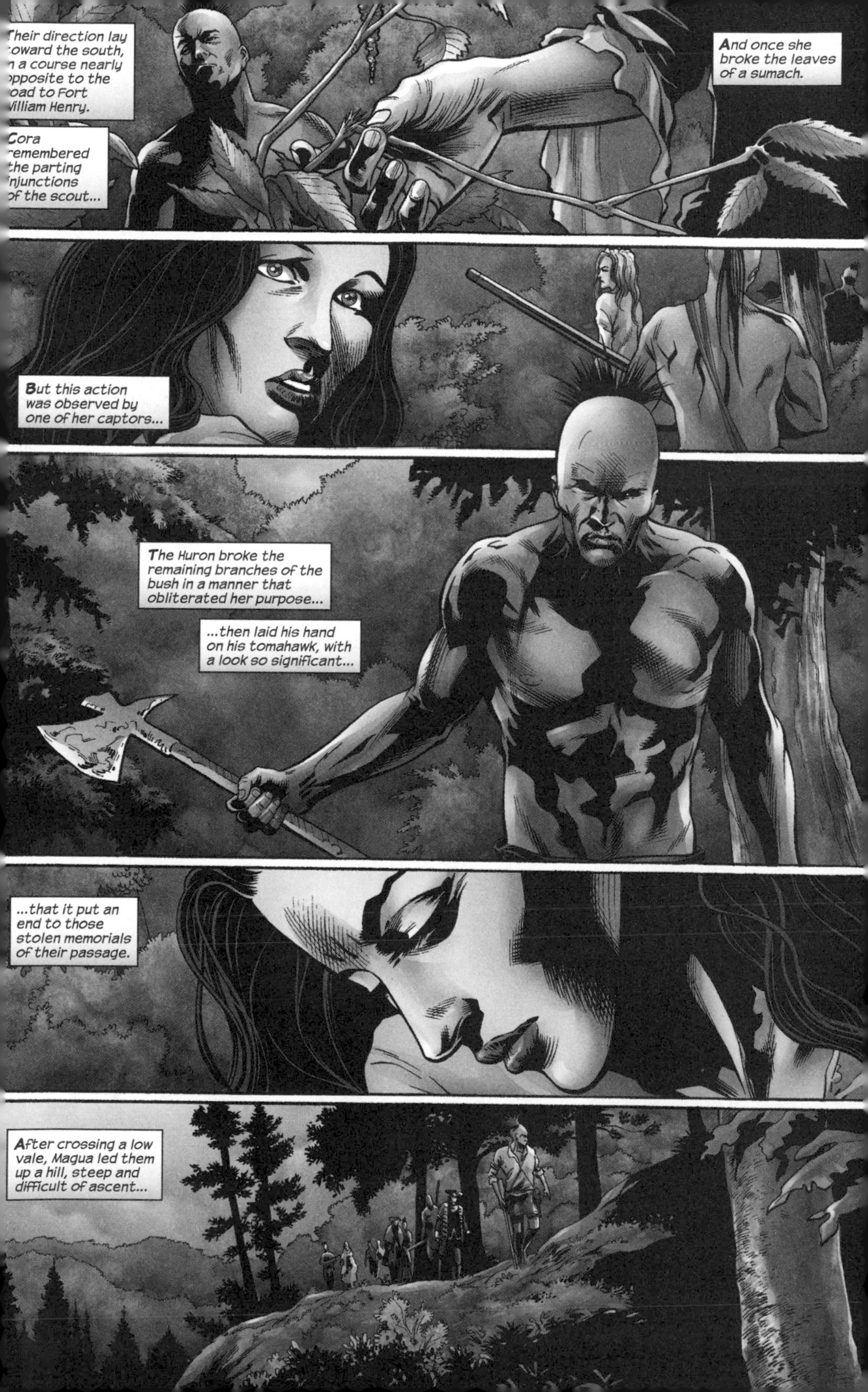
Their direction lay toward the south, in a course nearly opposite to the road to Fort William Henry.
Cora remembered the parting injunctions of the scout...
And once she broke the leaves of a sumach.
But this action was observed by one of her captors...
The Huron broke the remaining branches of the bush in a manner that obliterated her purpose...
...then laid his hand on his tomahawk, with a look so significant...
...that it put an end to those stolen memorials of their passage.
After crossing a low vale, Magua led them up a hill, steep and difficult of ascent...

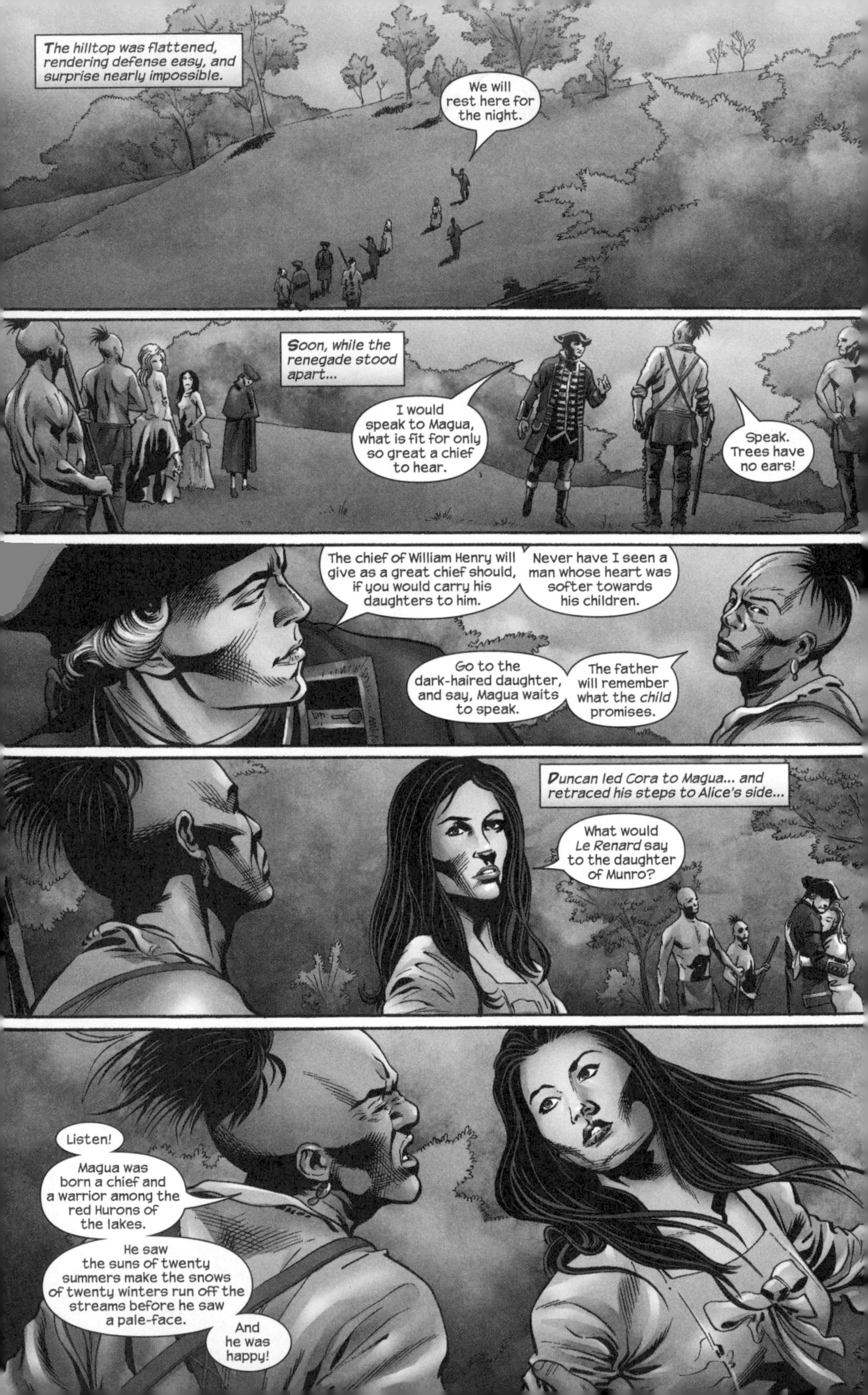

The hilltop was flattened, rendering defense easy, and surprise nearly impossible.
We will rest here for the night.
Soon, while the renegade stood apart...
I would speak to Magua, what is fit for only so great a chief to hear.
Speak. Trees have no ears!
The chief of William Henry will give as a great chief should, if you would carry his daughters to him.
Never have I seen a man whose heart was softer towards his children.
Go to the dark-haired daughter, and say, Magua waits to speak.
The father will remember what the *child* promises.
Duncan led Cora to Magua... and retraced his steps to Alice's side...
What would *Le Renard* say to the daughter of Munro?
Listen!
Magua was born a chief and a warrior among the red Hurons of the lakes.
He saw the suns of twenty summers make the snows of twenty winters run off the streams before he saw a pale-face.
And he was happy!

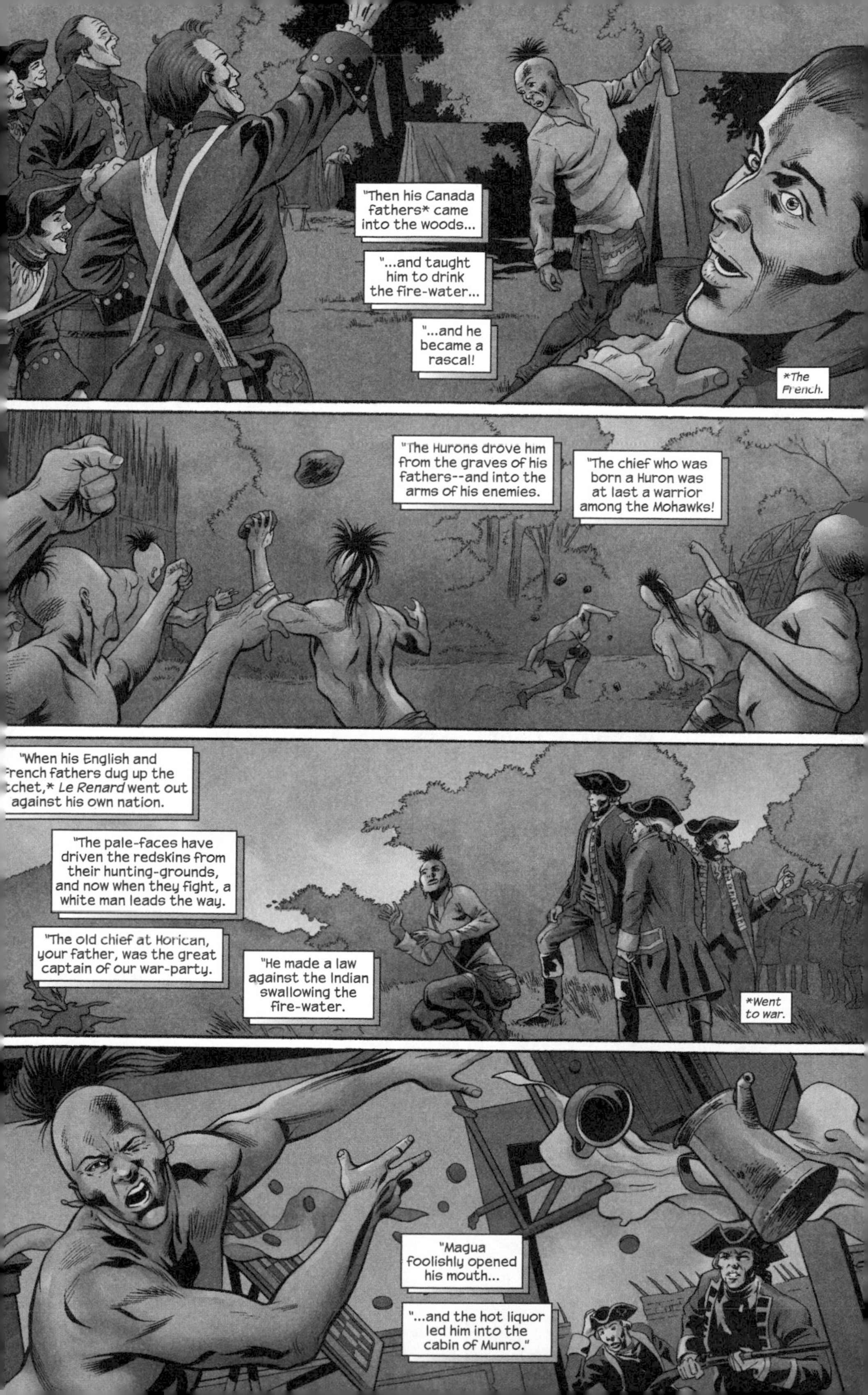
"Then his Canada fathers* came into the woods...
"...and taught him to drink the fire-water...
"...and he became a rascal!
*The French.
"The Hurons drove him from the graves of his fathers--and into the arms of his enemies.
"The chief who was born a Huron was at last a warrior among the Mohawks!
"When his English and French fathers dug up the tchet,* *Le Renard* went out against his own nation.
"The pale-faces have driven the redskins from their hunting-grounds, and now when they fight, a white man leads the way.
"The old chief at Horican, your father, was the great captain of our war-party.
"He made a law against the Indian swallowing the fire-water.
*Went to war.
"Magua foolishly opened his mouth...
"...and the hot liquor led him into the cabin of Munro."

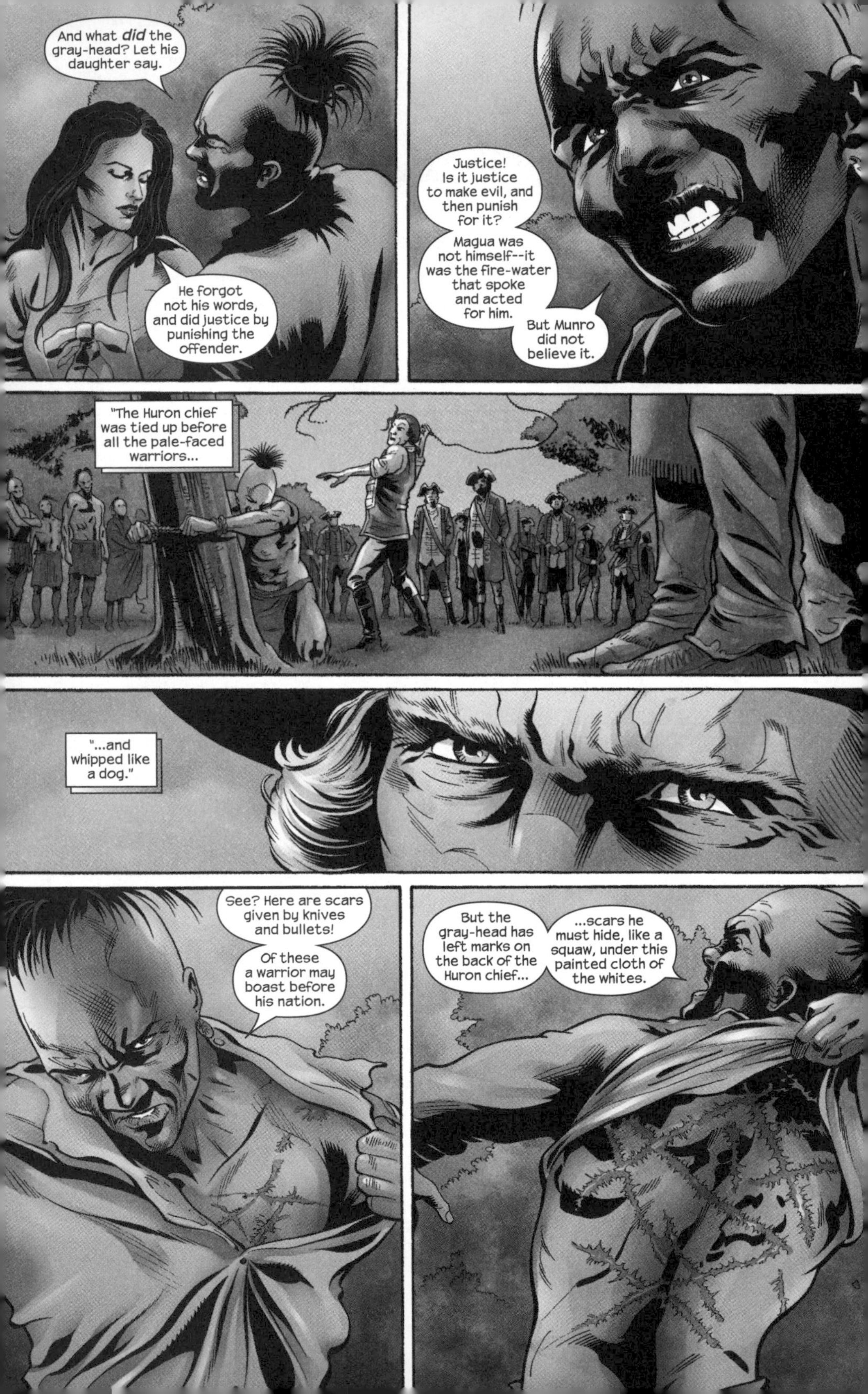
And what *did* the gray-head? Let his daughter say.
He forgot not his words, and did justice by punishing the offender.
Justice! Is it justice to make evil, and then punish for it?
Magua was not himself--it was the fire-water that spoke and acted for him.
But Munro did not believe it.
"The Huron chief was tied up before all the pale-faced warriors...
"...and whipped like a dog."
See? Here are scars given by knives and bullets!
Of these a warrior may boast before his nation.
But the gray-head has left marks on the back of the Huron chief...
...scars he must hide, like a squaw, under this painted cloth of the whites.

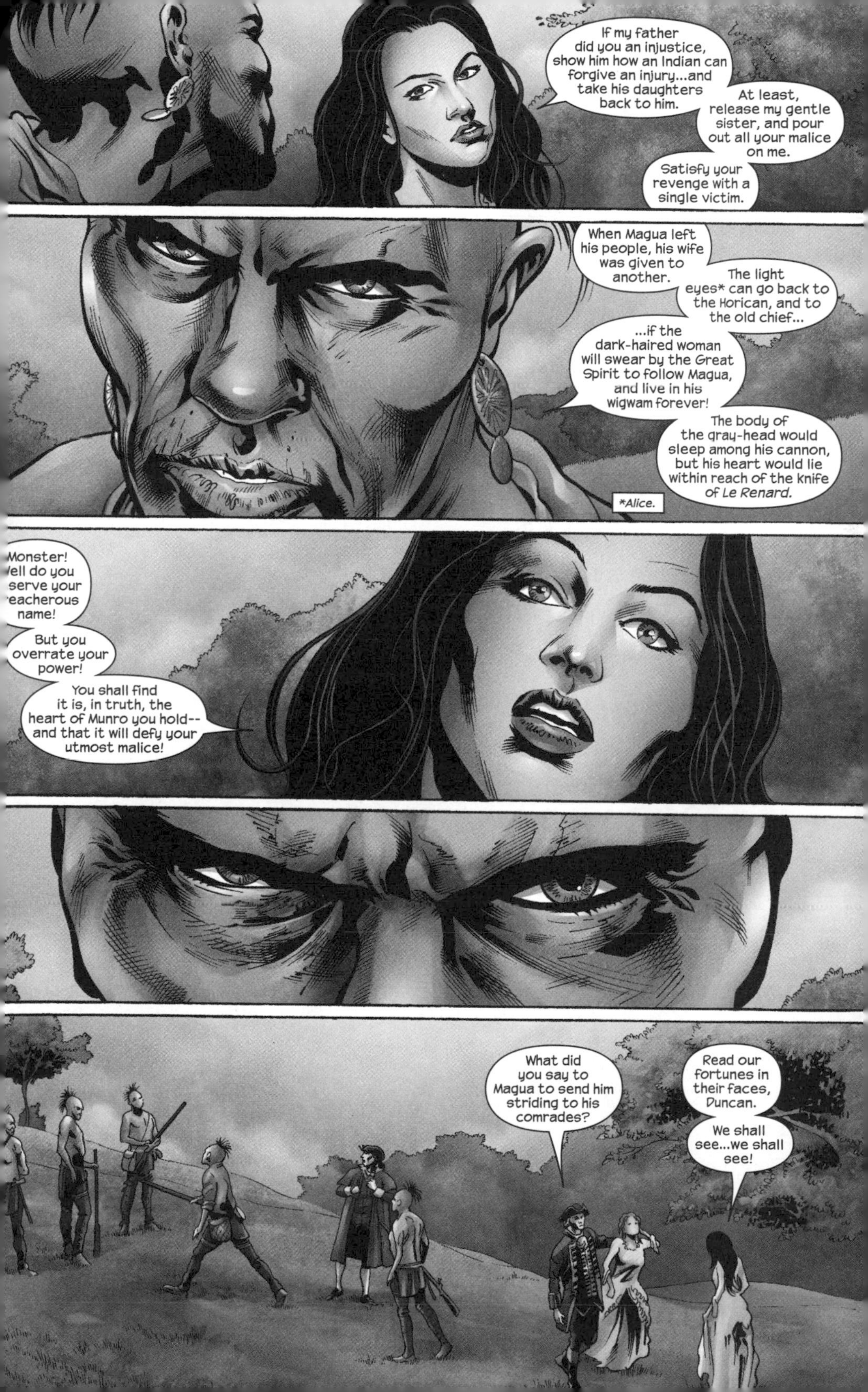
If my father did you an injustice, show him how an Indian can forgive an injury...and take his daughters back to him.
At least, release my gentle sister, and pour out all your malice on me.
Satisfy your revenge with a single victim.
When Magua left his people, his wife was given to another.
The light eyes* can go back to the Horican, and to the old chief...
...if the dark-haired woman will swear by the Great Spirit to follow Magua, and live in his wigwam forever!
The body of the gray-head would sleep among his cannon, but his heart would lie within reach of the knife of *Le Renard*.
*Alice.
Monster! ell do you serve your eacherous name!
But you overrate your power!
You shall find it is, in truth, the heart of Munro you hold--and that it will defy your utmost malice!
What did you say to Magua to send him striding to his comrades?
Read our fortunes in their faces, Duncan.
We shall see...we shall see!

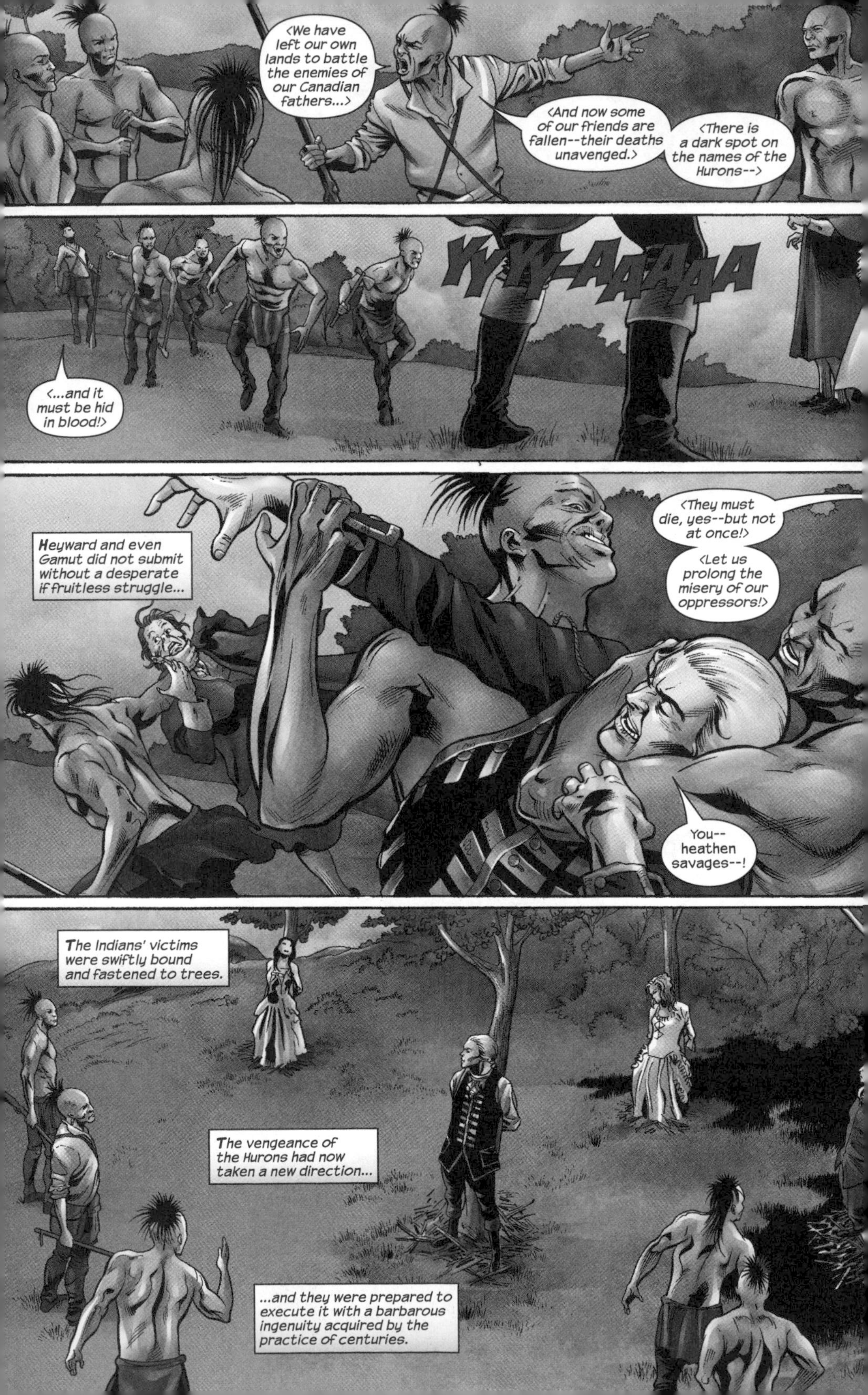

<We have left our own lands to battle the enemies of our Canadian fathers...>
<And now some of our friends are fallen--their deaths unavenged.>
<There is a dark spot on the names of the Hurons-->
YYY-AAAAA
<...and it must be hid in blood!>
Heyward and even Gamut did not submit without a desperate if fruitless struggle...
<They must die, yes--but not at once!>
<Let us prolong the misery of our oppressors!>
You--heathen savages--!
The Indians' victims were swiftly bound and fastened to trees.
The vengeance of the Hurons had now taken a new direction...
...and they were prepared to execute it with a barbarous ingenuity acquired by the practice of centuries.

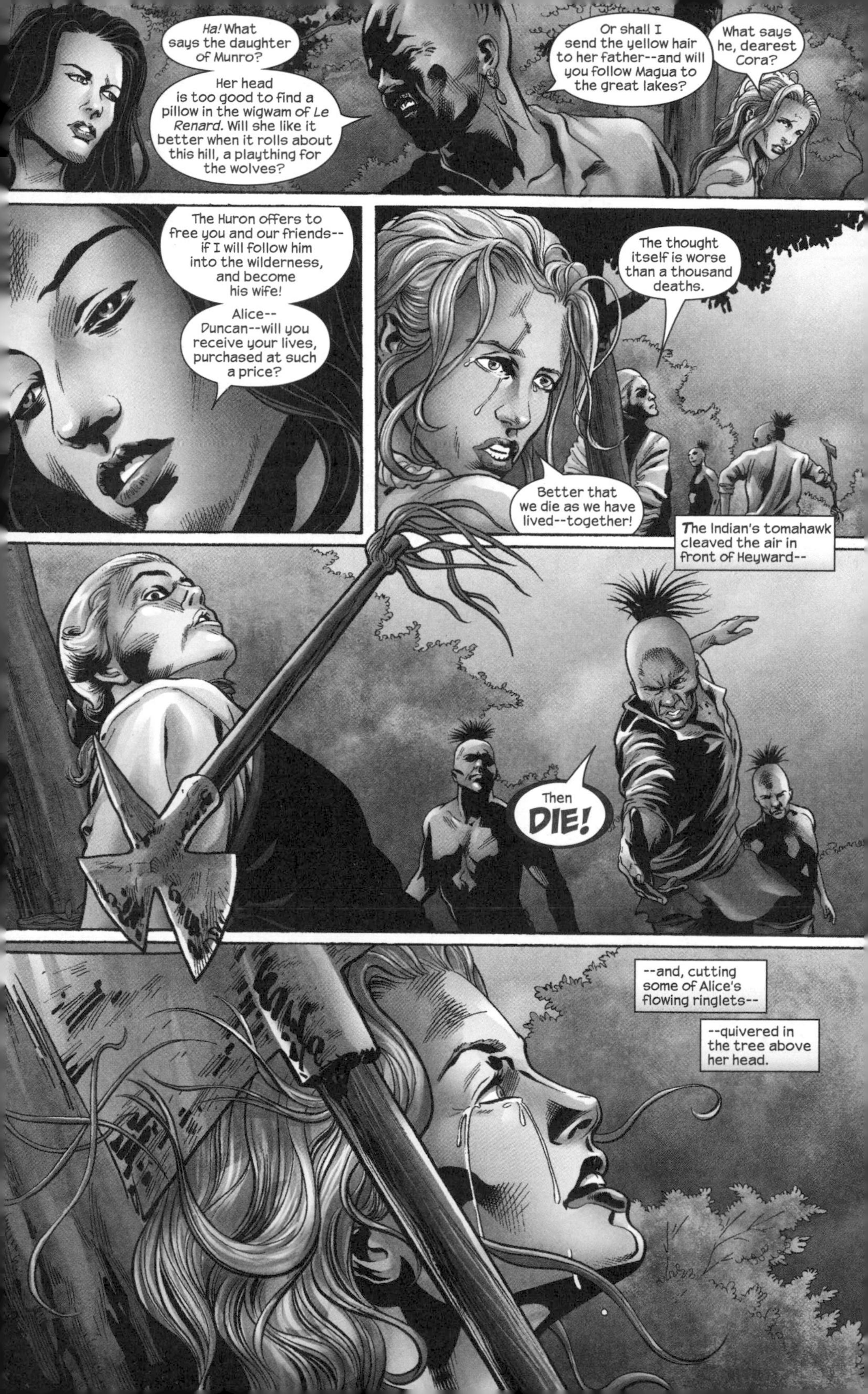
Ha! What says the daughter of Munro?
Her head is too good to find a pillow in the wigwam of *Le Renard.* Will she like it better when it rolls about this hill, a plaything for the wolves?
Or shall I send the yellow hair to her father--and will you follow Magua to the great lakes?
What says he, dearest Cora?
The Huron offers to free you and our friends--if I will follow him into the wilderness, and become his wife!
Alice--Duncan--will you receive your lives, purchased at such a price?
The thought itself is worse than a thousand deaths.
Better that we die as we have lived--together!
The Indian's tomahawk cleaved the air in front of Heyward--
Then DIE!
--and, cutting some of Alice's flowing ringlets--
--quivered in the tree above her head.

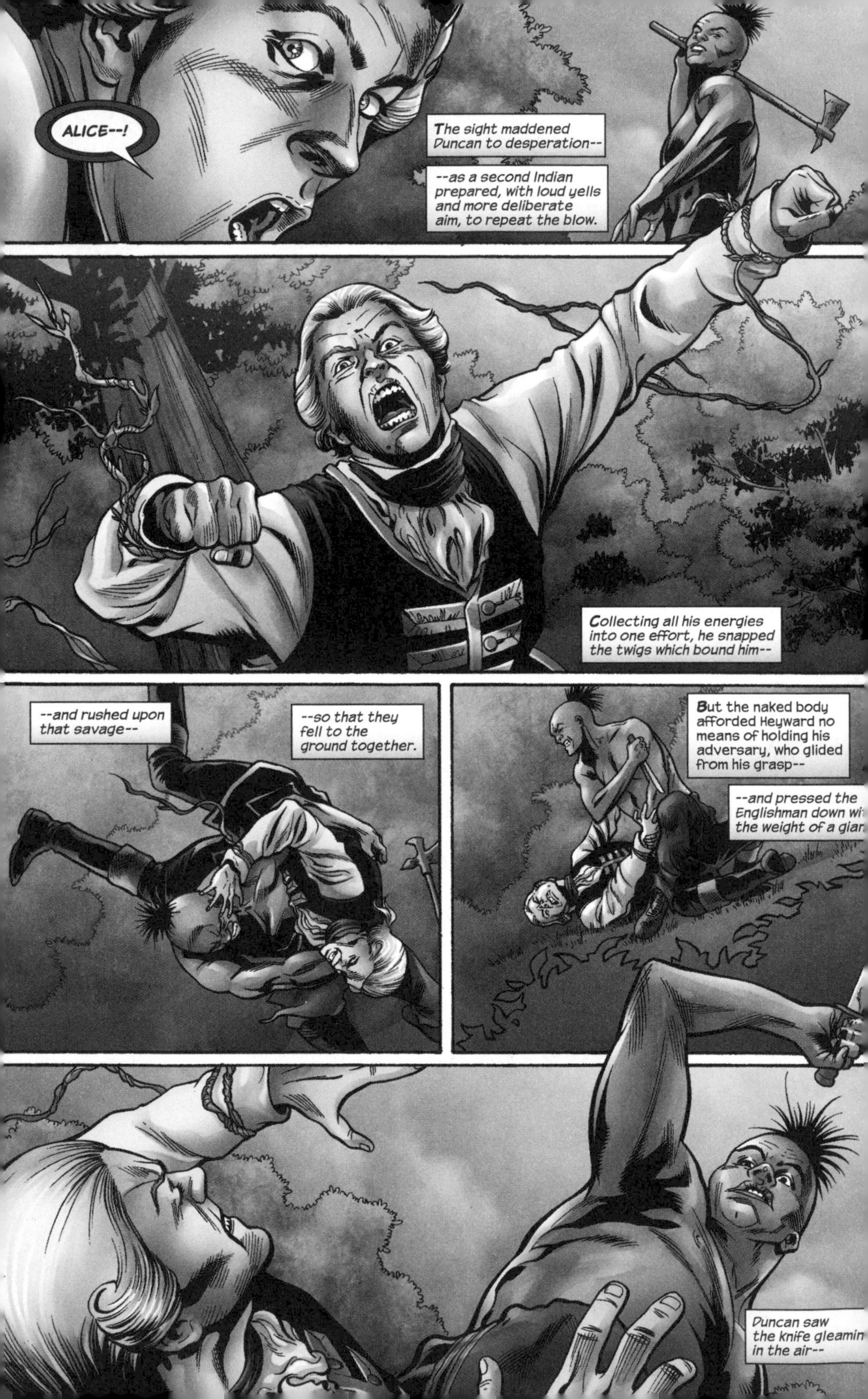
ALICE--!
The sight maddened Duncan to desperation--
--as a second Indian prepared, with loud yells and more deliberate aim, to repeat the blow.
Collecting all his energies into one effort, he snapped the twigs which bound him--
--and rushed upon that savage--
--so that they fell to the ground together.
But the naked body afforded Heyward no means of holding his adversary, who glided from his grasp--
--and pressed the Englishman down wi
the weight of a gian
Duncan saw the knife gleamin in the air--

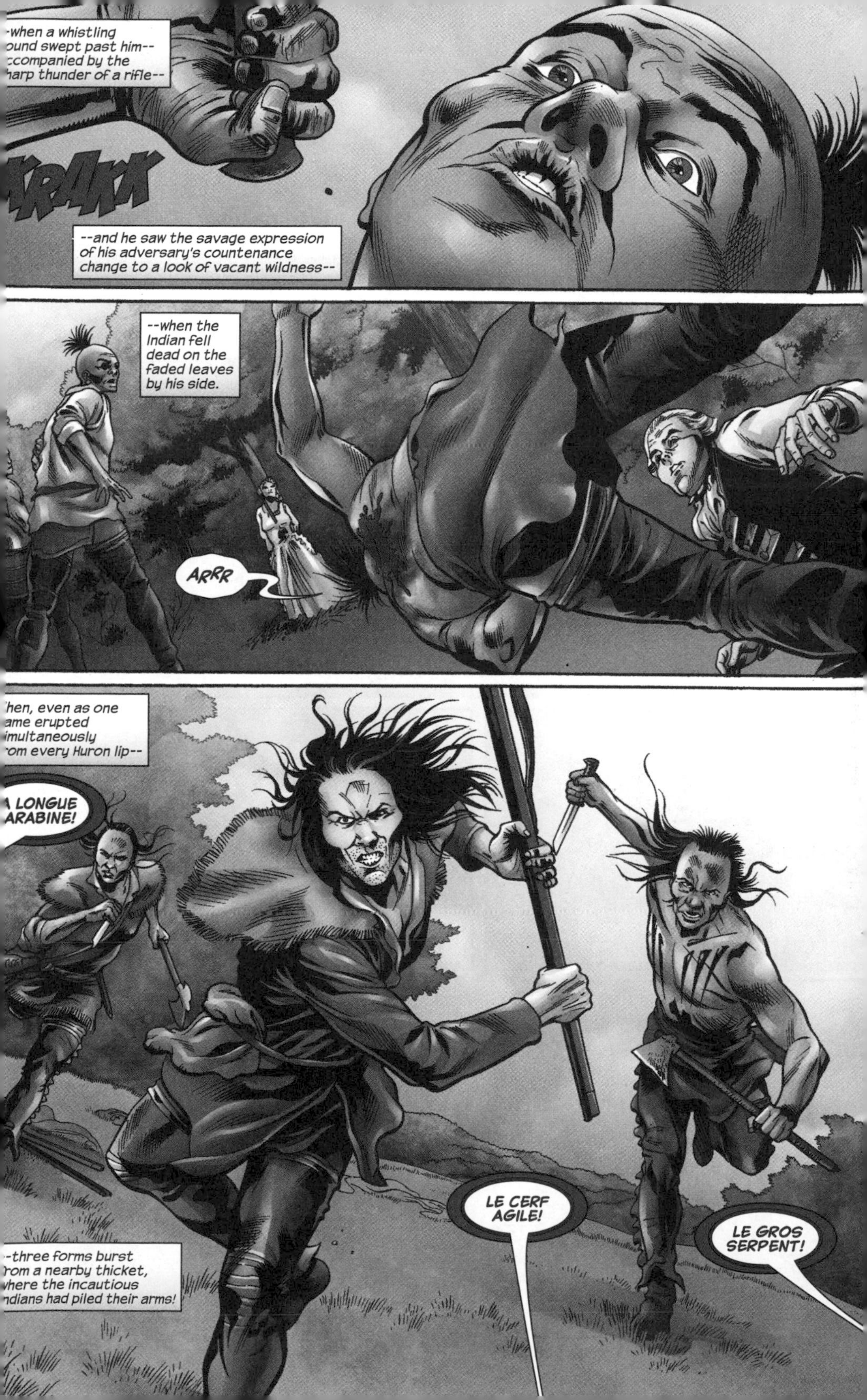

-when a whistling ound swept past him-- ccompanied by the harp thunder of a rifle--
KRAKK
--and he saw the savage expression of his adversary's countenance change to a look of vacant wildness--
--when the Indian fell dead on the faded leaves by his side.
ARRR
hen, even as one ame erupted imultaneously rom every Huron lip--
A LONGUE ARABINE!
LE CERF AGILE!
LE GROS SERPENT!
--three forms burst rom a nearby thicket, where the incautious ndians had piled their arms!

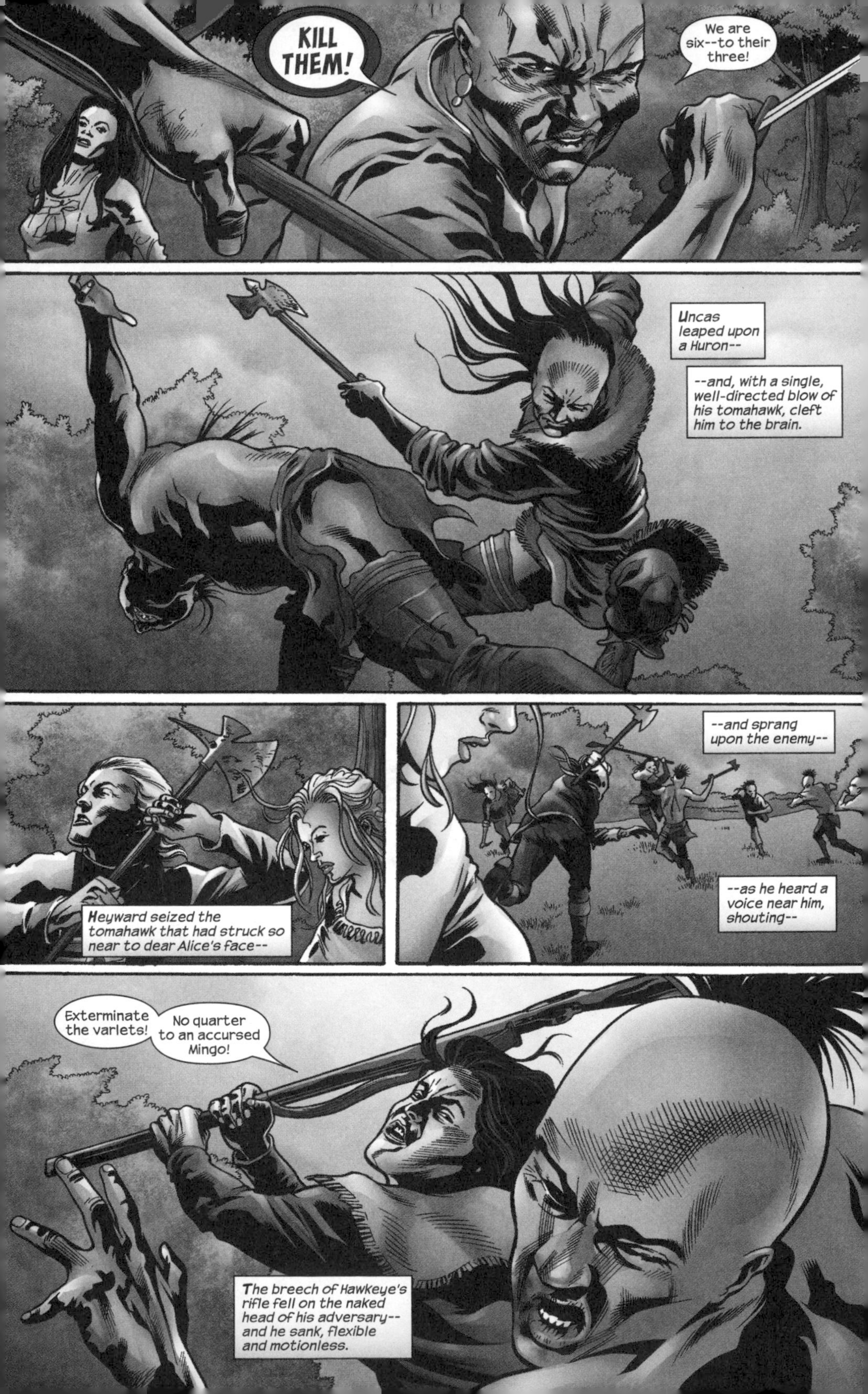
KILL THEM!
We are six--to their three!
Uncas leaped upon a Huron--
--and, with a single, well-directed blow of his tomahawk, cleft him to the brain.
Heyward seized the tomahawk that had struck so near to dear Alice's face--
--and sprang upon the enemy--
--as he heard a voice near him, shouting--
Exterminate the varlets!
No quarter to an accursed Mingo!
The breech of Hawkeye's rifle fell on the naked head of his adversary--and he sank, flexible and motionless.

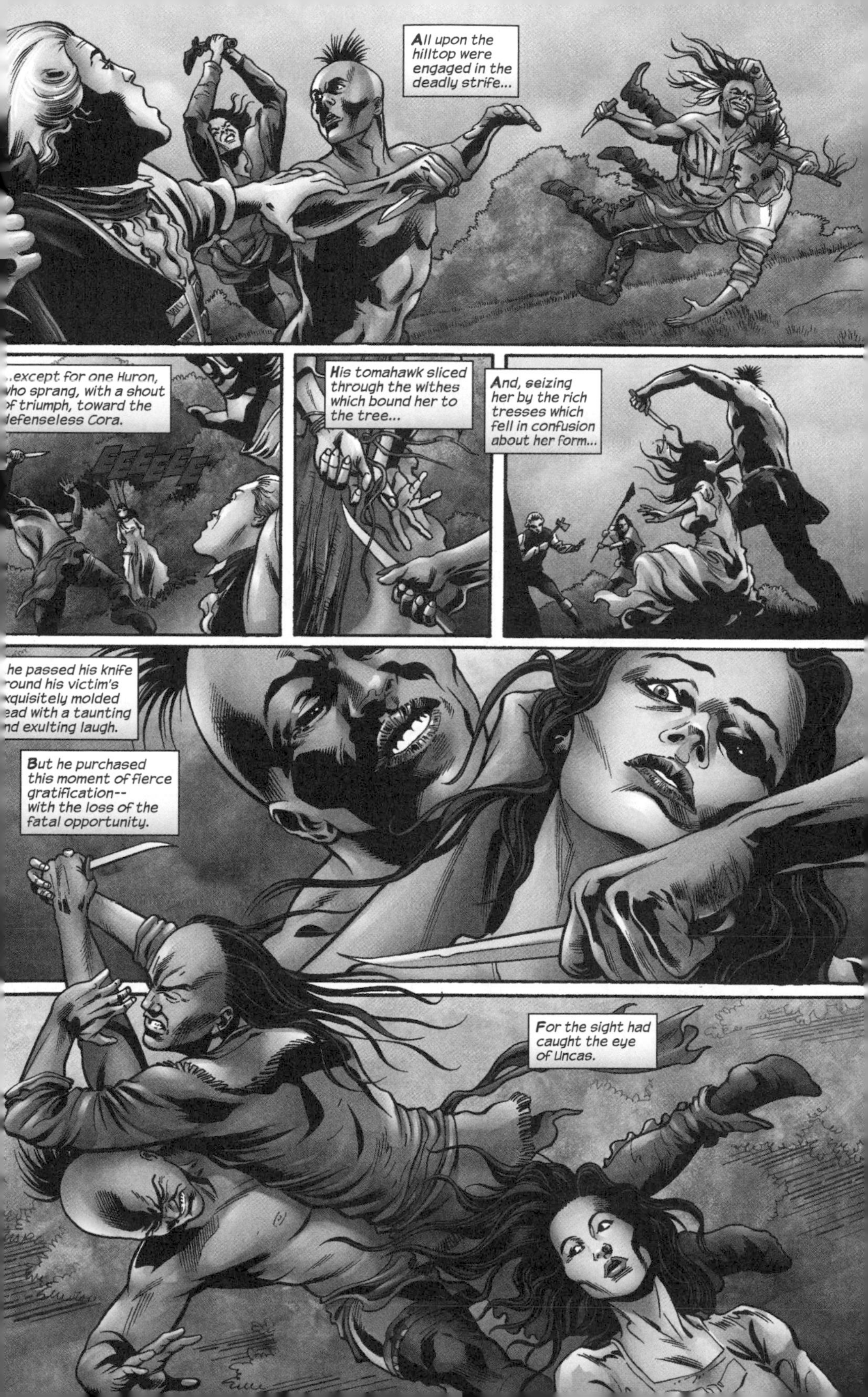
All upon the hilltop were engaged in the deadly strife...
..except for one Huron, who sprang, with a shout of triumph, toward the defenseless Cora.
EEEEEE
His tomahawk sliced through the withes which bound her to the tree...
And, seizing her by the rich tresses which fell in confusion about her form...
he passed his knife round his victim's exquisitely molded head with a taunting and exulting laugh.
But he purchased this moment of fierce gratification-- with the loss of the fatal opportunity.
For the sight had caught the eye of Uncas.

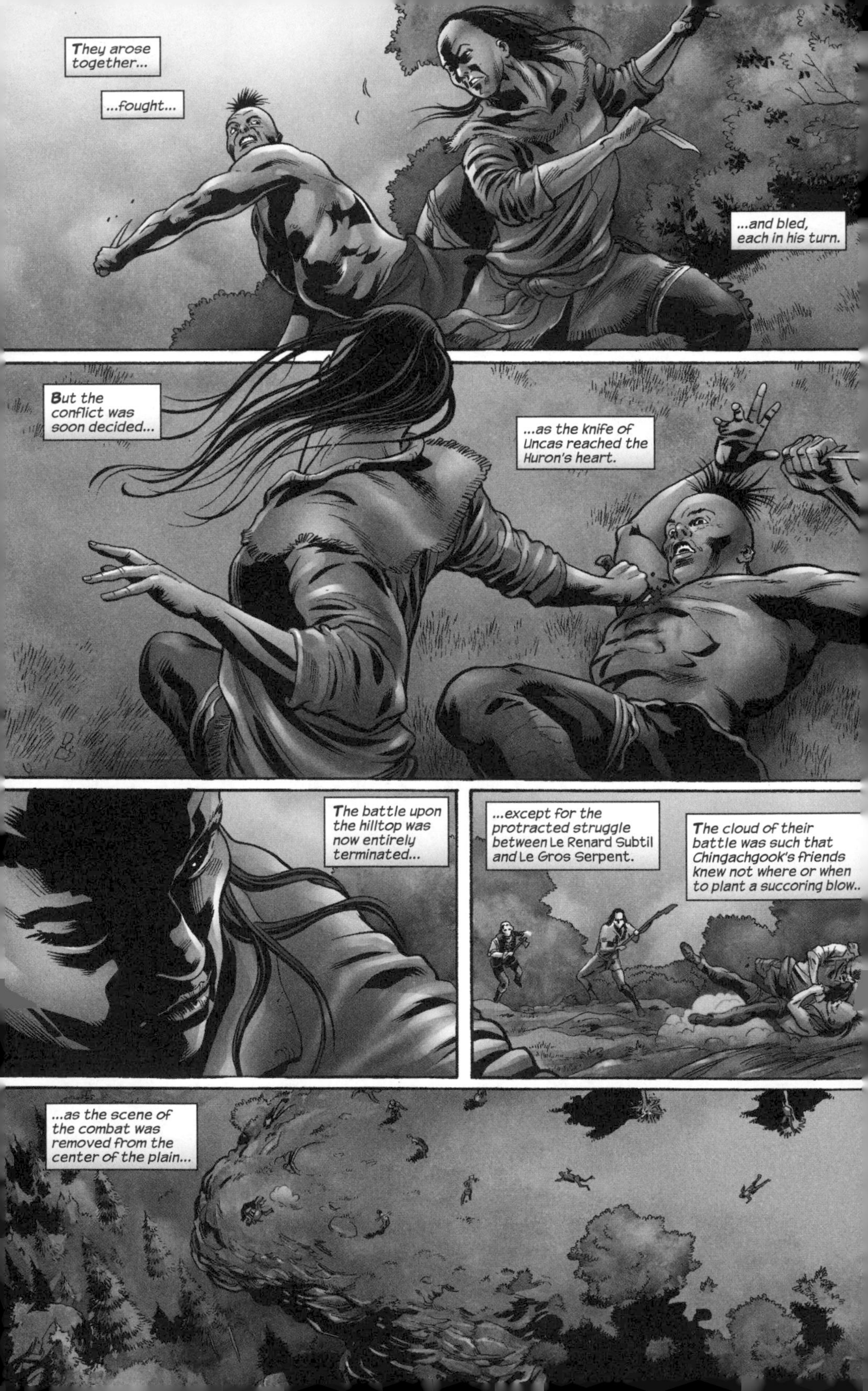

They arose together...
...fought...
...and bled, each in his turn.
But the conflict was soon decided...
...as the knife of Uncas reached the Huron's heart.
The battle upon the hilltop was now entirely terminated...
...except for the protracted struggle between Le Renard Subtil and Le Gros Serpent.
The cloud of their battle was such that Chingachgook's friends knew not where or when to plant a succoring blow..
...as the scene of the combat was removed from the center of the plain...

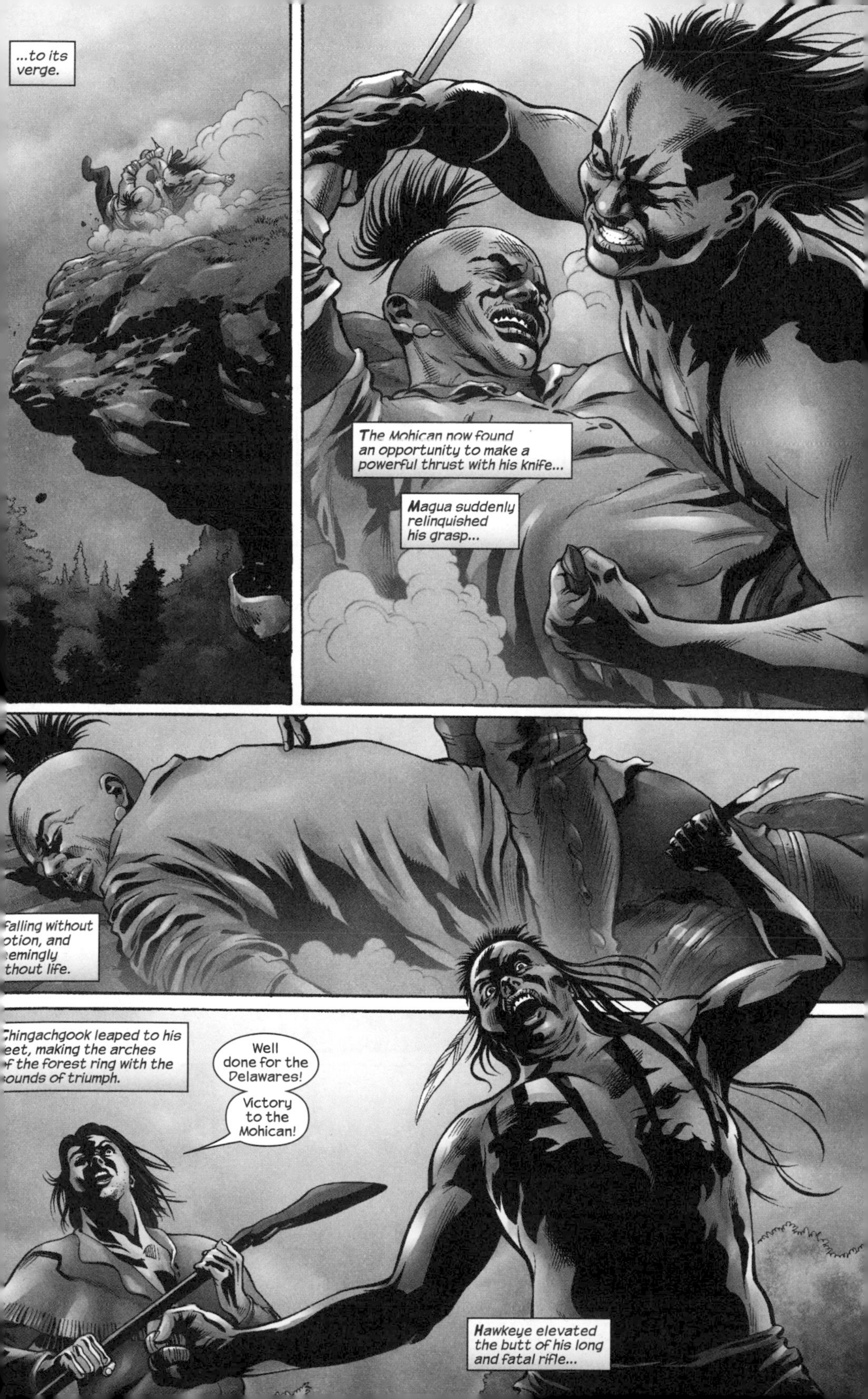
...to its verge.
The Mohican now found an opportunity to make a powerful thrust with his knife...
Magua suddenly relinquished his grasp...
falling without otion, and eemingly thout life.
Chingachgook leaped to his eet, making the arches f the forest ring with the ounds of triumph.
Well done for the Delawares!
Victory to the Mohican!
Hawkeye elevated the butt of his long and fatal rifle...

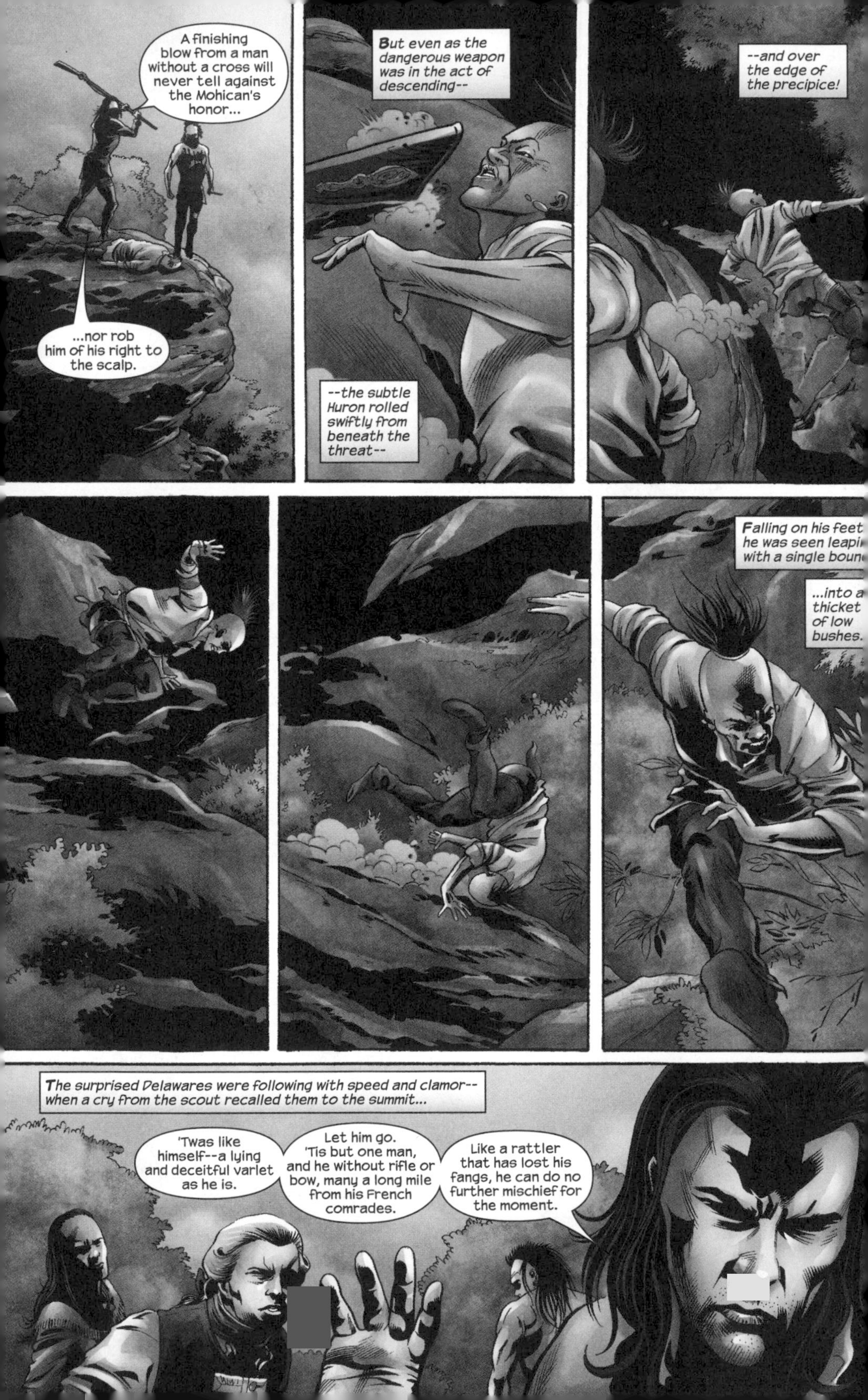
A finishing blow from a man without a cross will never tell against the Mohican's honor...
...nor rob him of his right to the scalp.
But even as the dangerous weapon was in the act of descending--
--the subtle Huron rolled swiftly from beneath the threat--
--and over the edge of the precipice!
Falling on his feet he was seen leapi with a single boun
...into a thicket of low bushes.
The surprised Delawares were following with speed and clamor-- when a cry from the scout recalled them to the summit...
'Twas like himself--a lying and deceitful varlet as he is.
Let him go. 'Tis but one man, and he without rifle or bow, many a long mile from his French comrades.
Like a rattler that has lost his fangs, he can do no further mischief for the moment.

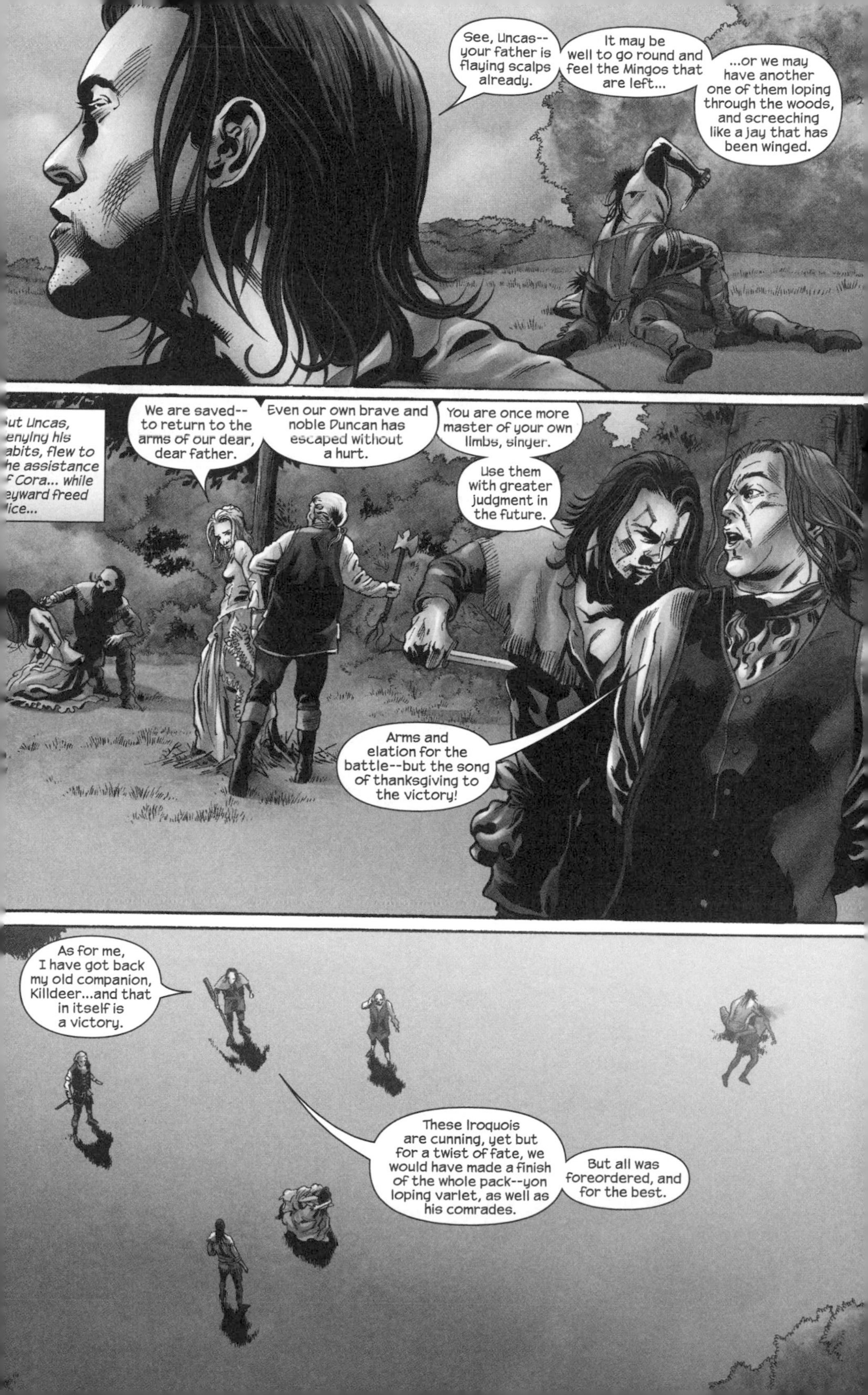

See, Uncas--your father is flaying scalps already.
It may be well to go round and feel the Mingos that are left...
...or we may have another one of them loping through the woods, and screeching like a jay that has been winged.
ut Uncas, enying his abits, flew to he assistance f Cora... while eyward freed lice...
We are saved--to return to the arms of our dear, dear father.
Even our own brave and noble Duncan has escaped without a hurt.
You are once more master of your own limbs, singer.
Use them with greater judgment in the future.
Arms and elation for the battle--but the song of thanksgiving to the victory!
As for me, I have got back my old companion, Killdeer...and that in itself is a victory.
These Iroquois are cunning, yet but for a twist of fate, we would have made a finish of the whole pack--yon loping varlet, as well as his comrades.
But all was foreordered, and for the best.

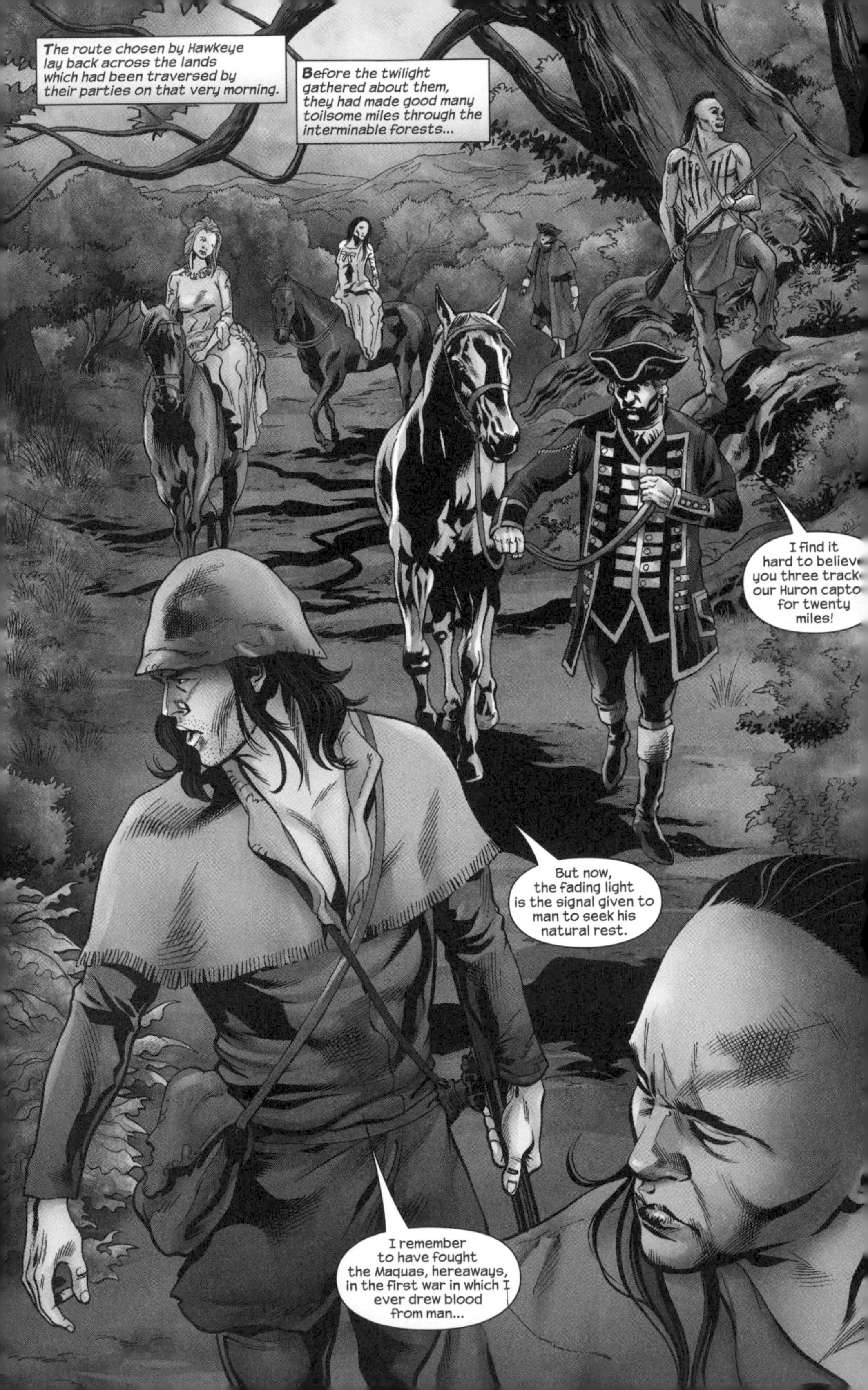
The route chosen by Hawkeye lay back across the lands which had been traversed by their parties on that very morning.
Before the twilight gathered about them, they had made good many toilsome miles through the interminable forests...
I find it hard to believe you three track our Huron capto for twenty miles!
But now, the fading light is the signal given to man to seek his natural rest.
I remember to have fought the Maquas, hereaways, in the first war in which I ever drew blood from man...

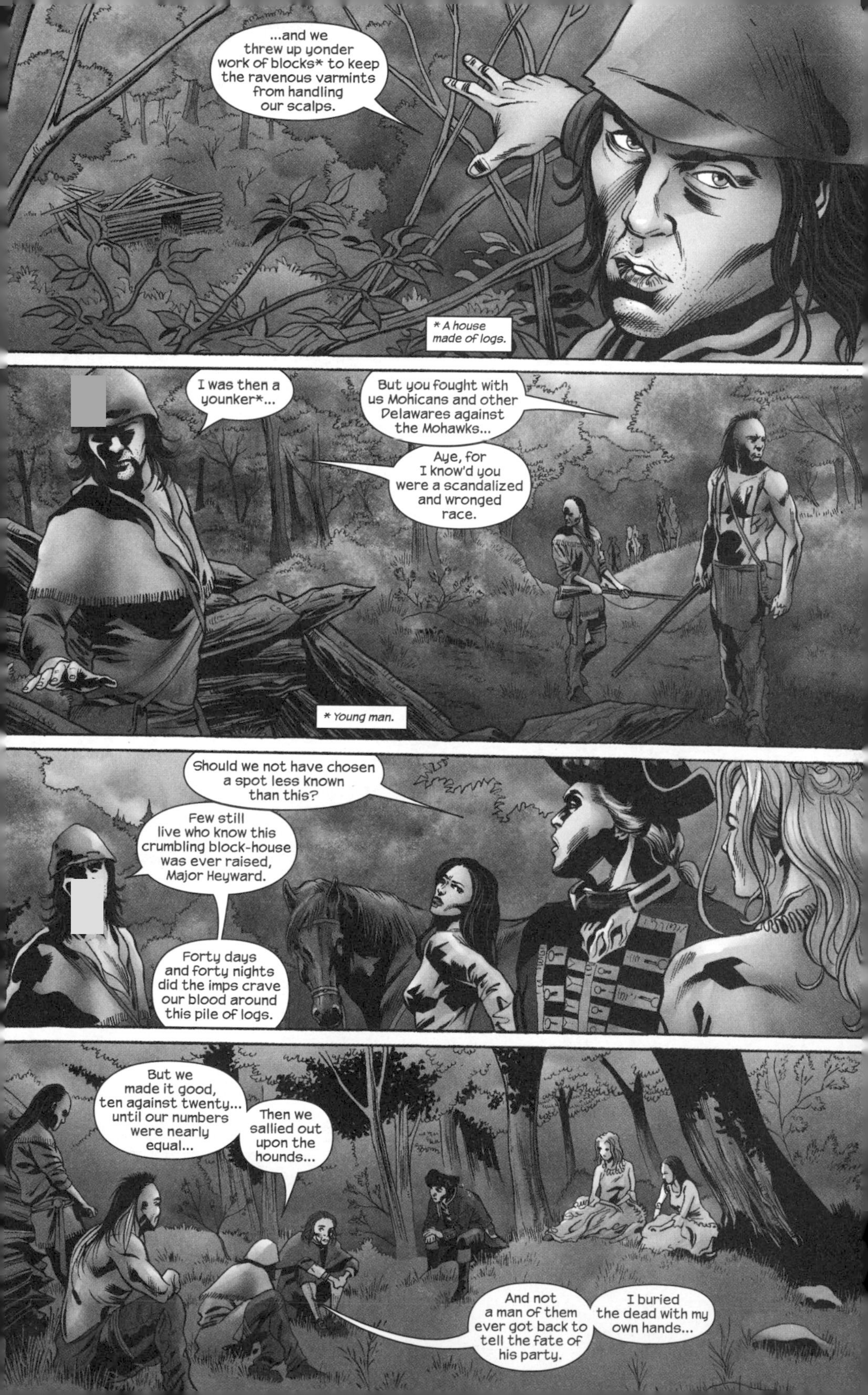
...and we threw up yonder work of blocks* to keep the ravenous varmints from handling our scalps.
* A house made of logs.
I was then a younker*...
But you fought with us Mohicans and other Delawares against the Mohawks...
Aye, for I know'd you were a scandalized and wronged race.
* Young man.
Should we not have chosen a spot less known than this?
Few still live who know this crumbling block-house was ever raised, Major Heyward.
Forty days and forty nights did the imps crave our blood around this pile of logs.
But we made it good, ten against twenty... until our numbers were nearly equal...
Then we sallied out upon the hounds...
And not a man of them ever got back to tell the fate of his party.
I buried the dead with my own hands...

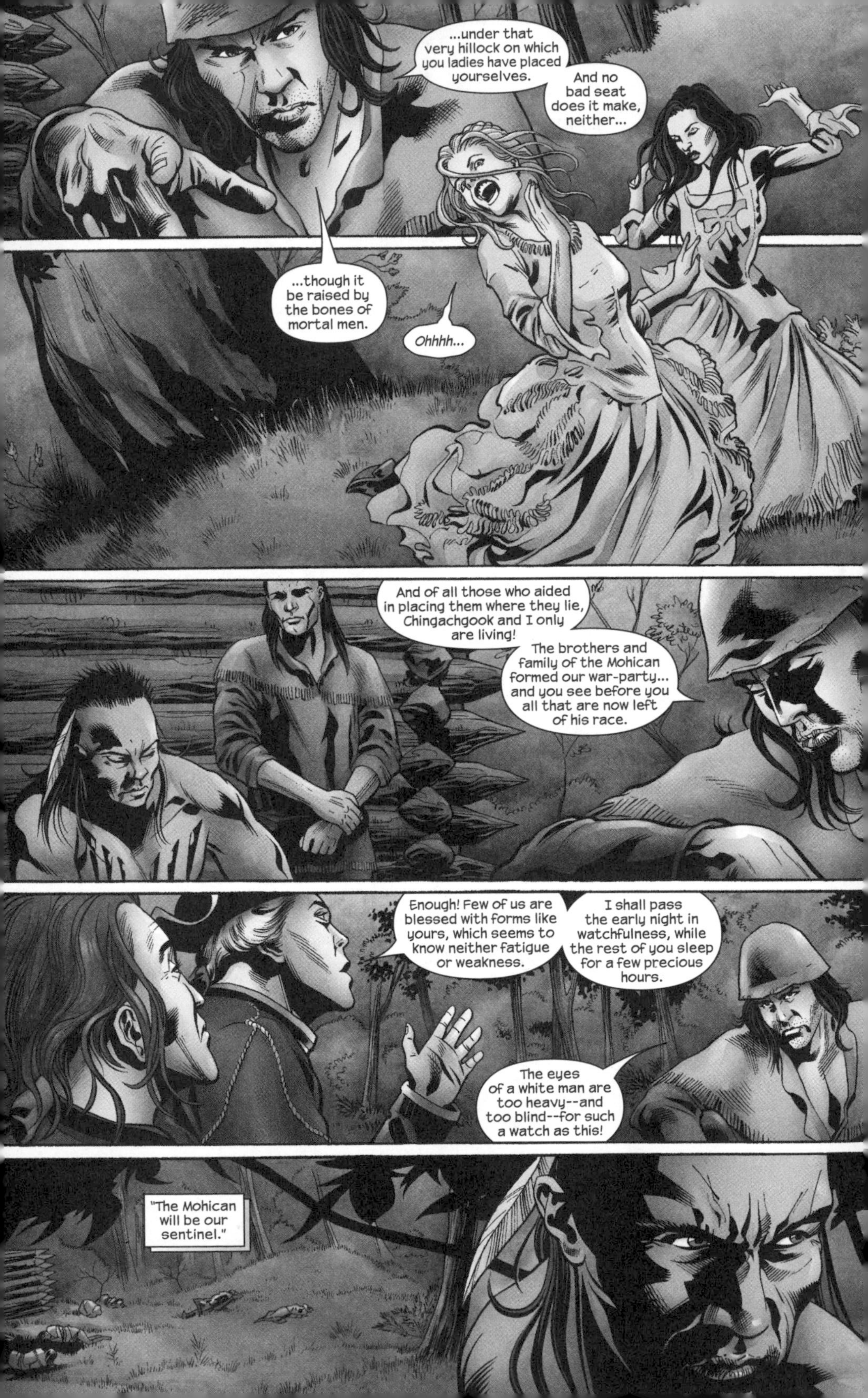

...under that very hillock on which you ladies have placed yourselves.
And no bad seat does it make, neither...
...though it be raised by the bones of mortal men.
Ohhhh...
And of all those who aided in placing them where they lie, Chingachgook and I only are living!
The brothers and family of the Mohican formed our war-party... and you see before you all that are now left of his race.
Enough! Few of us are blessed with forms like yours, which seems to know neither fatigue or weakness.
I shall pass the early night in watchfulness, while the rest of you sleep for a few precious hours.
The eyes of a white man are too heavy--and too blind--for such a watch as this!
"The Mohican will be our sentinel."

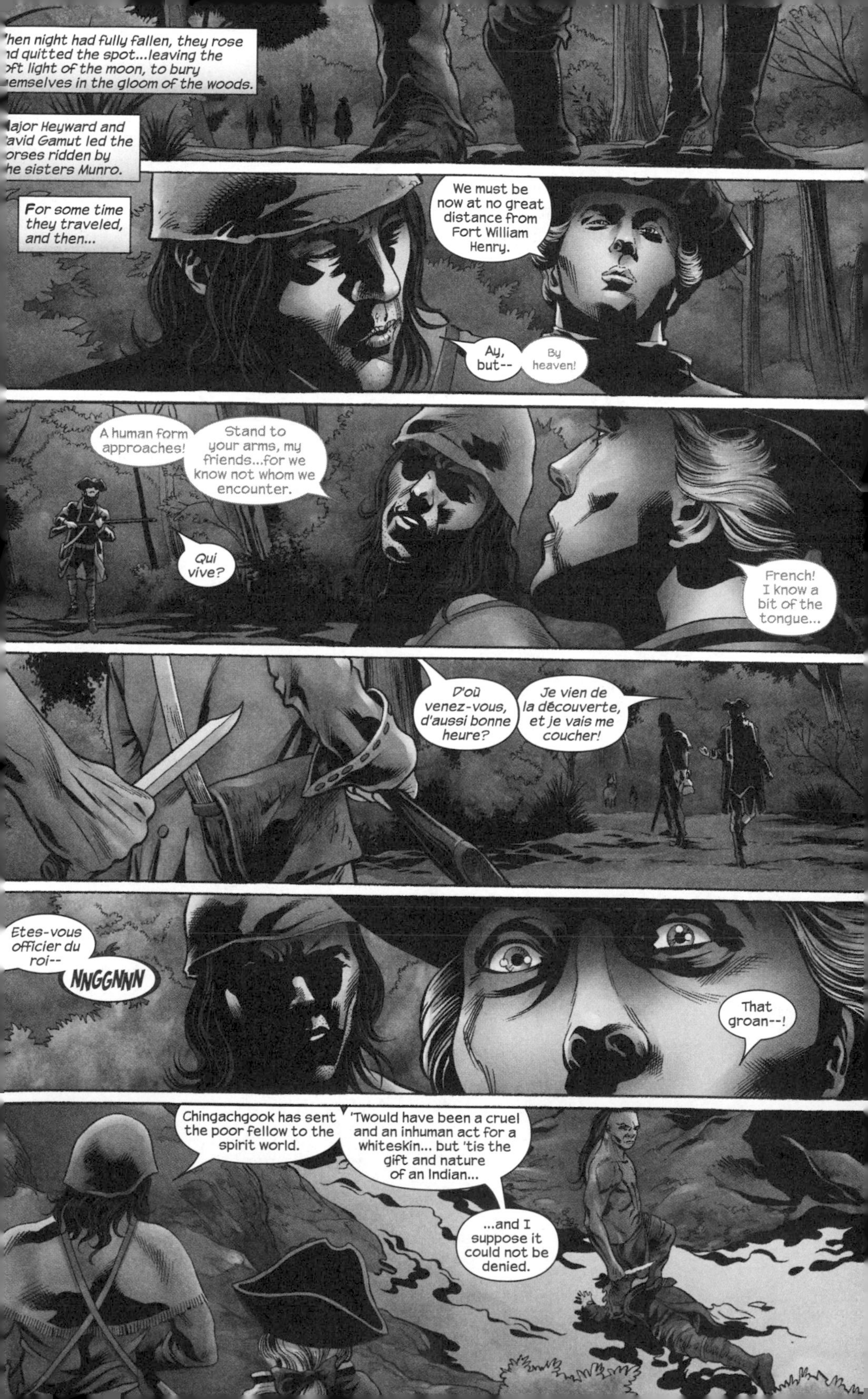
hen night had fully fallen, they rose nd quitted the spot...leaving the oft light of the moon, to bury emselves in the gloom of the woods.
ajor Heyward and avid Gamut led the orses ridden by he sisters Munro.
For some time they traveled, and then...
We must be now at no great distance from Fort William Henry.
Ay, but--
By heaven!
A human form approaches!
Stand to your arms, my friends...for we know not whom we encounter.
Qui vive?
French! I know a bit of the tongue...
D'où venez-vous, d'aussi bonne heure?
Je vien de la dĕcouverte, et je vais me coucher!
Etes-vous officier du roi--
NNGGNNN
That groan--!
Chingachgook has sent the poor fellow to the spirit world.
'Twould have been a cruel and an inhuman act for a whiteskin... but 'tis the gift and nature of an Indian...
...and I suppose it could not be denied.

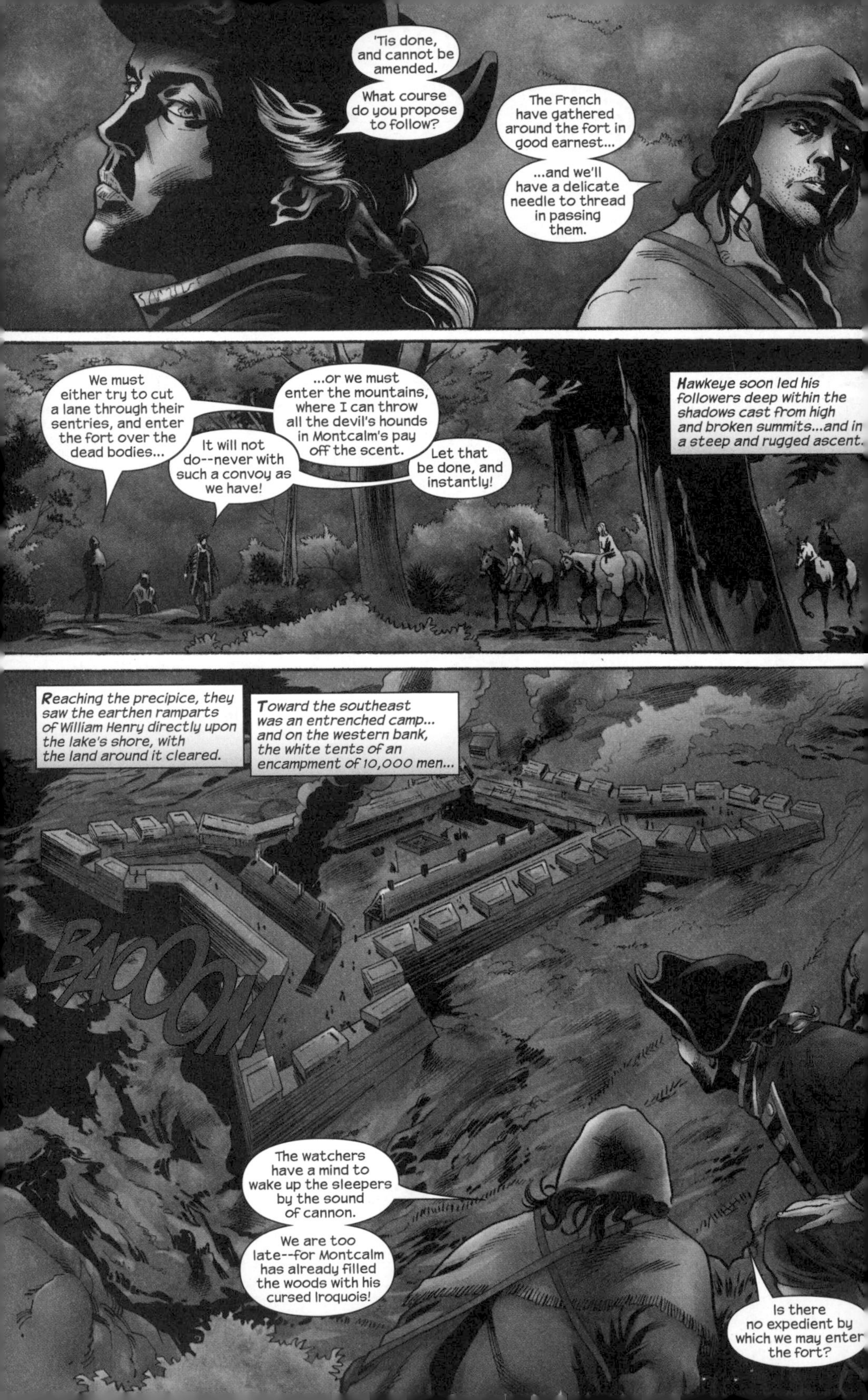
'Tis done, and cannot be amended.
What course do you propose to follow?
The French have gathered around the fort in good earnest...
...and we'll have a delicate needle to thread in passing them.
We must either try to cut a lane through their sentries, and enter the fort over the dead bodies...
...or we must enter the mountains, where I can throw all the devil's hounds in Montcalm's pay off the scent.
It will not do--never with such a convoy as we have!
Let that be done, and instantly!
Hawkeye soon led his followers deep within the shadows cast from high and broken summits...and in a steep and rugged ascent.
Reaching the precipice, they saw the earthen ramparts of William Henry directly upon the lake's shore, with the land around it cleared.
Toward the southeast was an entrenched camp... and on the western bank, the white tents of an encampment of 10,000 men...
BAOOOM
The watchers have a mind to wake up the sleepers by the sound of cannon.
We are too late--for Montcalm has already filled the woods with his cursed Iroquois!
Is there no expedient by which we may enter the fort?

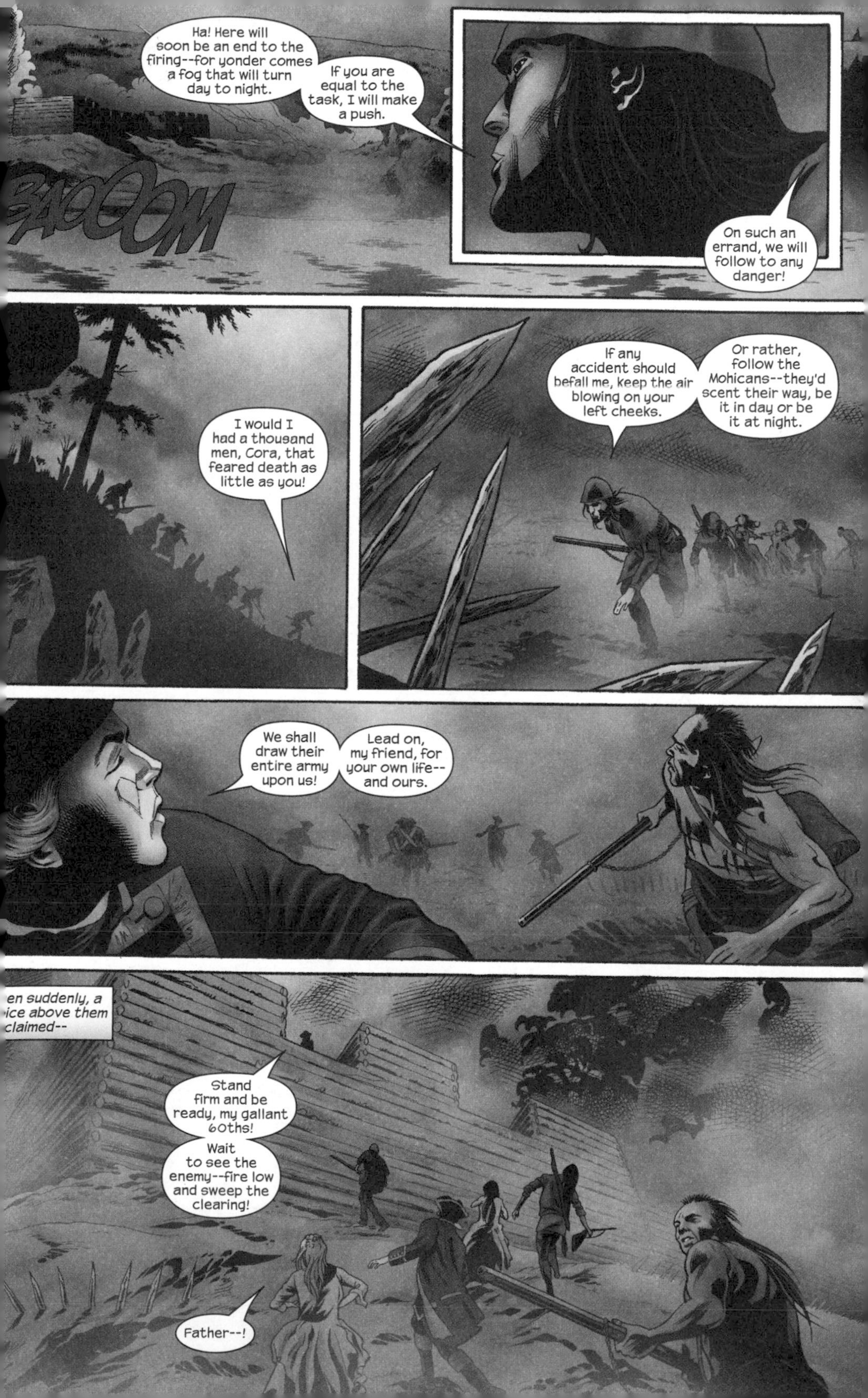
Ha! Here will soon be an end to the firing--for yonder comes a fog that will turn day to night.
If you are equal to the task, I will make a push.
BAOOOOM
On such an errand, we will follow to any danger!
I would I had a thousand men, Cora, that feared death as little as you!
If any accident should befall me, keep the air blowing on your left cheeks.
Or rather, follow the Mohicans--they'd scent their way, be it in day or be it at night.
We shall draw their entire army upon us!
Lead on, my friend, for your own life--and ours.
en suddenly, a
ice above them
claimed--
Stand firm and be ready, my gallant 60ths!
Wait to see the enemy--fire low and sweep the clearing!
Father--!

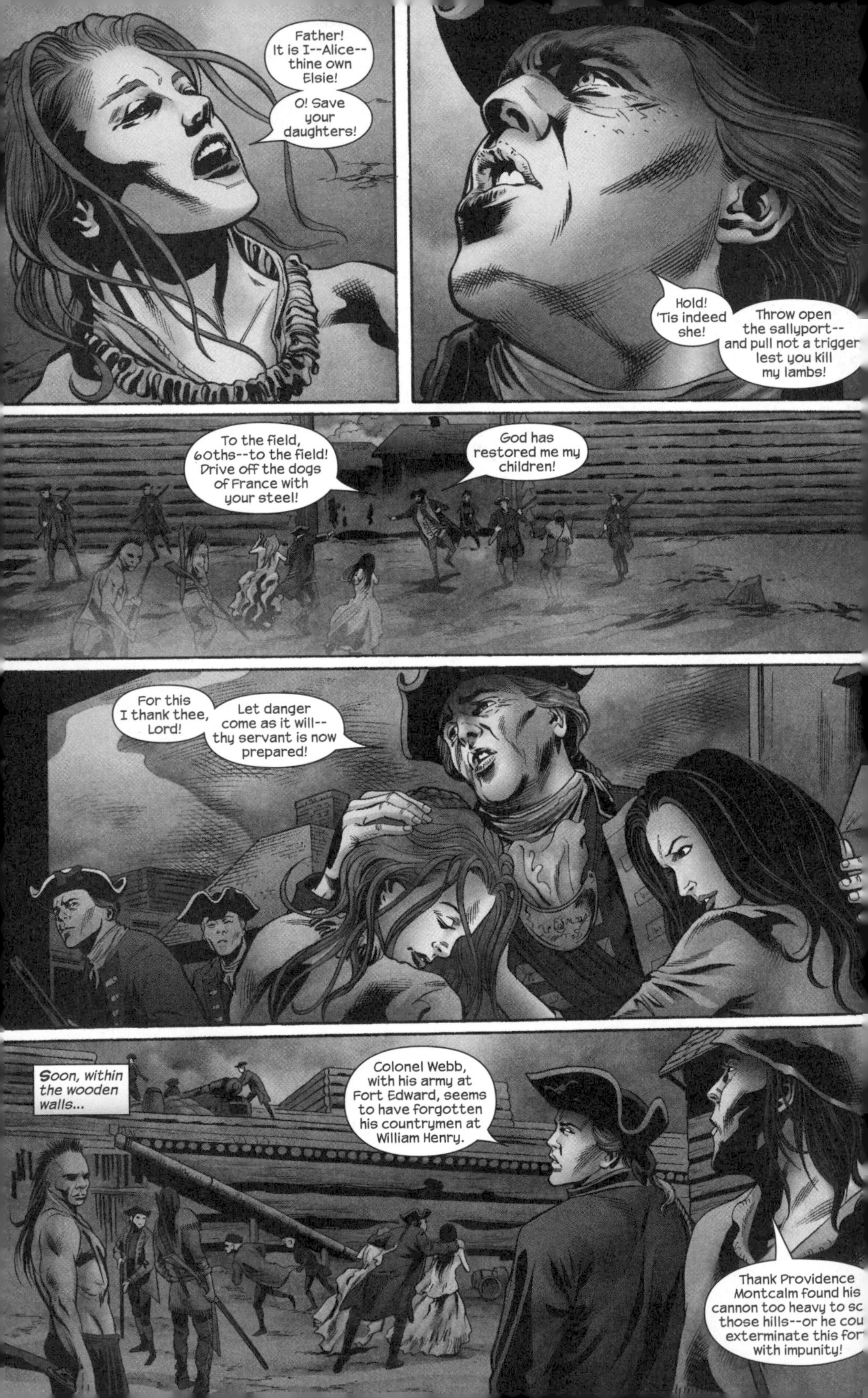

Father! It is I--Alice--thine own Elsie!
O! Save your daughters!
Hold! 'Tis indeed she!
Throw open the sallyport--and pull not a trigger lest you kill my lambs!
To the field, 60ths--to the field! Drive off the dogs of France with your steel!
God has restored me my children!
For this I thank thee, Lord!
Let danger come as it will--thy servant is now prepared!
Soon, within the wooden walls...
Colonel Webb, with his army at Fort Edward, seems to have forgotten his countrymen at William Henry.
Thank Providence Montcalm found his cannon too heavy to sc those hills--or he cou exterminate this for with impunity!

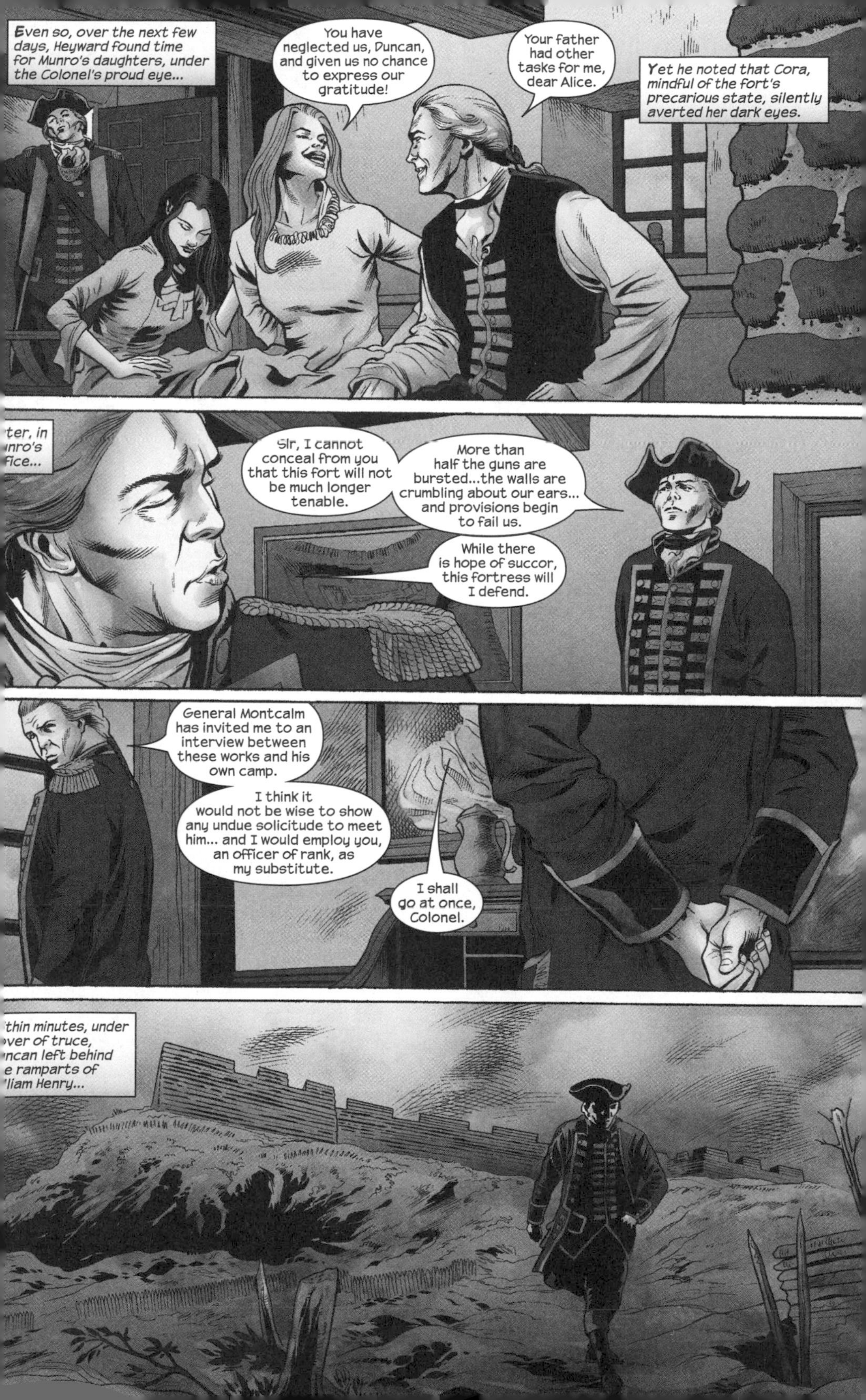
Even so, over the next few days, Heyward found time for Munro's daughters, under the Colonel's proud eye...
You have neglected us, Duncan, and given us no chance to express our gratitude!
Your father had other tasks for me, dear Alice.
Yet he noted that Cora, mindful of the fort's precarious state, silently averted her dark eyes.
ter, in
nro's
fice...
Sir, I cannot conceal from you that this fort will not be much longer tenable.
More than half the guns are bursted...the walls are crumbling about our ears... and provisions begin to fail us.
While there is hope of succor, this fortress will I defend.
General Montcalm has invited me to an interview between these works and his own camp.
I think it would not be wise to show any undue solicitude to meet him... and I would employ you, an officer of rank, as my substitute.
I shall go at once, Colonel.
thin minutes, under
ver of truce,
ncan left behind
e ramparts of
liam Henry...

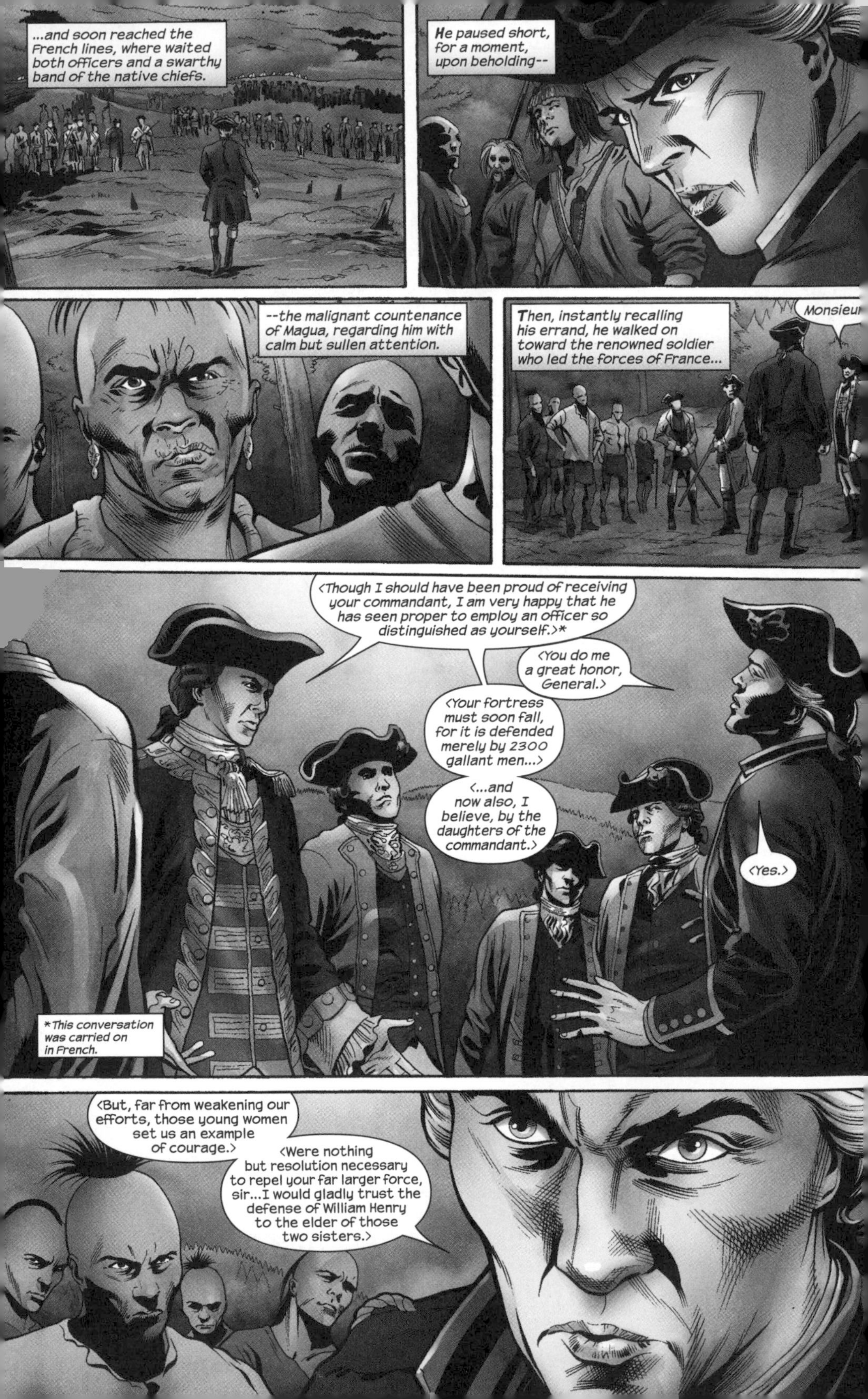

...and soon reached the French lines, where waited both officers and a swarthy band of the native chiefs.
He paused short, for a moment, upon beholding--
--the malignant countenance of Magua, regarding him with calm but sullen attention.
Then, instantly recalling his errand, he walked on toward the renowned soldier who led the forces of France...
Monsieur
<Though I should have been proud of receiving your commandant, I am very happy that he has seen proper to employ an officer so distinguished as yourself.>*
<You do me a great honor, General.>
<Your fortress must soon fall, for it is defended merely by 2300 gallant men...>
<...and now also, I believe, by the daughters of the commandant.>
<Yes.>
*This conversation was carried on in French.
<But, far from weakening our efforts, those young women set us an example of courage.>
<Were nothing but resolution necessary to repel your far larger force, sir...I would gladly trust the defense of William Henry to the elder of those two sisters.>

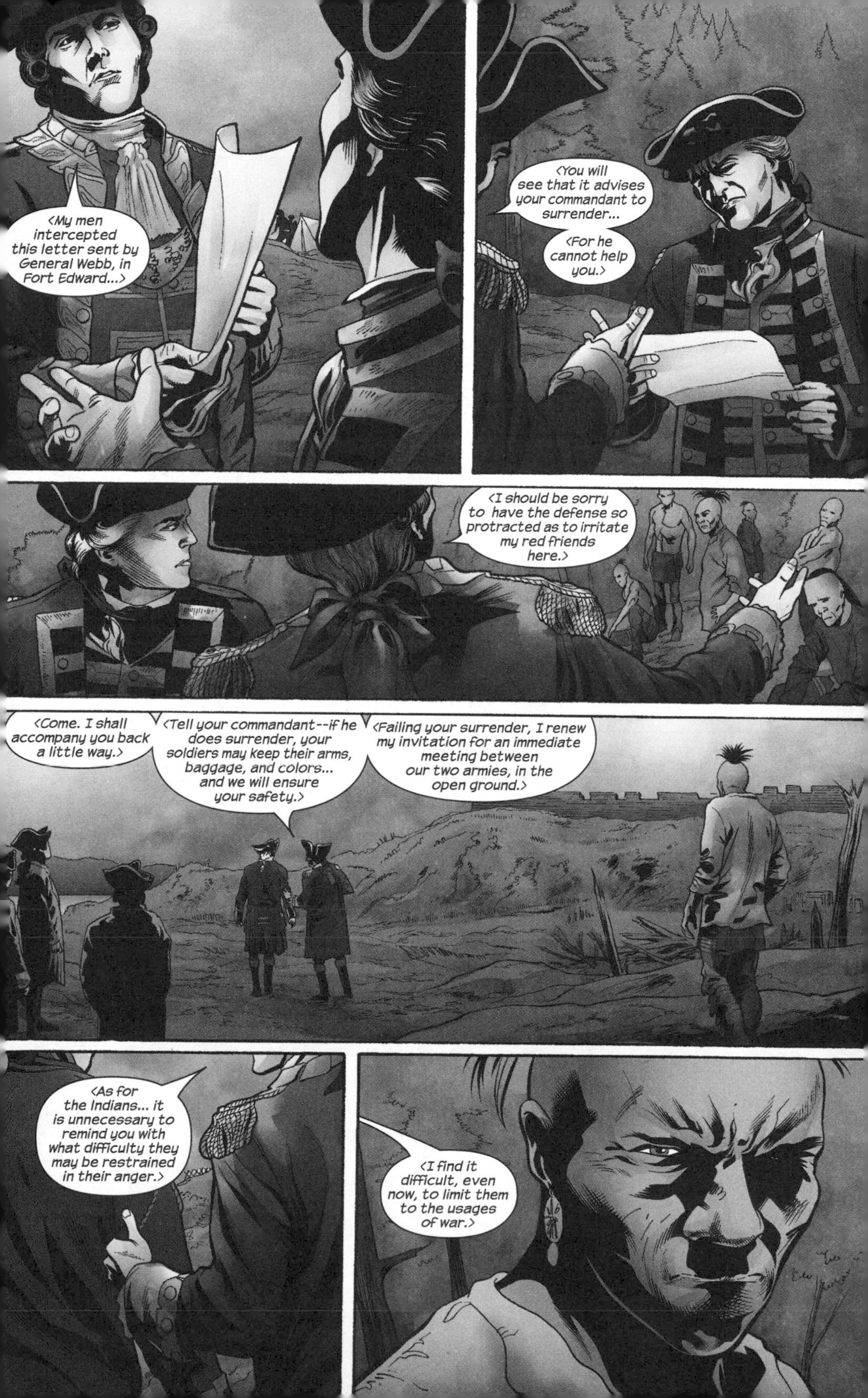
<My men intercepted this letter sent by General Webb, in Fort Edward...>
<You will see that it advises your commandant to surrender...
<For he cannot help you.>
<I should be sorry to have the defense so protracted as to irritate my red friends here.>
<Come. I shall accompany you back a little way.>
<Tell your commandant--if he does surrender, your soldiers may keep their arms, baggage, and colors... and we will ensure your safety.>
<Failing your surrender, I renew my invitation for an immediate meeting between our two armies, in the open ground.>
<As for the Indians... it is unnecessary to remind you with what difficulty they may be restrained in their anger.>
<I find it difficult, even now, to limit them to the usages of war.>

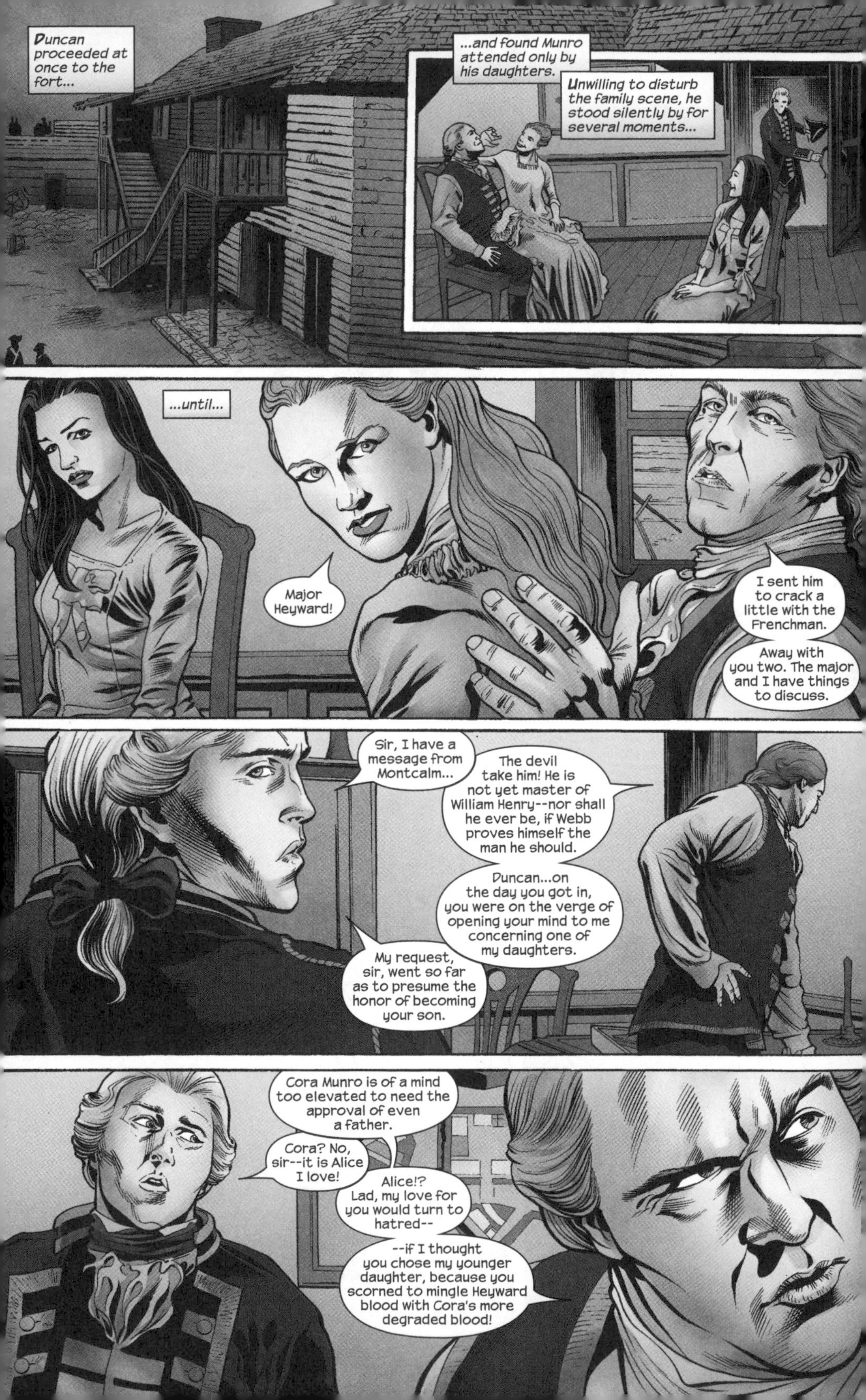
Duncan proceeded at once to the fort...
...and found Munro attended only by his daughters.
Unwilling to disturb the family scene, he stood silently by for several moments...
...until...
Major Heyward!
I sent him to crack a little with the Frenchman.
Away with you two. The major and I have things to discuss.
Sir, I have a message from Montcalm...
The devil take him! He is not yet master of William Henry--nor shall he ever be, if Webb proves himself the man he should.
Duncan...on the day you got in, you were on the verge of opening your mind to me concerning one of my daughters.
My request, sir, went so far as to presume the honor of becoming your son.
Cora Munro is of a mind too elevated to need the approval of even a father.
Cora? No, sir--it is Alice I love!
Alice!? Lad, my love for you would turn to hatred--
--if I thought you chose my younger daughter, because you scorned to mingle Heyward blood with Cora's more degraded blood!

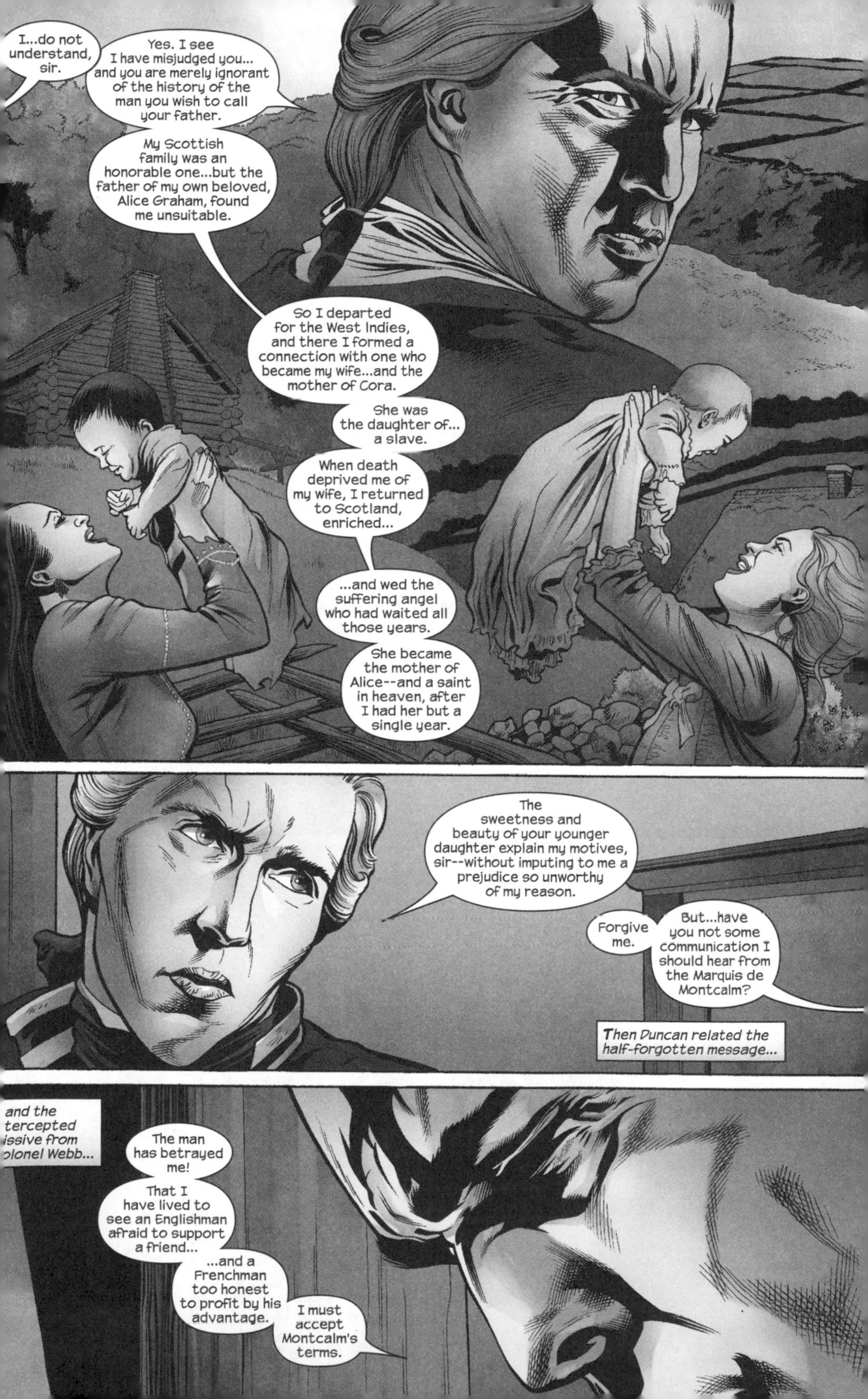
I...do not understand, sir.
Yes. I see I have misjudged you... and you are merely ignorant of the history of the man you wish to call your father.
My Scottish family was an honorable one...but the father of my own beloved, Alice Graham, found me unsuitable.
So I departed for the West Indies, and there I formed a connection with one who became my wife...and the mother of Cora.
She was the daughter of... a slave.
When death deprived me of my wife, I returned to Scotland, enriched...
...and wed the suffering angel who had waited all those years.
She became the mother of Alice--and a saint in heaven, after I had her but a single year.
The sweetness and beauty of your younger daughter explain my motives, sir--without imputing to me a prejudice so unworthy of my reason.
Forgive me.
But...have you not some communication I should hear from the Marquis de Montcalm?
Then Duncan related the half-forgotten message...
and the tercepted issive from olonel Webb...
The man has betrayed me!
That I have lived to see an Englishman afraid to support a friend...
...and a Frenchman too honest to profit by his advantage.
I must accept Montcalm's terms.

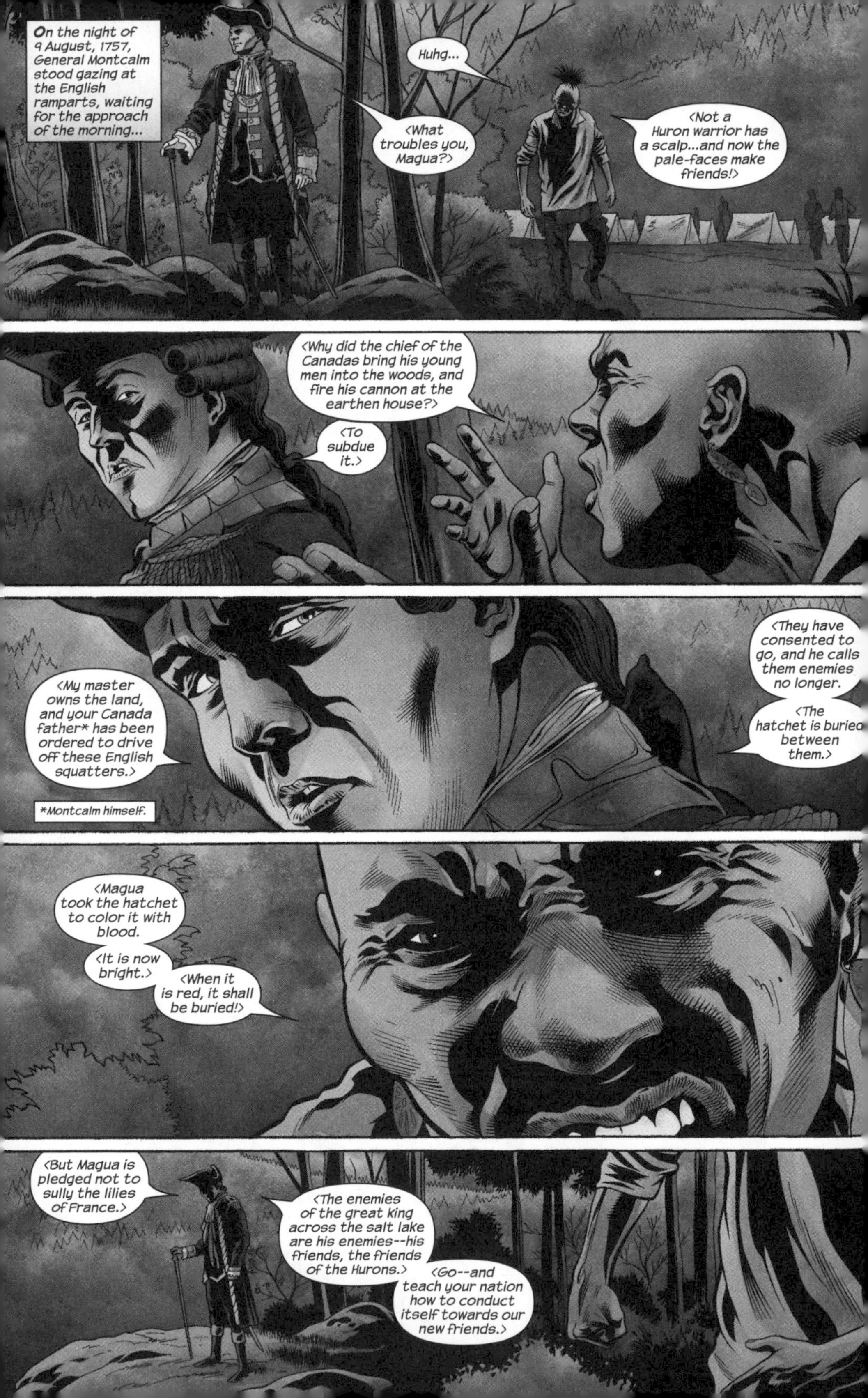
On the night of 9 August, 1757, General Montcalm stood gazing at the English ramparts, waiting for the approach of the morning...
Huhg...
<What troubles you, Magua?>
<Not a Huron warrior has a scalp...and now the pale-faces make friends!>
<Why did the chief of the Canadas bring his young men into the woods, and fire his cannon at the earthen house?>
<To subdue it.>
<My master owns the land, and your Canada father* has been ordered to drive off these English squatters.>
*Montcalm himself.
<They have consented to go, and he calls them enemies no longer.
<The hatchet is buried between them.>
<Magua took the hatchet to color it with blood.
<It is now bright.>
<When it is red, it shall be buried!>
<But Magua is pledged not to sully the lilies of France.>
<The enemies of the great king across the salt lake are his enemies--his friends, the friends of the Hurons.>
<Go--and teach your nation how to conduct itself towards our new friends.>

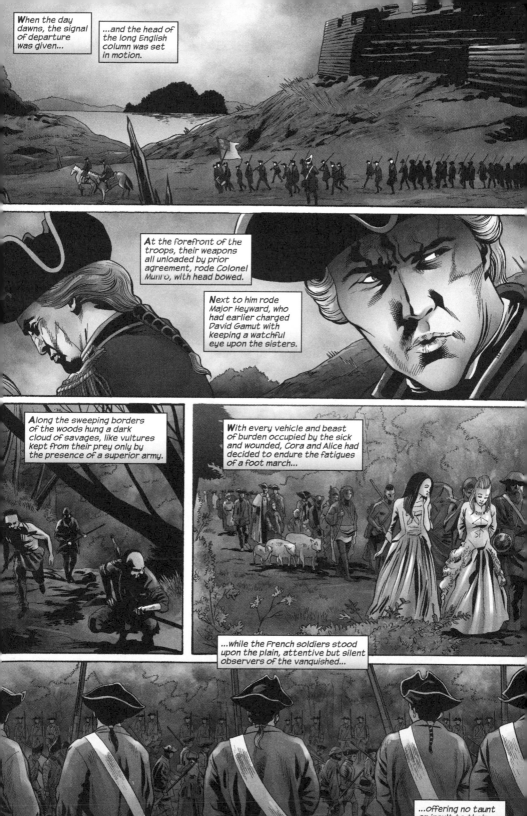

When the day dawns, the signal of departure was given...

...and the head of the long English column was set in motion.

At the forefront of the troops, their weapons all unloaded by prior agreement, rode Colonel Munro, with head bowed.

Next to him rode Major Heyward, who had earlier charged David Gamut with keeping a watchful eye upon the sisters.

Along the sweeping borders of the woods hung a dark cloud of savages, like vultures kept from their prey only by the presence of a superior army.

With every vehicle and beast of burden occupied by the sick and wounded, Cora and Alice had decided to endure the fatigues of a foot march...

...while the French soldiers stood upon the plain, attentive but silent observers of the vanquished...

...offering no taunt or insult to their less fortunate foes.

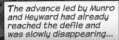

The advance led by Munro and Heyward had already reached the defile and was slowly disappearing...

...as a few of the sullen Hurons straggled among the conquered columns...as yet, only passive observers.

It was then that Cora saw the form of Magua gliding among his countrymen...

...and speaking with his fatal and artful eloquence.

The savages seemed content to let their enemies pass without further molestation.

But, as the female crowd approached, the gaudy colors of a shawl attracted the eyes of a wild and untutored Huron...

No--!

Give him the shawl, woman!

Take the shawl-- everything-- but give me my babe!

The Indian flourished the infant over his head, as if weighing its ransom--

--then dashed its head against a rock--

--and cast its remains to her very feet.

For an instant, the mother looked wildly down at the unseemly object...

Then she raised her eyes to Heaven, as if to call on God to curse the perpetrator of the foul deed.

She was spared the sin of such a prayer...

...when the Huron mercifully drove his tomahawk into her brain.

She fell, grasping at her child in death...

...with the same engrossing love that had caused her to cherish it when living.

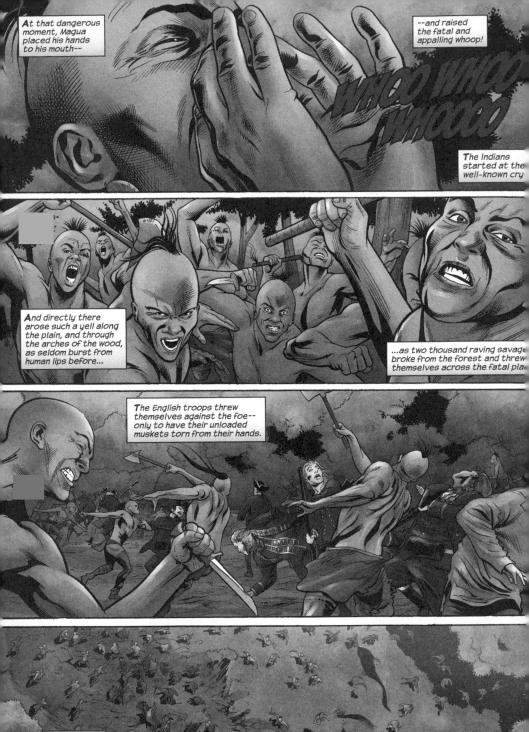

At that dangerous moment, Magua placed his hands to his mouth--

--and raised the fatal and appalling whoop!

WHOO WHOO WHOOO

The Indians started at the well-known cry

And directly there arose such a yell along the plain, and through the arches of the wood, as seldom burst from human lips before...

...as two thousand raving savages broke from the forest and threw themselves across the fatal plain

The English troops threw themselves against the foe-- only to have their unloaded muskets torn from their hands.

Death was everywhere...

...and in his most terrific and disgusting aspects.

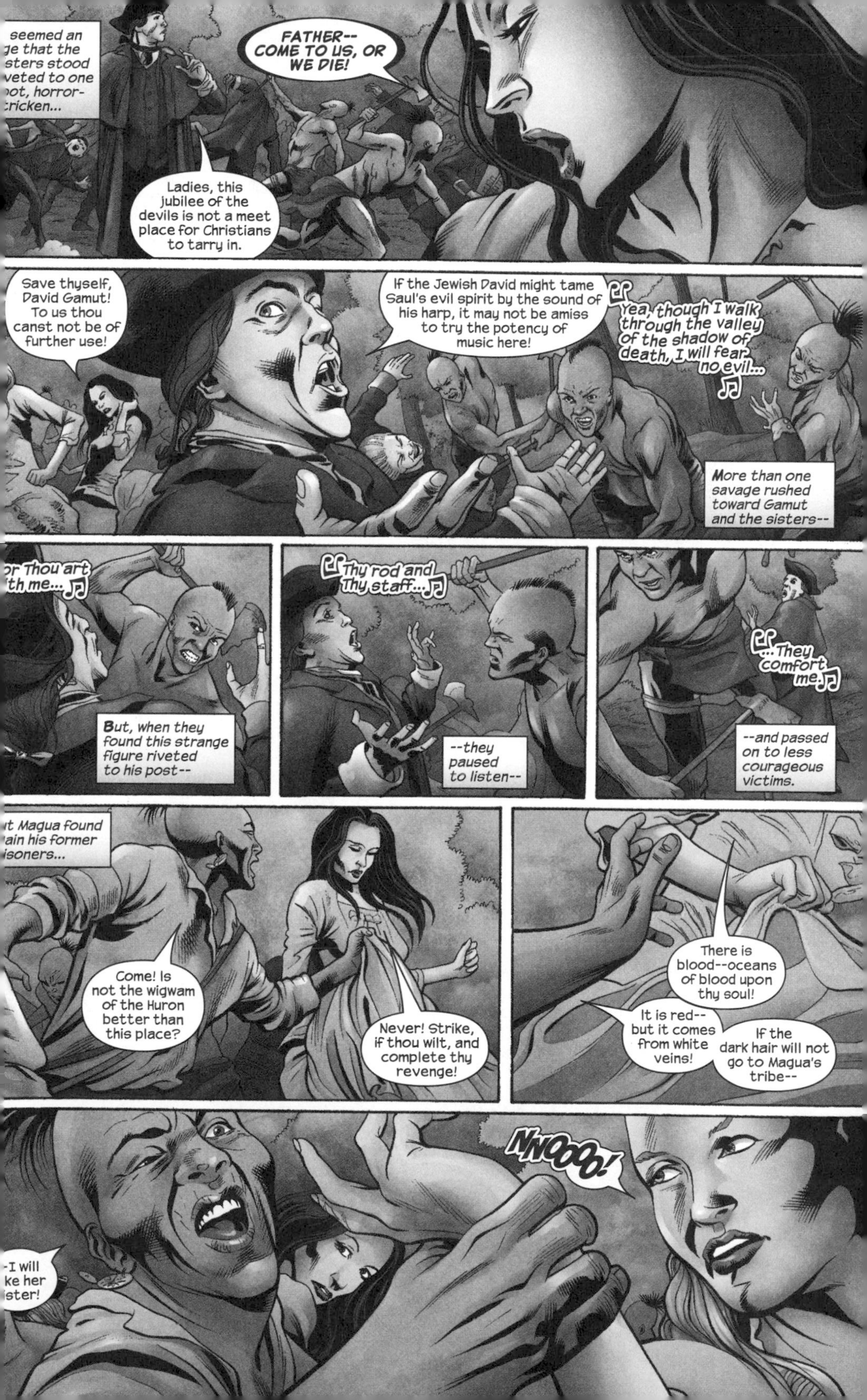
seemed an
ge that the
sters stood
veted to one
oot, horror-
ricken...
FATHER--
COME TO US, OR
WE DIE!
Ladies, this
jubilee of the
devils is not a meet
place for Christians
to tarry in.
Save thyself,
David Gamut!
To us thou
canst not be of
further use!
If the Jewish David might tame
Saul's evil spirit by the sound of
his harp, it may not be amiss
to try the potency of
music here!
Yea, though I walk
through the valley
of the shadow of
death, I will fear
no evil...
More than one
savage rushed
toward Gamut
and the sisters--
or Thou art
ith me...
But, when they
found this strange
figure riveted
to his post--
Thy rod and
Thy staff...
--they
paused
to listen--
...They
comfort
me.
--and passed
on to less
courageous
victims.
t Magua found
ain his former
isoners...
Come! Is
not the wigwam
of the Huron
better than
this place?
Never! Strike,
if thou wilt, and
complete thy
revenge!
There is
blood--oceans
of blood upon
thy soul!
It is red--
but it comes
from white
veins!
If the
dark hair will not
go to Magua's
tribe--
NNOOOO!
-I will
ke her
ister!

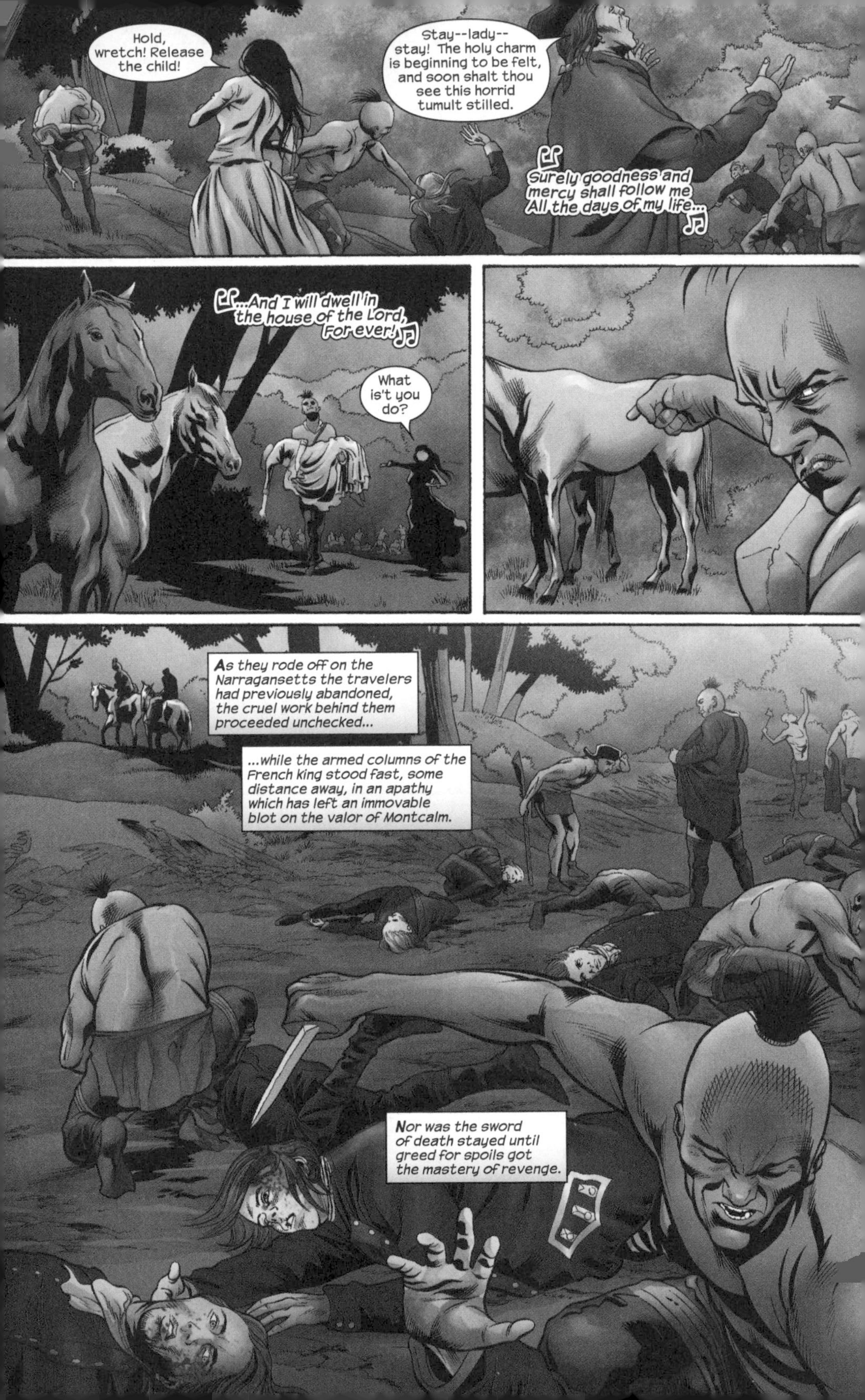
Hold, wretch! Release the child!
Stay--lady--stay! The holy charm is beginning to be felt, and soon shalt thou see this horrid tumult stilled.
Surely goodness and mercy shall follow me All the days of my life...
...And I will dwell in the house of the Lord, For ever!
What is't you do?
As they rode off on the Narragansetts the travelers had previously abandoned, the cruel work behind them proceeded unchecked...
...while the armed columns of the French king stood fast, some distance away, in an apathy which has left an immovable blot on the valor of Montcalm.
Nor was the sword of death stayed until greed for spoils got the mastery of revenge.

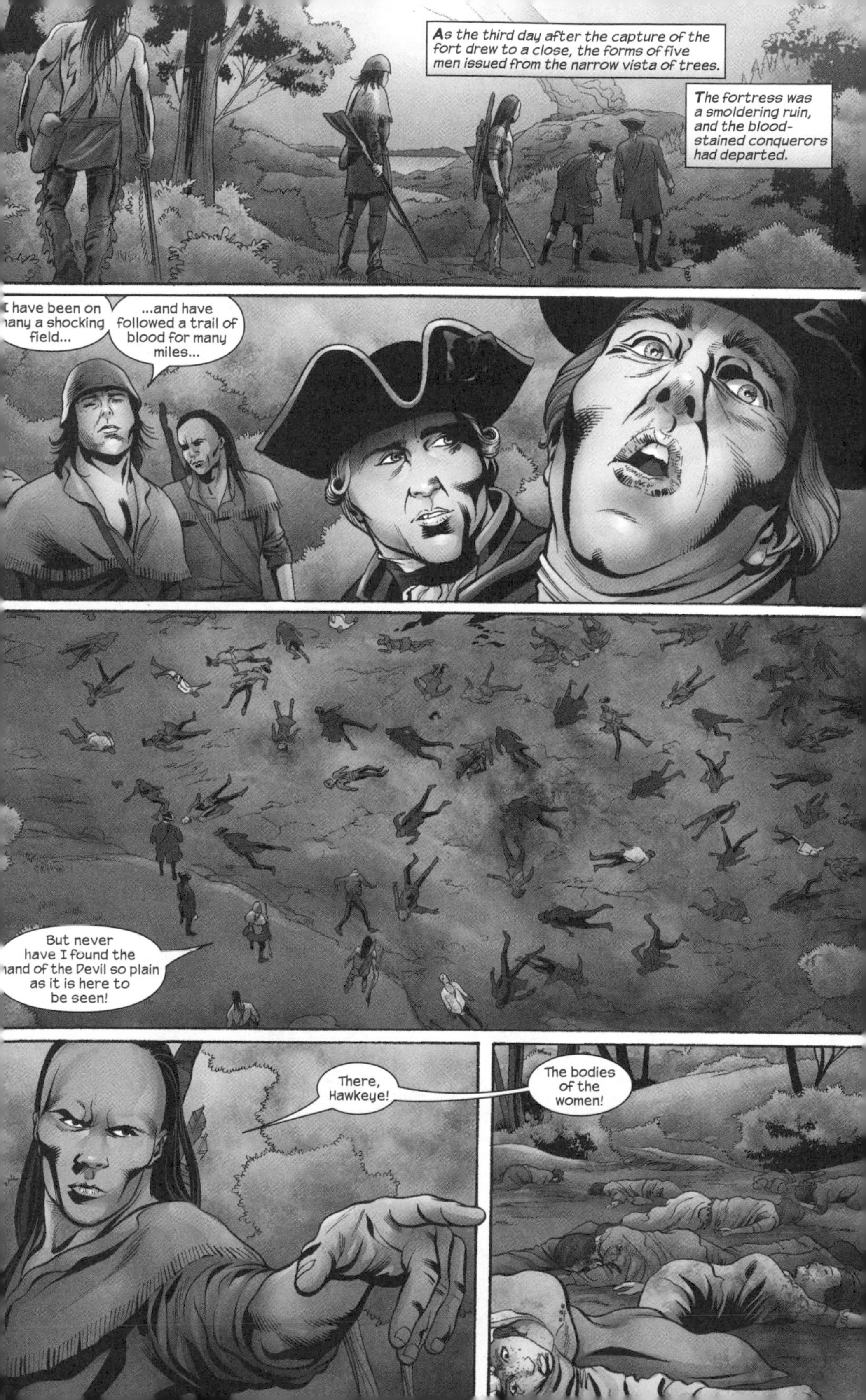
As the third day after the capture of the fort drew to a close, the forms of five men issued from the narrow vista of trees.
The fortress was a smoldering ruin, and the blood-stained conquerors had departed.
I have been on many a shocking field...
...and have followed a trail of blood for many miles...
But never have I found the hand of the Devil so plain as it is here to be seen!
There, Hawkeye!
The bodies of the women!

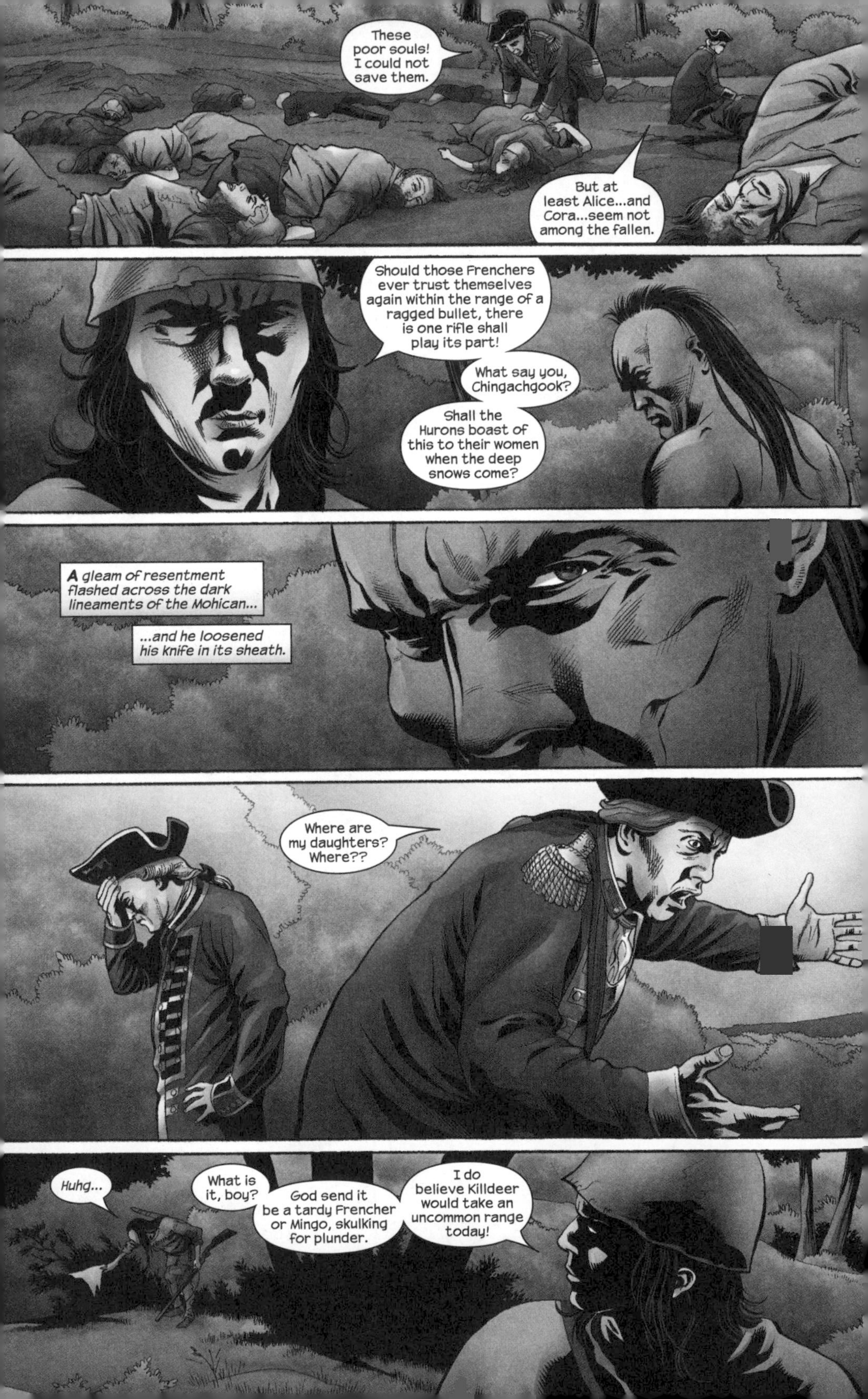
These poor souls! I could not save them.
But at least Alice...and Cora...seem not among the fallen.
Should those Frenchers ever trust themselves again within the range of a ragged bullet, there is one rifle shall play its part!
What say you, Chingachgook?
Shall the Hurons boast of this to their women when the deep snows come?
A gleam of resentment flashed across the dark lineaments of the Mohican...
...and he loosened his knife in its sheath.
Where are my daughters? Where??
Huhg...
What is it, boy?
God send it be a tardy Frencher or Mingo, skulking for plunder.
I do believe Killdeer would take an uncommon range today!

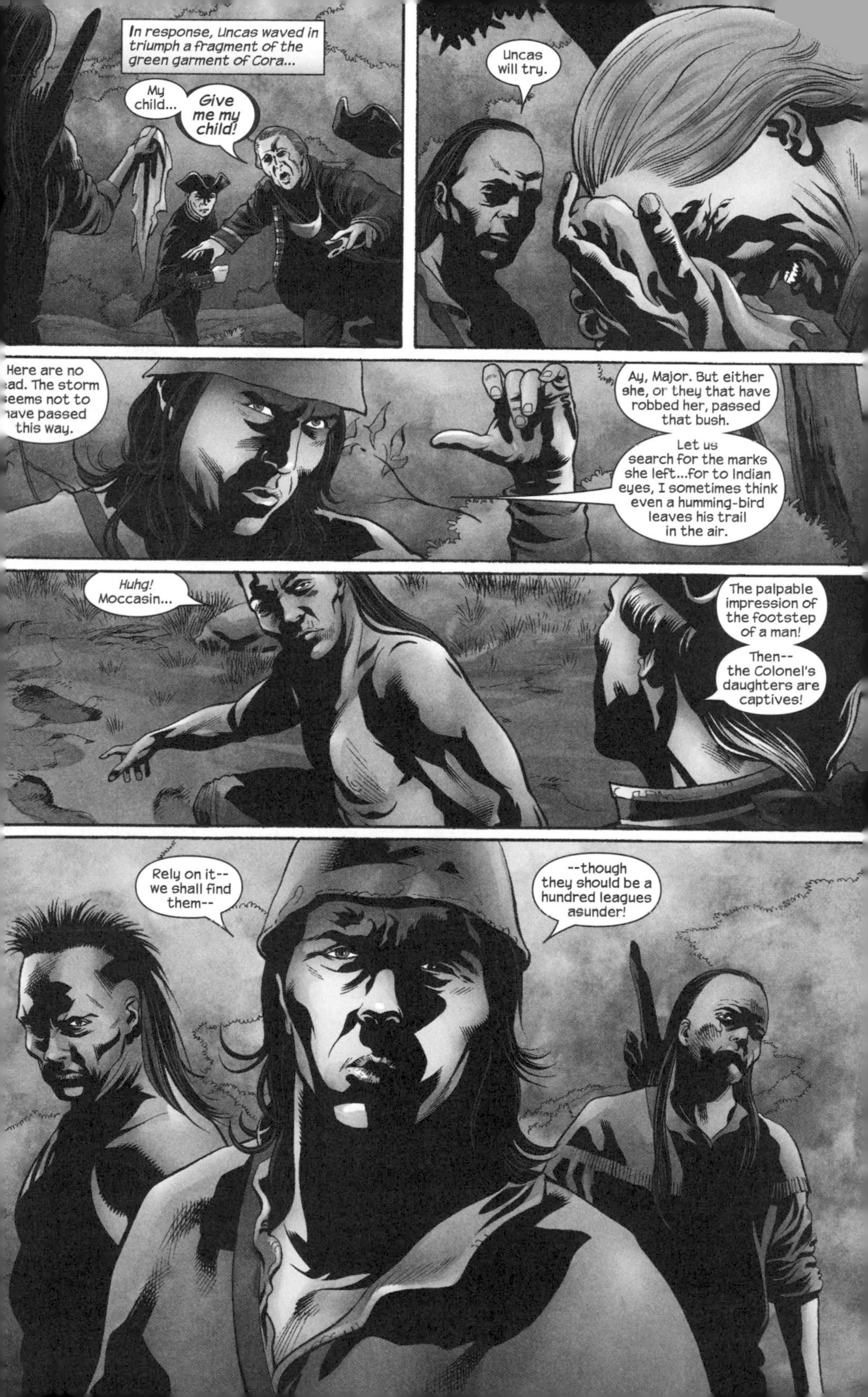

In response, Uncas waved in triumph a fragment of the green garment of Cora...
My child...
Give me my child!
Uncas will try.
Here are no ead. The storm seems not to have passed this way.
Ay, Major. But either she, or they that have robbed her, passed that bush.
Let us search for the marks she left...for to Indian eyes, I sometimes think even a humming-bird leaves his trail in the air.
Huhg! Moccasin...
The palpable impression of the footstep of a man!
Then-- the Colonel's daughters are captives!
Rely on it-- we shall find them--
--though they should be a hundred leagues asunder!

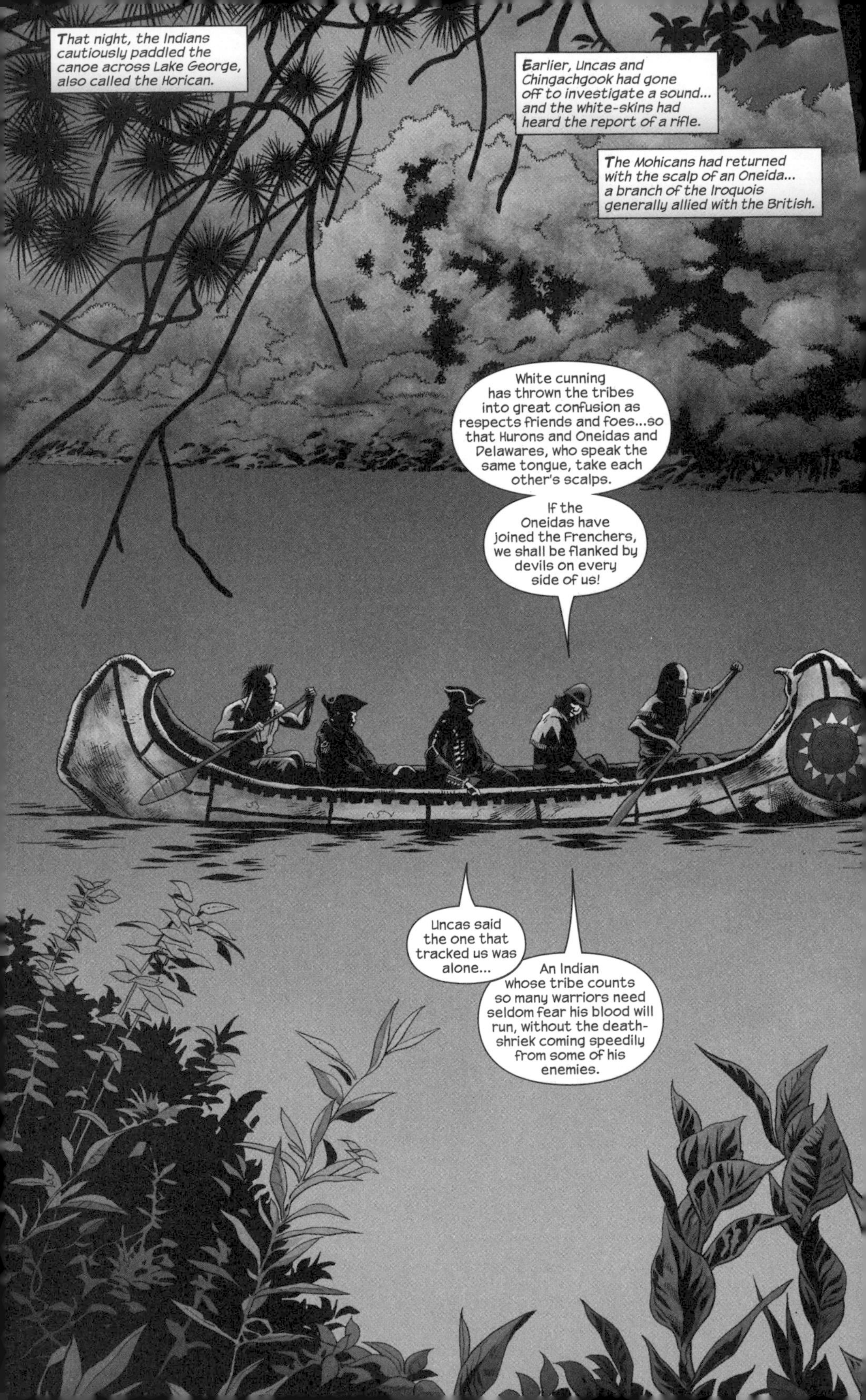
That night, the Indians cautiously paddled the canoe across Lake George, also called the Horican.
Earlier, Uncas and Chingachgook had gone off to investigate a sound... and the white-skins had heard the report of a rifle.
The Mohicans had returned with the scalp of an Oneida... a branch of the Iroquois generally allied with the British.
White cunning has thrown the tribes into great confusion as respects friends and foes...so that Hurons and Oneidas and Delawares, who speak the same tongue, take each other's scalps.
If the Oneidas have joined the Frenchers, we shall be flanked by devils on every side of us!
Uncas said the one that tracked us was alone...
An Indian whose tribe counts so many warriors need seldom fear his blood will run, without the death-shriek coming speedily from some of his enemies.

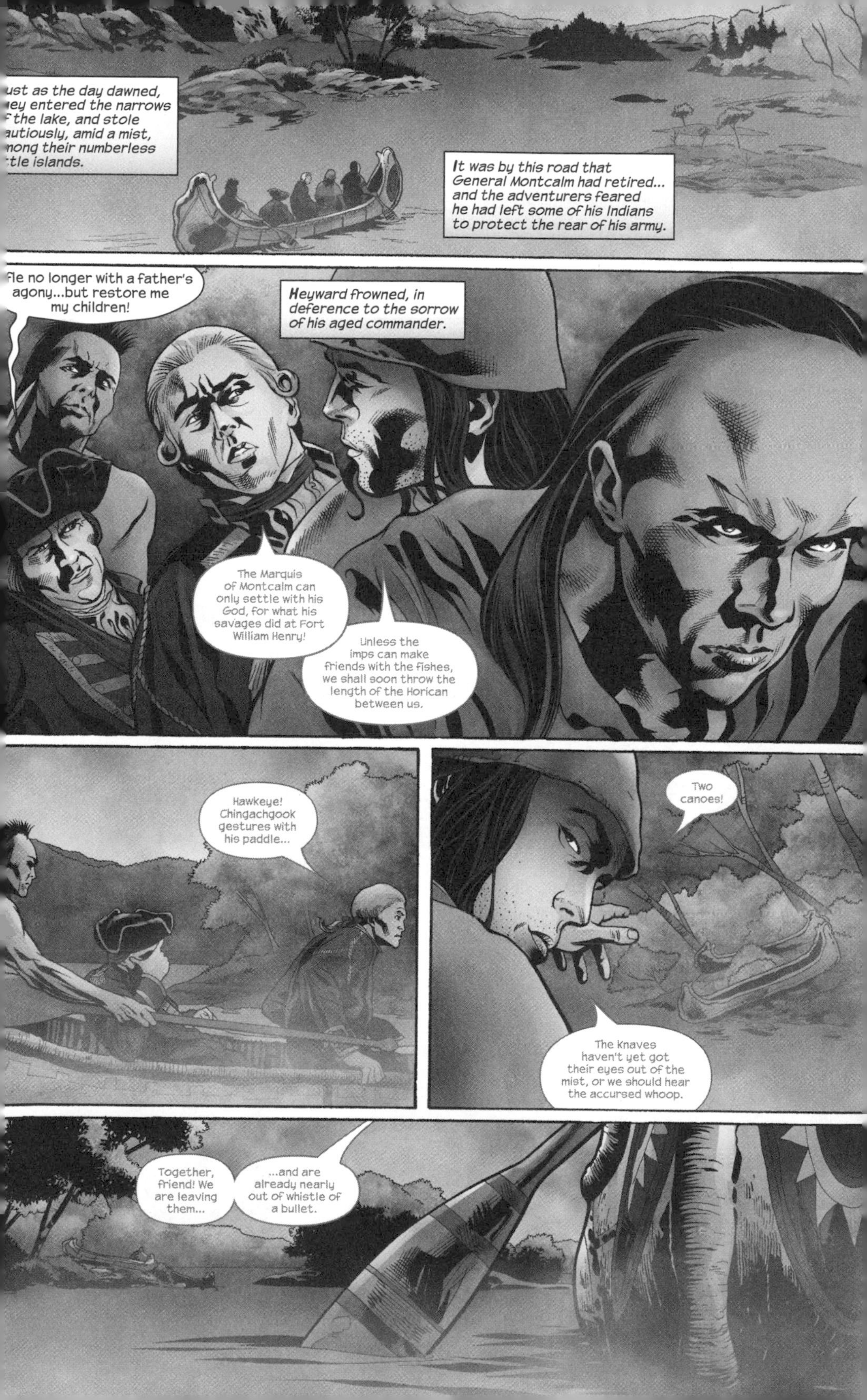
ust as the day dawned, ey entered the narrows f the lake, and stole autiously, amid a mist, nong their numberless ttle islands.
It was by this road that General Montcalm had retired... and the adventurers feared he had left some of his Indians to protect the rear of his army.
le no longer with a father's agony...but restore me my children!
Heyward frowned, in deference to the sorrow of his aged commander.
The Marquis of Montcalm can only settle with his God, for what his savages did at Fort William Henry!
Unless the imps can make friends with the fishes, we shall soon throw the length of the Horican between us.
Hawkeye! Chingachgook gestures with his paddle...
Two canoes!
The knaves haven't yet got their eyes out of the mist, or we should hear the accursed whoop.
Together, friend! We are leaving them...
...and are already nearly out of whistle of a bullet.

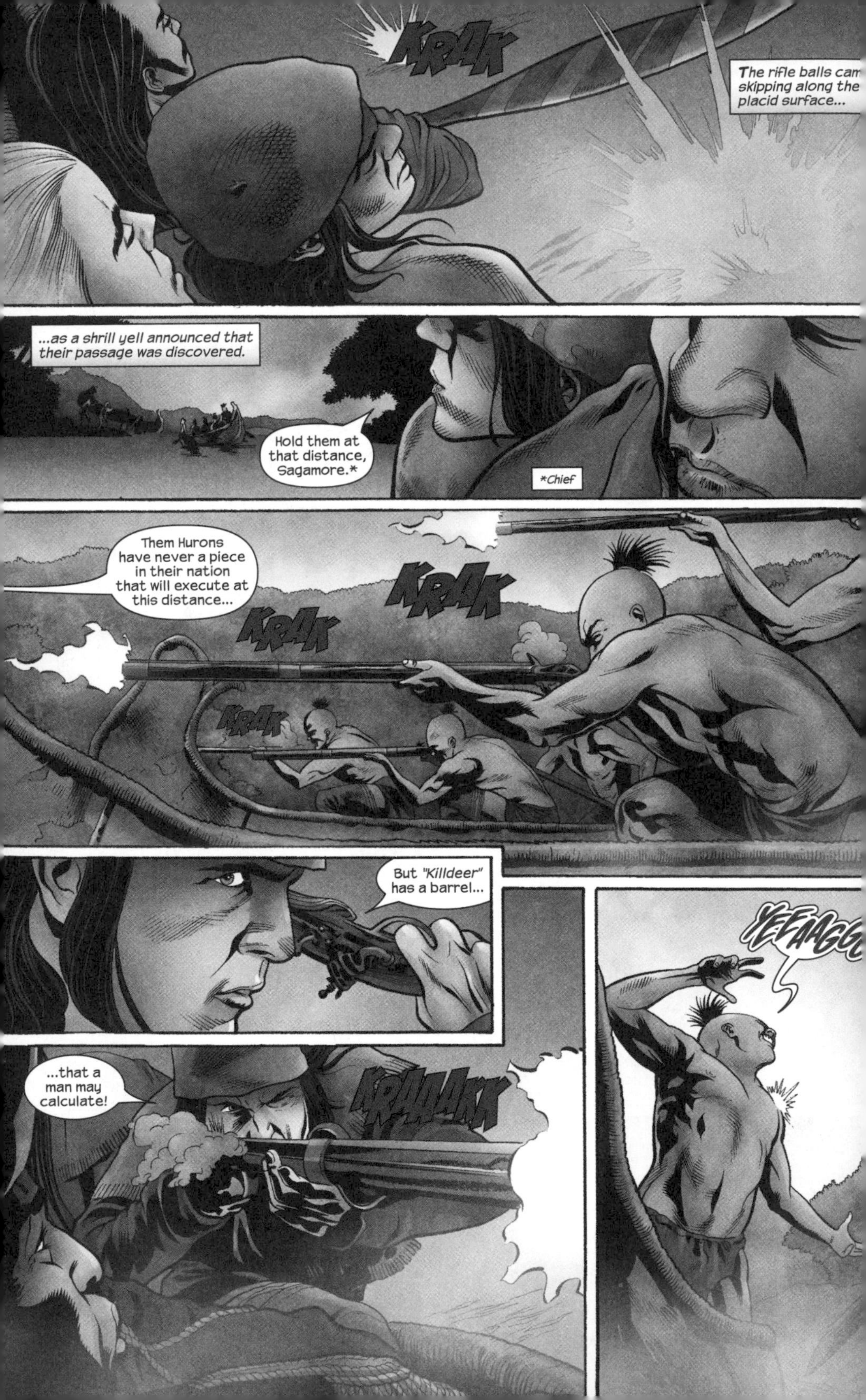
KRAK
The rifle balls cam
skipping along the
placid surface...
...as a shrill yell announced that their passage was discovered.
Hold them at that distance, Sagamore.*
*Chief
Them Hurons have never a piece in their nation that will execute at this distance...
KRAK
KRAK
KRAK
But "Killdeer" has a barrel...
...that a man may calculate!
KRAAAKK

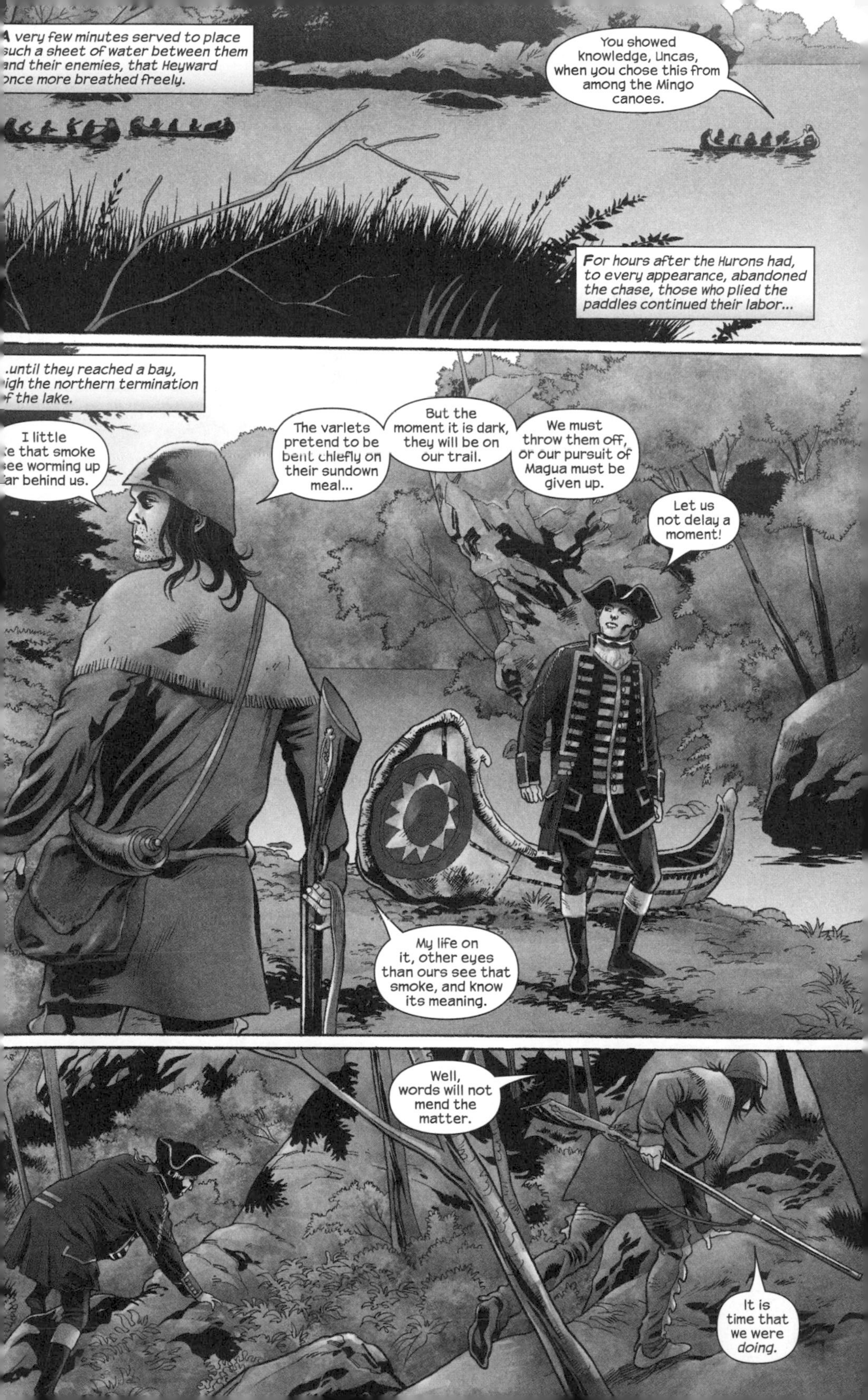

A very few minutes served to place such a sheet of water between them and their enemies, that Heyward once more breathed freely.
You showed knowledge, Uncas, when you chose this from among the Mingo canoes.
For hours after the Hurons had, to every appearance, abandoned the chase, those who plied the paddles continued their labor...
..until they reached a bay, nigh the northern termination of the lake.
I little like that smoke I see worming up far behind us.
The varlets pretend to be bent chiefly on their sundown meal...
But the moment it is dark, they will be on our trail.
We must throw them off, or our pursuit of Magua must be given up.
Let us not delay a moment!
My life on it, other eyes than ours see that smoke, and know its meaning.
Well, words will not mend the matter.
It is time that we were doing.

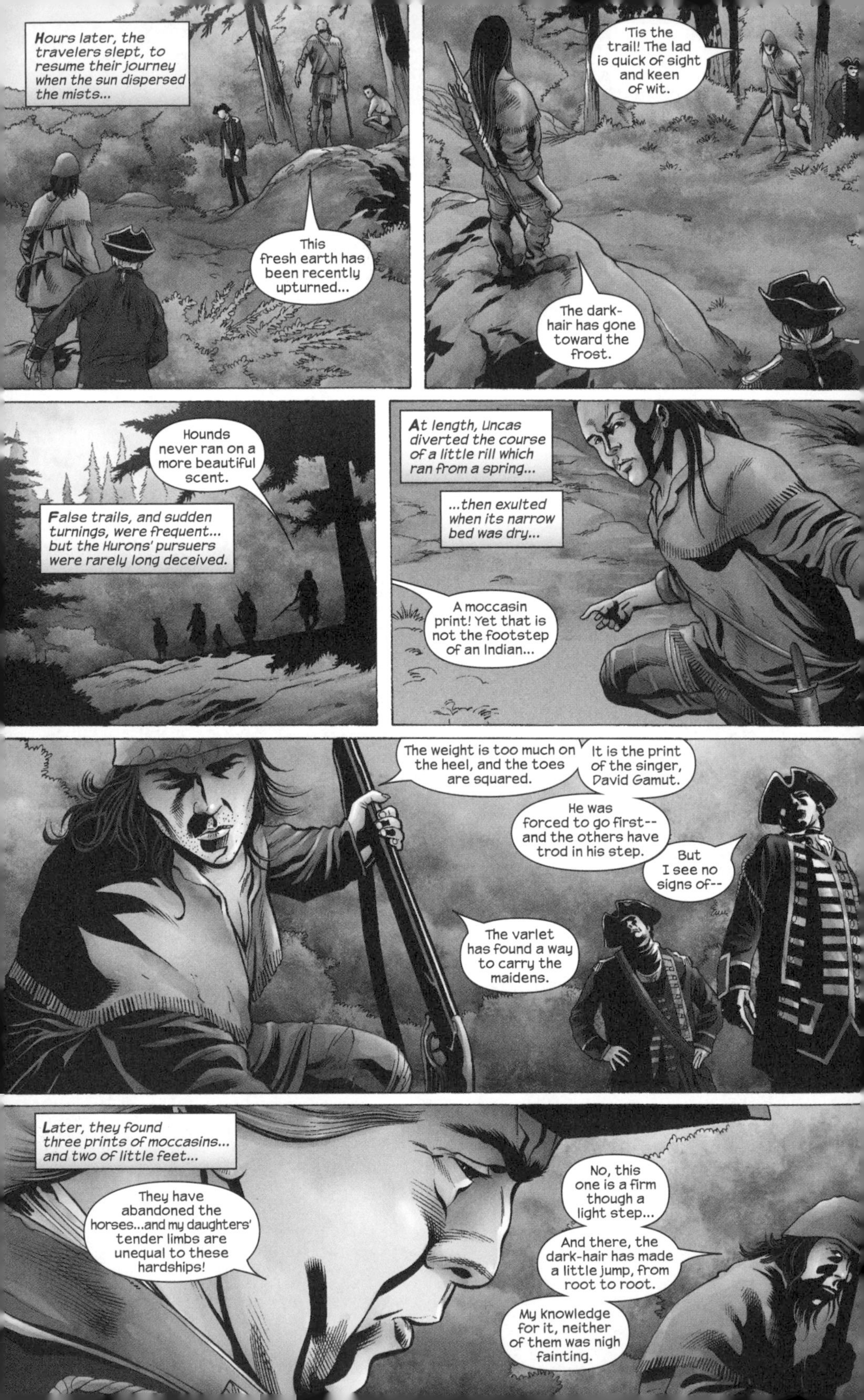

Hours later, the travelers slept, to resume their journey when the sun dispersed the mists...
This fresh earth has been recently upturned...
'Tis the trail! The lad is quick of sight and keen of wit.
The dark-hair has gone toward the frost.
Hounds never ran on a more beautiful scent.
False trails, and sudden turnings, were frequent... but the Hurons' pursuers were rarely long deceived.
At length, Uncas diverted the course of a little rill which ran from a spring...
...then exulted when its narrow bed was dry...
A moccasin print! Yet that is not the footstep of an Indian...
The weight is too much on the heel, and the toes are squared.
It is the print of the singer, David Gamut.
He was forced to go first--and the others have trod in his step.
But I see no signs of--
The varlet has found a way to carry the maidens.
Later, they found three prints of moccasins... and two of little feet...
They have abandoned the horses...and my daughters' tender limbs are unequal to these hardships!
No, this one is a firm though a light step...
And there, the dark-hair has made a little jump, from root to root.
My knowledge for it, neither of them was nigh fainting.

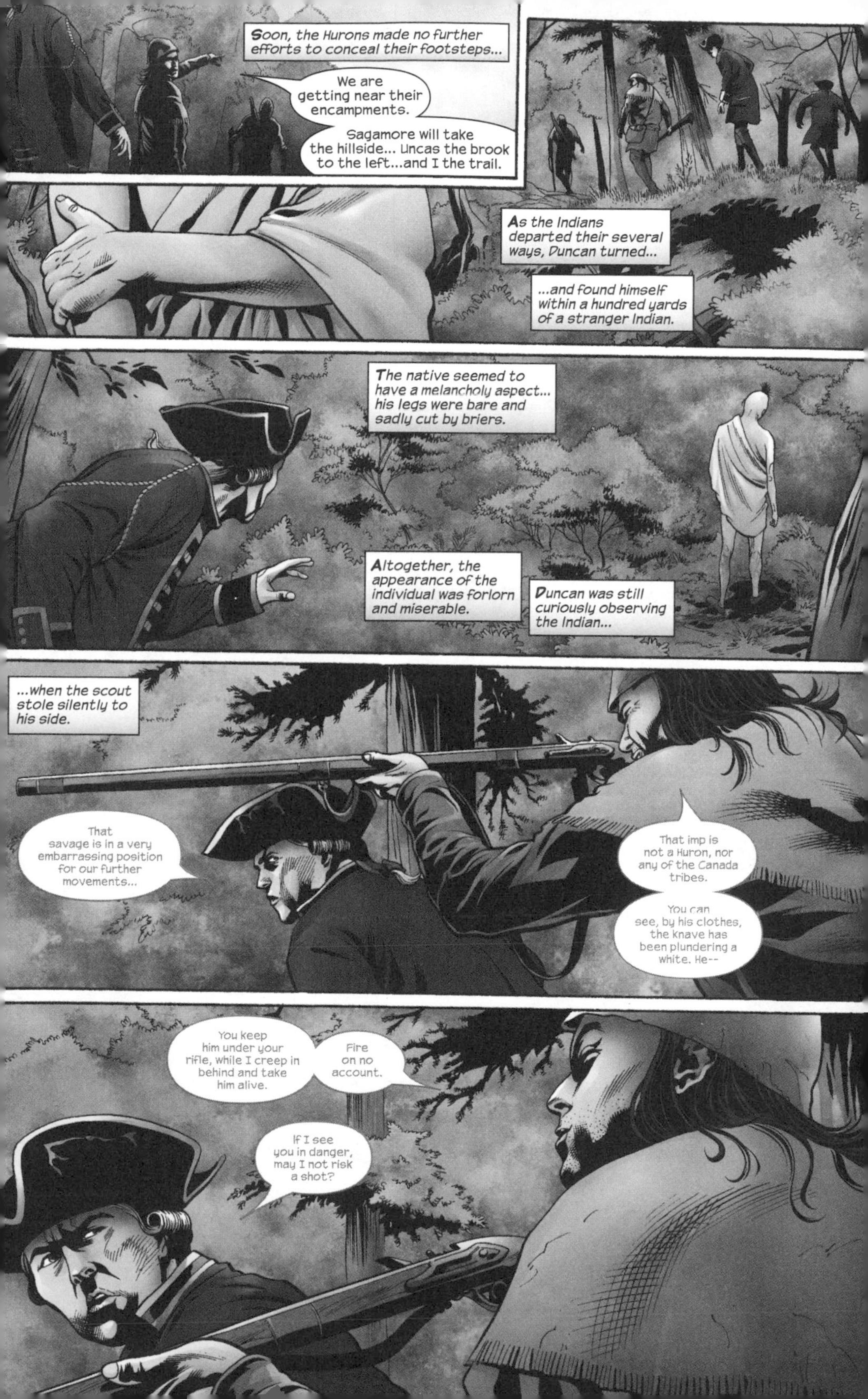
Soon, the Hurons made no further efforts to conceal their footsteps...
We are getting near their encampments.
Sagamore will take the hillside... Uncas the brook to the left...and I the trail.
As the Indians departed their several ways, Duncan turned...
...and found himself within a hundred yards of a stranger Indian.
The native seemed to have a melancholy aspect... his legs were bare and sadly cut by briers.
Altogether, the appearance of the individual was forlorn and miserable.
Duncan was still curiously observing the Indian...
...when the scout stole silently to his side.
That savage is in a very embarrassing position for our further movements...
That imp is not a Huron, nor any of the Canada tribes.
You can see, by his clothes, the knave has been plundering a white. He--
You keep him under your rifle, while I creep in behind and take him alive.
Fire on no account.
If I see you in danger, may I not risk a shot?

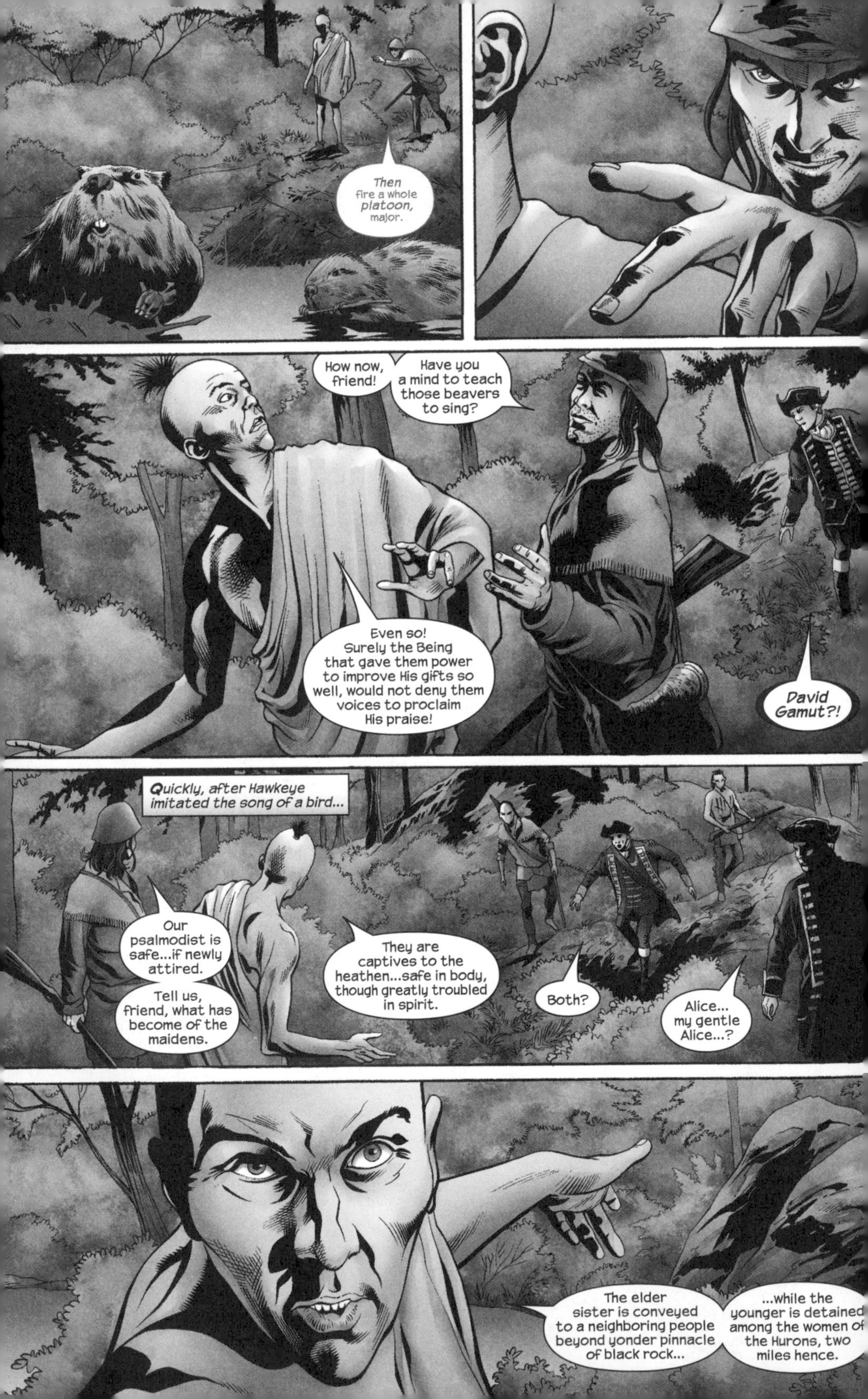
Then fire a whole platoon, major.
How now, friend!
Have you a mind to teach those beavers to sing?
Even so! Surely the Being that gave them power to improve His gifts so well, would not deny them voices to proclaim His praise!
David Gamut?!
Quickly, after Hawkeye imitated the song of a bird...
Our psalmodist is safe...if newly attired.
Tell us, friend, what has become of the maidens.
They are captives to the heathen...safe in body, though greatly troubled in spirit.
Both?
Alice... my gentle Alice...?
The elder sister is conveyed to a neighboring people beyond yonder pinnacle of black rock...
...while the younger is detained among the women of the Hurons, two miles hence.

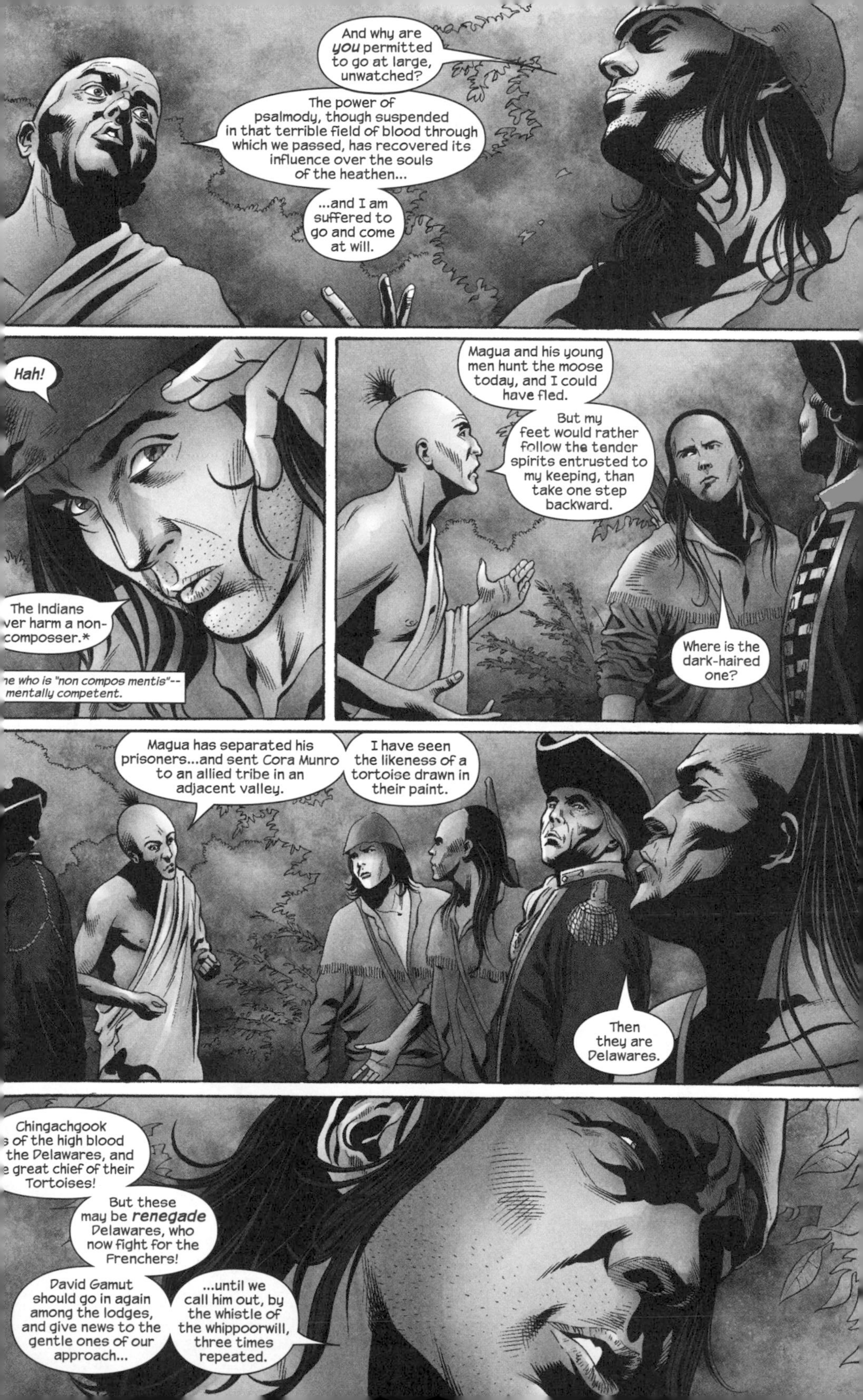
And why are *you* permitted to go at large, unwatched?
The power of psalmody, though suspended in that terrible field of blood through which we passed, has recovered its influence over the souls of the heathen...
...and I am suffered to go and come at will.
Hah!
The Indians ver harm a non-composser.*
ne who is "non compos mentis"-- mentally competent.
Magua and his young men hunt the moose today, and I could have fled.
But my feet would rather follow the tender spirits entrusted to my keeping, than take one step backward.
Where is the dark-haired one?
Magua has separated his prisoners...and sent Cora Munro to an allied tribe in an adjacent valley.
I have seen the likeness of a tortoise drawn in their paint.
Then they are Delawares.
Chingachgook s of the high blood the Delawares, and great chief of their Tortoises!
But these may be *renegade* Delawares, who now fight for the Frenchers!
David Gamut should go in again among the lodges, and give news to the gentle ones of our approach...
...until we call him out, by the whistle of the whippoorwill, three times repeated.

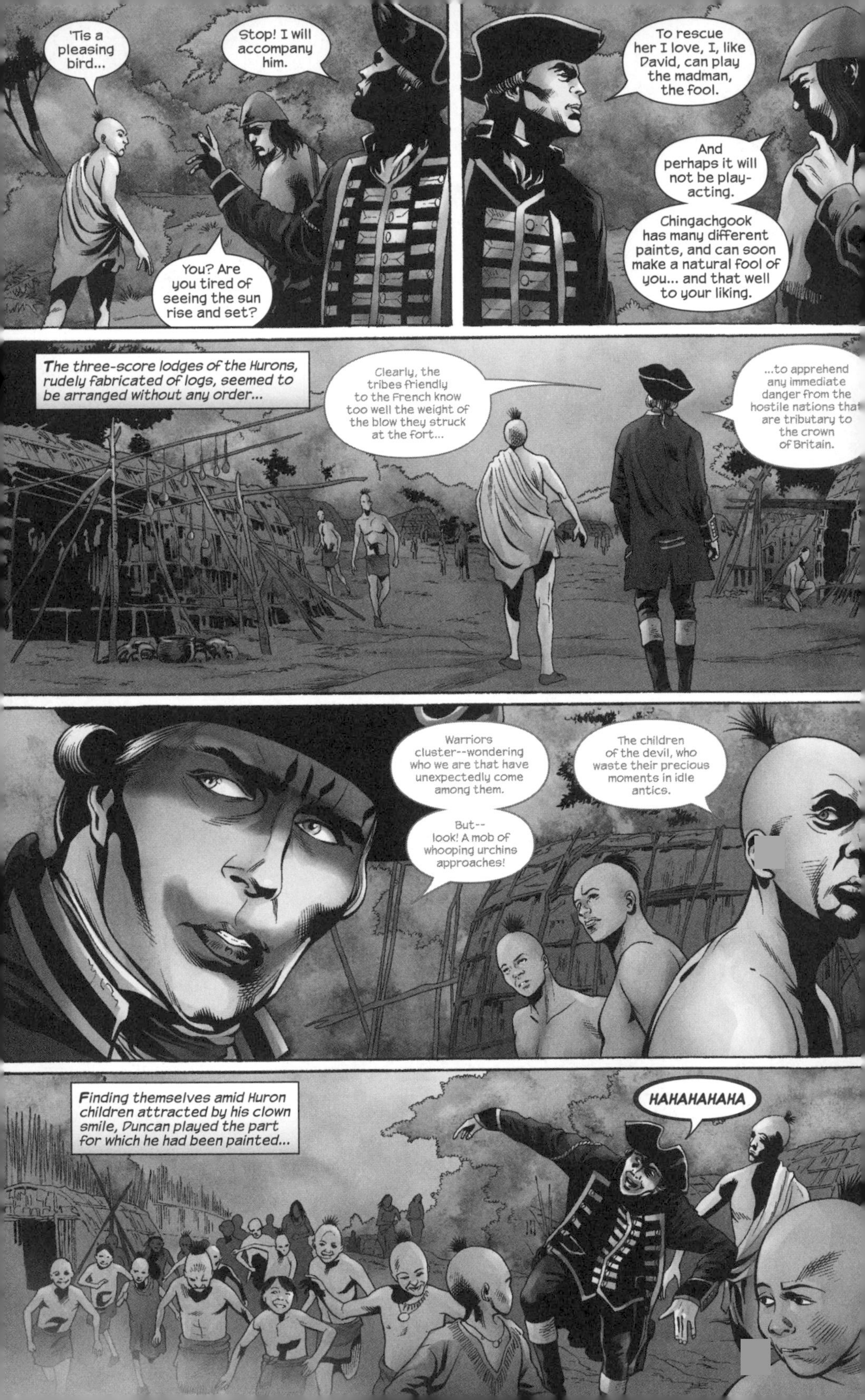
'Tis a pleasing bird...
Stop! I will accompany him.
You? Are you tired of seeing the sun rise and set?
To rescue her I love, I, like David, can play the madman, the fool.
And perhaps it will not be play-acting.
Chingachgook has many different paints, and can soon make a natural fool of you... and that well to your liking.
The three-score lodges of the Hurons, rudely fabricated of logs, seemed to be arranged without any order...
Clearly, the tribes friendly to the French know too well the weight of the blow they struck at the fort...
...to apprehend any immediate danger from the hostile nations that are tributary to the crown of Britain.
Warriors cluster--wondering who we are that have unexpectedly come among them.
But--look! A mob of whooping urchins approaches!
The children of the devil, who waste their precious moments in idle antics.
Finding themselves amid Huron children attracted by his clown smile, Duncan played the part for which he had been painted...
HAHAHAHAHA

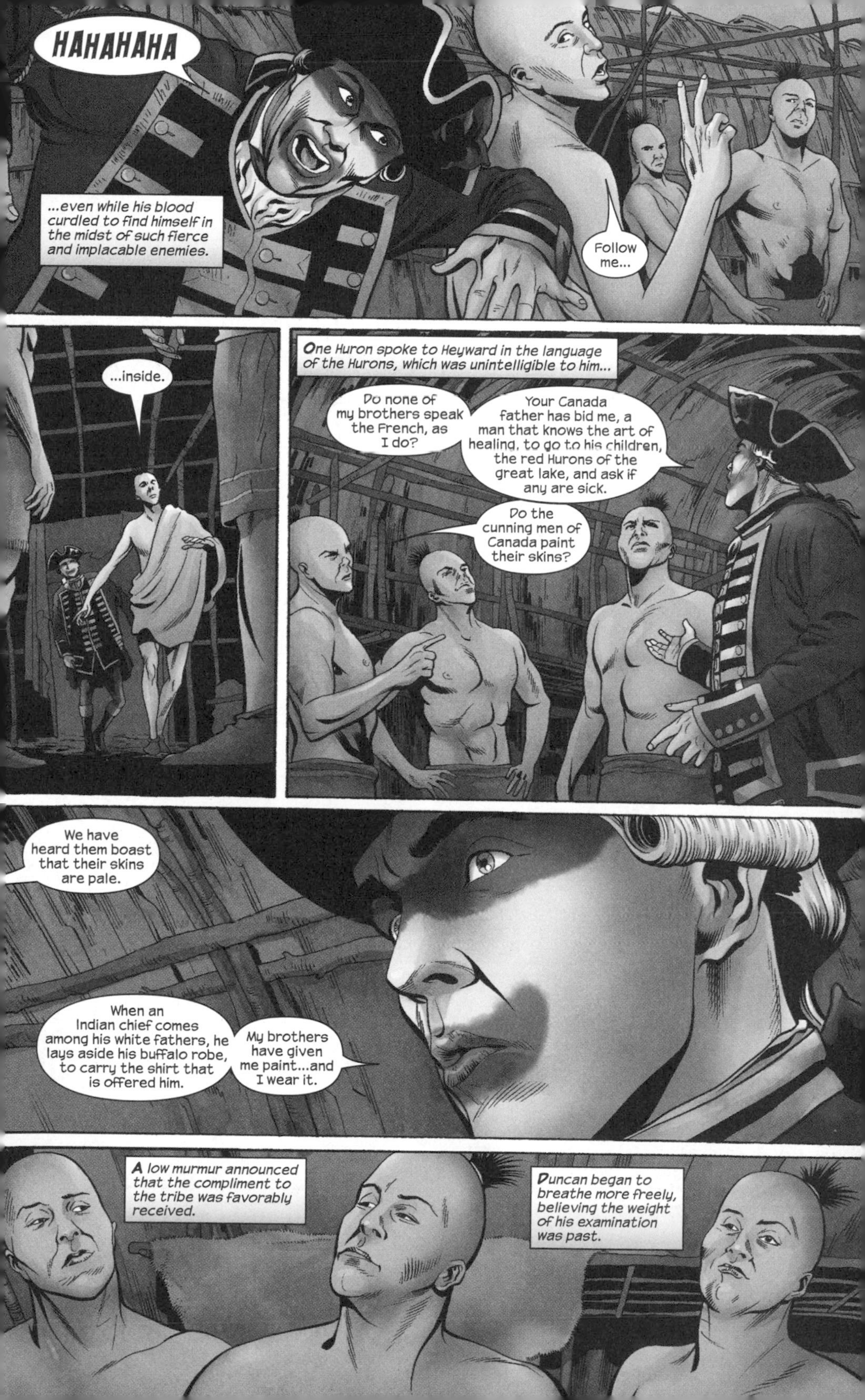
HAHAHAHA
...even while his blood curdled to find himself in the midst of such fierce and implacable enemies.
Follow me...
...inside.
One Huron spoke to Heyward in the language of the Hurons, which was unintelligible to him...
Do none of my brothers speak the French, as I do?
Your Canada father has bid me, a man that knows the art of healing, to go to his children, the red Hurons of the great lake, and ask if any are sick.
Do the cunning men of Canada paint their skins?
We have heard them boast that their skins are pale.
When an Indian chief comes among his white fathers, he lays aside his buffalo robe, to carry the shirt that is offered him.
My brothers have given me paint...and I wear it.
A low murmur announced that the compliment to the tribe was favorably received.
Duncan began to breathe more freely, believing the weight of his examination was past.

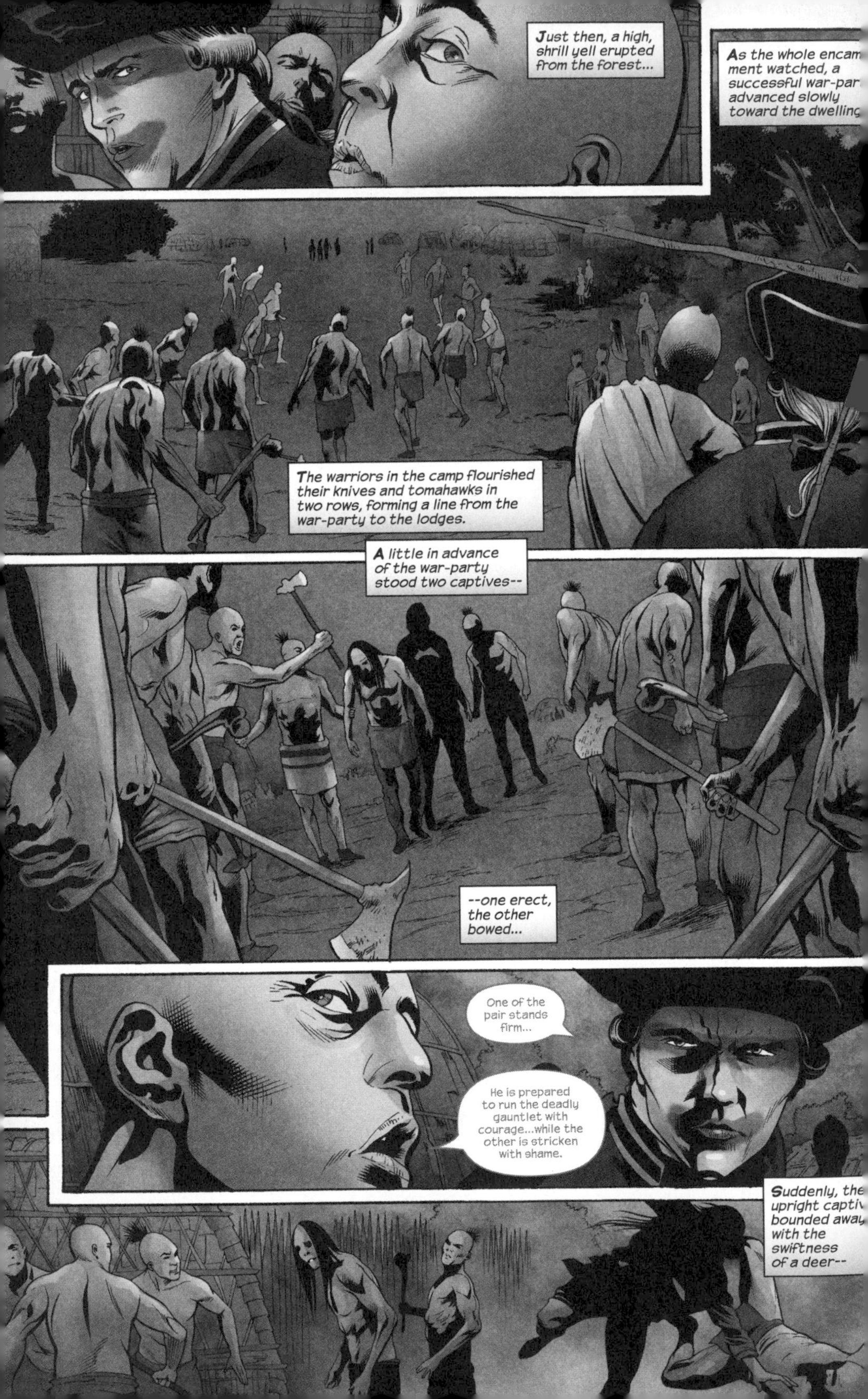
Just then, a high, shrill yell erupted from the forest...
As the whole encam ment watched, a successful war-par advanced slowly toward the dwelling
The warriors in the camp flourished their knives and tomahawks in two rows, forming a line from the war-party to the lodges.
A little in advance of the war-party stood two captives--
--one erect, the other bowed...
One of the pair stands firm...
He is prepared to run the deadly gauntlet with courage...while the other is stricken with shame.
Suddenly, the upright captiv bounded away with the swiftness of a deer--

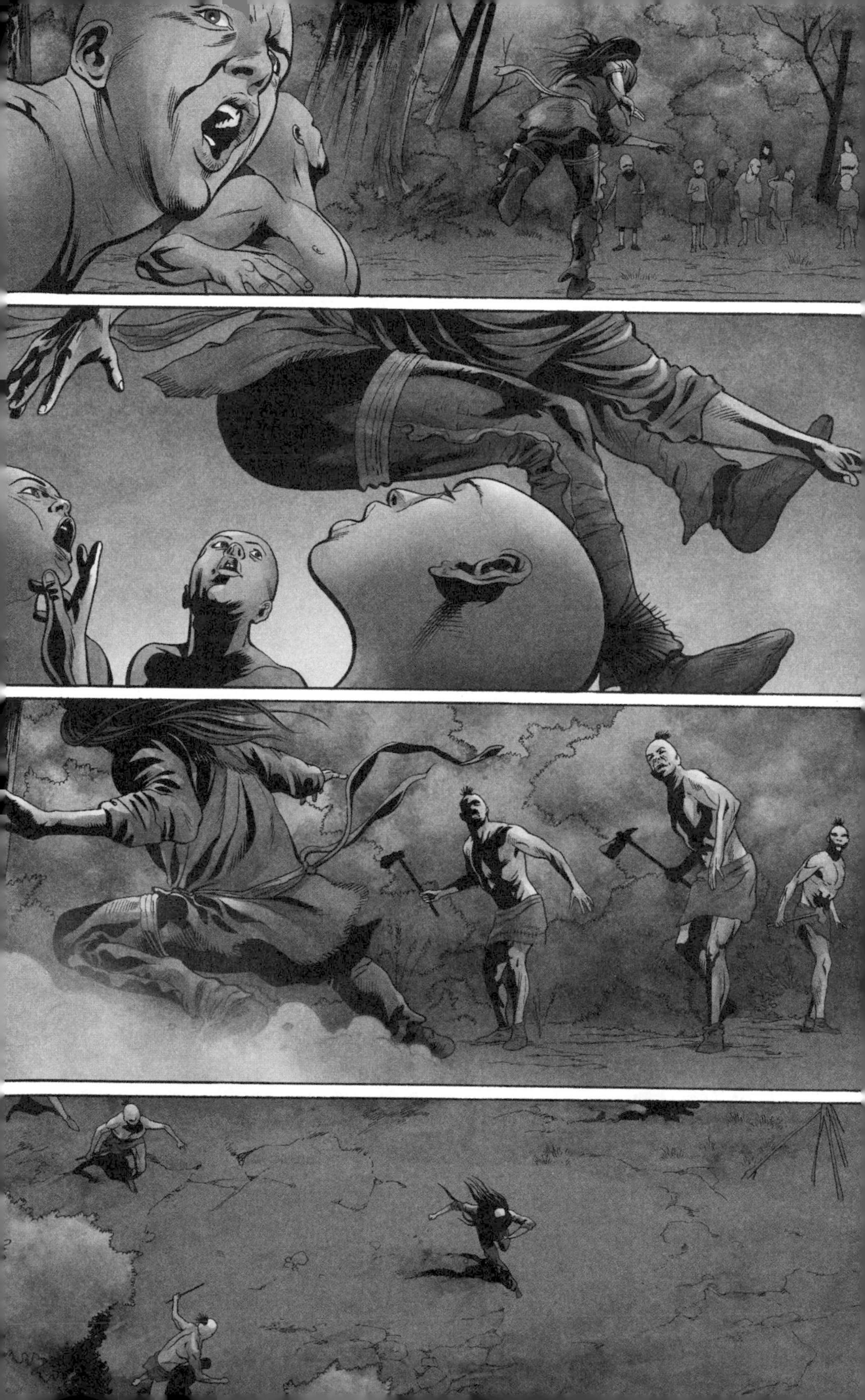

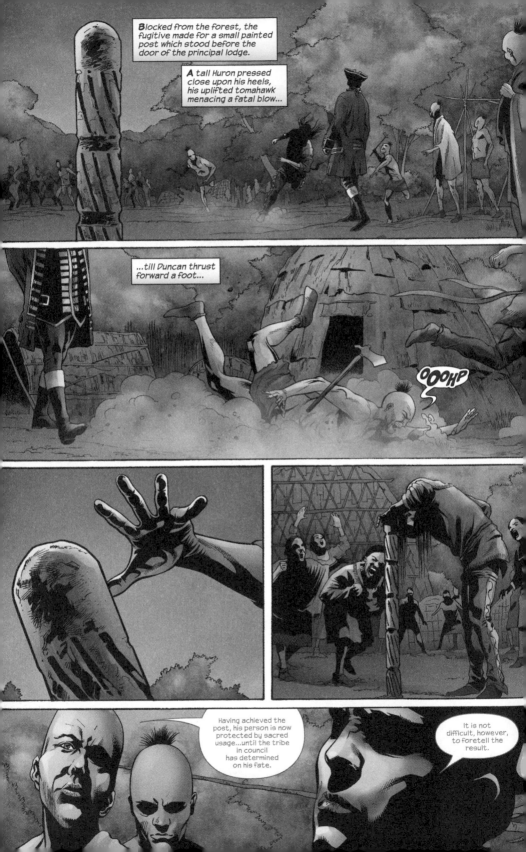

Blocked from the forest, the fugitive made for a small painted post which stood before the door of the principal lodge.

A tall Huron pressed close upon his heels, his uplifted tomahawk menacing a fatal blow...

...till Duncan thrust forward a foot...

OOOHP

Having achieved the post, his person is now protected by sacred usage...until the tribe in council has determined on his fate.

It is not difficult, however, to foretell the result.

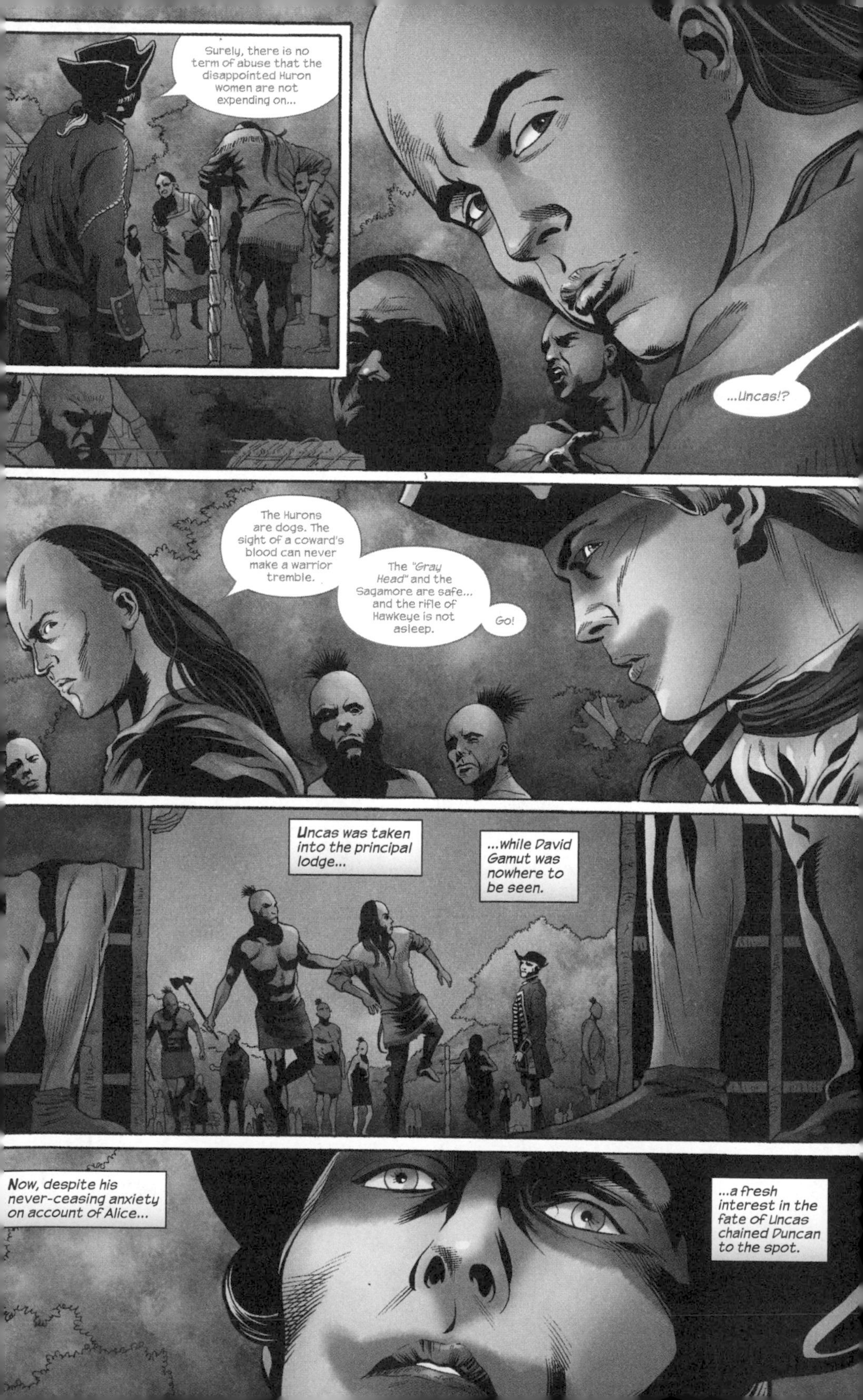
Surely, there is no term of abuse that the disappointed Huron women are not expending on...
...Uncas!?
The Hurons are dogs. The sight of a coward's blood can never make a warrior tremble.
The "Gray Head" and the Sagamore are safe... and the rifle of Hawkeye is not asleep.
Go!
Uncas was taken into the principal lodge...
...while David Gamut was nowhere to be seen.
Now, despite his never-ceasing anxiety on account of Alice...
...a fresh interest in the fate of Uncas chained Duncan to the spot.

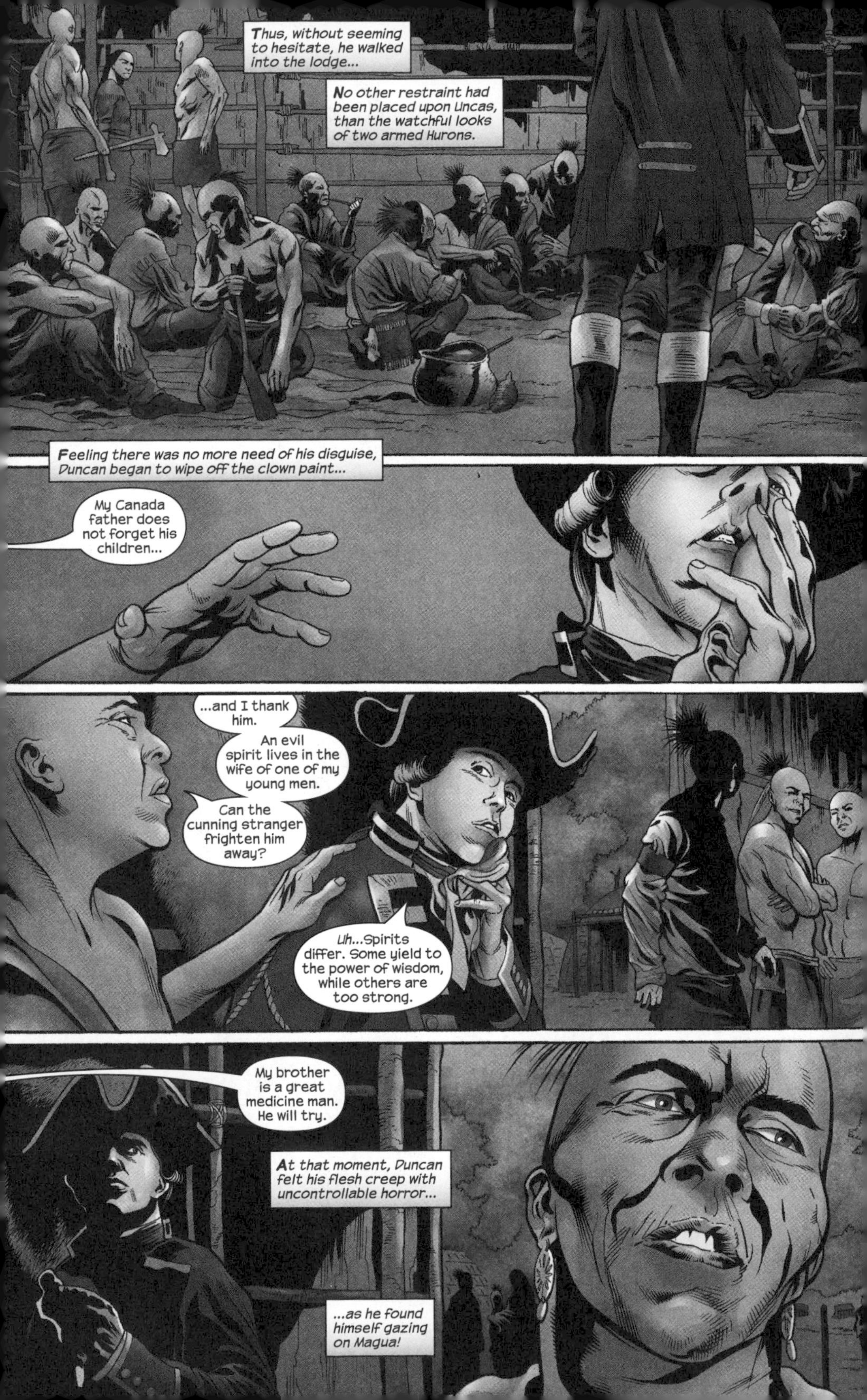
Thus, without seeming to hesitate, he walked into the lodge...
No other restraint had been placed upon Uncas, than the watchful looks of two armed Hurons.
Feeling there was no more need of his disguise, Duncan began to wipe off the clown paint...
My Canada father does not forget his children...
...and I thank him.
An evil spirit lives in the wife of one of my young men.
Can the cunning stranger frighten him away?
Uh...Spirits differ. Some yield to the power of wisdom, while others are too strong.
My brother is a great medicine man. He will try.
At that moment, Duncan felt his flesh creep with uncontrollable horror...
...as he found himself gazing on Magua!

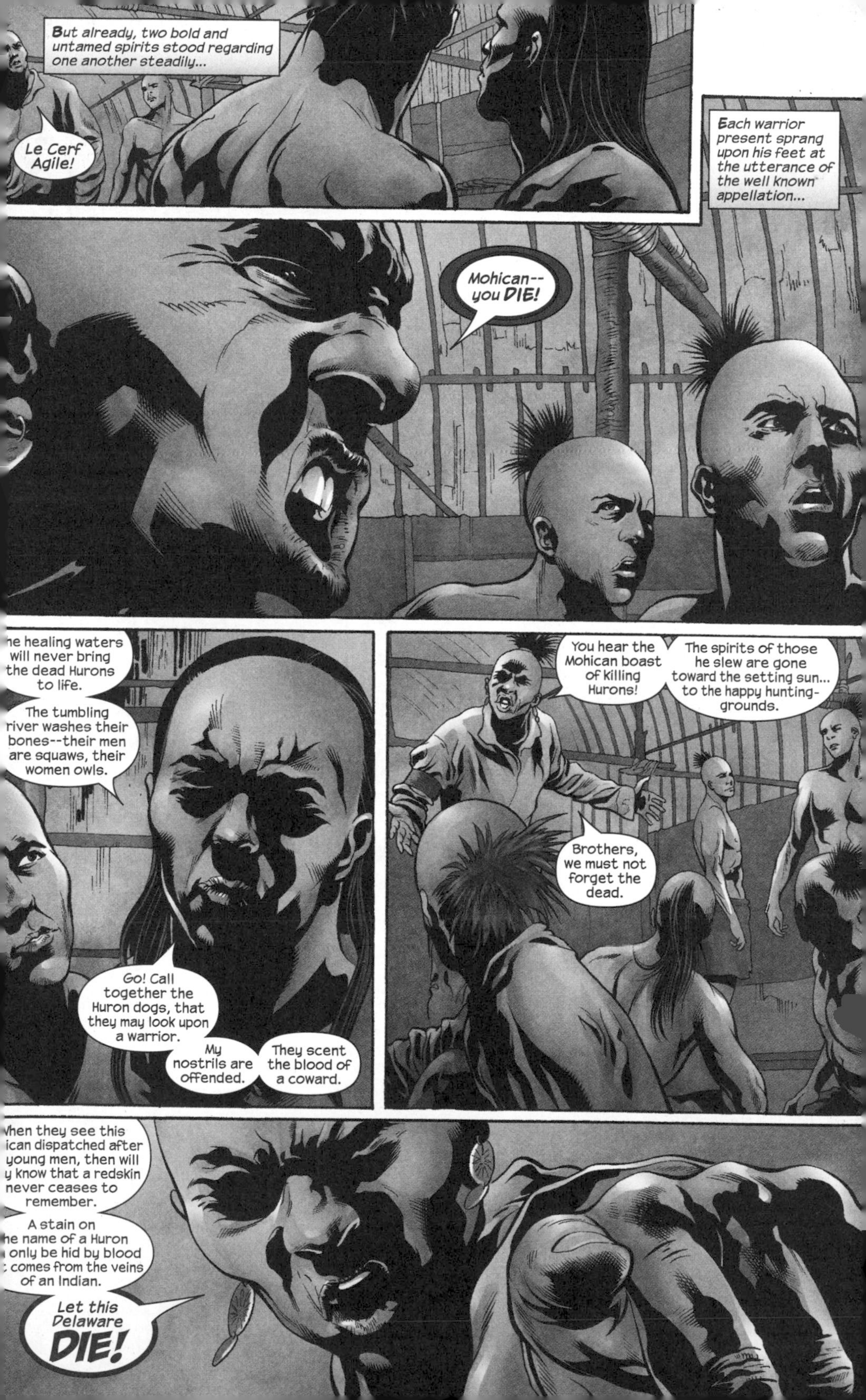

But already, two bold and untamed spirits stood regarding one another steadily...
Le Cerf Agile!
Each warrior present sprang upon his feet at the utterance of the well known appellation...
Mohican-- you DIE!
he healing waters will never bring the dead Hurons to life.
The tumbling river washes their bones--their men are squaws, their women owls.
Go! Call together the Huron dogs, that they may look upon a warrior.
My nostrils are offended.
They scent the blood of a coward.
You hear the Mohican boast of killing Hurons!
The spirits of those he slew are gone toward the setting sun... to the happy hunting-grounds.
Brothers, we must not forget the dead.
hen they see this ican dispatched after young men, then will know that a redskin never ceases to remember.
A stain on he name of a Huron only be hid by blood comes from the veins of an Indian.
Let this Delaware DIE!

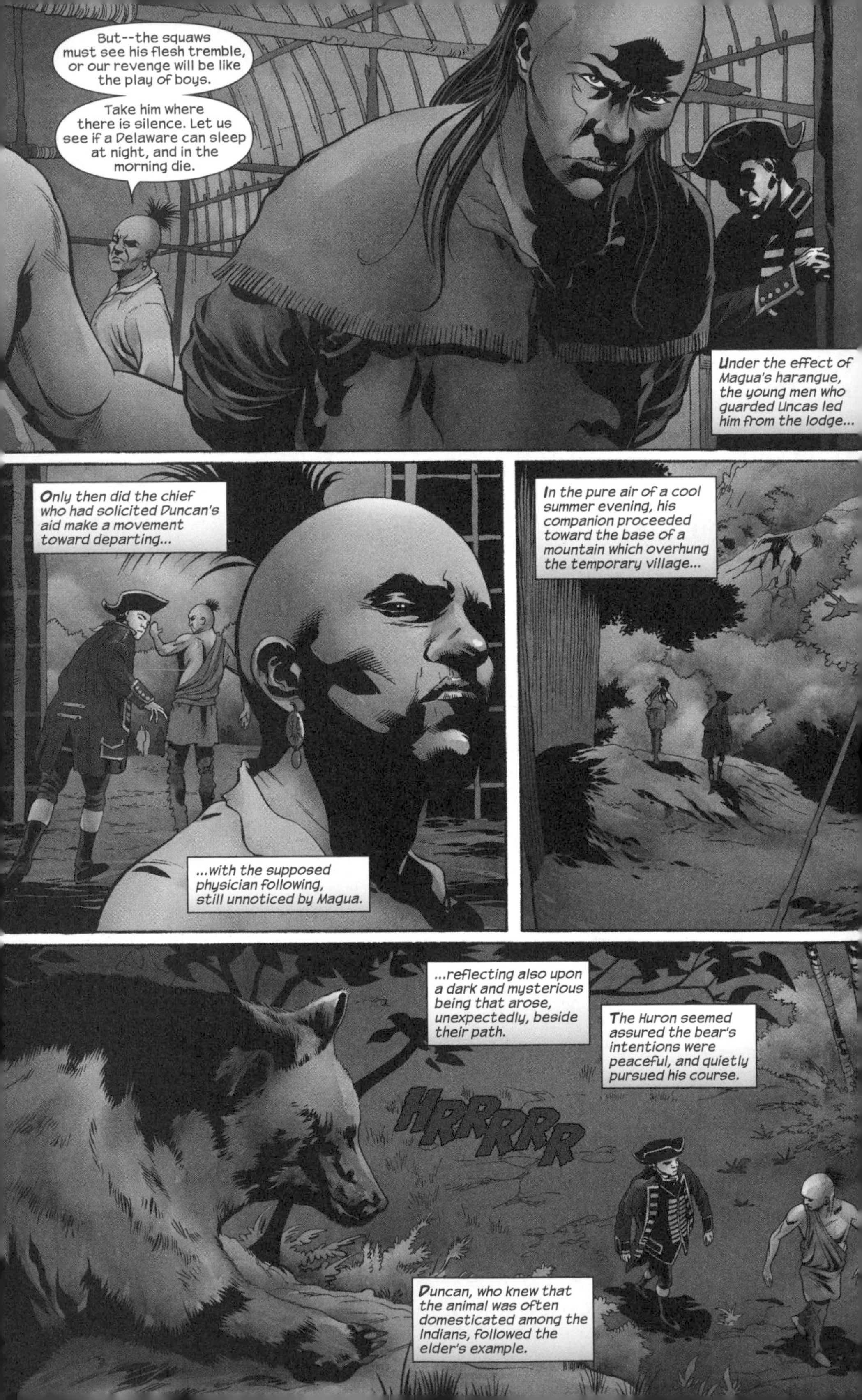
But--the squaws must see his flesh tremble, or our revenge will be like the play of boys.
Take him where there is silence. Let us see if a Delaware can sleep at night, and in the morning die.
Under the effect of Magua's harangue, the young men who guarded Uncas led him from the lodge...
Only then did the chief who had solicited Duncan's aid make a movement toward departing...
...with the supposed physician following, still unnoticed by Magua.
In the pure air of a cool summer evening, his companion proceeded toward the base of a mountain which overhung the temporary village...
...reflecting also upon a dark and mysterious being that arose, unexpectedly, beside their path.
The Huron seemed assured the bear's intentions were peaceful, and quietly pursued his course.
HRRRRRR
Duncan, who knew that the animal was often domesticated among the Indians, followed the elder's example.

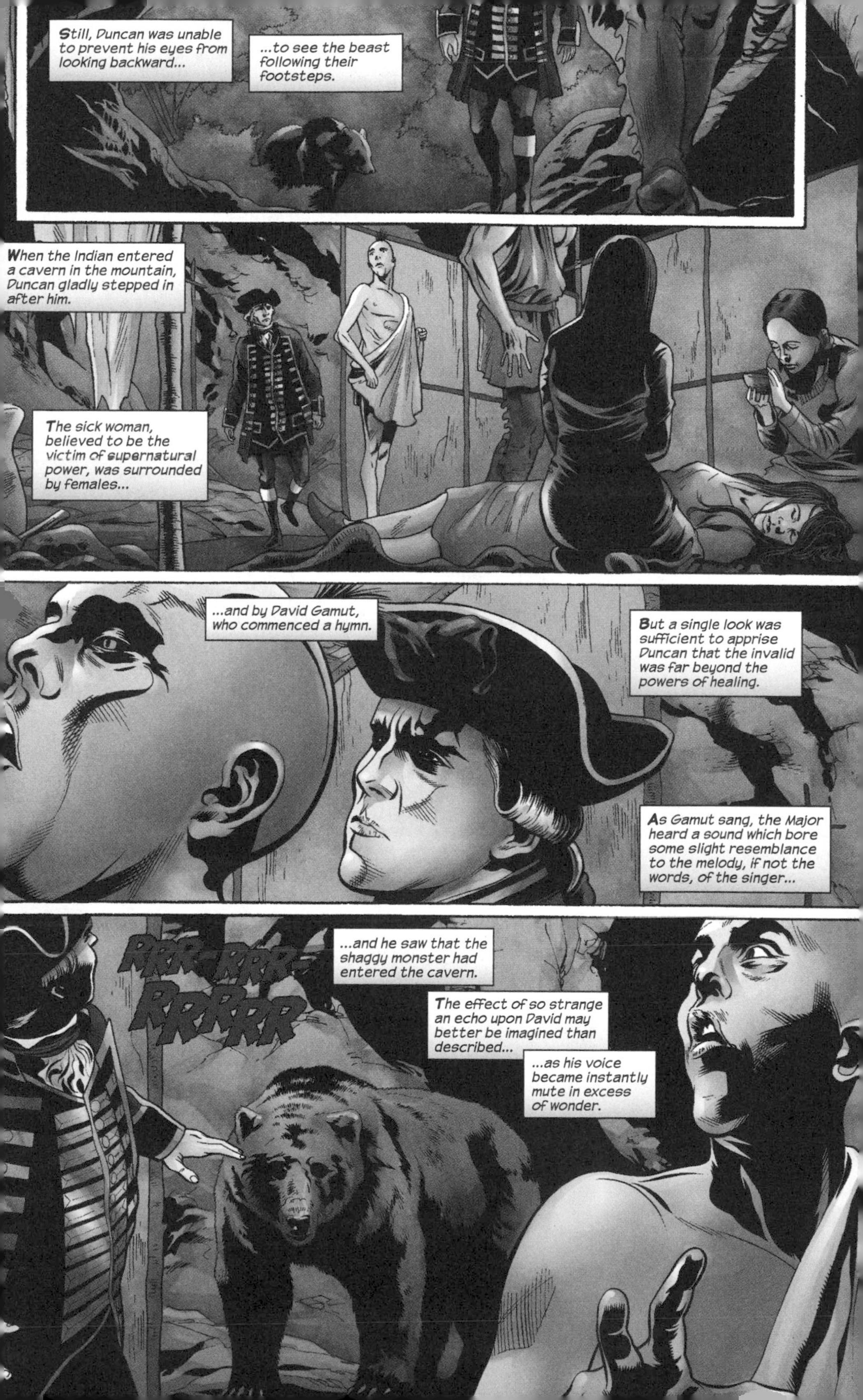
Still, Duncan was unable to prevent his eyes from looking backward...
...to see the beast following their footsteps.
When the Indian entered a cavern in the mountain, Duncan gladly stepped in after him.
The sick woman, believed to be the victim of supernatural power, was surrounded by females...
...and by David Gamut, who commenced a hymn.
But a single look was sufficient to apprise Duncan that the invalid was far beyond the powers of healing.
As Gamut sang, the Major heard a sound which bore some slight resemblance to the melody, if not the words, of the singer...
RRR-RRR-RRRRR
...and he saw that the shaggy monster had entered the cavern.
The effect of so strange an echo upon David may better be imagined than described...
...as his voice became instantly mute in excess of wonder.

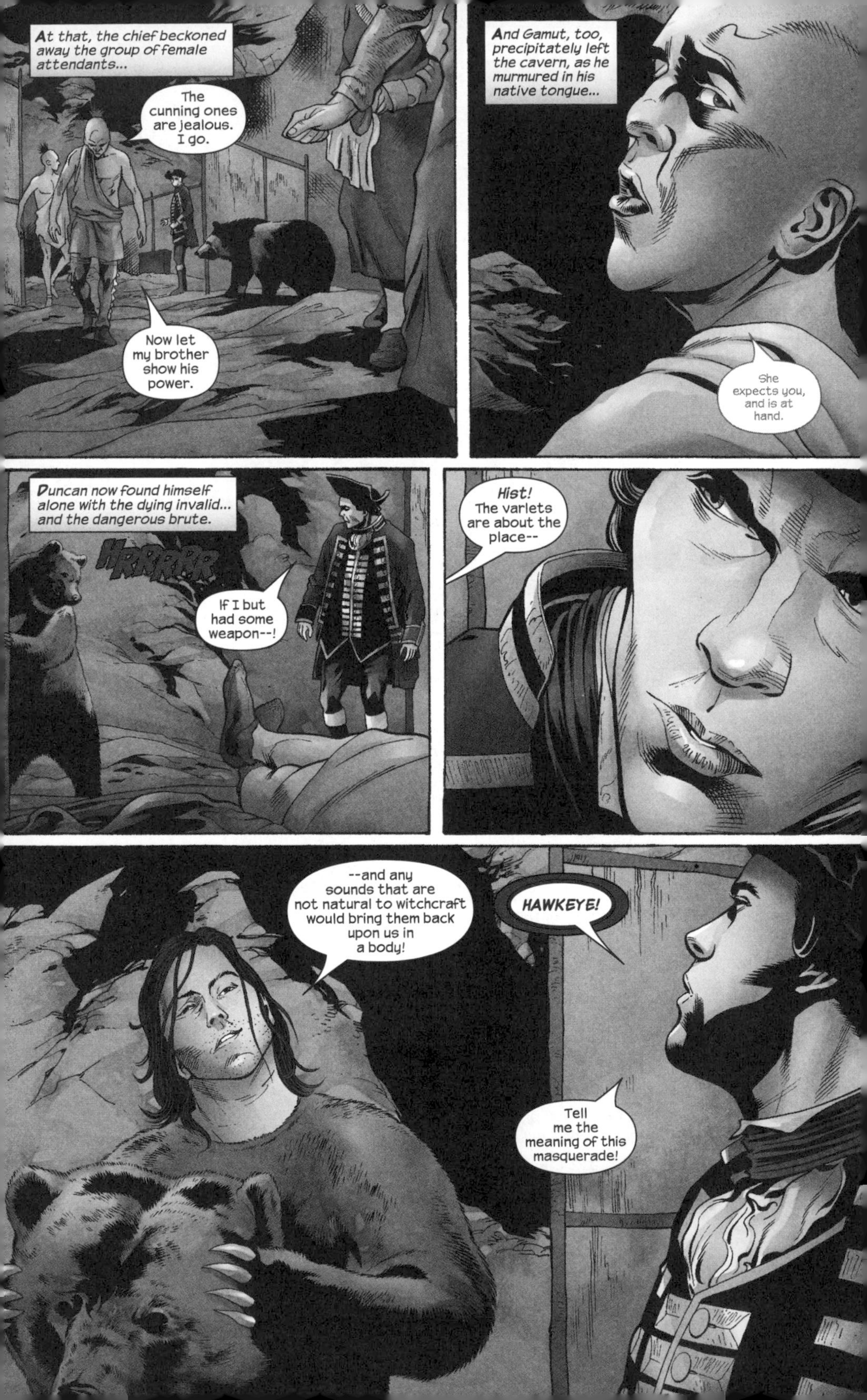
At that, the chief beckoned away the group of female attendants...
The cunning ones are jealous. I go.
Now let my brother show his power.
And Gamut, too, precipitately left the cavern, as he murmured in his native tongue...
She expects you, and is at hand.
Duncan now found himself alone with the dying invalid... and the dangerous brute.
HRRRRR
If I but had some weapon--!
Hist! The varlets are about the place--
--and any sounds that are not natural to witchcraft would bring them back upon us in a body!
HAWKEYE!
Tell me the meaning of this masquerade!

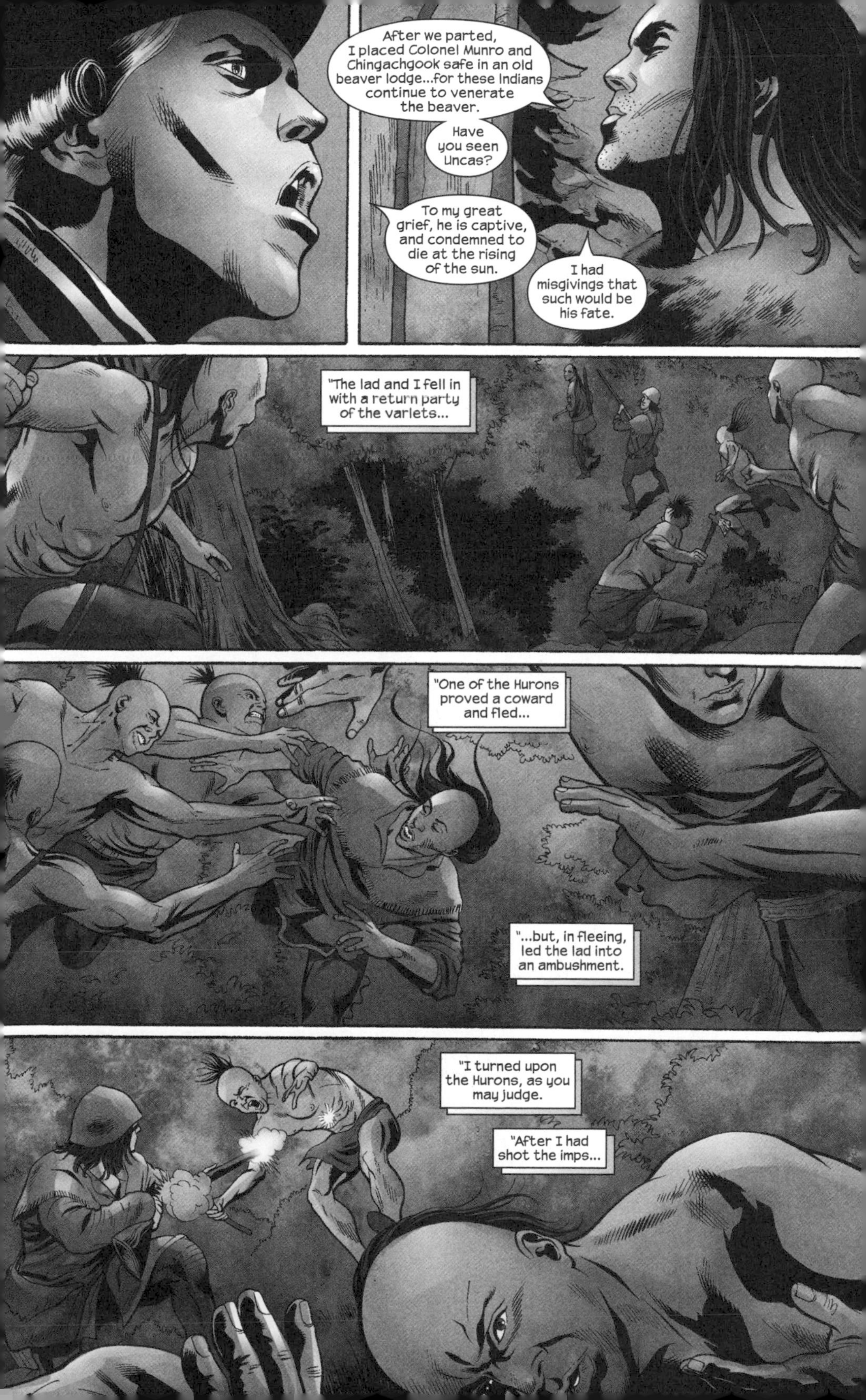
After we parted, I placed Colonel Munro and Chingachgook safe in an old beaver lodge...for these Indians continue to venerate the beaver.
Have you seen Uncas?
To my great grief, he is captive, and condemned to die at the rising of the sun.
I had misgivings that such would be his fate.
"The lad and I fell in with a return party of the varlets...
"One of the Hurons proved a coward and fled...
"...but, in fleeing, led the lad into an ambushment.
"I turned upon the Hurons, as you may judge.
"After I had shot the imps...

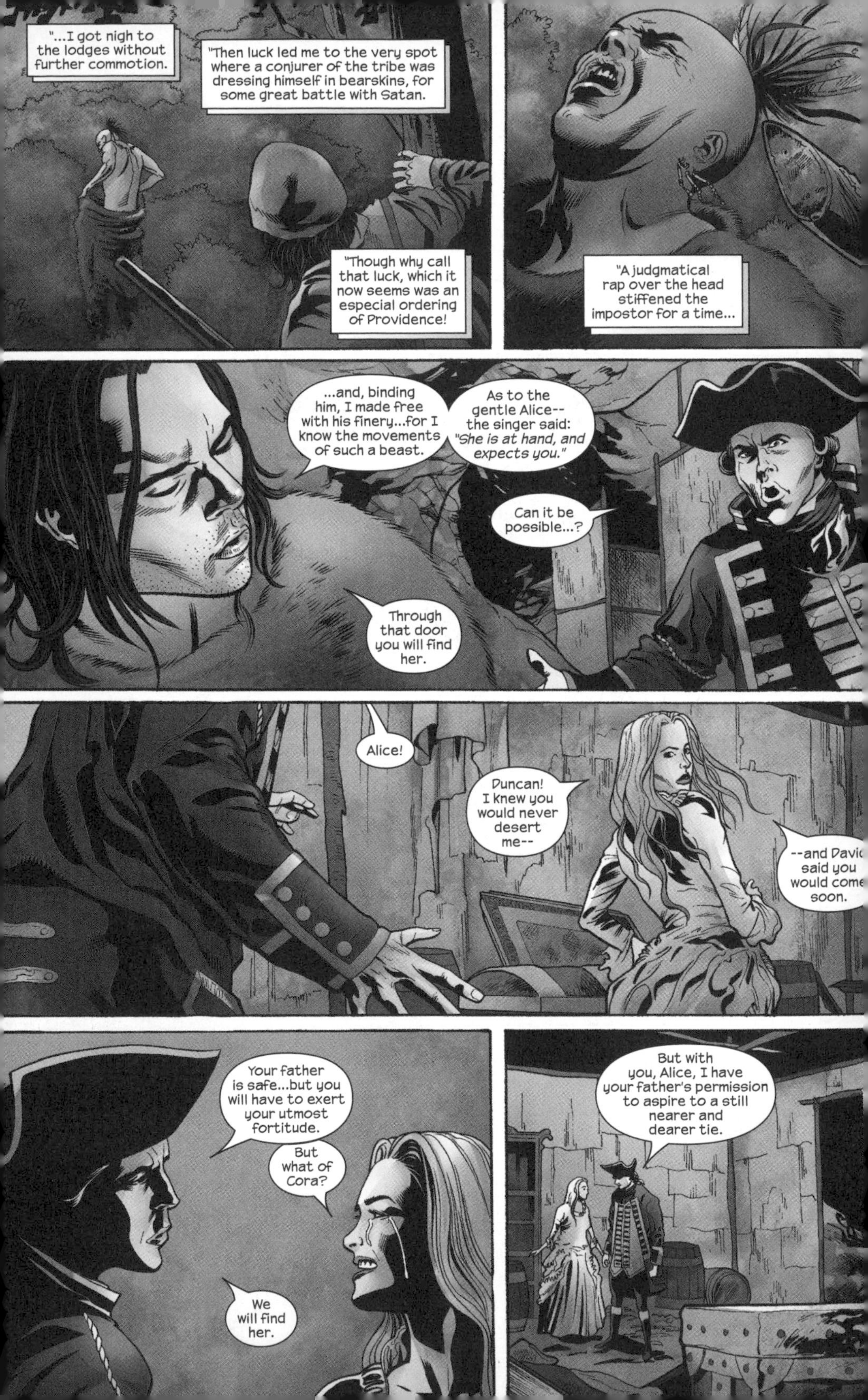
"...I got nigh to the lodges without further commotion.
"Then luck led me to the very spot where a conjurer of the tribe was dressing himself in bearskins, for some great battle with Satan.
"Though why call that luck, which it now seems was an especial ordering of Providence!
"A judgmatical rap over the head stiffened the impostor for a time...
...and, binding him, I made free with his finery...for I know the movements of such a beast.
As to the gentle Alice-- the singer said: *"She is at hand, and expects you."*
Can it be possible...?
Through that door you will find her.
Alice!
Duncan! I knew you would never desert me--
--and Davic said you would come soon.
Your father is safe...but you will have to exert your utmost fortitude.
But what of Cora?
We will find her.
But with you, Alice, I have your father's permission to aspire to a still nearer and dearer tie.

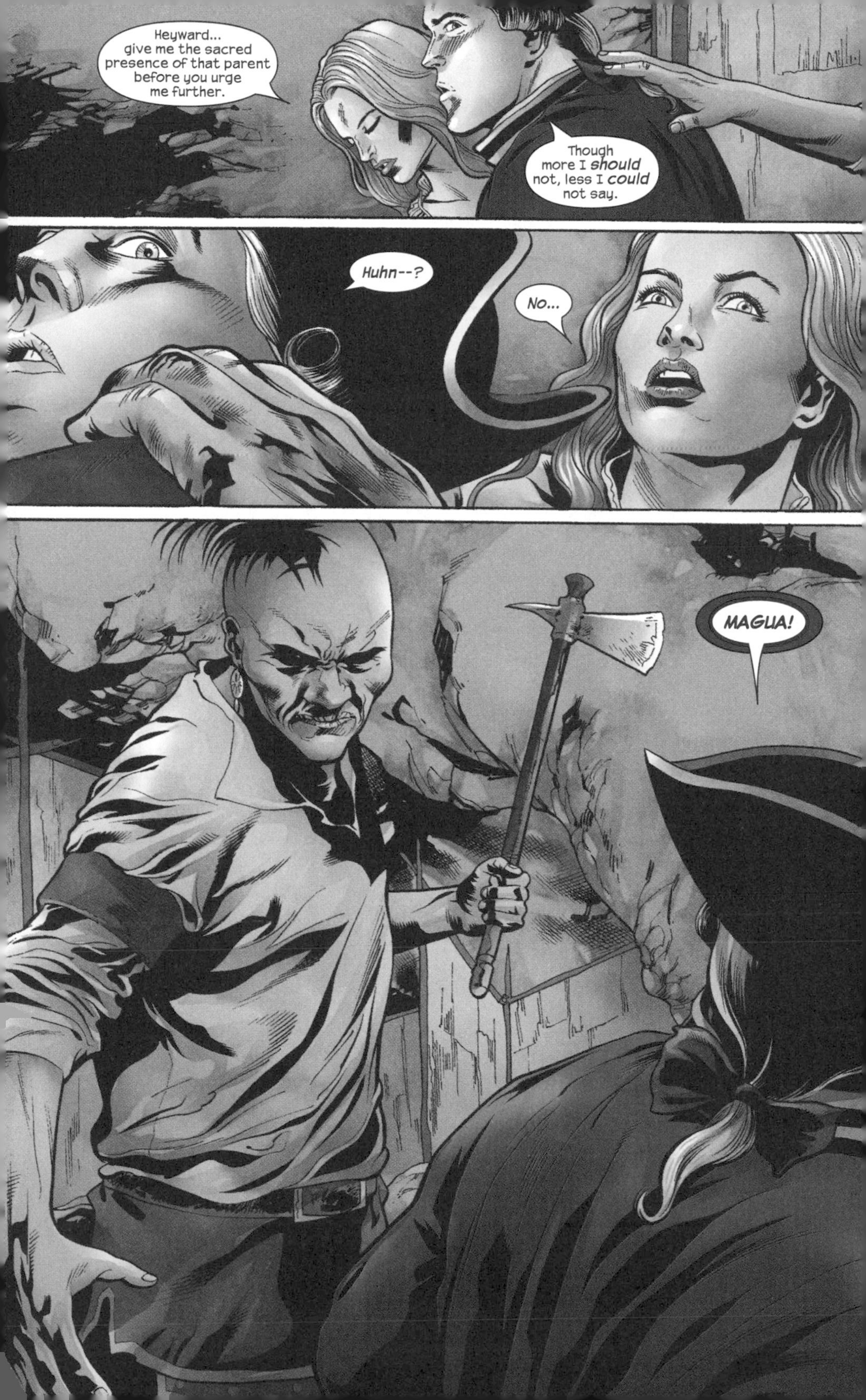
Heyward... give me the sacred presence of that parent before you urge me further.
Though more I *should* not, less I *could* not say.
Huhn--?
No...
MAGUA!

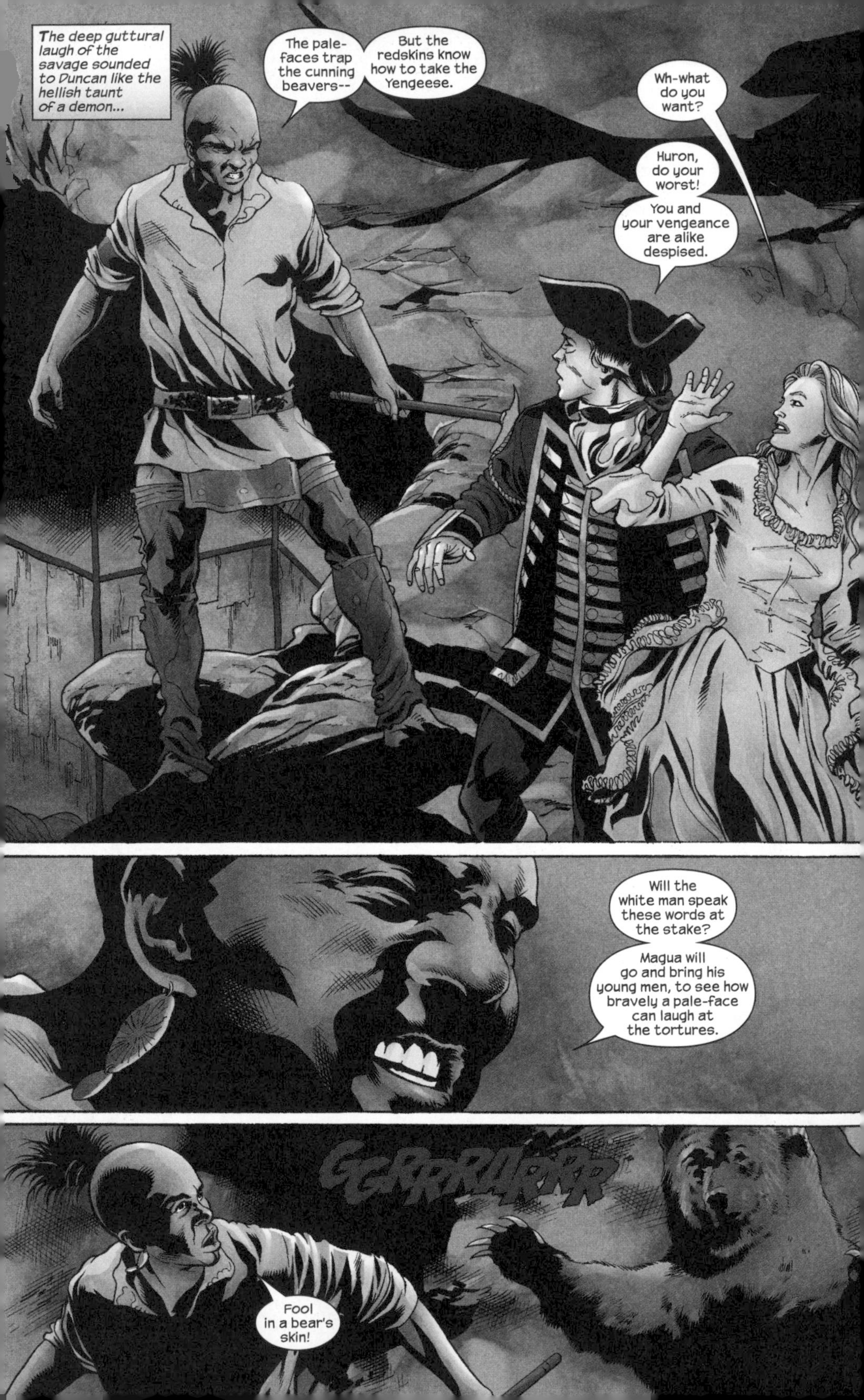
The deep guttural laugh of the savage sounded to Duncan like the hellish taunt of a demon...
The pale-faces trap the cunning beavers--
But the redskins know how to take the Yengeese.
Wh-what do you want?
Huron, do your worst!
You and your vengeance are alike despised.
Will the white man speak these words at the stake?
Magua will go and bring his young men, to see how bravely a pale-face can laugh at the tortures.
GGRRRRARRR
Fool in a bear's skin!

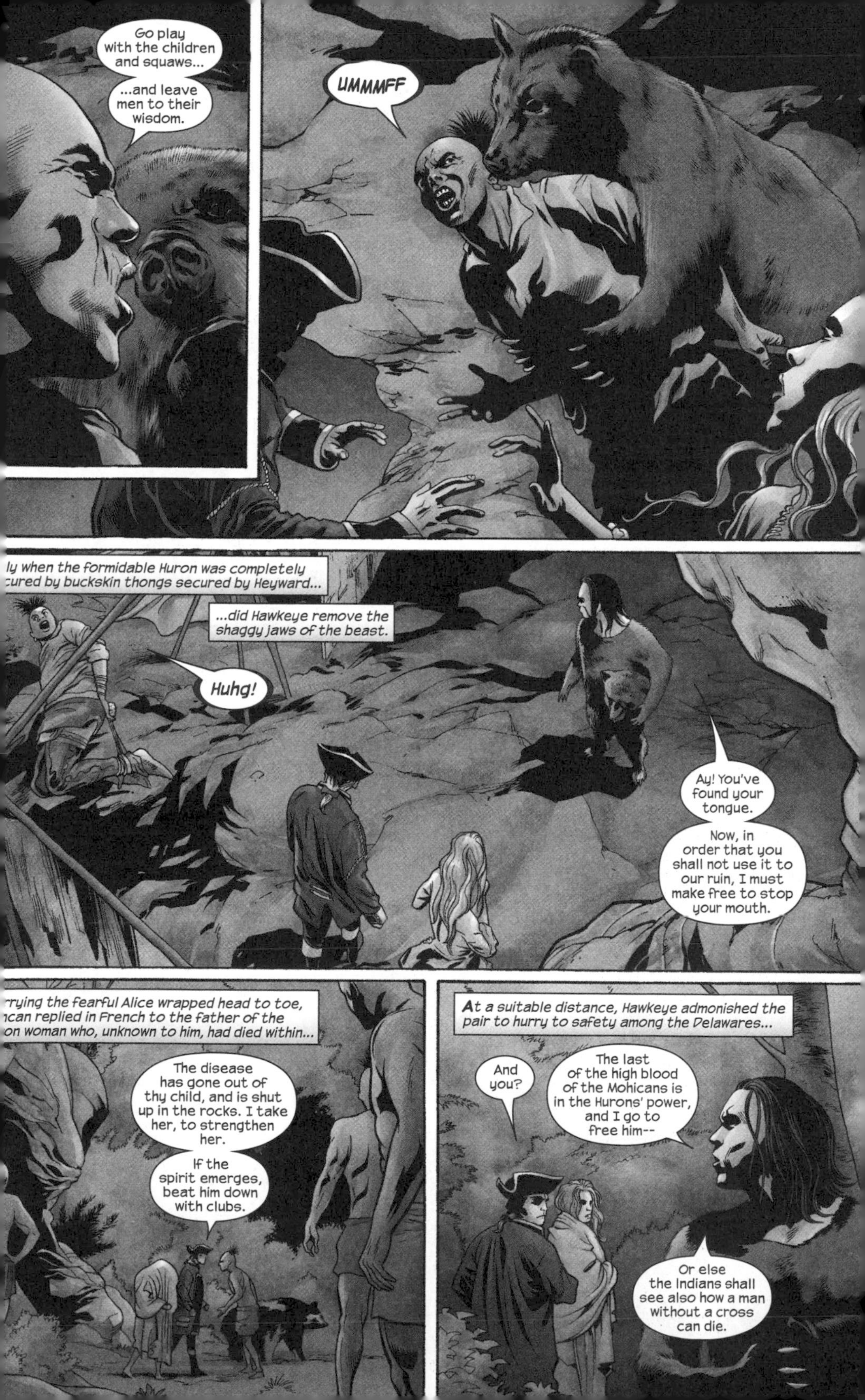
Go play with the children and squaws...
...and leave men to their wisdom.
UMMMFF
ly when the formidable Huron was completely
cured by buckskin thongs secured by Heyward...
...did Hawkeye remove the shaggy jaws of the beast.
Huhg!
Ay! You've found your tongue.
Now, in order that you shall not use it to our ruin, I must make free to stop your mouth.
rrying the fearful Alice wrapped head to toe,
ncan replied in French to the father of the
on woman who, unknown to him, had died within...
The disease has gone out of thy child, and is shut up in the rocks. I take her, to strengthen her.
If the spirit emerges, beat him down with clubs.
At a suitable distance, Hawkeye admonished the pair to hurry to safety among the Delawares...
And you?
The last of the high blood of the Mohicans is in the Hurons' power, and I go to free him--
Or else the Indians shall see also how a man without a cross can die.

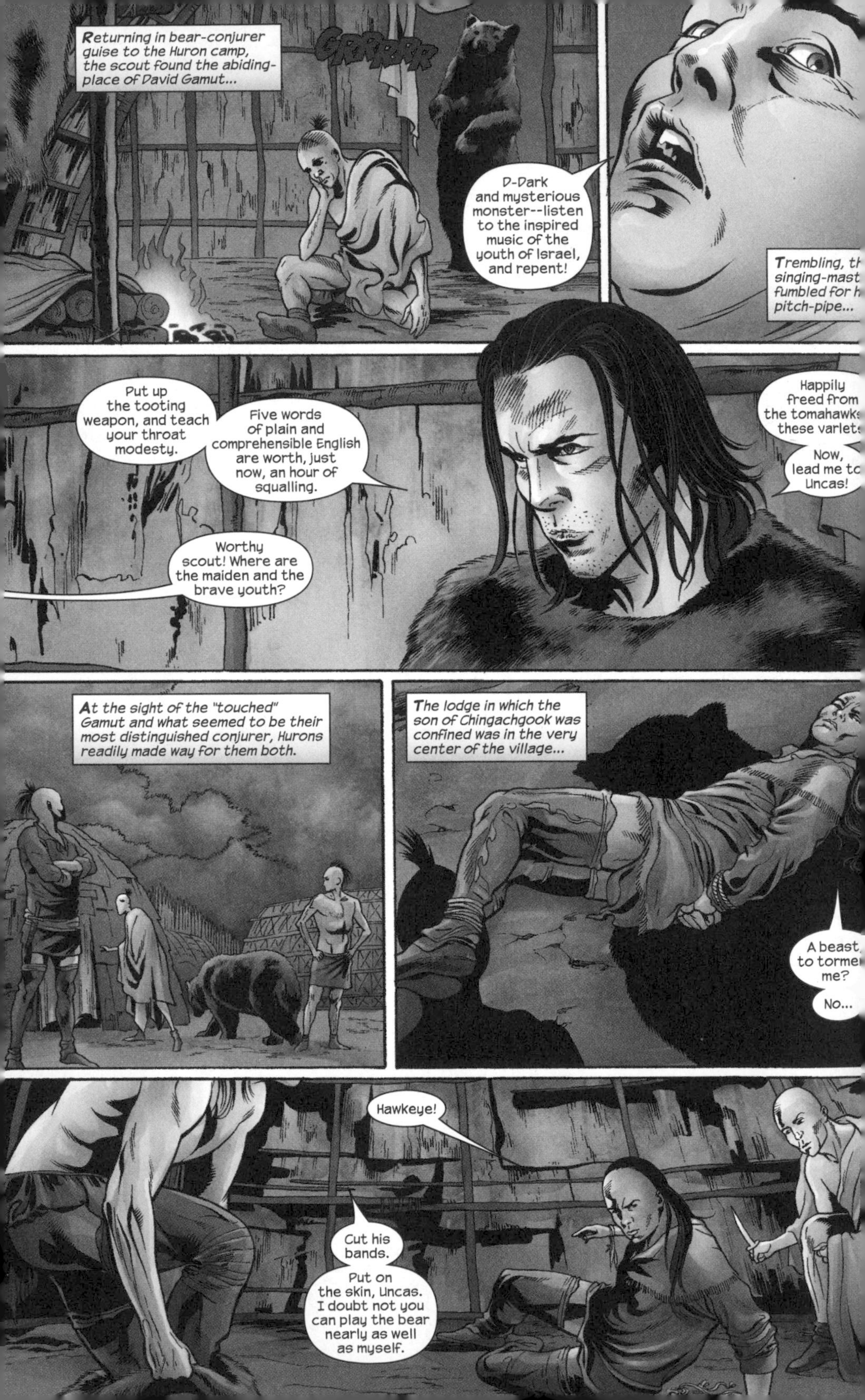
Returning in bear-conjurer guise to the Huron camp, the scout found the abiding-place of David Gamut...
GRRRRR
D-Dark and mysterious monster--listen to the inspired music of the youth of Israel, and repent!
Trembling, th singing-mast fumbled for h pitch-pipe...
Put up the tooting weapon, and teach your throat modesty.
Five words of plain and comprehensible English are worth, just now, an hour of squalling.
Happily freed from the tomahawks these varlets
Now, lead me to Uncas!
Worthy scout! Where are the maiden and the brave youth?
At the sight of the "touched" Gamut and what seemed to be their most distinguished conjurer, Hurons readily made way for them both.
The lodge in which the son of Chingachgook was confined was in the very center of the village...
A beast to torme me?
No...
Hawkeye!
Cut his bands.
Put on the skin, Uncas. I doubt not you can play the bear nearly as well as myself.

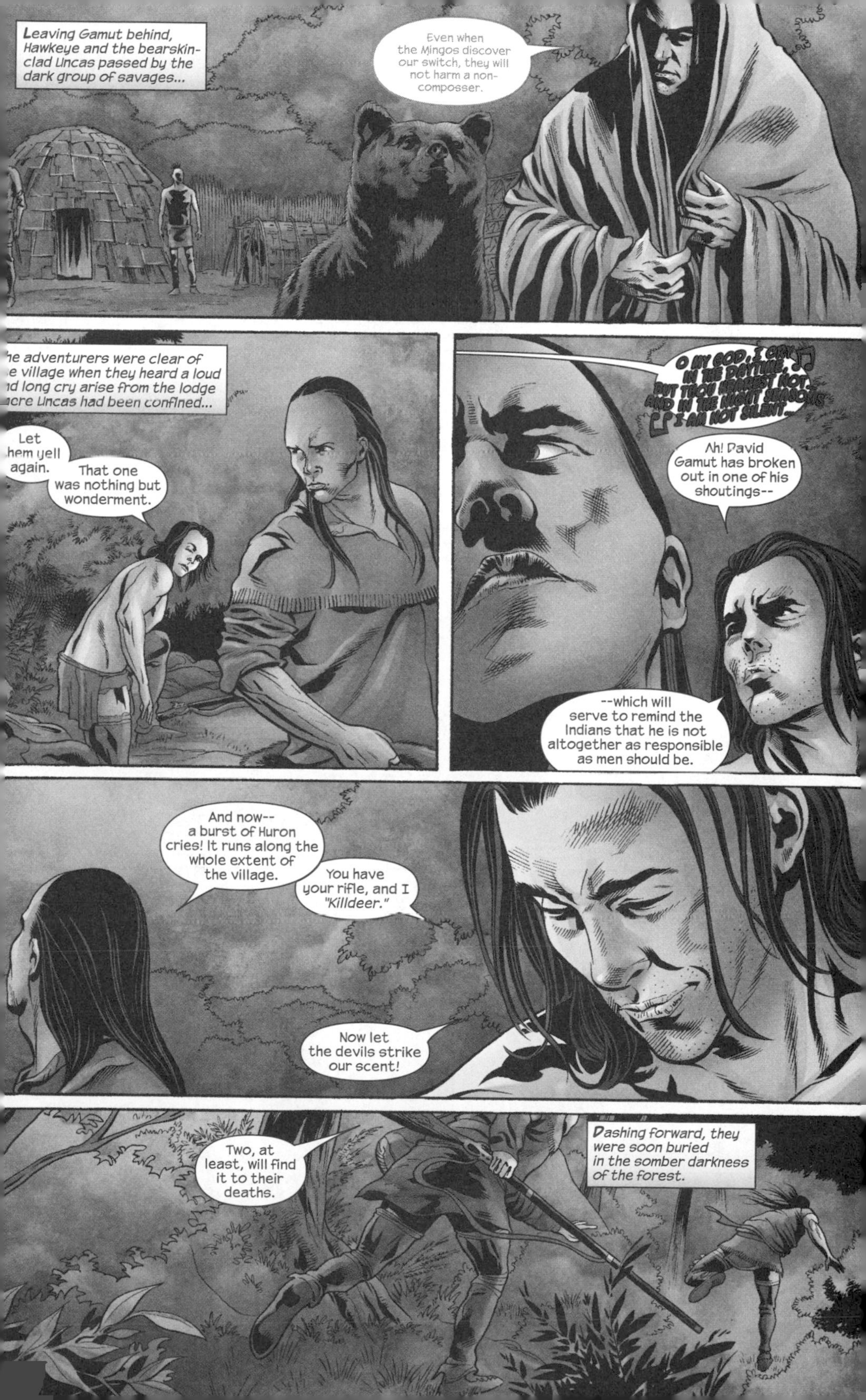
Leaving Gamut behind, Hawkeye and the bearskin-clad Uncas passed by the dark group of savages...
Even when the Mingos discover our switch, they will not harm a non-composser.
he adventurers were clear of e village when they heard a loud nd long cry arise from the lodge here Uncas had been confined...
Let hem yell again.
That one was nothing but wonderment.
O MY GOD, I CRY IN THE DAYTIME, BUT THOU HEAREST NOT... AND IN THE NIGHT SEASONS I AM NOT SILENT...
Ah! David Gamut has broken out in one of his shoutings--
--which will serve to remind the Indians that he is not altogether as responsible as men should be.
And now-- a burst of Huron cries! It runs along the whole extent of the village.
You have your rifle, and I "Killdeer."
Now let the devils strike our scent!
Two, at least, will find it to their deaths.
Dashing forward, they were soon buried in the somber darkness of the forest.

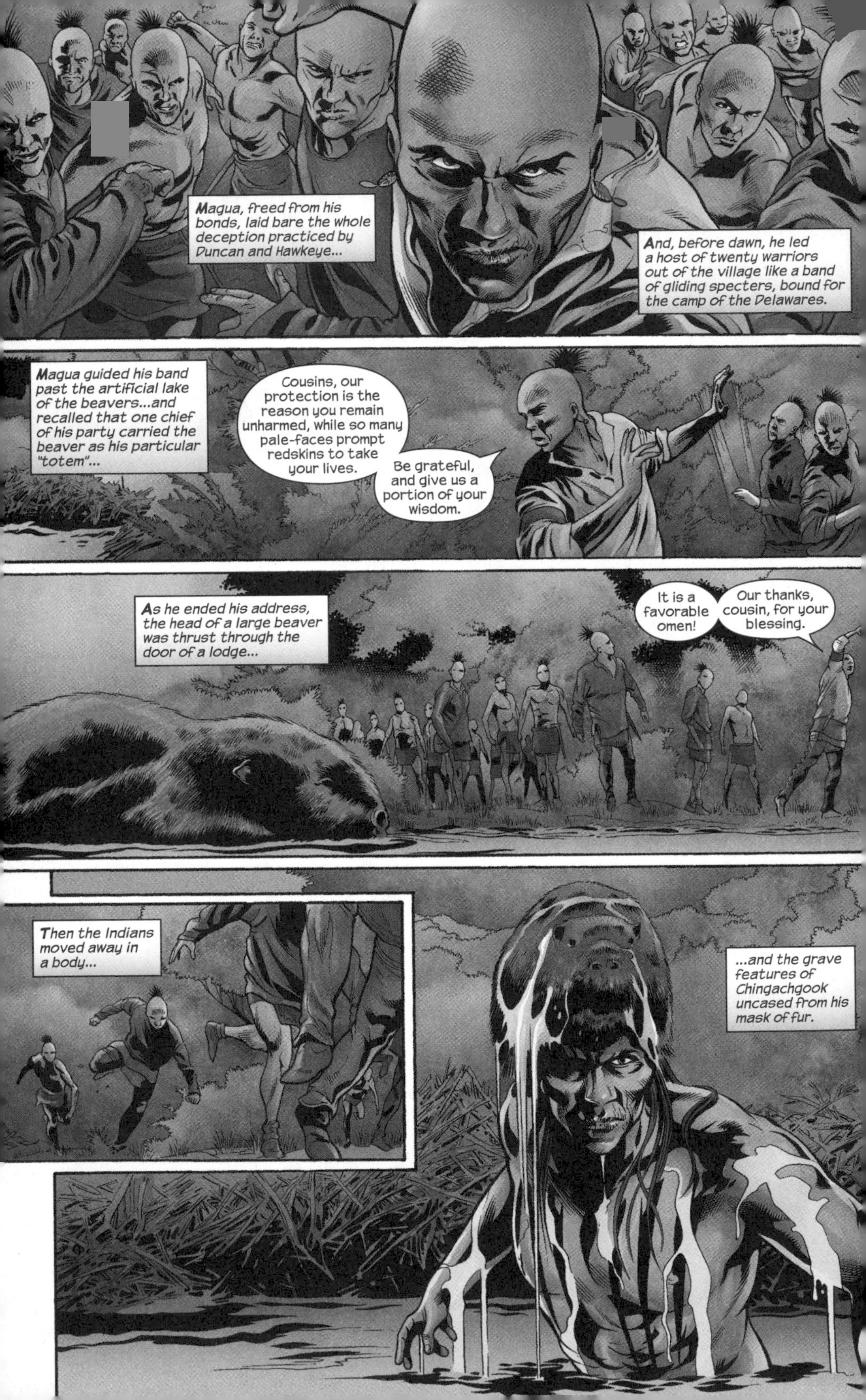

Magua, freed from his bonds, laid bare the whole deception practiced by Duncan and Hawkeye...
And, before dawn, he led a host of twenty warriors out of the village like a band of gliding specters, bound for the camp of the Delawares.
Magua guided his band past the artificial lake of the beavers...and recalled that one chief of his party carried the beaver as his particular "totem"...
Cousins, our protection is the reason you remain unharmed, while so many pale-faces prompt redskins to take your lives.
Be grateful, and give us a portion of your wisdom.
As he ended his address, the head of a large beaver was thrust through the door of a lodge...
It is a favorable omen!
Our thanks, cousin, for your blessing.
Then the Indians moved away in a body...
...and the grave features of Chingachgook uncased from his mask of fur.

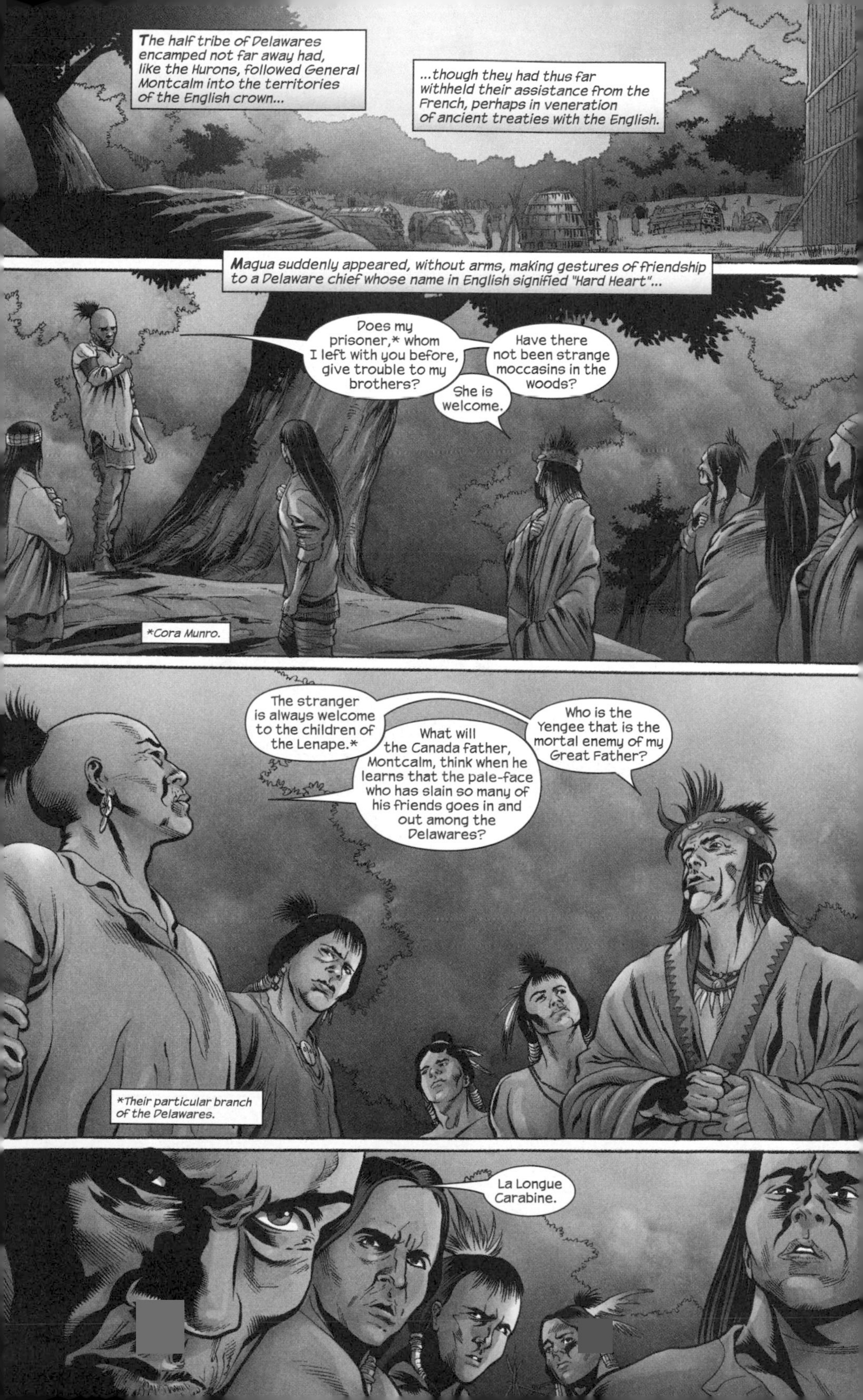
The half tribe of Delawares encamped not far away had, like the Hurons, followed General Montcalm into the territories of the English crown...
...though they had thus far withheld their assistance from the French, perhaps in veneration of ancient treaties with the English.
Magua suddenly appeared, without arms, making gestures of friendship to a Delaware chief whose name in English signified "Hard Heart"...
Does my prisoner,* whom I left with you before, give trouble to my brothers?
She is welcome.
Have there not been strange moccasins in the woods?
*Cora Munro.
The stranger is always welcome to the children of the Lenape.*
Who is the Yengee that is the mortal enemy of my Great Father?
What will the Canada father, Montcalm, think when he learns that the pale-face who has slain so many of his friends goes in and out among the Delawares?
*Their particular branch of the Delawares.
La Longue Carabine.

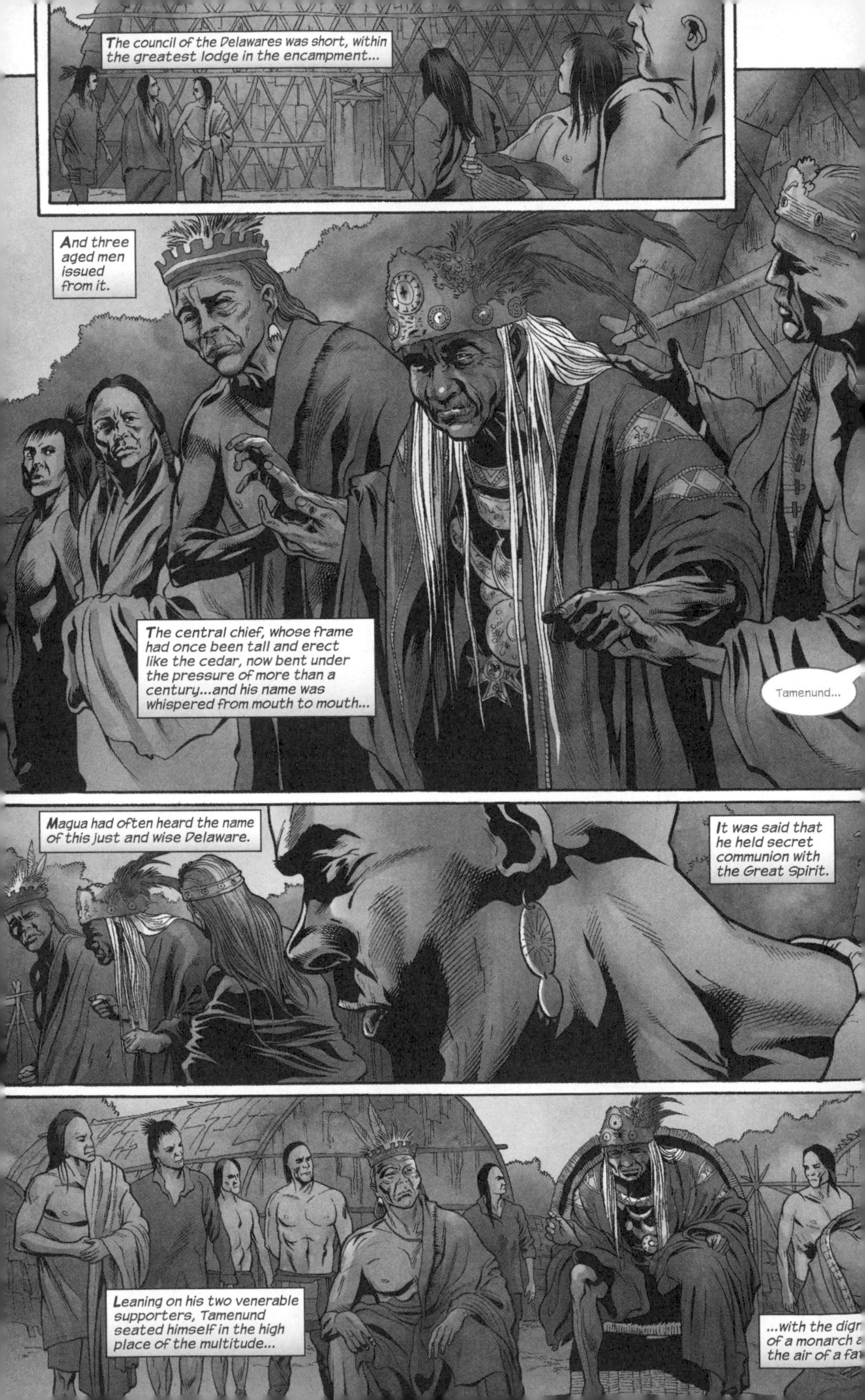

The council of the Delawares was short, within the greatest lodge in the encampment...
And three aged men issued from it.
The central chief, whose frame had once been tall and erect like the cedar, now bent under the pressure of more than a century...and his name was whispered from mouth to mouth...
Tamenund...
Magua had often heard the name of this just and wise Delaware.
It was said that he held secret communion with the Great Spirit.
Leaning on his two venerable supporters, Tamenund seated himself in the high place of the multitude...
...with the dig
of a monarch
the air of a fa

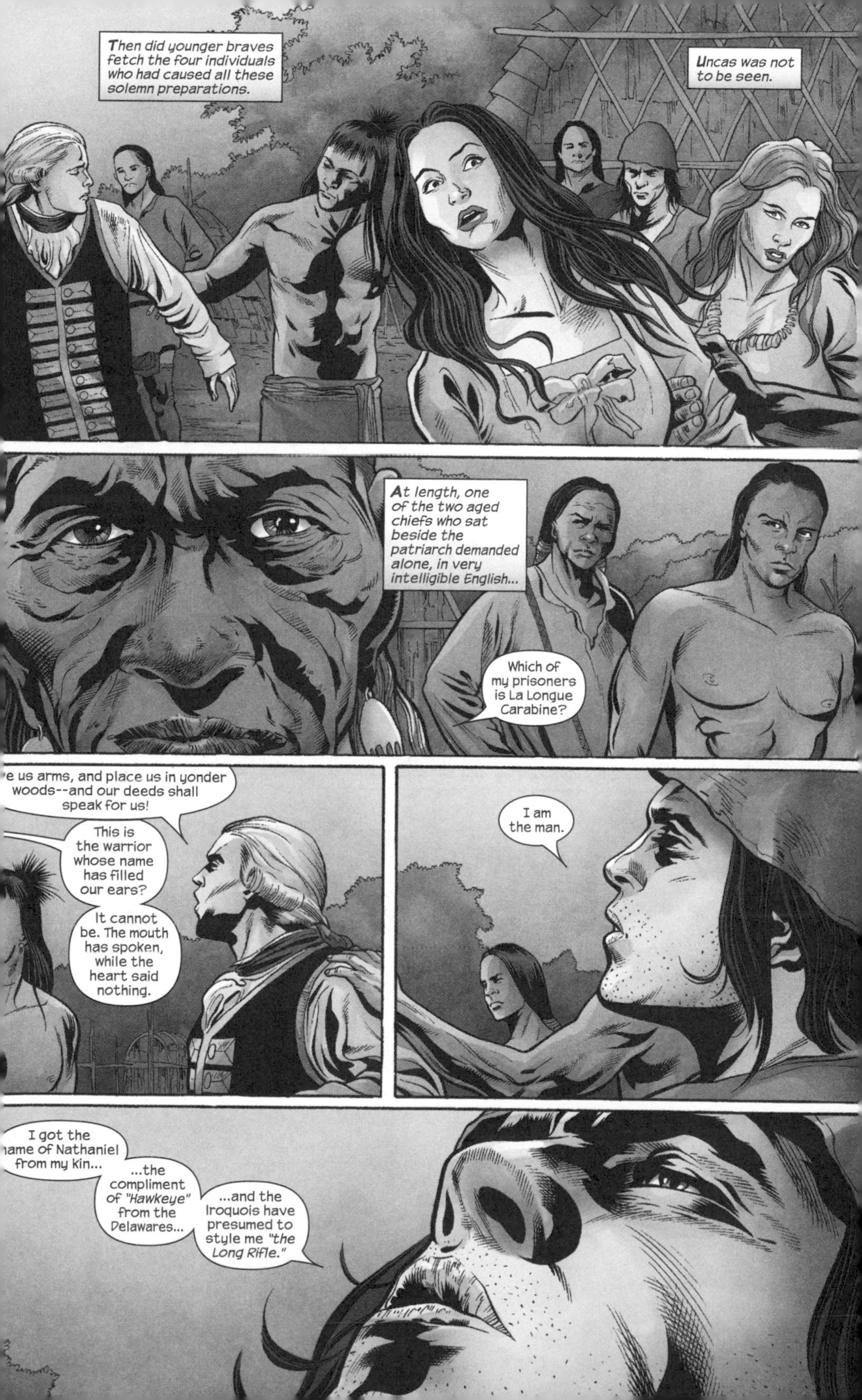
Then did younger braves fetch the four individuals who had caused all these solemn preparations.
Uncas was not to be seen.
At length, one of the two aged chiefs who sat beside the patriarch demanded alone, in very intelligible English...
Which of my prisoners is La Longue Carabine?
e us arms, and place us in yonder woods--and our deeds shall speak for us!
This is the warrior whose name has filled our ears?
It cannot be. The mouth has spoken, while the heart said nothing.
I am the man.
I got the ame of Nathaniel from my kin...
...the compliment of "Hawkeye" from the Delawares...
...and the Iroquois have presumed to style me "the Long Rifle."

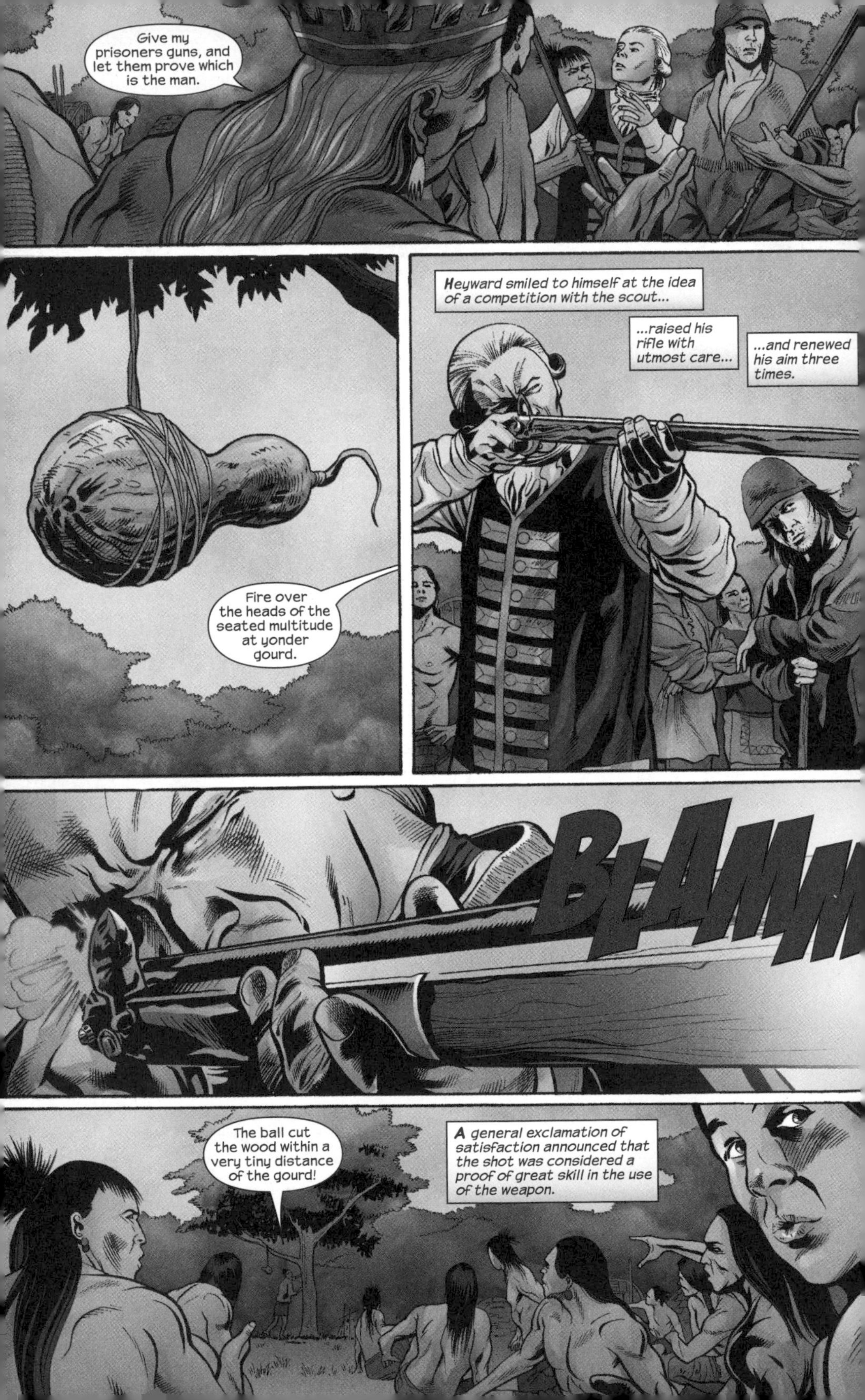
Give my prisoners guns, and let them prove which is the man.
Fire over the heads of the seated multitude at yonder gourd.
Heyward smiled to himself at the idea of a competition with the scout...
...raised his rifle with utmost care...
...and renewed his aim three times.
BLAMM
The ball cut the wood within a very tiny distance of the gourd!
A general exclamation of satisfaction announced that the shot was considered a proof of great skill in the use of the weapon.

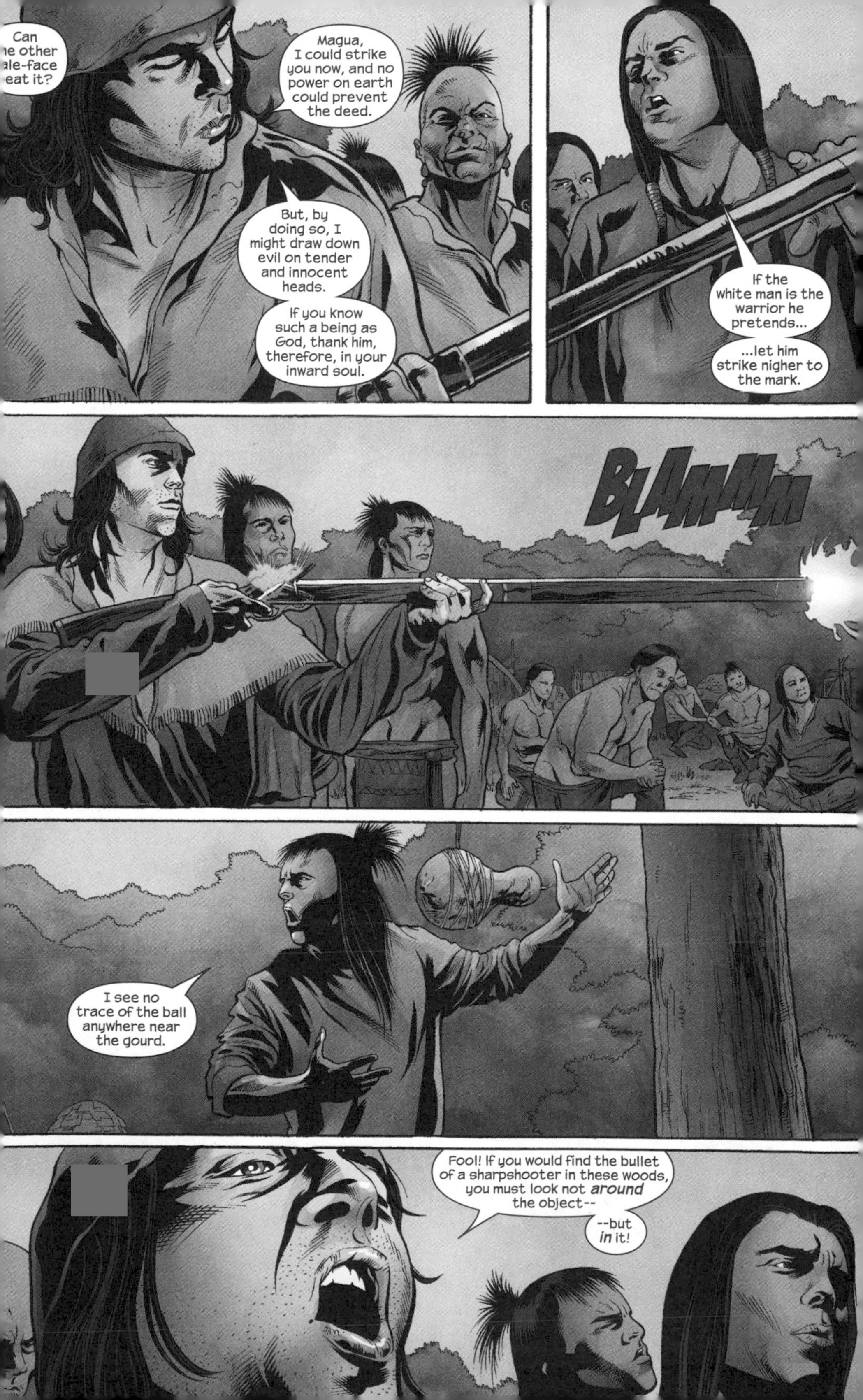

Can e other ale-face eat it?
Magua, I could strike you now, and no power on earth could prevent the deed.
But, by doing so, I might draw down evil on tender and innocent heads.
If you know such a being as God, thank him, therefore, in your inward soul.
If the white man is the warrior he pretends...
...let him strike nigher to the mark.
BLAMMM
I see no trace of the ball anywhere near the gourd.
Fool! If you would find the bullet of a sharpshooter in these woods, you must look not *around* the object--
--but *in* it!

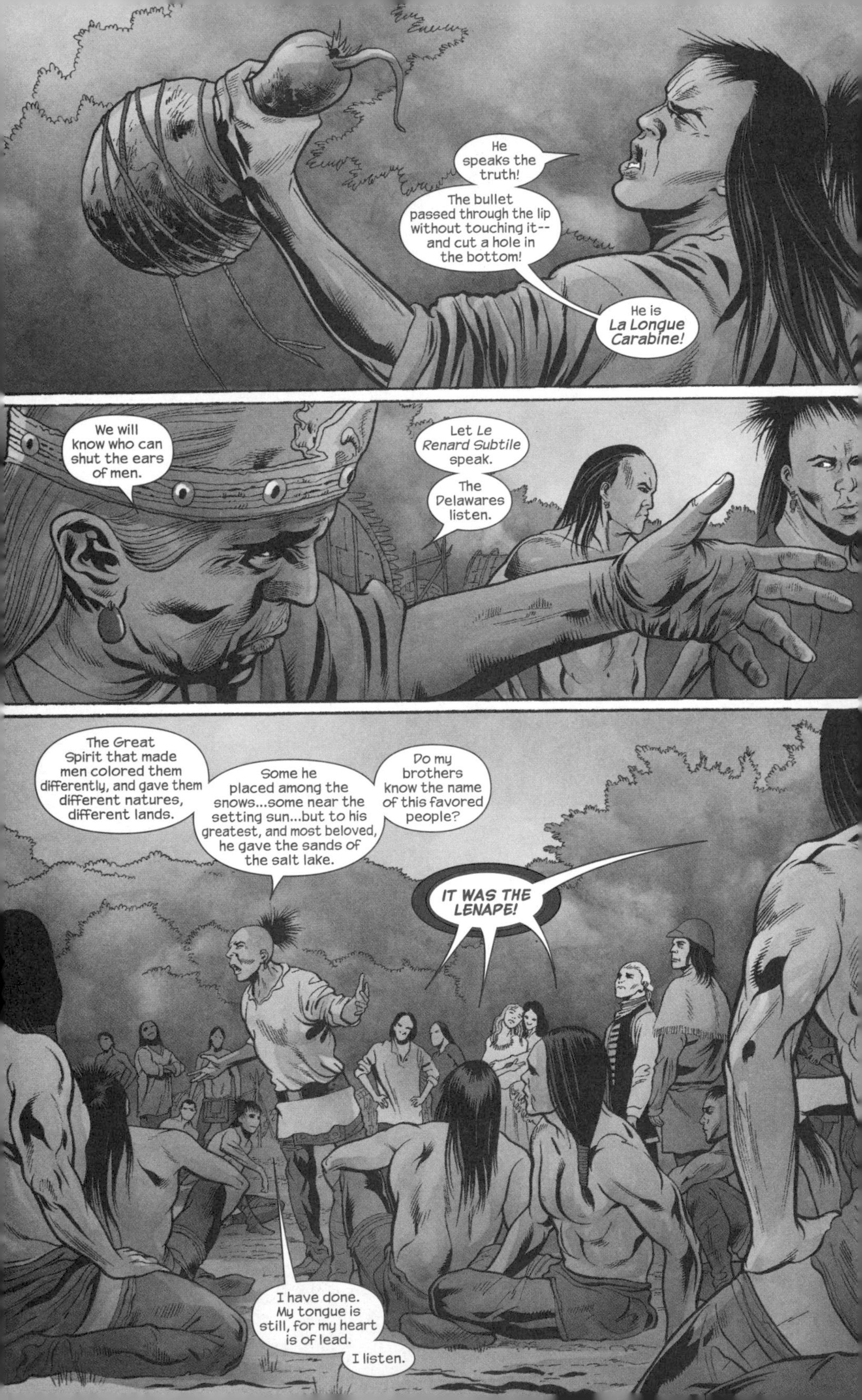
He speaks the truth!
The bullet passed through the lip without touching it-- and cut a hole in the bottom!
He is *La Longue Carabine!*
We will know who can shut the ears of men.
Let *Le Renard Subtile* speak.
The Delawares listen.
The Great Spirit that made men colored them differently, and gave them different natures, different lands.
Some he placed among the snows...some near the setting sun...but to his greatest, and most beloved, he gave the sands of the salt lake.
Do my brothers know the name of this favored people?
IT WAS THE LENAPE!
I have done. My tongue is still, for my heart is of lead.
I listen.

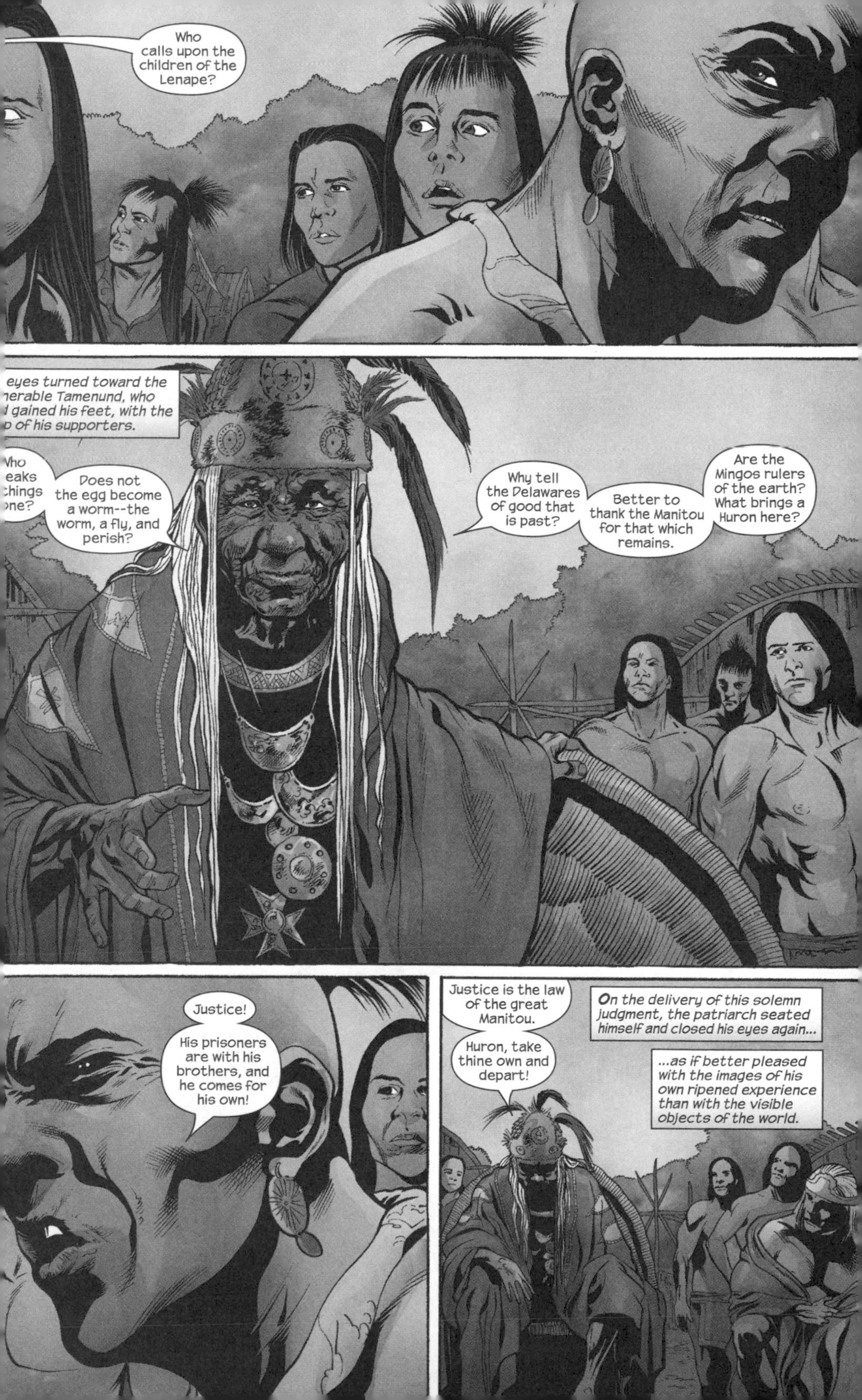
Who calls upon the children of the Lenape?
eyes turned toward the nerable Tamenund, who d gained his feet, with the o of his supporters.
Who eaks things one?
Does not the egg become a worm--the worm, a fly, and perish?
Why tell the Delawares of good that is past?
Better to thank the Manitou for that which remains.
Are the Mingos rulers of the earth? What brings a Huron here?
Justice!
His prisoners are with his brothers, and he comes for his own!
Justice is the law of the great Manitou.
Huron, take thine own and depart!
On the delivery of this solemn judgment, the patriarch seated himself and closed his eyes again...
...as if better pleased with the images of his own ripened experience than with the visible objects of the world.

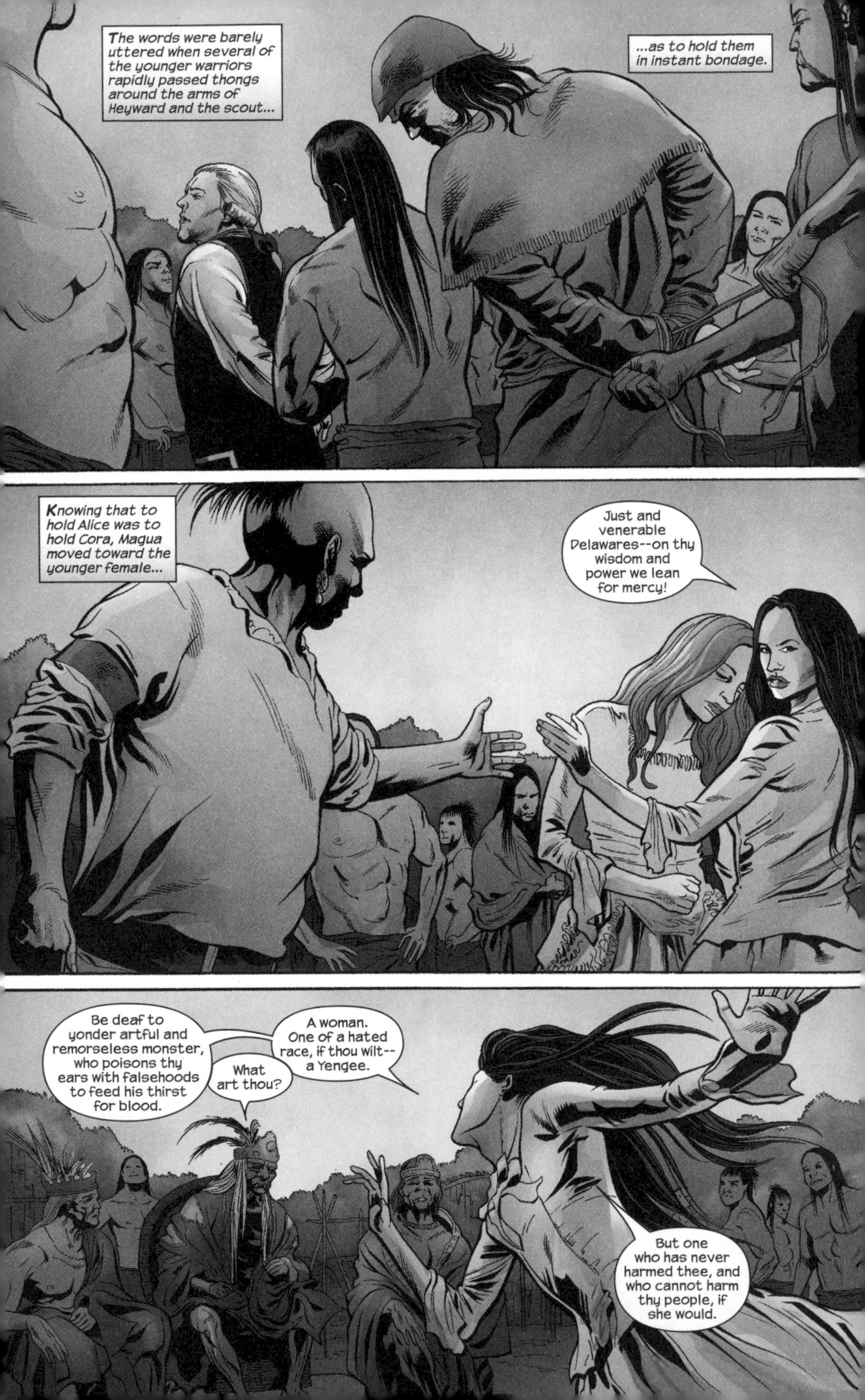
The words were barely uttered when several of the younger warriors rapidly passed thongs around the arms of Heyward and the scout...
...as to hold them in instant bondage.
Knowing that to hold Alice was to hold Cora, Magua moved toward the younger female...
Just and venerable Delawares--on thy wisdom and power we lean for mercy!
Be deaf to yonder artful and remorseless monster, who poisons thy ears with falsehoods to feed his thirst for blood.
What art thou?
A woman. One of a hated race, if thou wilt--a Yengee.
But one who has never harmed thee, and who cannot harm thy people, if she would.

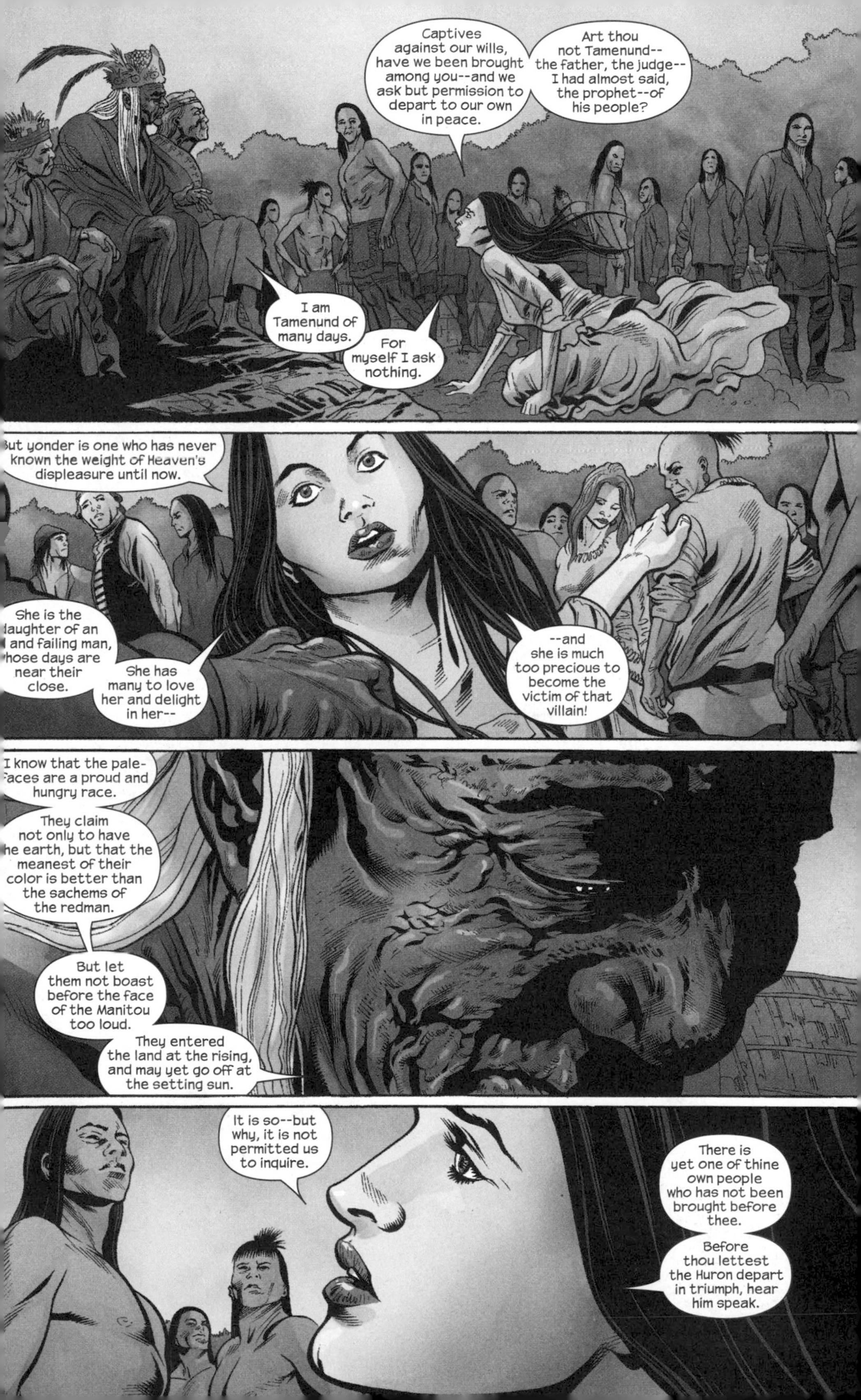
Captives against our wills, have we been brought among you--and we ask but permission to depart to our own in peace.
Art thou not Tamenund-- the father, the judge-- I had almost said, the prophet--of his people?
I am Tamenund of many days.
For myself I ask nothing.
ut yonder is one who has never known the weight of Heaven's displeasure until now.
She is the aughter of an and failing man, hose days are near their close.
She has many to love her and delight in her--
--and she is much too precious to become the victim of that villain!
I know that the pale- aces are a proud and hungry race.
They claim not only to have he earth, but that the meanest of their color is better than the sachems of the redman.
But let them not boast before the face of the Manitou too loud.
They entered the land at the rising, and may yet go off at the setting sun.
It is so--but why, it is not permitted us to inquire.
There is yet one of thine own people who has not been brought before thee.
Before thou lettest the Huron depart in triumph, hear him speak.

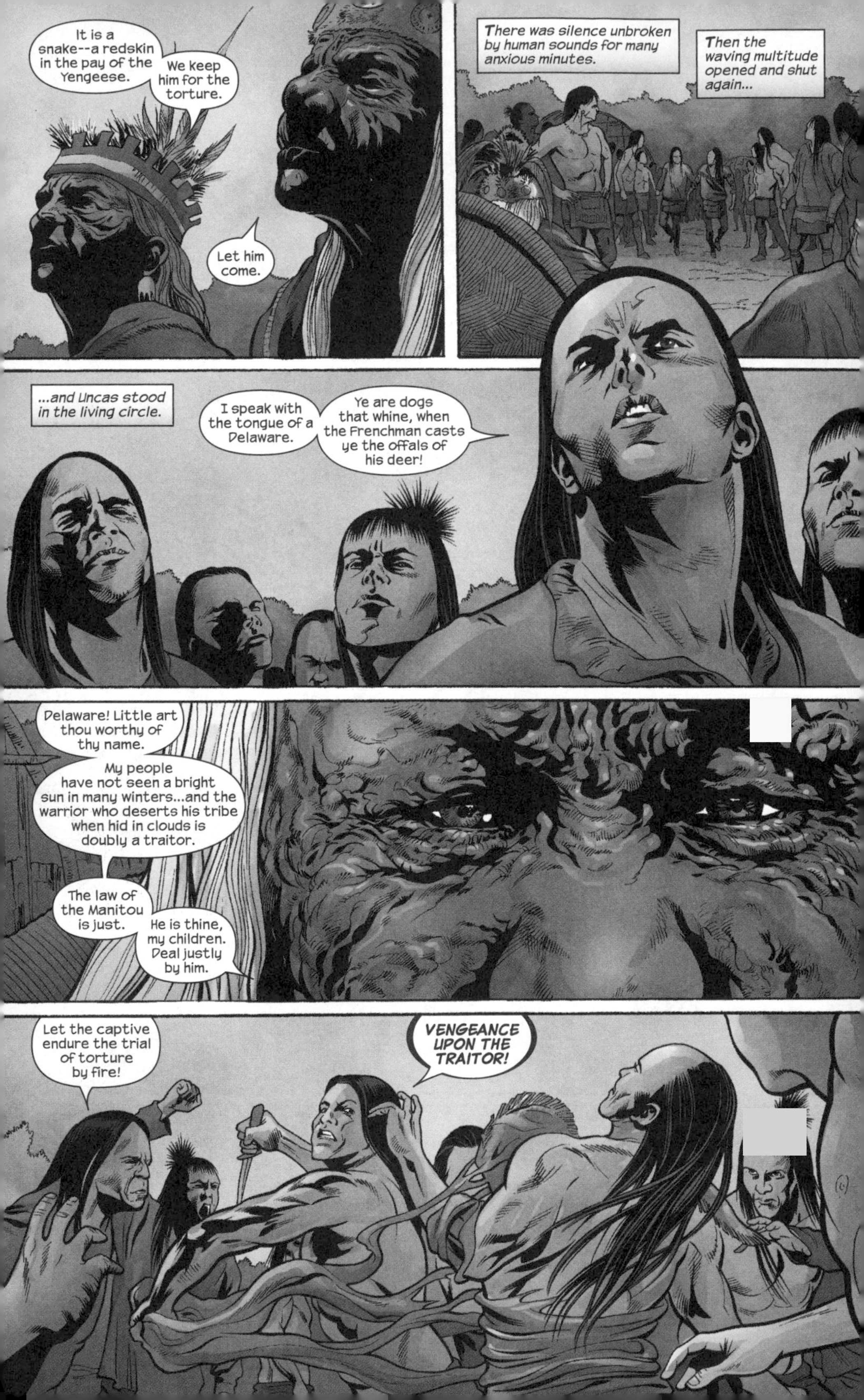
It is a snake--a redskin in the pay of the Yengeese.
We keep him for the torture.
Let him come.
There was silence unbroken by human sounds for many anxious minutes.
Then the waving multitude opened and shut again...
...and Uncas stood in the living circle.
I speak with the tongue of a Delaware.
Ye are dogs that whine, when the Frenchman casts ye the offals of his deer!
Delaware! Little art thou worthy of thy name.
My people have not seen a bright sun in many winters...and the warrior who deserts his tribe when hid in clouds is doubly a traitor.
The law of the Manitou is just.
He is thine, my children. Deal justly by him.
Let the captive endure the trial of torture by fire!
VENGEANCE UPON THE TRAITOR!

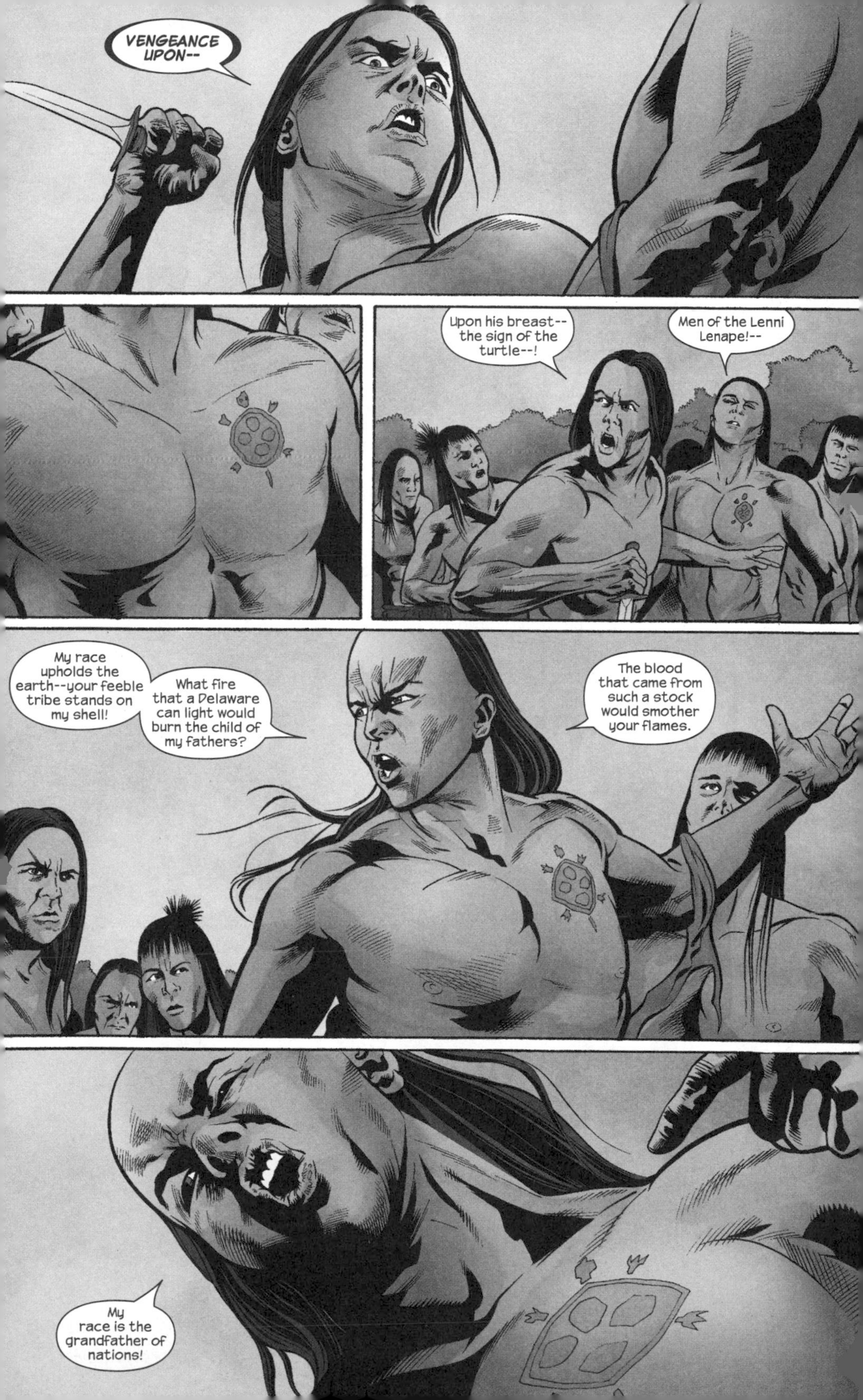
VENGEANCE UPON--
Upon his breast-- the sign of the turtle--!
Men of the Lenni Lenape!--
My race upholds the earth--your feeble tribe stands on my shell!
What fire that a Delaware can light would burn the child of my fathers?
The blood that came from such a stock would smother your flames.
My race is the grandfather of nations!

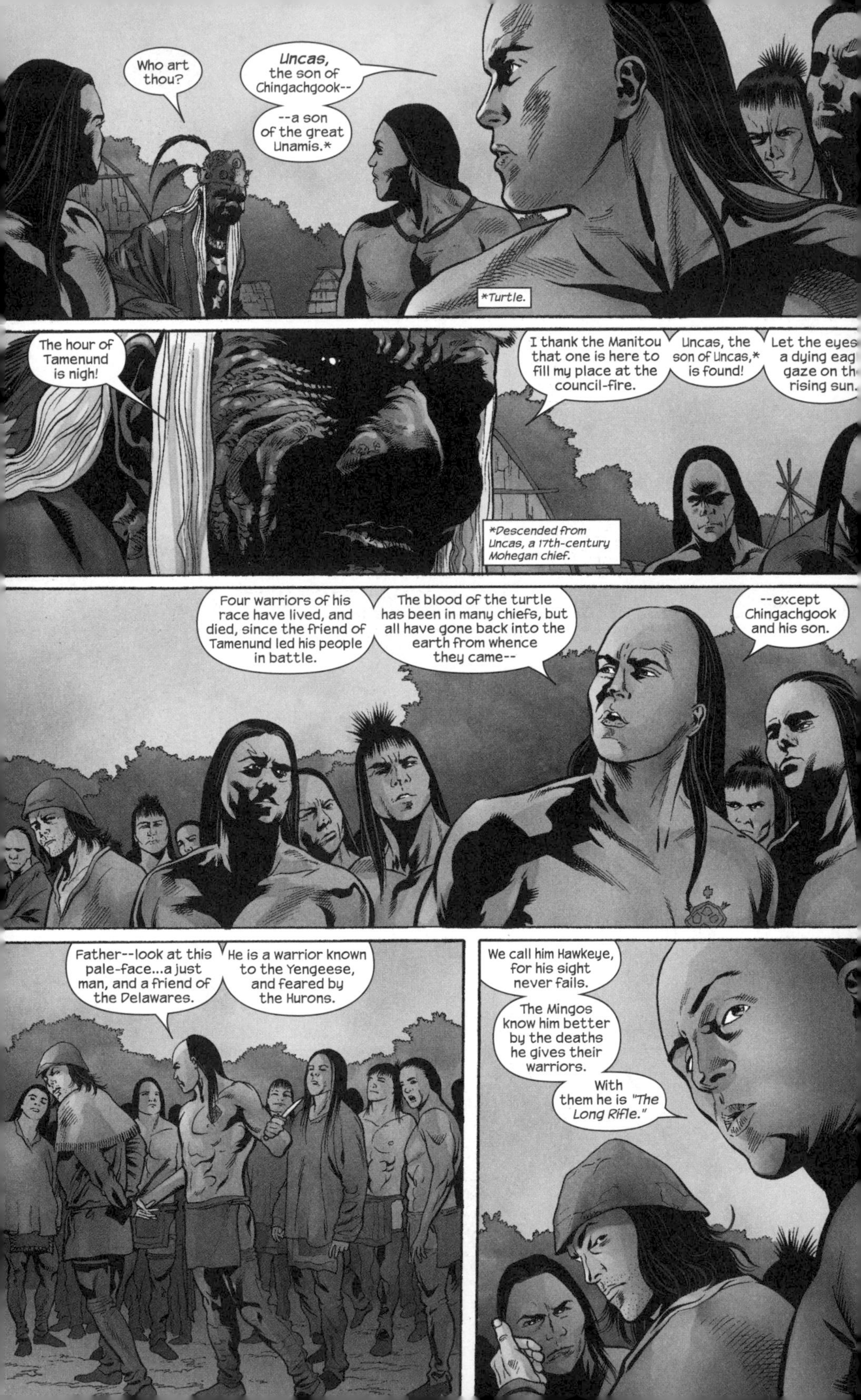

Who art thou?
Uncas, the son of Chingachgook--
--a son of the great Unamis.*
*Turtle.
The hour of Tamenund is nigh!
I thank the Manitou that one is here to fill my place at the council-fire.
Uncas, the son of Uncas,* is found!
Let the eyes a dying eag gaze on th rising sun.
*Descended from Uncas, a 17th-century Mohegan chief.
Four warriors of his race have lived, and died, since the friend of Tamenund led his people in battle.
The blood of the turtle has been in many chiefs, but all have gone back into the earth from whence they came--
--except Chingachgook and his son.
Father--look at this pale-face...a just man, and a friend of the Delawares.
He is a warrior known to the Yengeese, and feared by the Hurons.
We call him Hawkeye, for his sight never fails.
The Mingos know him better by the deaths he gives their warriors.
With them he is "The Long Rifle."

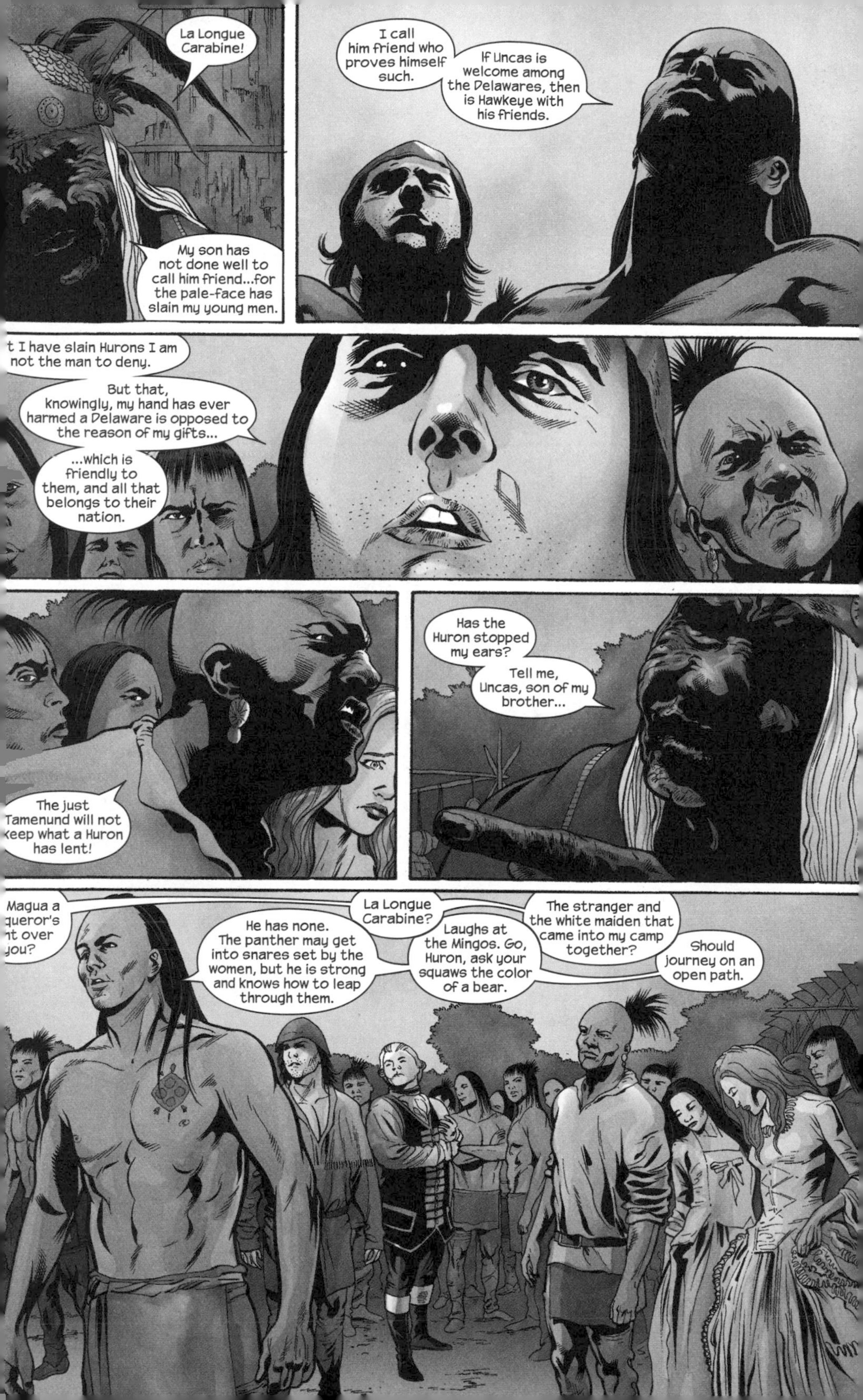
La Longue Carabine!
My son has not done well to call him friend...for the pale-face has slain my young men.
I call him friend who proves himself such.
If Uncas is welcome among the Delawares, then is Hawkeye with his friends.
t I have slain Hurons I am not the man to deny.
But that, knowingly, my hand has ever harmed a Delaware is opposed to the reason of my gifts...
...which is friendly to them, and all that belongs to their nation.
The just Tamenund will not keep what a Huron has lent!
Has the Huron stopped my ears?
Tell me, Uncas, son of my brother...
Magua a queror's nt over you?
He has none. The panther may get into snares set by the women, but he is strong and knows how to leap through them.
La Longue Carabine?
Laughs at the Mingos. Go, Huron, ask your squaws the color of a bear.
The stranger and the white maiden that came into my camp together?
Should journey on an open path.

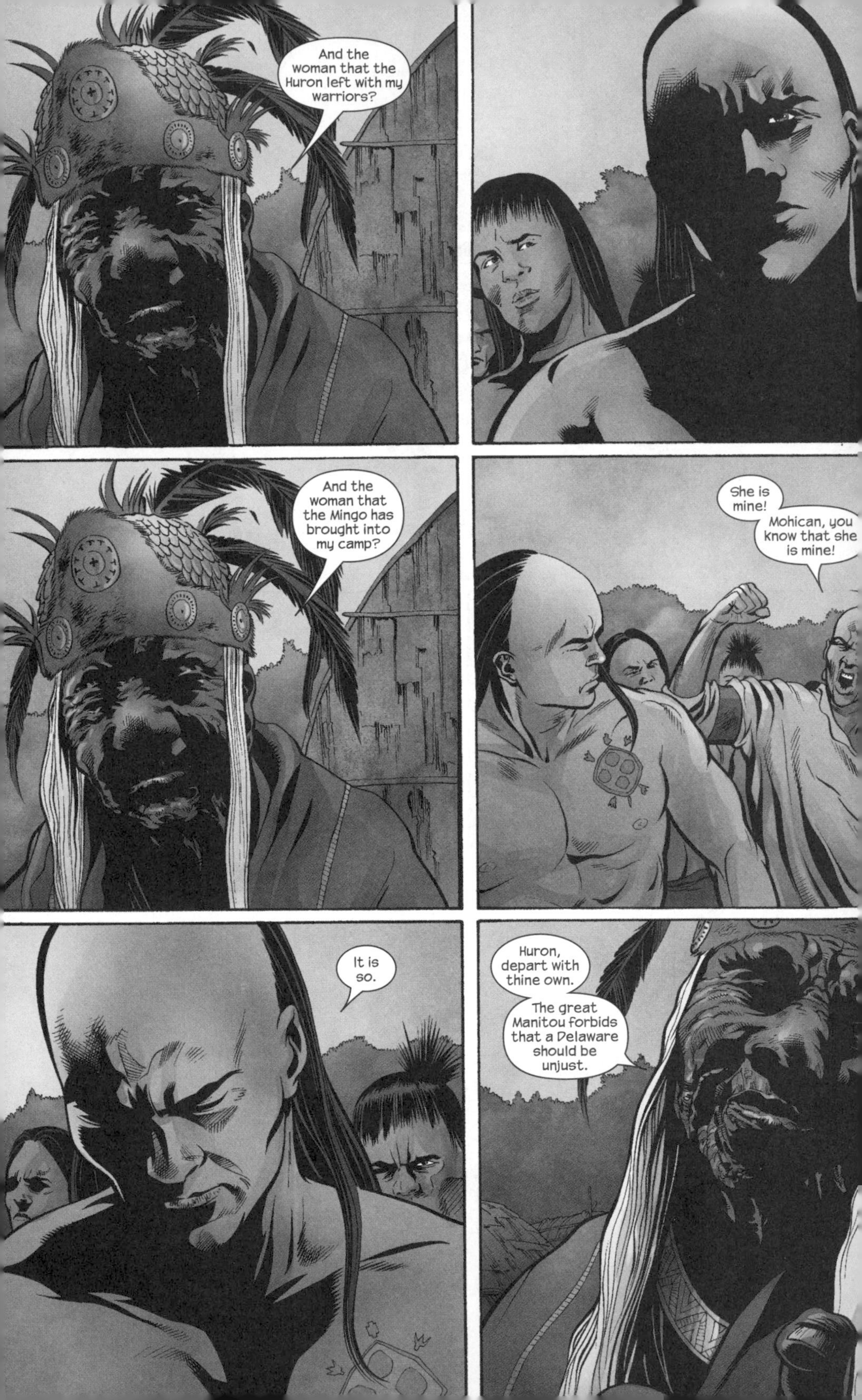
And the woman that the Huron left with my warriors?
And the woman that the Mingo has brought into my camp?
She is mine!
Mohican, you know that she is mine!
It is so.
Huron, depart with thine own.
The great Manitou forbids that a Delaware should be unjust.

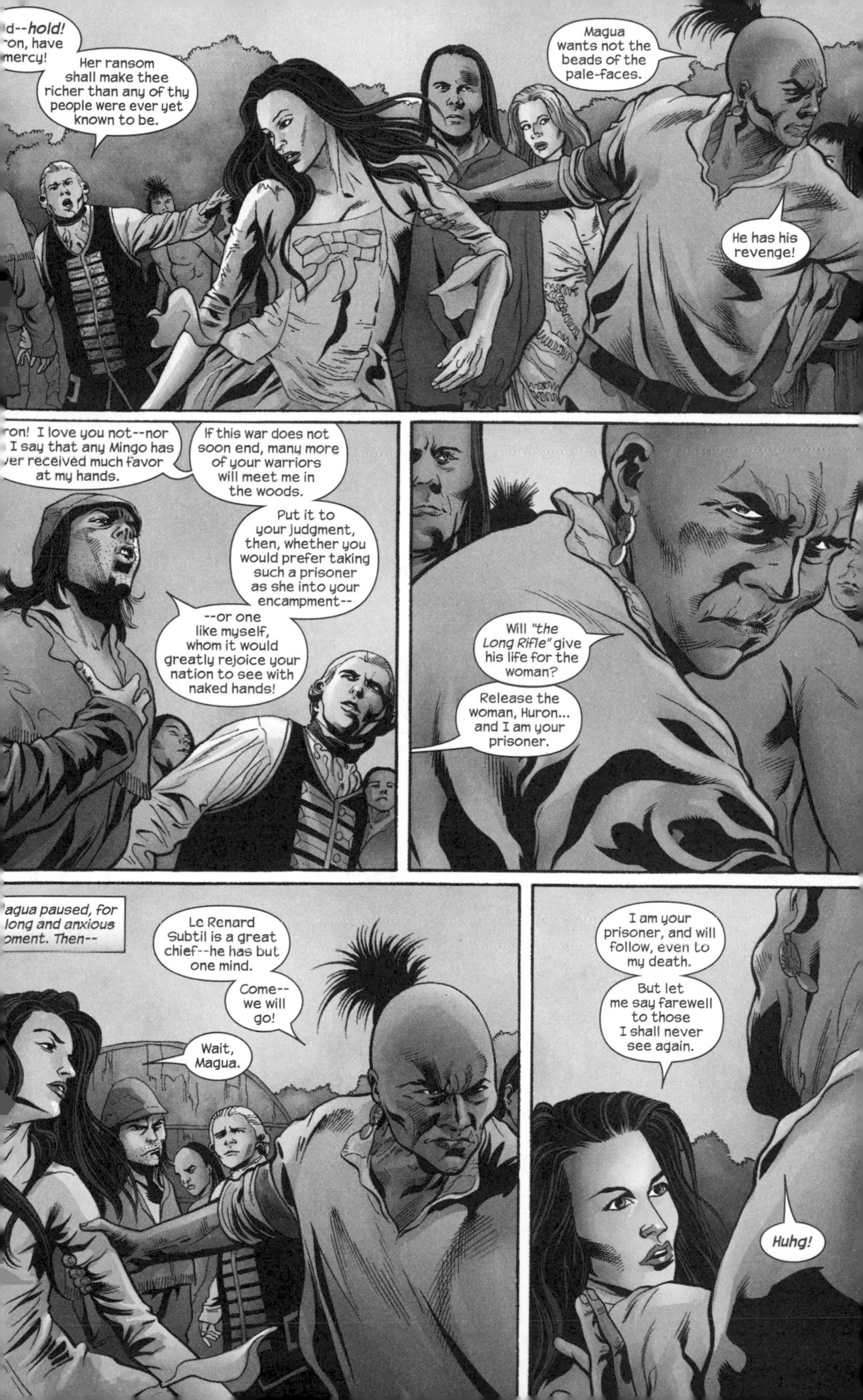
d--hold! ron, have mercy!
Her ransom shall make thee richer than any of thy people were ever yet known to be.
Magua wants not the beads of the pale-faces.
He has his revenge!
ron! I love you not--nor I say that any Mingo has ver received much favor at my hands.
If this war does not soon end, many more of your warriors will meet me in the woods.
Put it to your judgment, then, whether you would prefer taking such a prisoner as she into your encampment--
--or one like myself, whom it would greatly rejoice your nation to see with naked hands!
Will "the Long Rifle" give his life for the woman?
Release the woman, Huron... and I am your prisoner.
agua paused, for long and anxious oment. Then--
Le Renard Subtil is a great chief--he has but one mind.
Come-- we will go!
Wait, Magua.
I am your prisoner, and will follow, even to my death.
But let me say farewell to those I shall never see again.
Huhg!

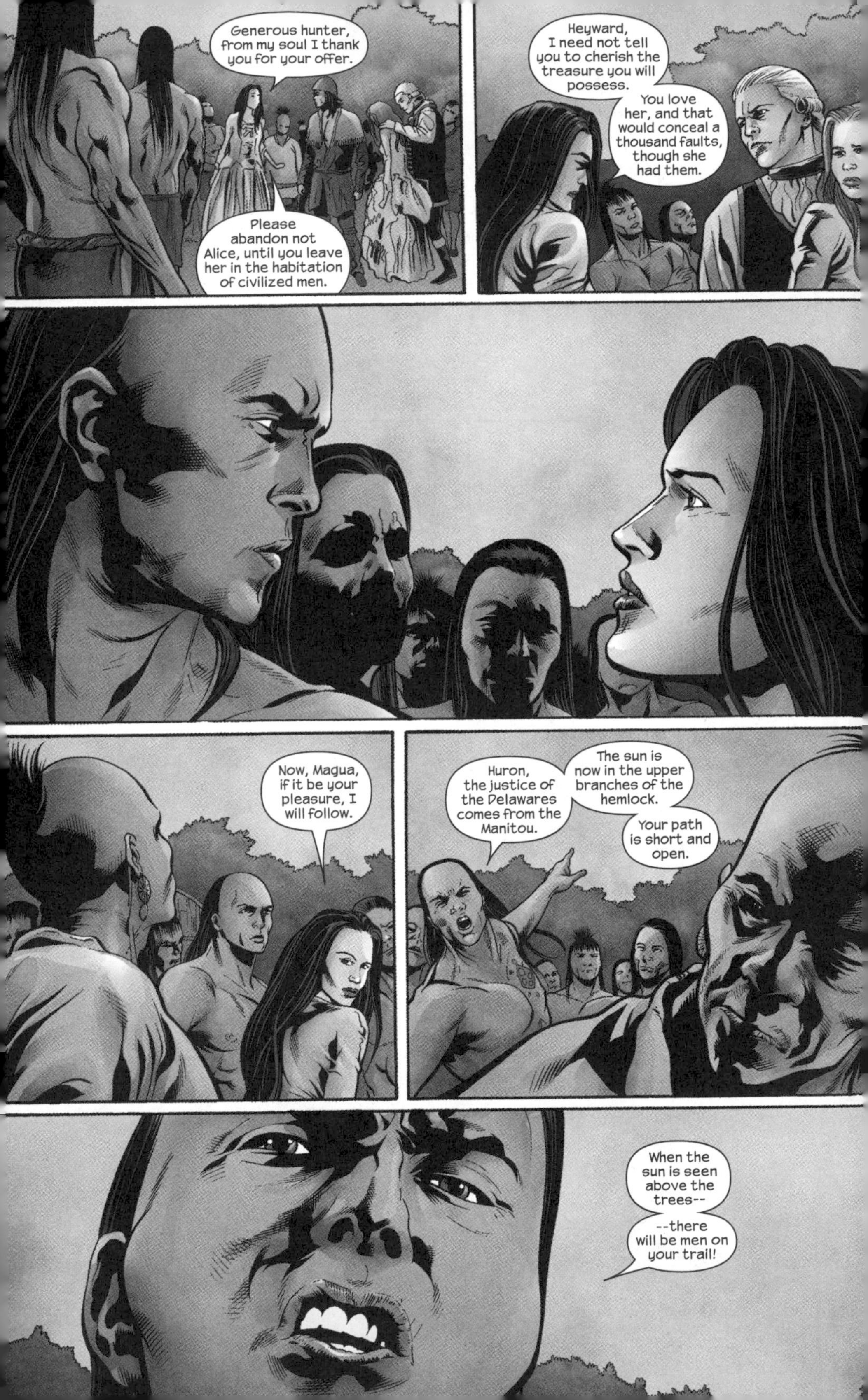
Generous hunter, from my soul I thank you for your offer.
Please abandon not Alice, until you leave her in the habitation of civilized men.
Heyward, I need not tell you to cherish the treasure you will possess.
You love her, and that would conceal a thousand faults, though she had them.
Now, Magua, if it be your pleasure, I will follow.
Huron, the justice of the Delawares comes from the Manitou.
The sun is now in the upper branches of the hemlock.
Your path is short and open.
When the sun is seen above the trees--
--there will be men on your trail!

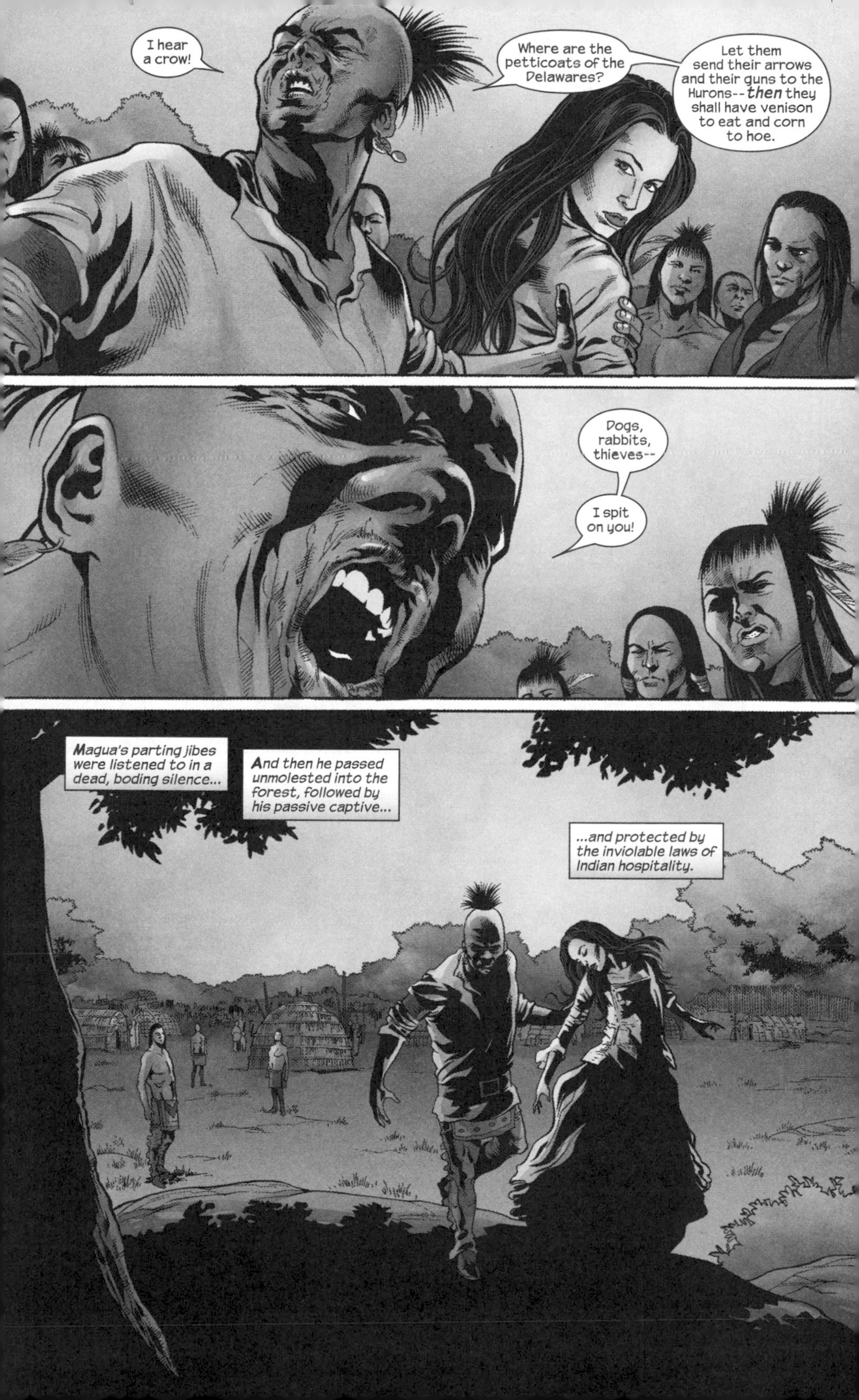

I hear a crow!
Where are the petticoats of the Delawares?
Let them send their arrows and their guns to the Hurons--*then* they shall have venison to eat and corn to hoe.
Dogs, rabbits, thieves--
I spit on you!
Magua's parting jibes were listened to in a dead, boding silence...
And then he passed unmolested into the forest, followed by his passive captive...
...and protected by the inviolable laws of Indian hospitality.

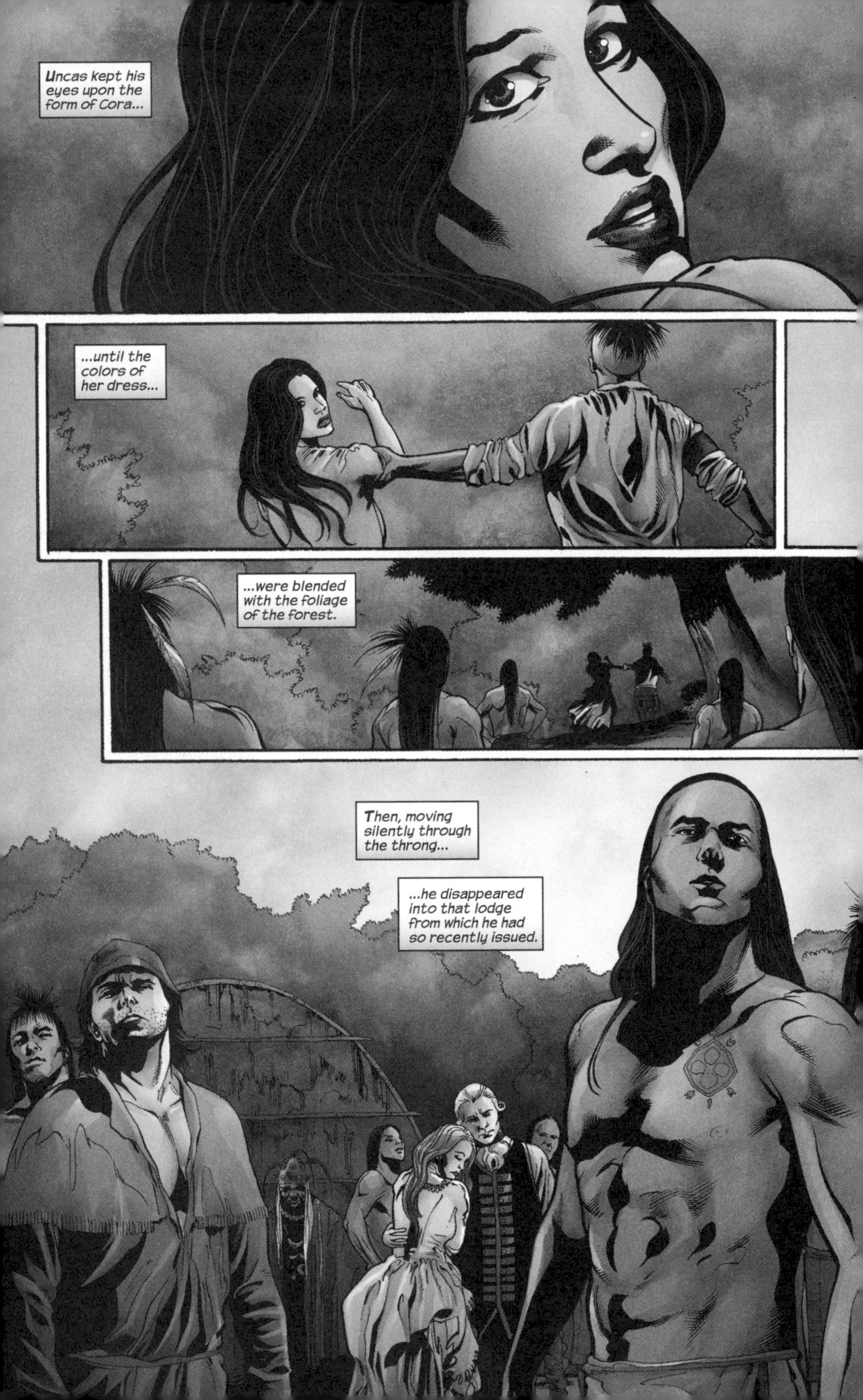
Uncas kept his eyes upon the form of Cora...
...until the colors of her dress...
...were blended with the foliage of the forest.
Then, moving silently through the throng...
...he disappeared into that lodge from which he had so recently issued.

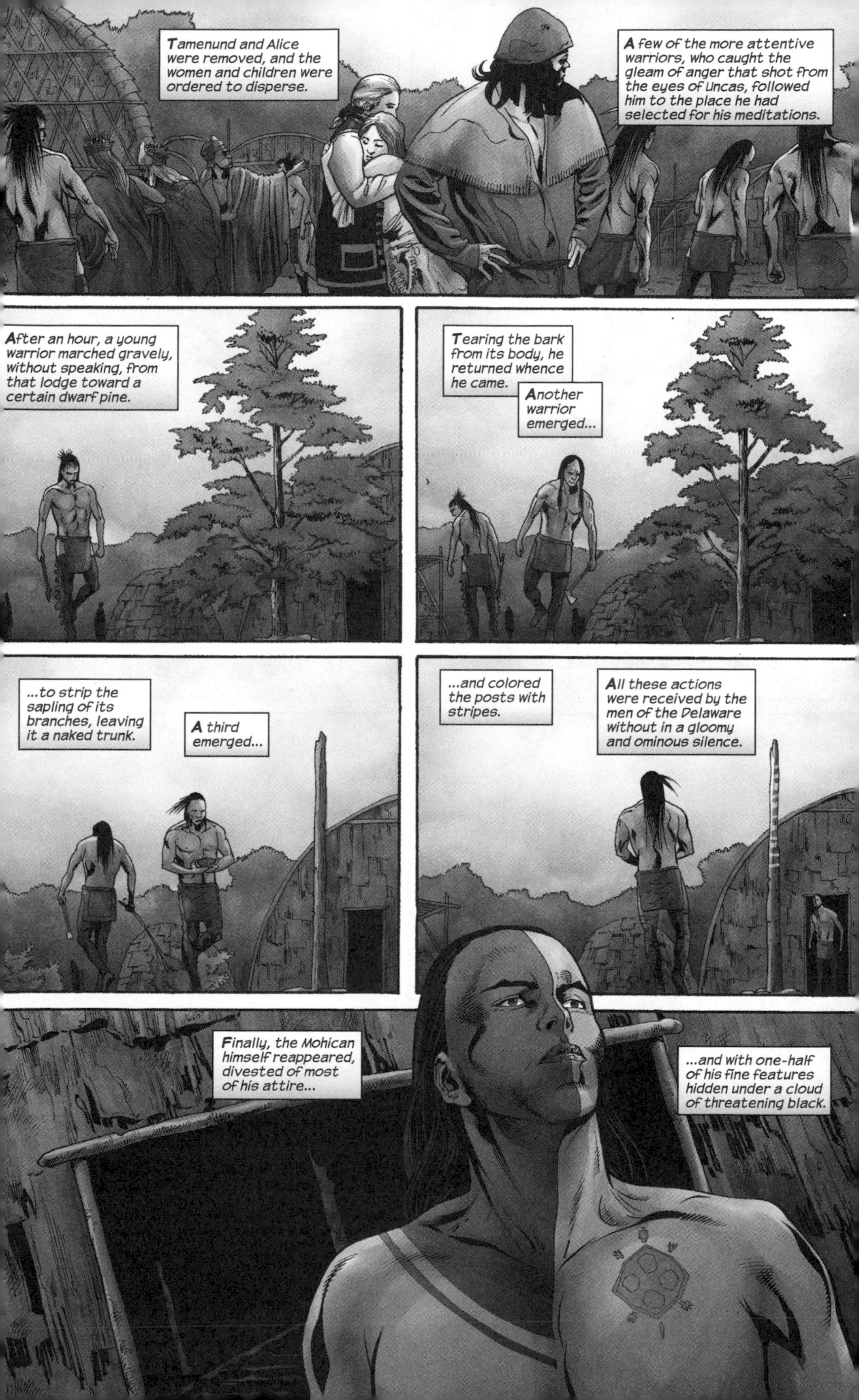
Tamenund and Alice were removed, and the women and children were ordered to disperse.
A few of the more attentive warriors, who caught the gleam of anger that shot from the eyes of Uncas, followed him to the place he had selected for his meditations.
After an hour, a young warrior marched gravely, without speaking, from that lodge toward a certain dwarf pine.
Tearing the bark from its body, he returned whence he came.
Another warrior emerged...
...to strip the sapling of its branches, leaving it a naked trunk.
A third emerged...
...and colored the posts with stripes.
All these actions were received by the men of the Delaware without in a gloomy and ominous silence.
Finally, the Mohican himself reappeared, divested of most of his attire...
...and with one-half of his fine features hidden under a cloud of threatening black.

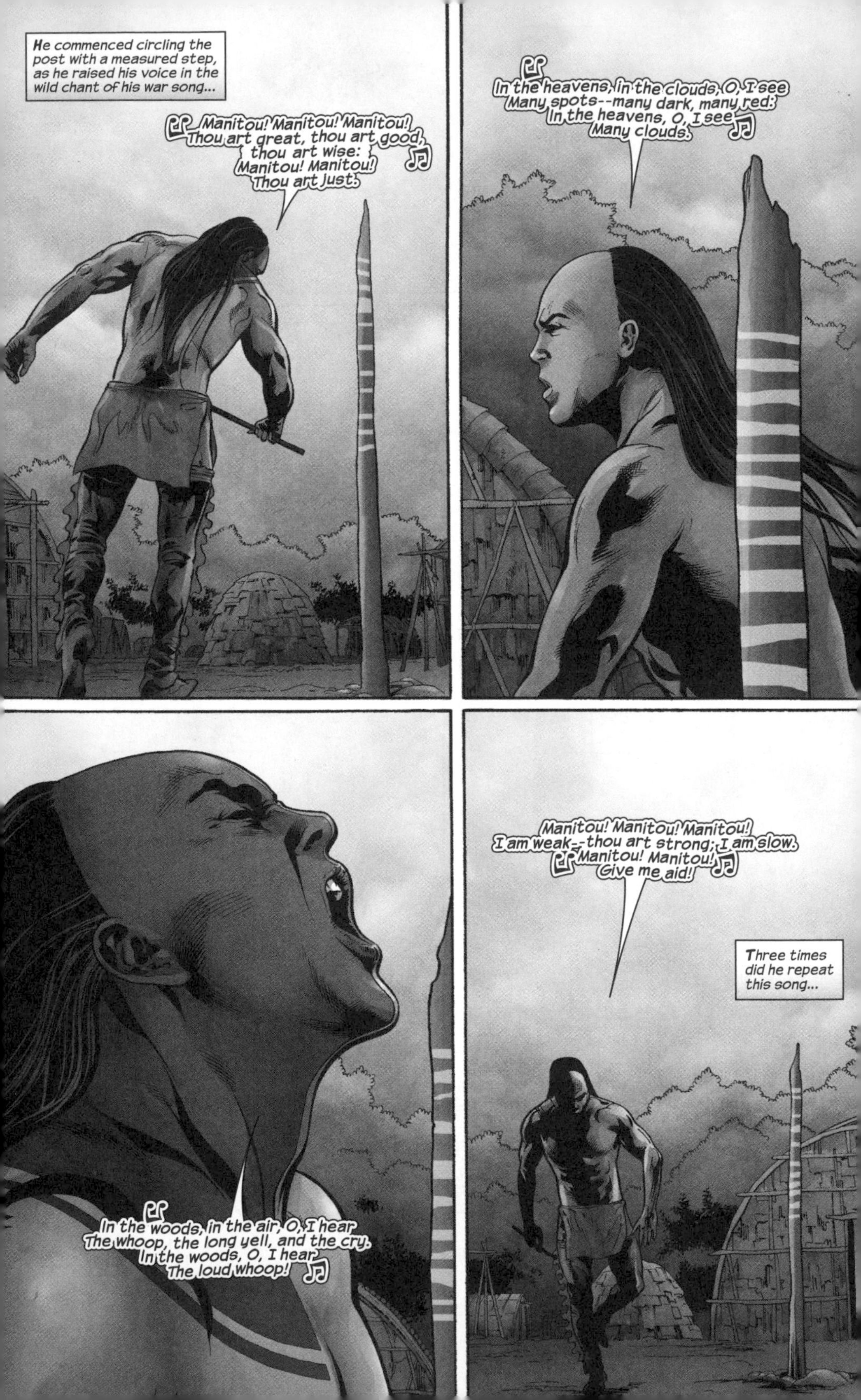
He commenced circling the post with a measured step, as he raised his voice in the wild chant of his war song...
Manitou! Manitou! Manitou! Thou art great, thou art good, thou art wise: Manitou! Manitou! Thou art just.
In the heavens, in the clouds, O, I see Many spots--many dark, many red: In the heavens, O, I see Many clouds.
In the woods, in the air, O, I hear The whoop, the long yell, and the cry. In the woods, O, I hear The loud whoop!
Manitou! Manitou! Manitou! I am weak--thou art strong; I am slow. Manitou! Manitou! Give me aid!
Three times did he repeat this song...

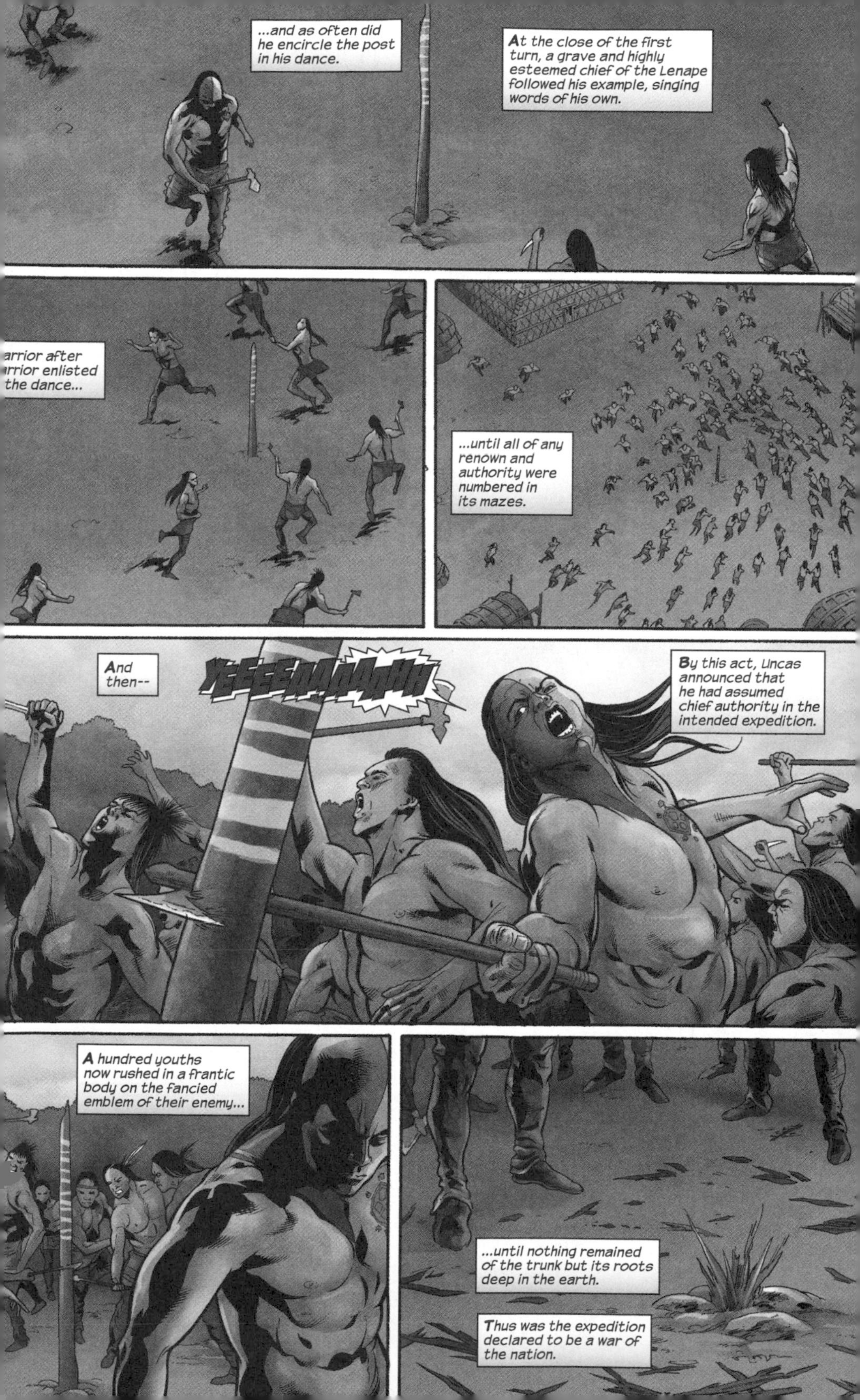

...and as often did he encircle the post in his dance.
At the close of the first turn, a grave and highly esteemed chief of the Lenape followed his example, singing words of his own.
arrior after
rrior enlisted
the dance...
...until all of any renown and authority were numbered in its mazes.
And then--
YEEEAAAAAHH
By this act, Uncas announced that he had assumed chief authority in the intended expedition.
A hundred youths now rushed in a frantic body on the fancied emblem of their enemy...
...until nothing remained of the trunk but its roots deep in the earth.
Thus was the expedition declared to be a war of the nation.

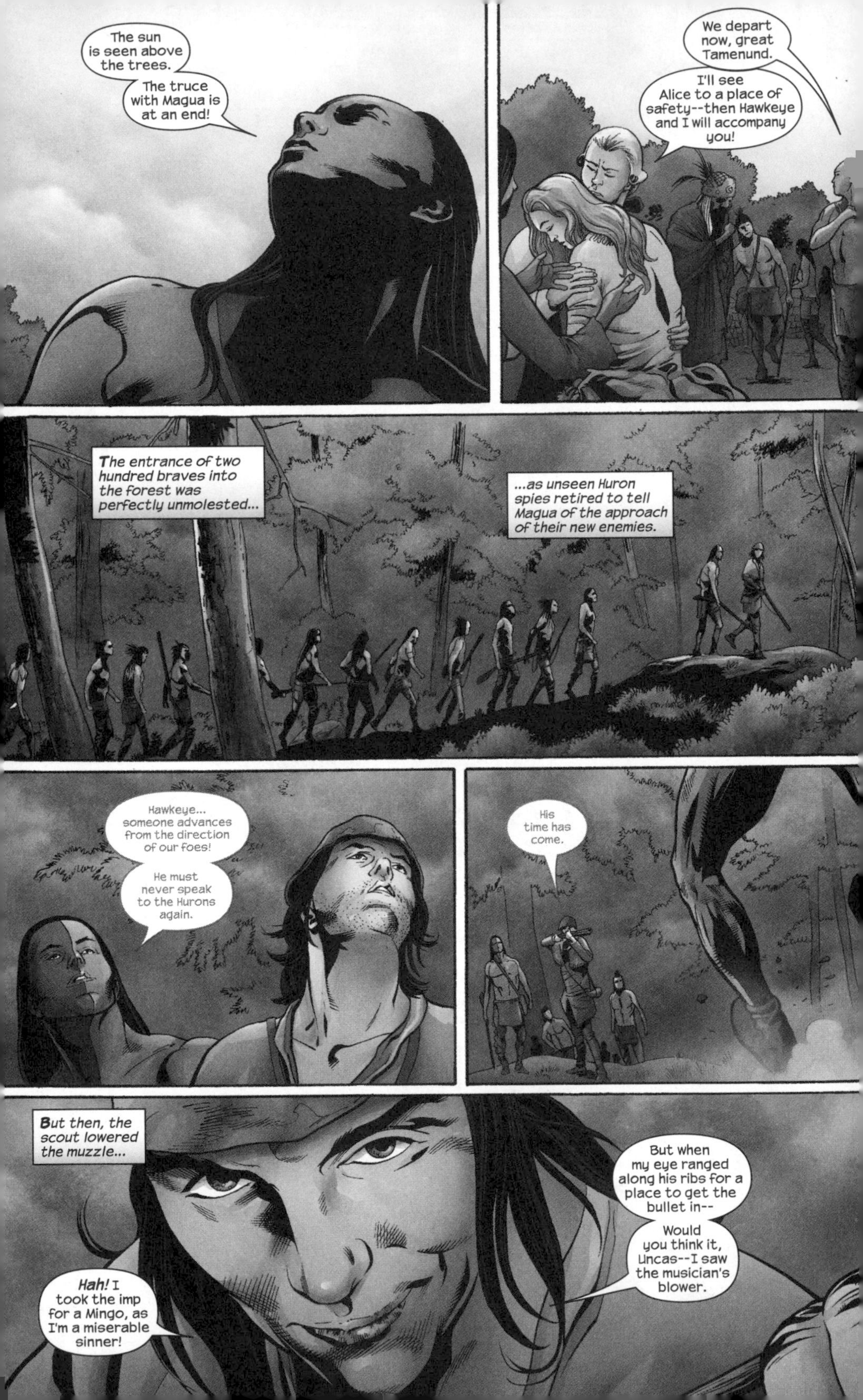

The sun is seen above the trees.
The truce with Magua is at an end!
We depart now, great Tamenund.
I'll see Alice to a place of safety--then Hawkeye and I will accompany you!
The entrance of two hundred braves into the forest was perfectly unmolested...
...as unseen Huron spies retired to tell Magua of the approach of their new enemies.
Hawkeye... someone advances from the direction of our foes!
He must never speak to the Hurons again.
His time has come.
But then, the scout lowered the muzzle...
But when my eye ranged along his ribs for a place to get the bullet in--
Would you think it, Uncas--I saw the musician's blower.
Hah! I took the imp for a Mingo, as I'm a miserable sinner!

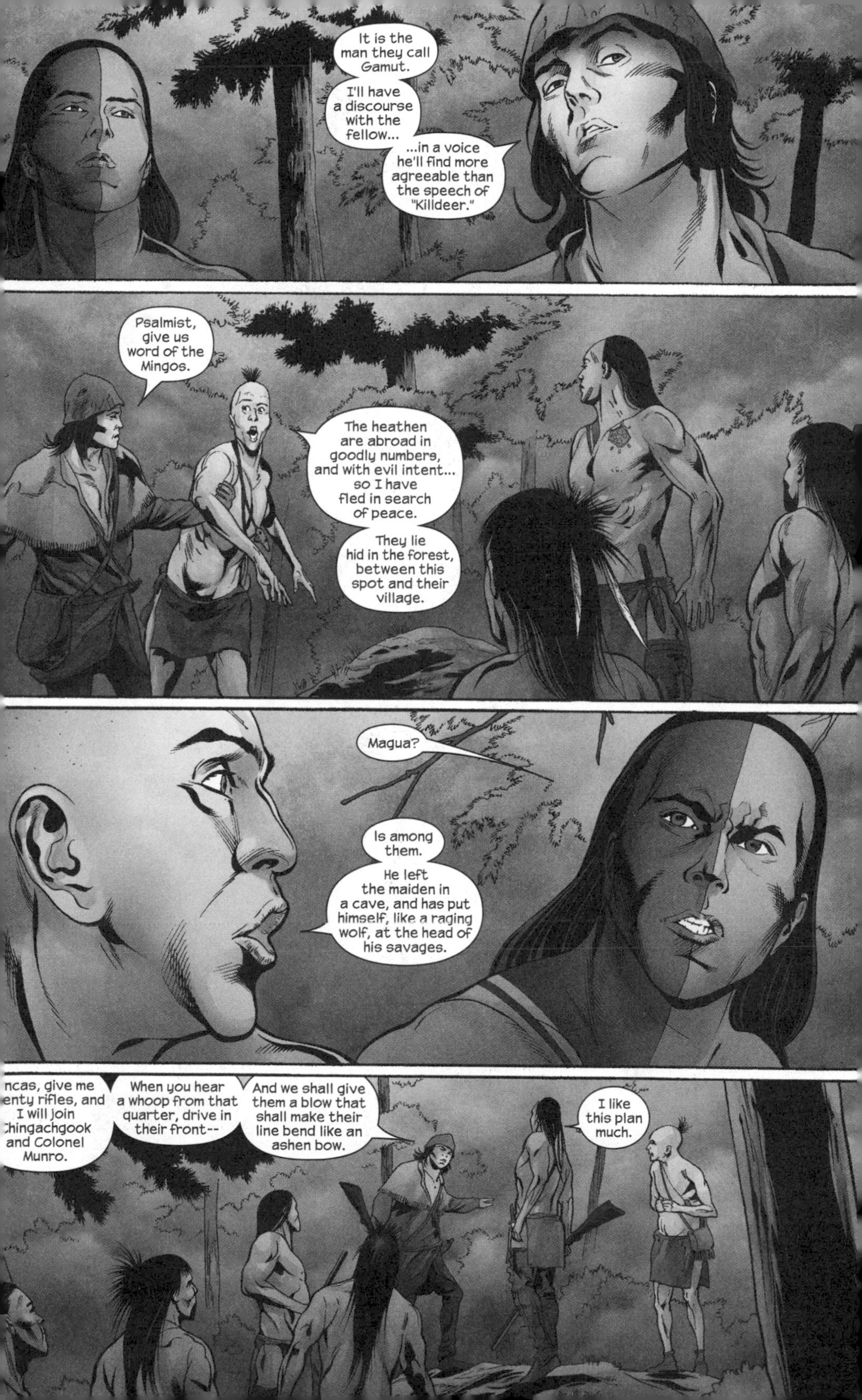
It is the man they call Gamut.
I'll have a discourse with the fellow...
...in a voice he'll find more agreeable than the speech of "Killdeer."
Psalmist, give us word of the Mingos.
The heathen are abroad in goodly numbers, and with evil intent... so I have fled in search of peace.
They lie hid in the forest, between this spot and their village.
Magua?
Is among them.
He left the maiden in a cave, and has put himself, like a raging wolf, at the head of his savages.
ncas, give me enty rifles, and I will join Chingachgook and Colonel Munro.
When you hear a whoop from that quarter, drive in their front--
And we shall give them a blow that shall make their line bend like an ashen bow.
I like this plan much.

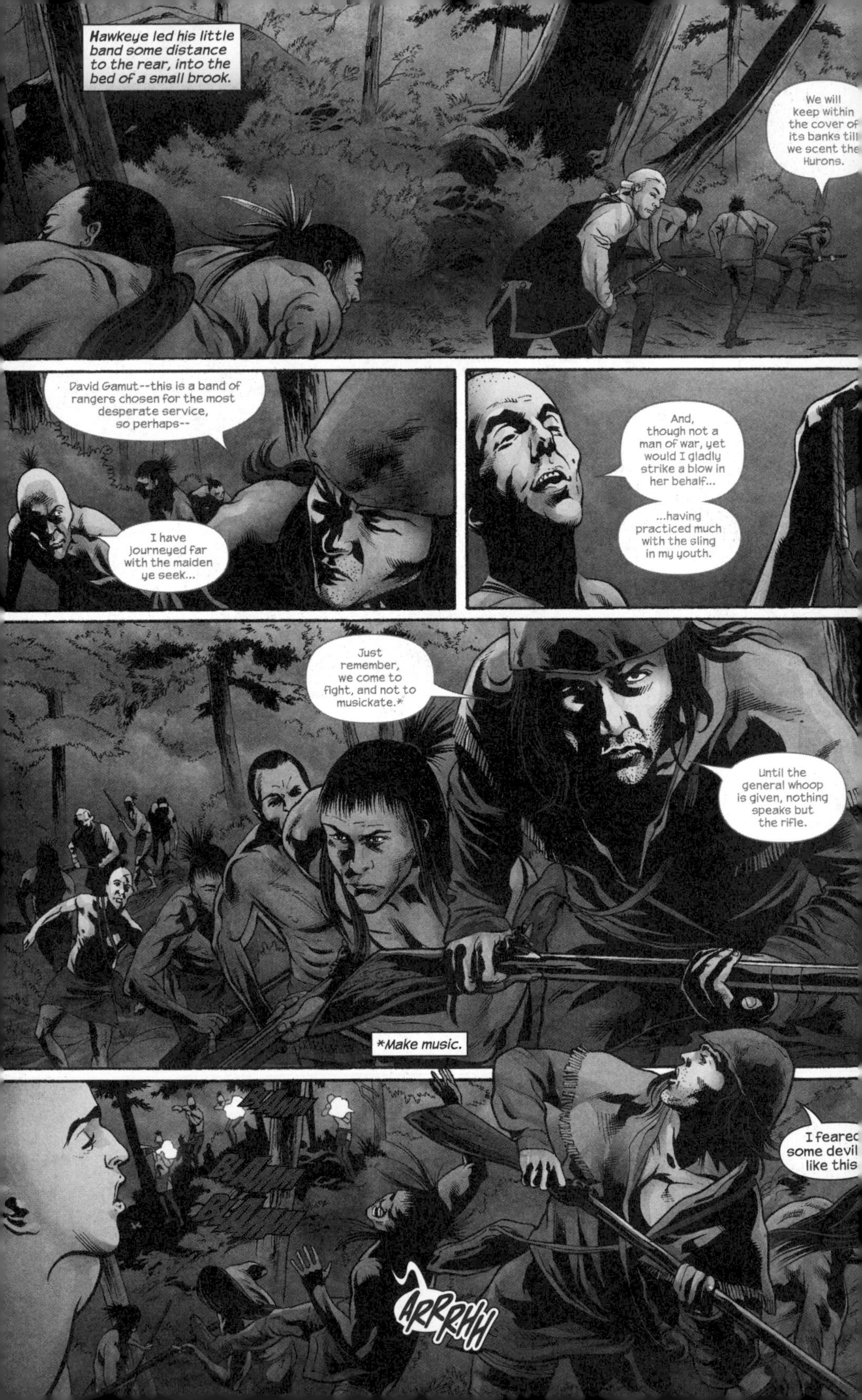
Hawkeye led his little band some distance to the rear, into the bed of a small brook.
We will keep within the cover of its banks till we scent the Hurons.
David Gamut--this is a band of rangers chosen for the most desperate service, so perhaps--
I have journeyed far with the maiden ye seek...
And, though not a man of war, yet would I gladly strike a blow in her behalf...
...having practiced much with the sling in my youth.
Just remember, we come to fight, and not to musickate.*
Until the general whoop is given, nothing speaks but the rifle.
*Make music.
I feare some devil like this
ARRRHH

cover,
en-- --and
CHARGE!

The Hurons slowly
yielded ground--but
the scout pressed
their retreat--

BLAMMM

BLAMMM
BLAMM

--discharging
his rifle, and darting
from tree to tree.

It was
only a small party
of ambushers--but as
they fall back, they
are joined by their
comrades!

the return fire of the
ons became nearly equal
hat maintained by the
ancing Delawares--

--even as he
found his enemy
throwing out
men on his flank.

--Hawkeye knew
t would be more
dangerous to
retreat than to
stand his ground--

, at that
ment--

YEEE-YAAAH!

BLAMM
BLAMM

The
band of
Uncas has
struck!

The Hurons
thought we were the
main force--and left too
small a force to resist the
Mohican's attack from
their rear!

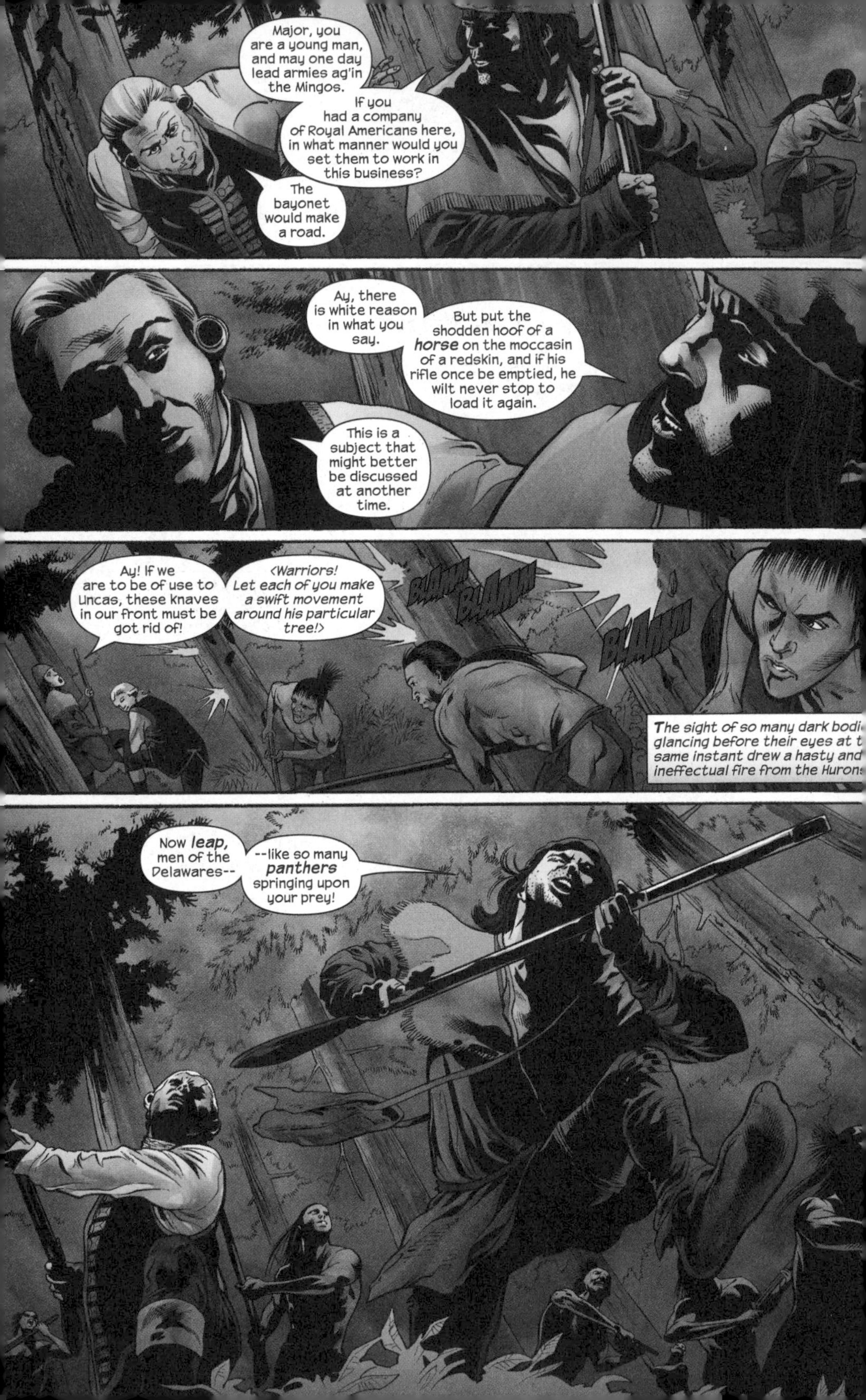
Major, you are a young man, and may one day lead armies ag'in the Mingos.
If you had a company of Royal Americans here, in what manner would you set them to work in this business?
The bayonet would make a road.
Ay, there is white reason in what you say.
But put the shodden hoof of a *horse* on the moccasin of a redskin, and if his rifle once be emptied, he wilt never stop to load it again.
This is a subject that might better be discussed at another time.
Ay! If we are to be of use to Uncas, these knaves in our front must be got rid of!
<Warriors! Let each of you make a swift movement around his particular tree!>
BLAMM BLAMM
BLAMM
The sight of so many dark bodi glancing before their eyes at t same instant drew a hasty and ineffectual fire from the Huron
Now *leap,* men of the Delawares--
--like so many *panthers* springing upon your prey!

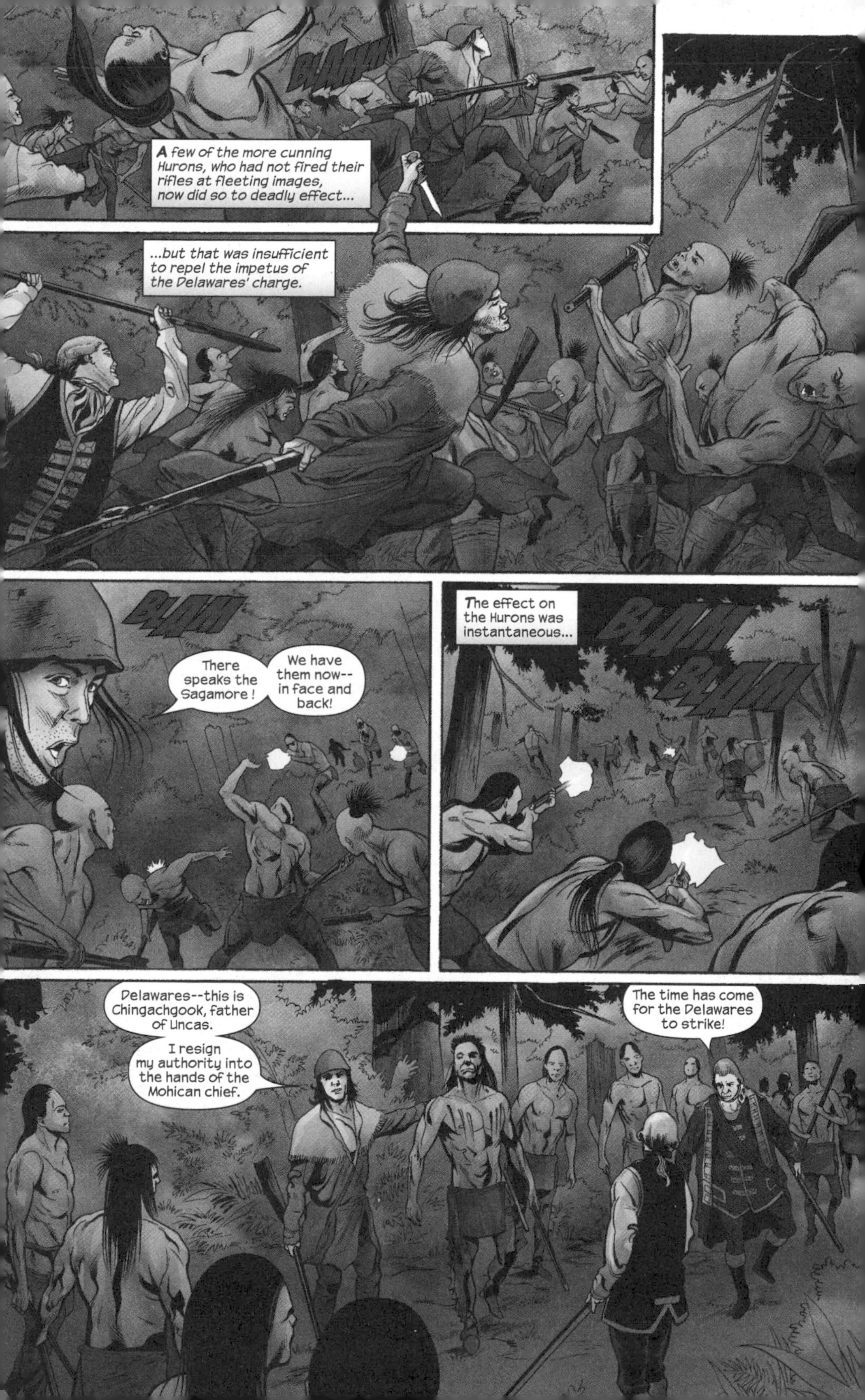
BLAAAM
A few of the more cunning Hurons, who had not fired their rifles at fleeting images, now did so to deadly effect...
...but that was insufficient to repel the impetus of the Delawares' charge.
BLAM
There speaks the Sagamore!
We have them now-- in face and back!
The effect on the Hurons was instantaneous...
BLAM
BLAM
Delawares--this is Chingachgook, father of Uncas.
I resign my authority into the hands of the Mohican chief.
The time has come for the Delawares to strike!

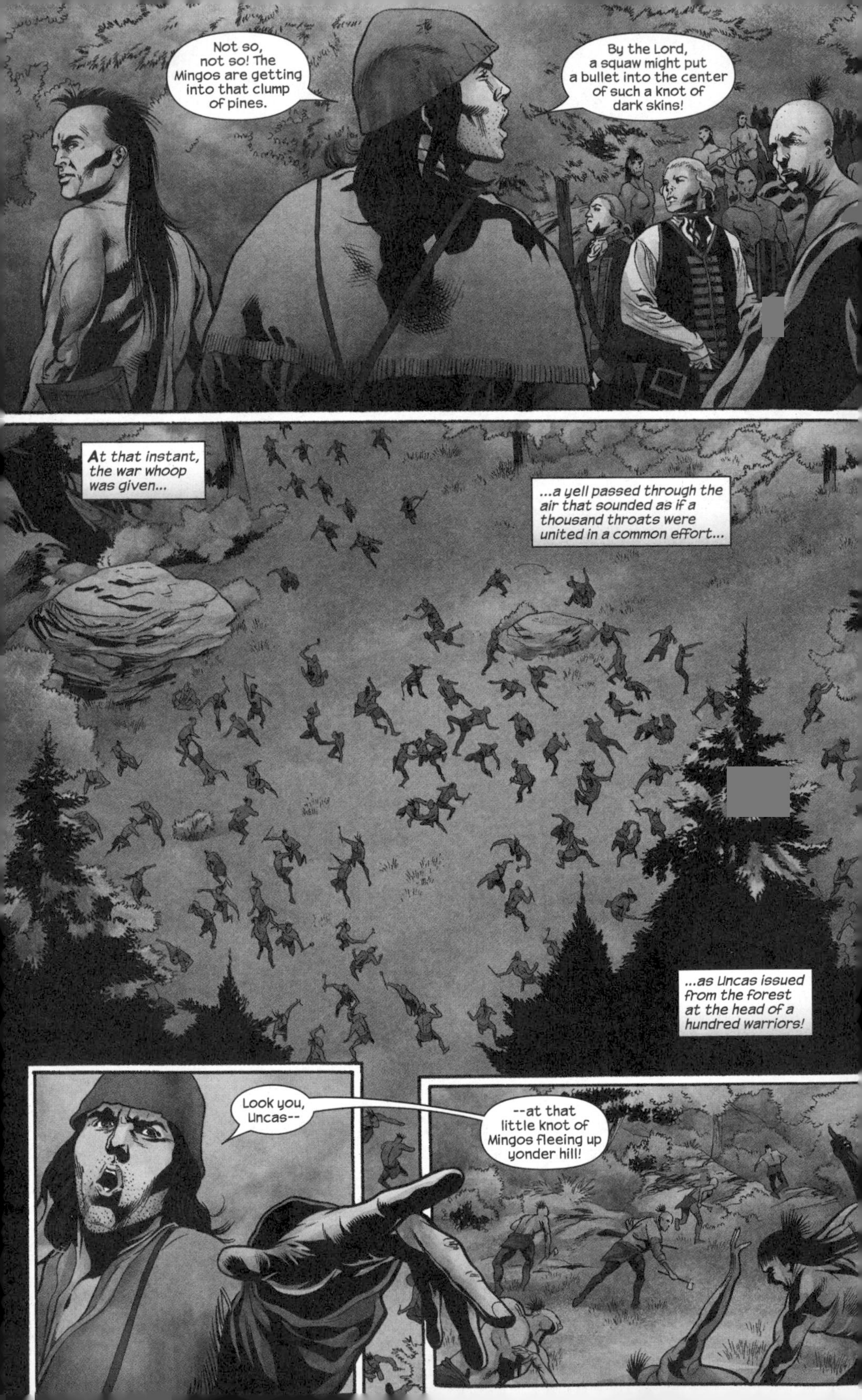
Not so, not so! The Mingos are getting into that clump of pines.
By the Lord, a squaw might put a bullet into the center of such a knot of dark skins!
At that instant, the war whoop was given...
...a yell passed through the air that sounded as if a thousand throats were united in a common effort...
...as Uncas issued from the forest at the head of a hundred warriors!
Look you, Uncas--
--at that little knot of Mingos fleeing up yonder hill!

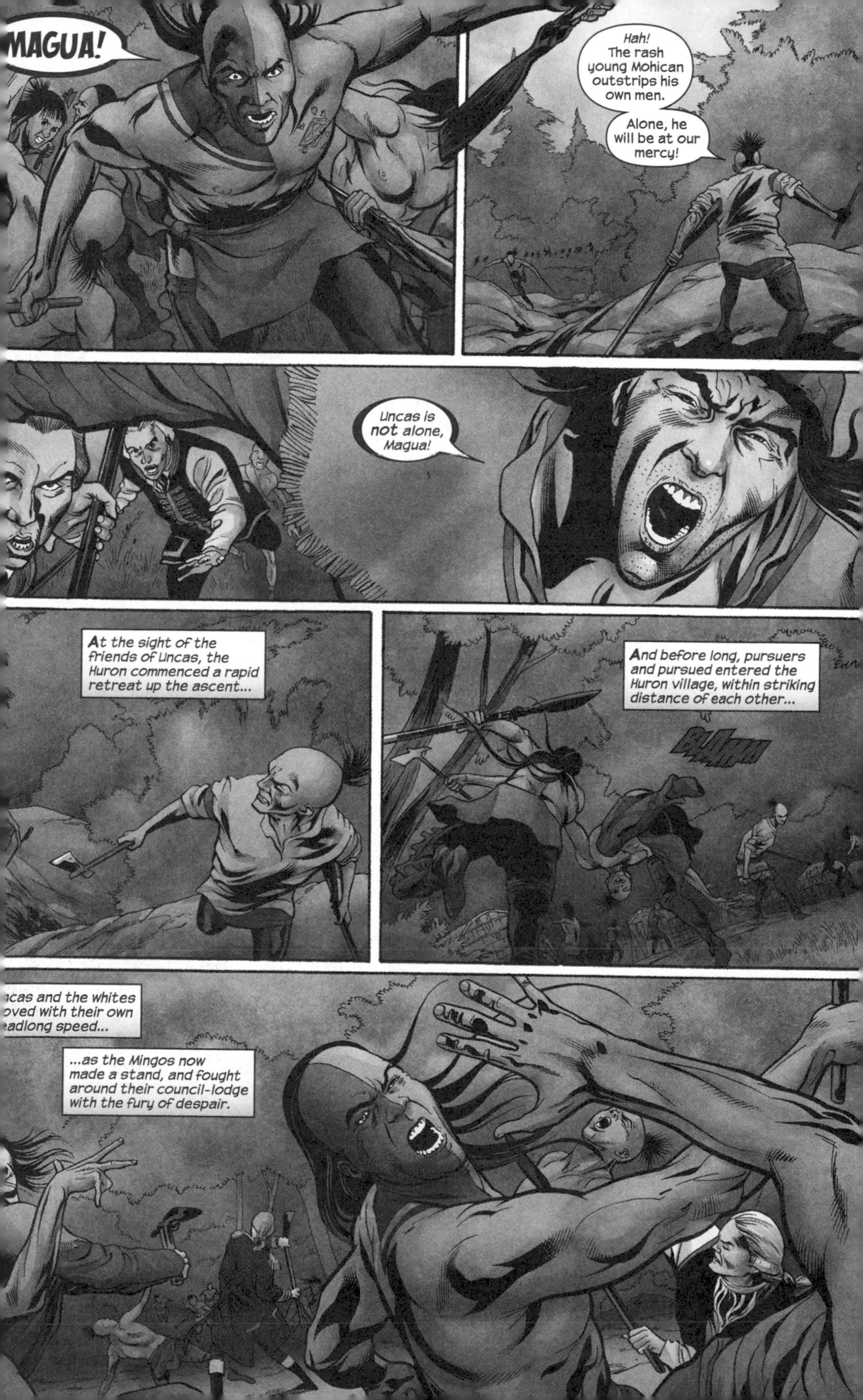
MAGUA!
Hah! The rash young Mohican outstrips his own men.
Alone, he will be at our mercy!
Uncas is **not** alone, Magua!
At the sight of the friends of Uncas, the Huron commenced a rapid retreat up the ascent...
And before long, pursuers and pursued entered the Huron village, within striking distance of each other...
ncas and the whites
oved with their own
eadlong speed...
...as the Mingos now made a stand, and fought around their council-lodge with the fury of despair.

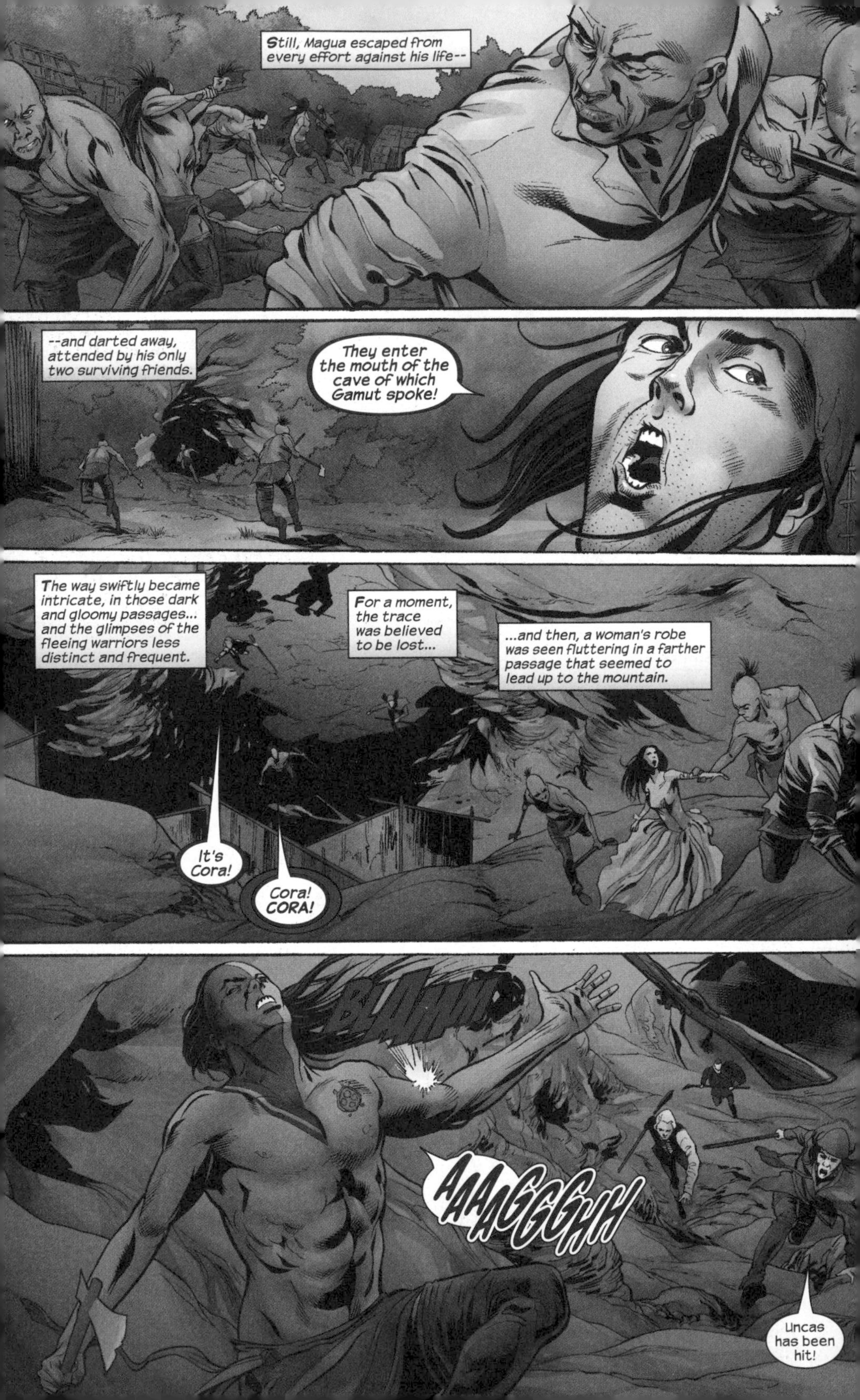
Still, Magua escaped from every effort against his life--
--and darted away, attended by his only two surviving friends.
They enter the mouth of the cave of which Gamut spoke!
The way swiftly became intricate, in those dark and gloomy passages... and the glimpses of the fleeing warriors less distinct and frequent.
For a moment, the trace was believed to be lost...
...and then, a woman's robe was seen fluttering in a farther passage that seemed to lead up to the mountain.
It's Cora!
Cora! CORA!
BLAMM
AAAAGGGHH
Uncas has been hit!

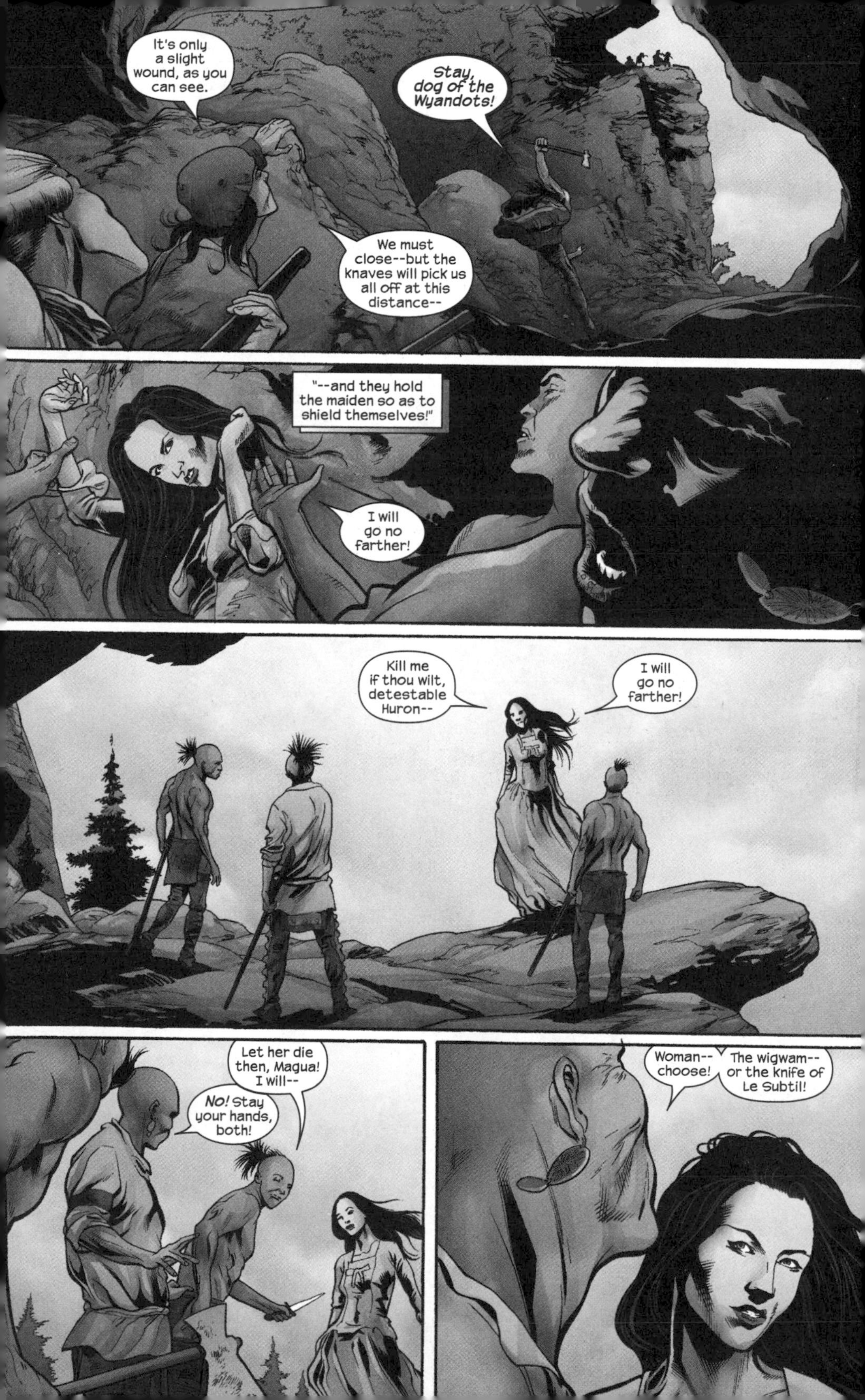
It's only a slight wound, as you can see.
Stay, dog of the Wyandots!
We must close--but the knaves will pick us all off at this distance--
"--and they hold the maiden so as to shield themselves!"
I will go no farther!
Kill me if thou wilt, detestable Huron--
I will go no farther!
Let her die then, Magua! I will--
No! Stay your hands, both!
Woman-- choose!
The wigwam-- or the knife of Le Subtil!

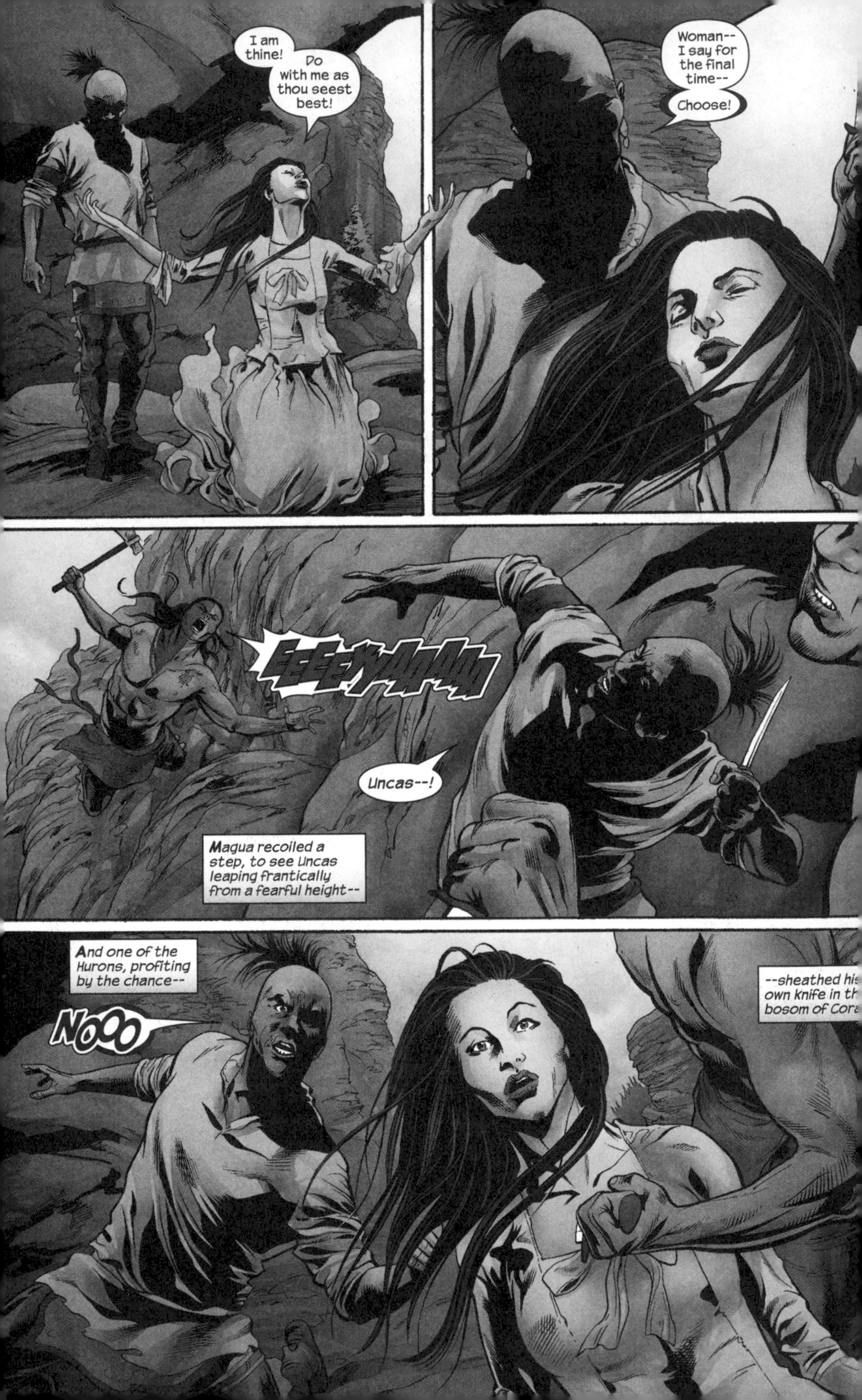
I am thine!
Do with me as thou seest best!
Woman-- I say for the final time--
Choose!
Uncas--!
Magua recoiled a step, to see Uncas leaping frantically from a fearful height--
And one of the Hurons, profiting by the chance--
NOOO
--sheathed his own knife in the bosom of Cora

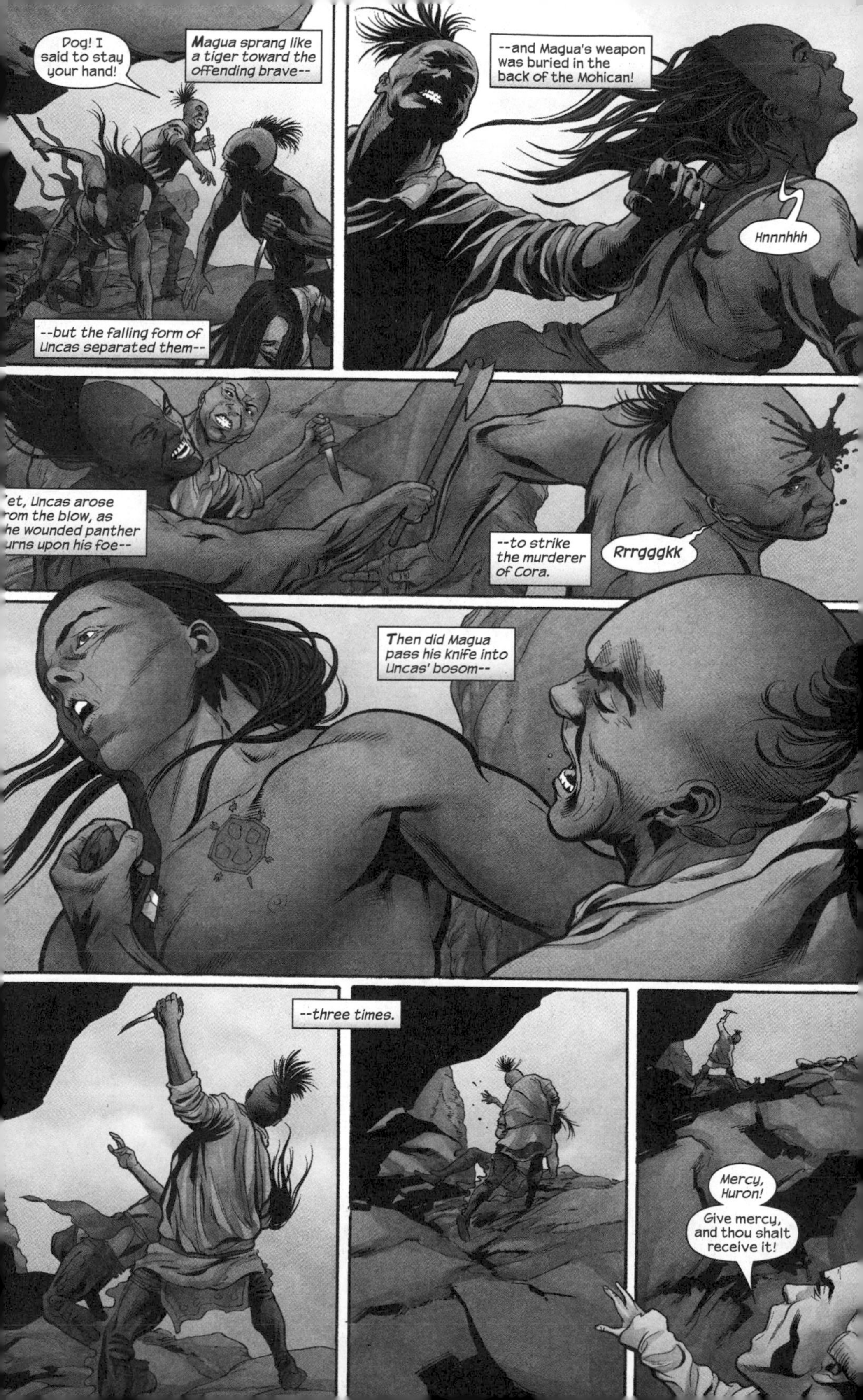
Dog! I said to stay your hand!
Magua sprang like a tiger toward the offending brave--
--but the falling form of Uncas separated them--
--and Magua's weapon was buried in the back of the Mohican!
Hnnnhhh
et, Uncas arose rom the blow, as he wounded panther urns upon his foe--
--to strike the murderer of Cora.
Rrrgggkk
Then did Magua pass his knife into Uncas' bosom--
--three times.
Mercy, Huron!
Give mercy, and thou shalt receive it!

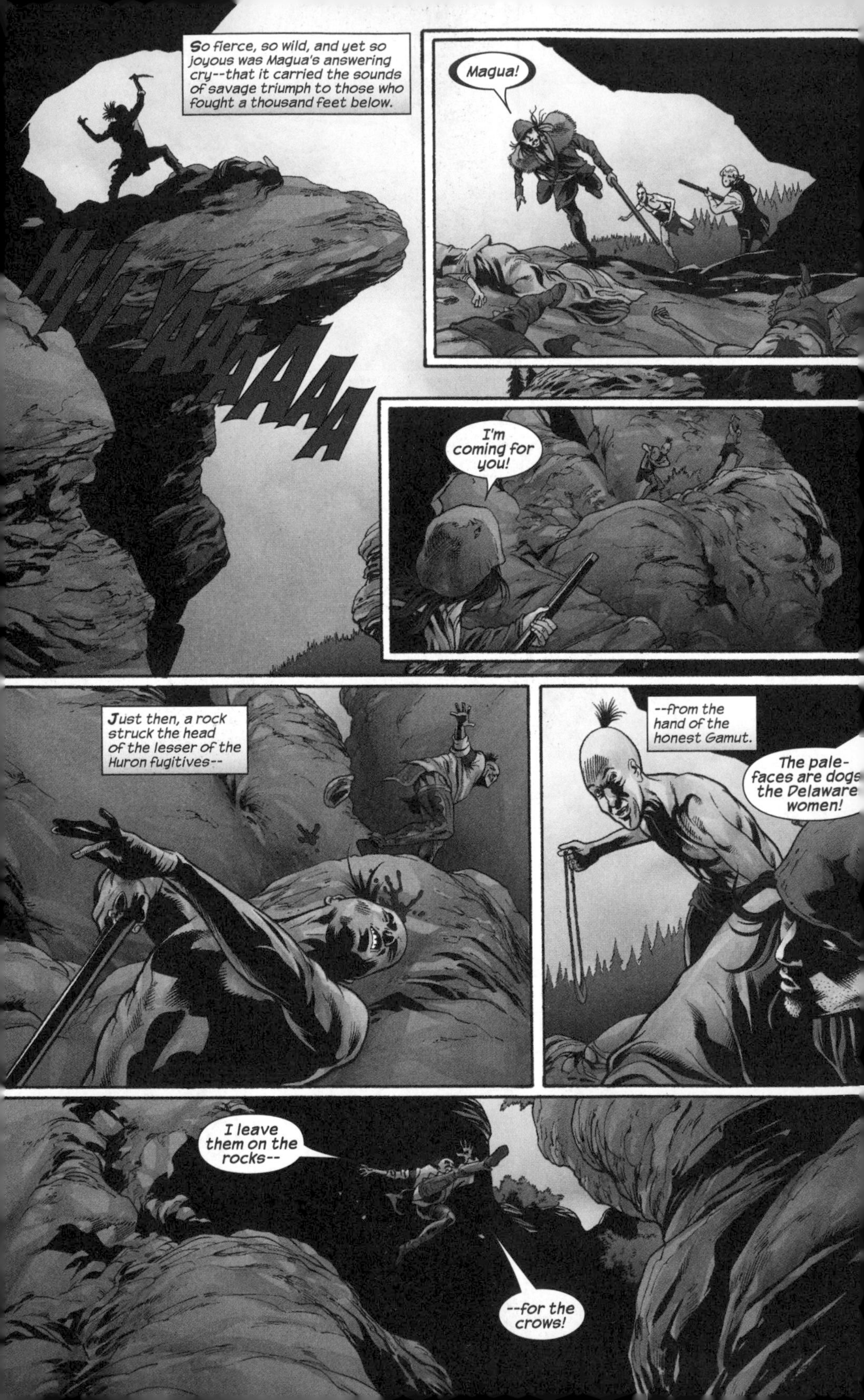
So fierce, so wild, and yet so joyous was Magua's answering cry--that it carried the sounds of savage triumph to those who fought a thousand feet below.
HIIEYAAAAAA
Magua!
I'm coming for you!
Just then, a rock struck the head of the lesser of the Huron fugitives--
--from the hand of the honest Gamut.
The pale-faces are dogs the Delaware women!
I leave them on the rocks--
--for the crows!

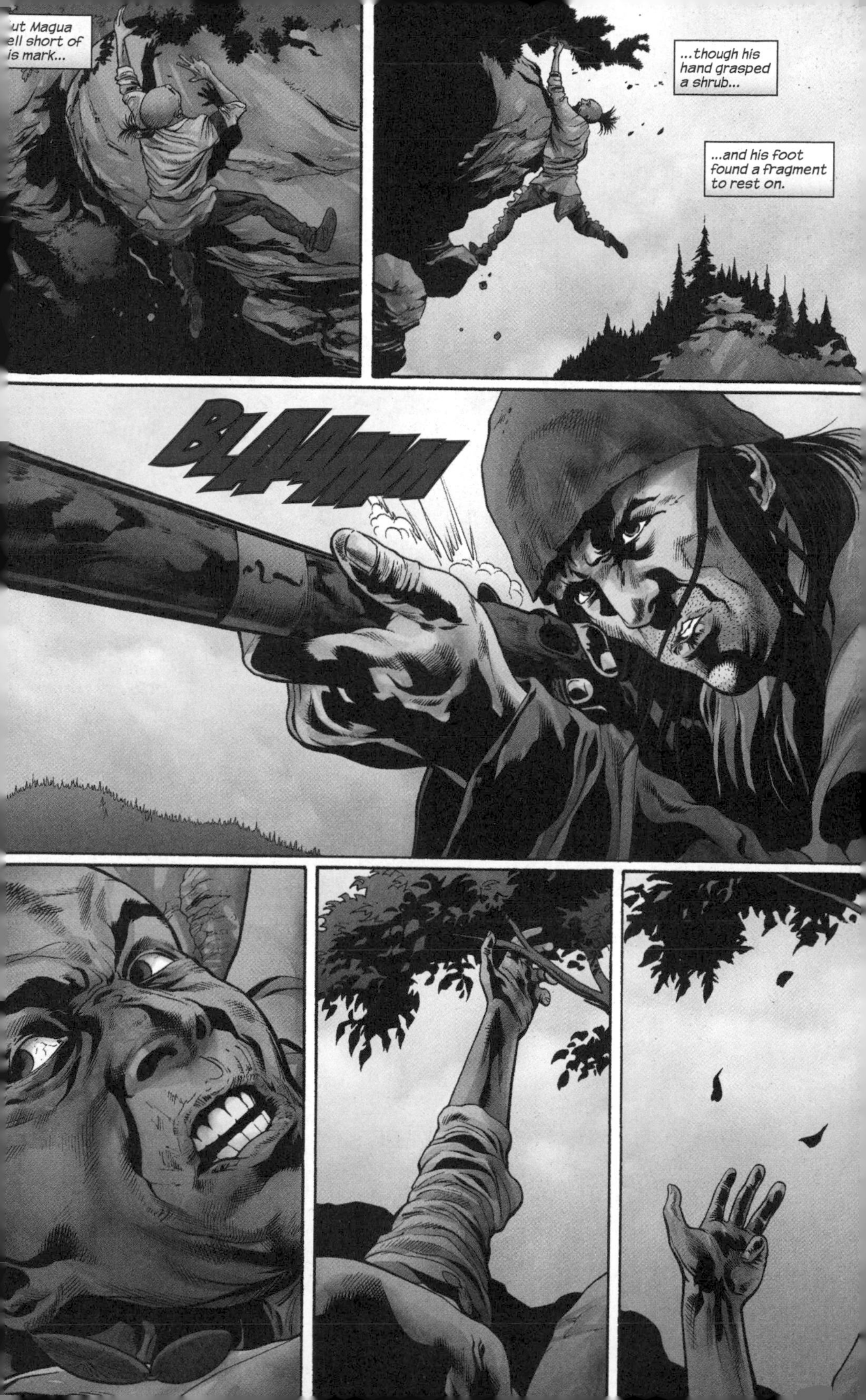

ut Magua
ell short of
is mark...
...though his
hand grasped
a shrub...
...and his foot
found a fragment
to rest on.
BLAAMM

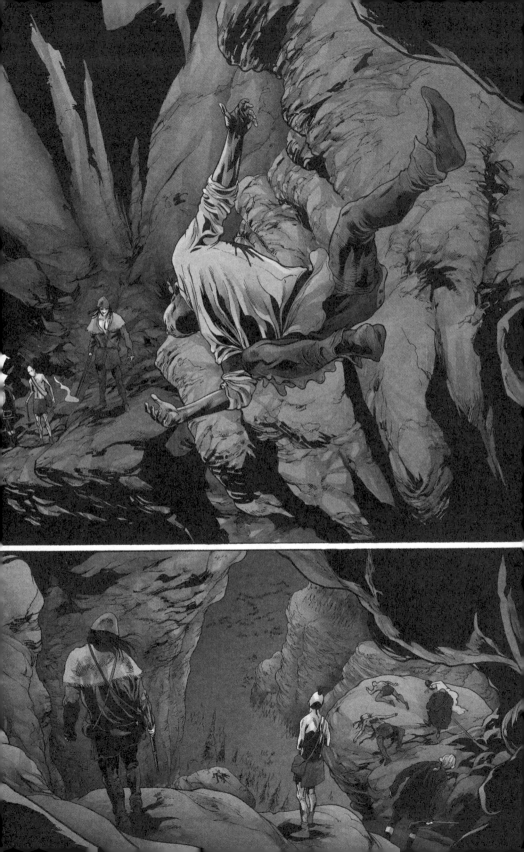

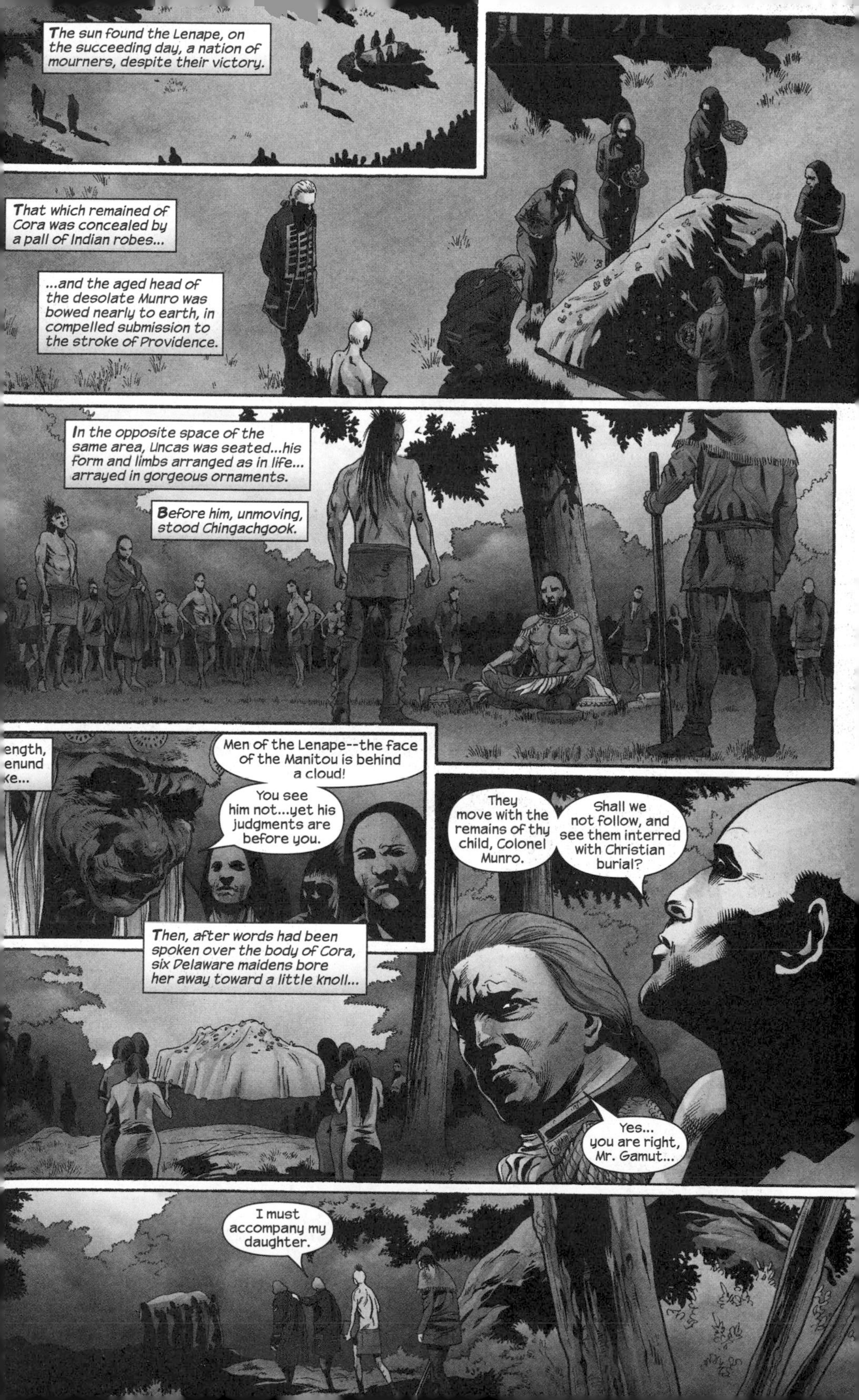

The sun found the Lenape, on the succeeding day, a nation of mourners, despite their victory.
That which remained of Cora was concealed by a pall of Indian robes...
...and the aged head of the desolate Munro was bowed nearly to earth, in compelled submission to the stroke of Providence.
In the opposite space of the same area, Uncas was seated...his form and limbs arranged as in life... arrayed in gorgeous ornaments.
Before him, unmoving, stood Chingachgook.
Men of the Lenape--the face of the Manitou is behind a cloud!
You see him not...yet his judgments are before you.
Then, after words had been spoken over the body of Cora, six Delaware maidens bore her away toward a little knoll...
They move with the remains of thy child, Colonel Munro.
Shall we not follow, and see them interred with Christian burial?
Yes... you are right, Mr. Gamut...
I must accompany my daughter.

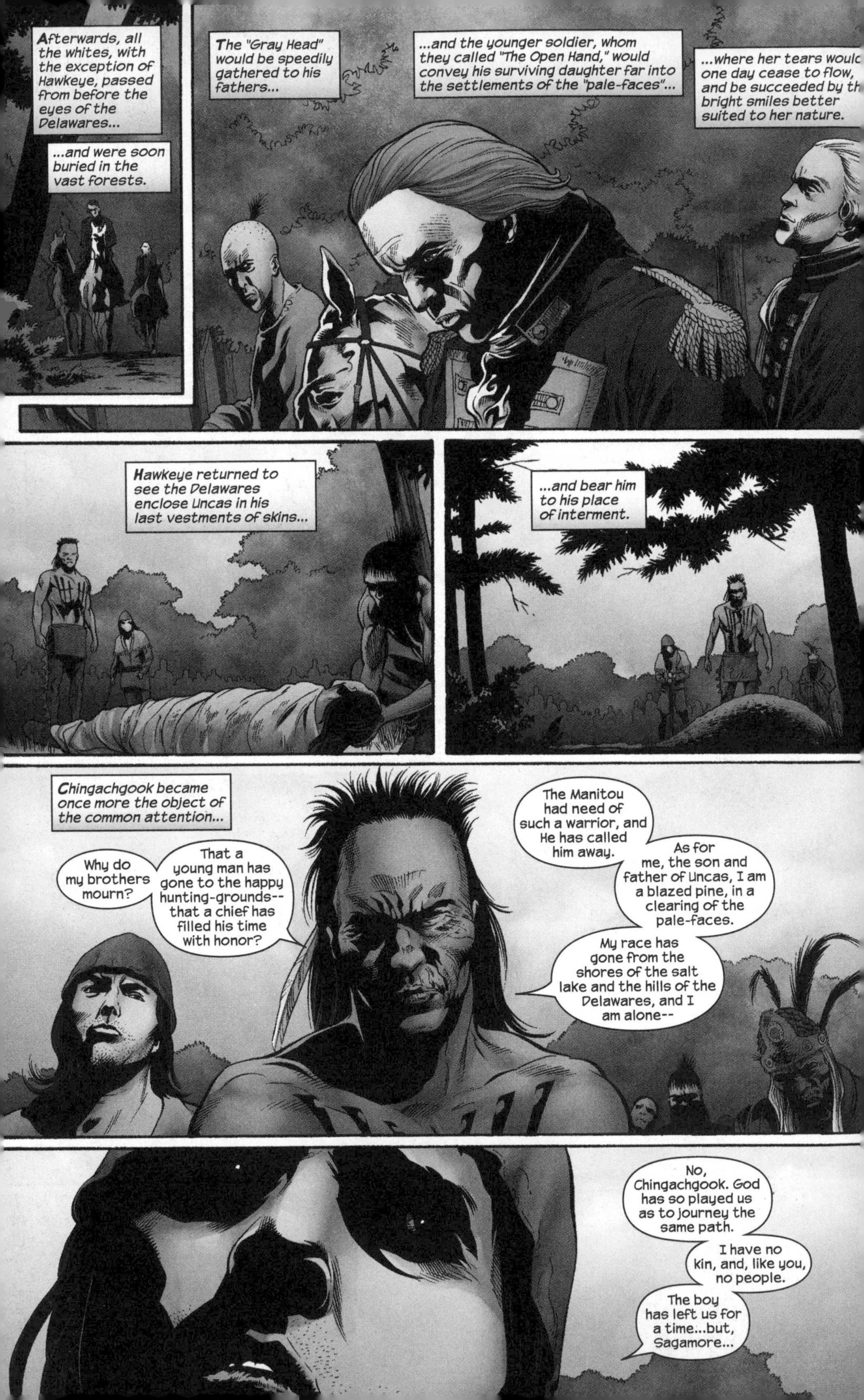
Afterwards, all the whites, with the exception of Hawkeye, passed from before the eyes of the Delawares...
...and were soon buried in the vast forests.
The "Gray Head" would be speedily gathered to his fathers...
...and the younger soldier, whom they called "The Open Hand," would convey his surviving daughter far into the settlements of the "pale-faces"...
...where her tears would one day cease to flow, and be succeeded by the bright smiles better suited to her nature.
Hawkeye returned to see the Delawares enclose Uncas in his last vestments of skins...
...and bear him to his place of interment.
Chingachgook became once more the object of the common attention...
Why do my brothers mourn?
That a young man has gone to the happy hunting-grounds-- that a chief has filled his time with honor?
The Manitou had need of such a warrior, and He has called him away.
As for me, the son and father of Uncas, I am a blazed pine, in a clearing of the pale-faces.
My race has gone from the shores of the salt lake and the hills of the Delawares, and I am alone--
No, Chingachgook. God has so played us as to journey the same path.
I have no kin, and, like you, no people.
The boy has left us for a time...but, Sagamore...

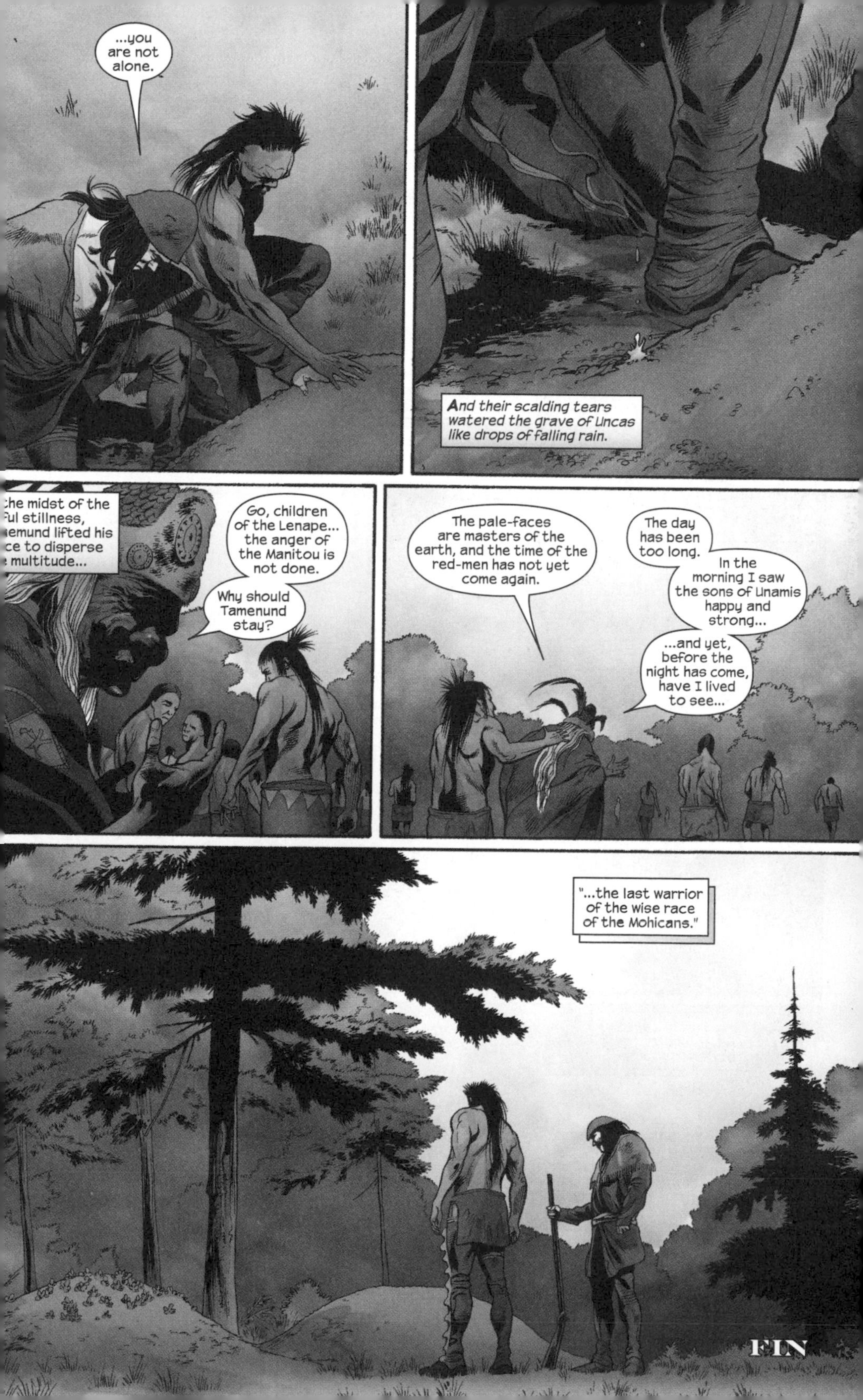
...you are not alone.
And their scalding tears watered the grave of Uncas like drops of falling rain.
he midst of the ful stillness, emund lifted his ce to disperse multitude...
Go, children of the Lenape... the anger of the Manitou is not done.
Why should Tamenund stay?
The pale-faces are masters of the earth, and the time of the red-men has not yet come again.
The day has been too long.
In the morning I saw the sons of Unamis happy and strong...
...and yet, before the night has come, have I lived to see...
"...the last warrior of the wise race of the Mohicans."
FIN

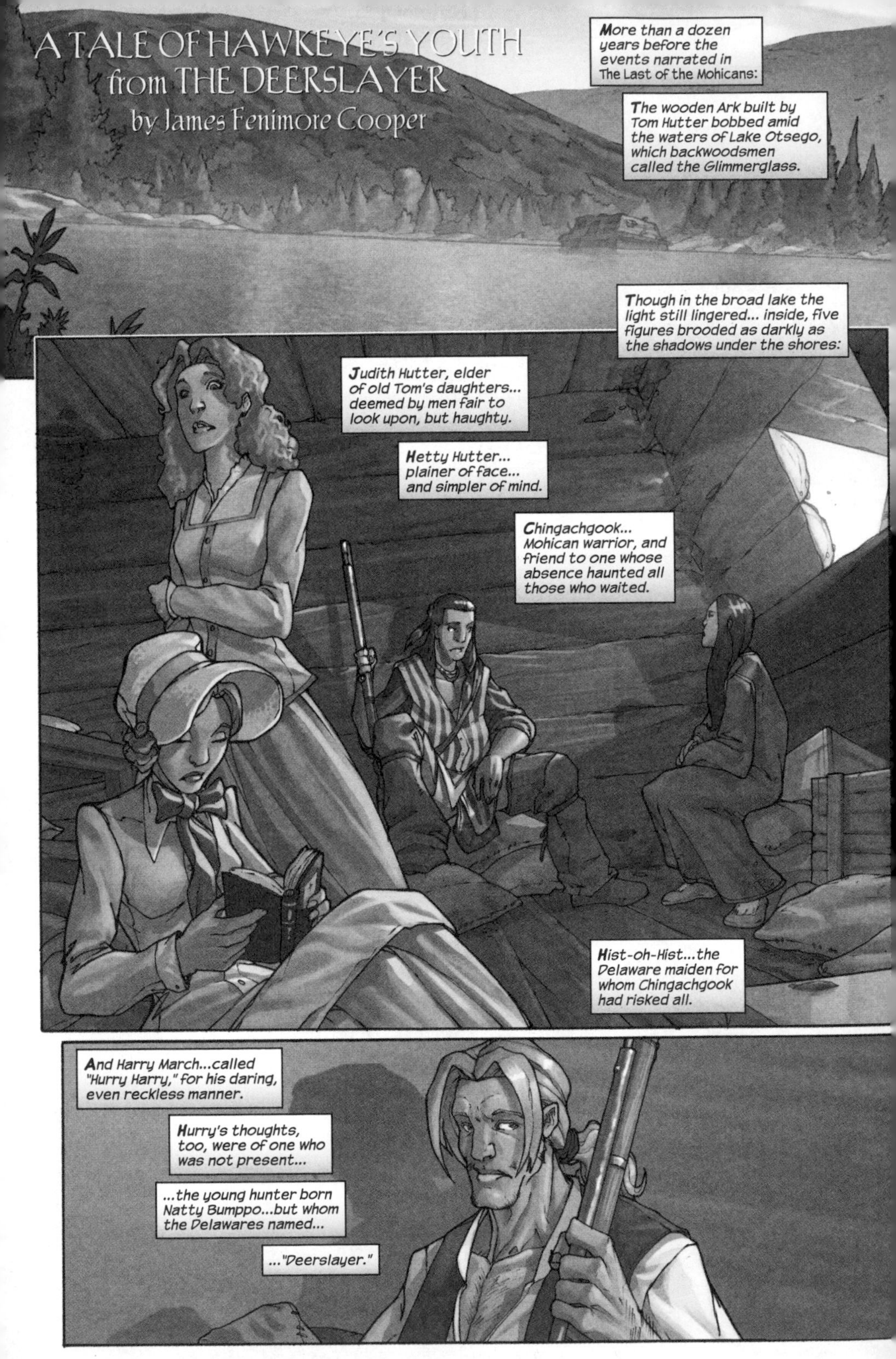

A TALE OF HAWKEYE'S YOUTH
from THE DEERSLAYER
by James Fenimore Cooper
More than a dozen years before the events narrated in The Last of the Mohicans:
The wooden Ark built by Tom Hutter bobbed amid the waters of Lake Otsego, which backwoodsmen called the Glimmerglass.
Though in the broad lake the light still lingered... inside, five figures brooded as darkly as the shadows under the shores:
Judith Hutter, elder of old Tom's daughters... deemed by men fair to look upon, but haughty.
Hetty Hutter... plainer of face... and simpler of mind.
Chingachgook... Mohican warrior, and friend to one whose absence haunted all those who waited.
Hist-oh-Hist...the Delaware maiden for whom Chingachgook had risked all.
And Harry March...called "Hurry Harry," for his daring, even reckless manner.
Hurry's thoughts, too, were of one who was not present...
...the young hunter born Natty Bumppo...but whom the Delawares named...
..."Deerslayer."

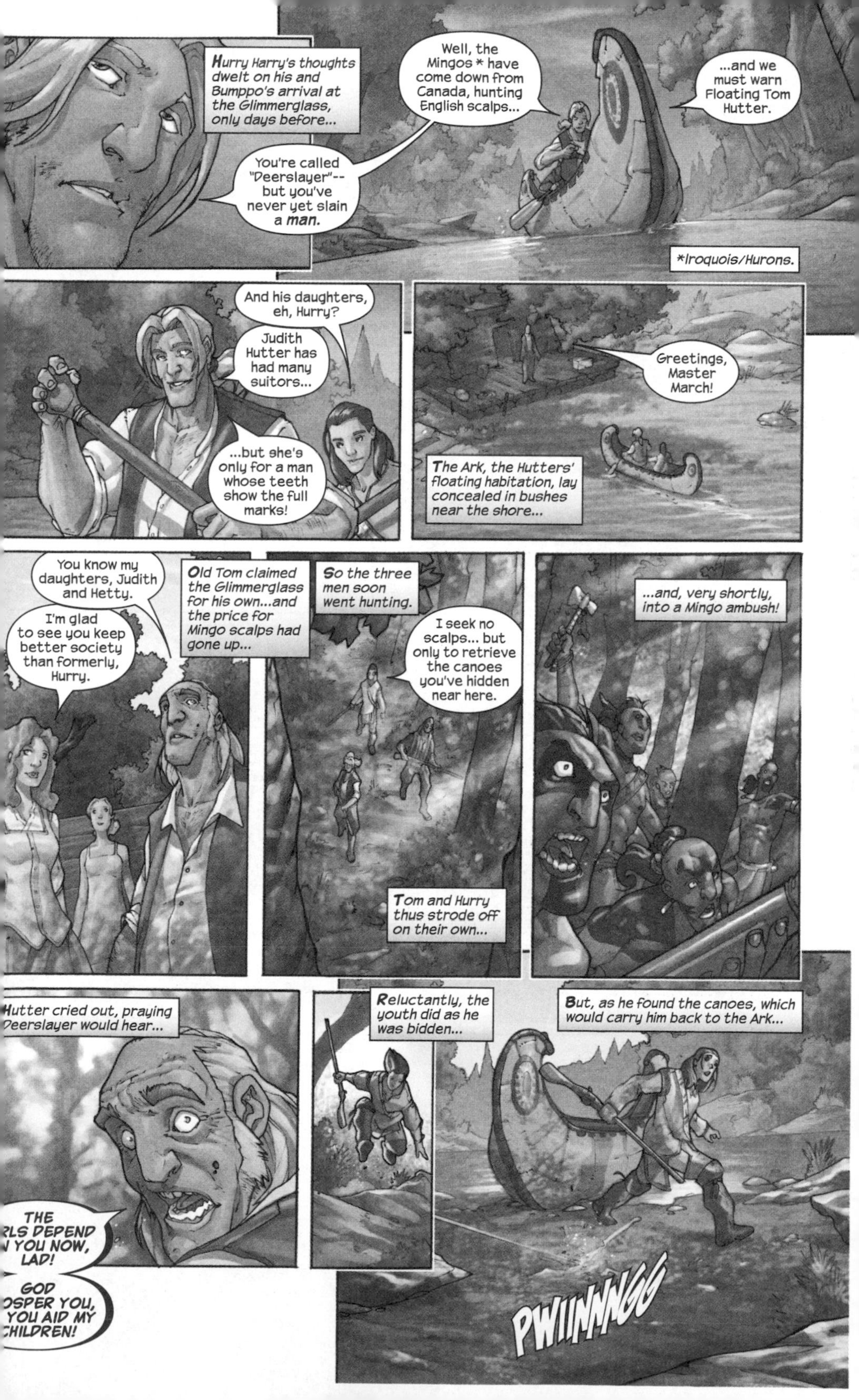
Hurry Harry's thoughts dwelt on his and Bumppo's arrival at the Glimmerglass, only days before...
You're called "Deerslayer"-- but you've never yet slain a man.
Well, the Mingos * have come down from Canada, hunting English scalps...
...and we must warn Floating Tom Hutter.
*Iroquois/Hurons.
And his daughters, eh, Hurry?
Judith Hutter has had many suitors...
...but she's only for a man whose teeth show the full marks!
Greetings, Master March!
The Ark, the Hutters' floating habitation, lay concealed in bushes near the shore...
You know my daughters, Judith and Hetty.
I'm glad to see you keep better society than formerly, Hurry.
Old Tom claimed the Glimmerglass for his own...and the price for Mingo scalps had gone up...
So the three men soon went hunting.
I seek no scalps... but only to retrieve the canoes you've hidden near here.
Tom and Hurry thus strode off on their own...
...and, very shortly, into a Mingo ambush!
Hutter cried out, praying Deerslayer would hear...
THE RLS DEPEND N YOU NOW, LAD!
GOD OSPER YOU, YOU AID MY CHILDREN!
Reluctantly, the youth did as he was bidden...
But, as he found the canoes, which would carry him back to the Ark...
PWIINNNGG

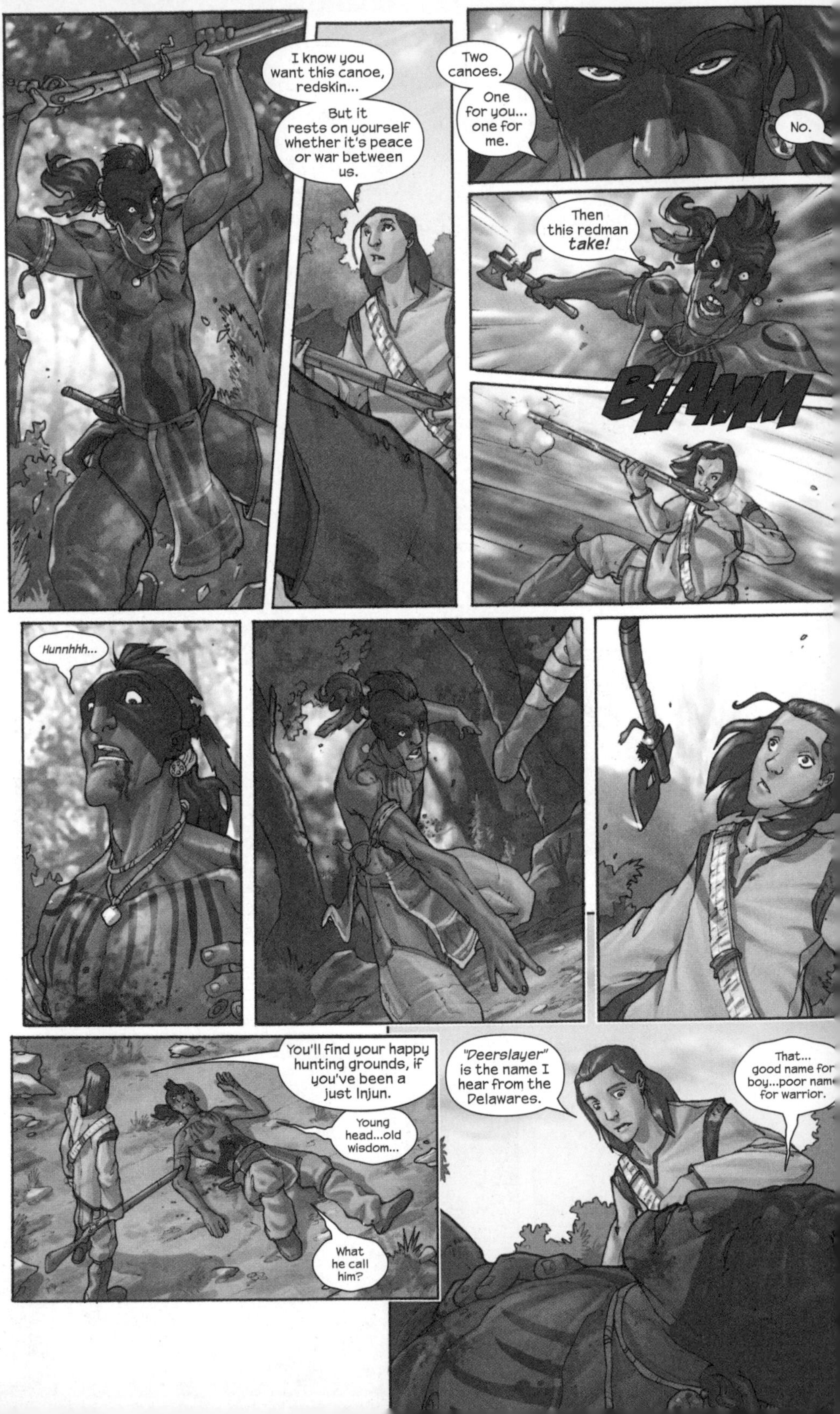
I know you want this canoe, redskin...
But it rests on yourself whether it's peace or war between us.
Two canoes.
One for you... one for me.
No.
Then this redman *take!*
BLAMM
Hunnhhh...
You'll find your happy hunting grounds, if you've been a just Injun.
Young head...old wisdom...
What he call him?
"Deerslayer" is the name I hear from the Delawares.
That... good name for boy...poor name for warrior.

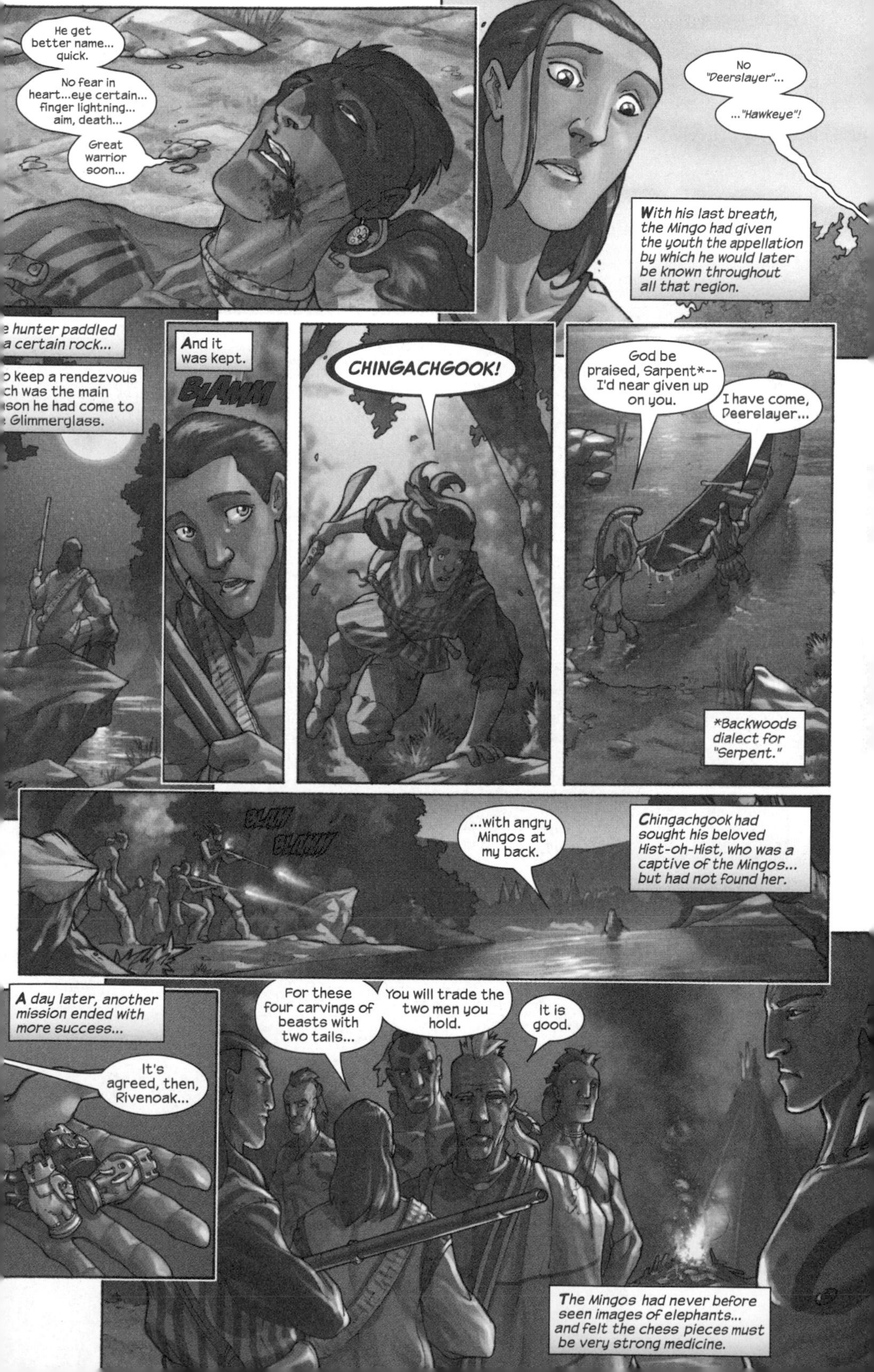

He get better name... quick.
No fear in heart...eye certain... finger lightning... aim, death...
Great warrior soon...
No "Deerslayer"...
..."Hawkeye"!
With his last breath, the Mingo had given the youth the appellation by which he would later be known throughout all that region.
e hunter paddled a certain rock...
o keep a rendezvous ch was the main son he had come to Glimmerglass.
And it was kept.
BLAMM
CHINGACHGOOK!
God be praised, Sarpent*-- I'd near given up on you.
I have come, Deerslayer...
*Backwoods dialect for "Serpent."
BLAM
BLAMM
...with angry Mingos at my back.
Chingachgook had sought his beloved Hist-oh-Hist, who was a captive of the Mingos... but had not found her.
A day later, another mission ended with more success...
It's agreed, then, Rivenoak...
For these four carvings of beasts with two tails...
You will trade the two men you hold.
It is good.
The Mingos had never before seen images of elephants... and felt the chess pieces must be very strong medicine.

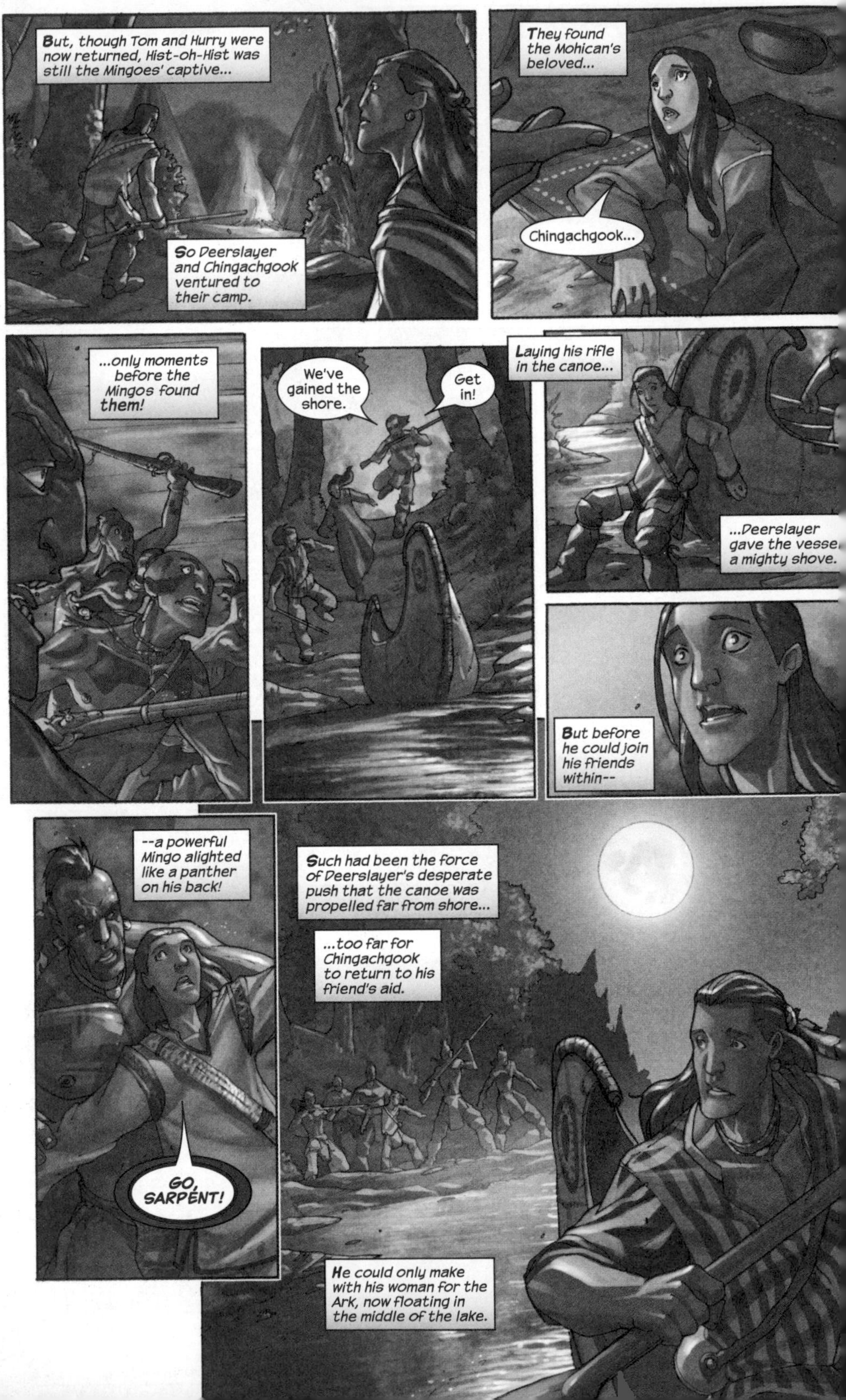
But, though Tom and Hurry were now returned, Hist-oh-Hist was still the Mingoes' captive...
So Deerslayer and Chingachgook ventured to their camp.
They found the Mohican's beloved...
Chingachgook...
...only moments before the Mingos found them!
We've gained the shore.
Get in!
Laying his rifle in the canoe...
...Deerslayer gave the vesse a mighty shove.
But before he could join his friends within--
--a powerful Mingo alighted like a panther on his back!
GO, SARPENT!
Such had been the force of Deerslayer's desperate push that the canoe was propelled far from shore...
...too far for Chingachgook to return to his friend's aid.
He could only make with his woman for the Ark, now floating in the middle of the lake.

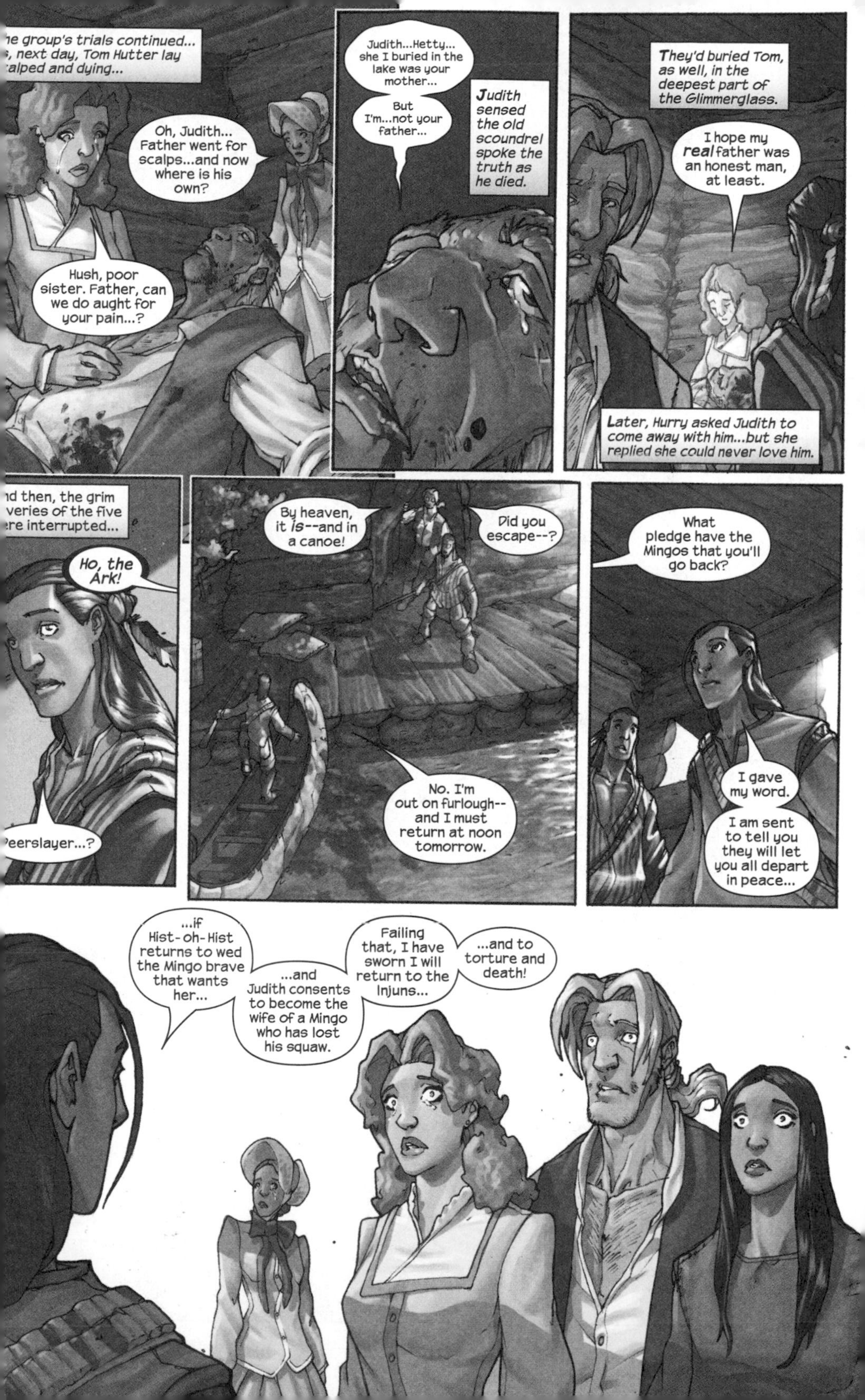
he group's trials continued... s, next day, Tom Hutter lay calped and dying...
Oh, Judith... Father went for scalps...and now where is his own?
Hush, poor sister. Father, can we do aught for your pain...?
Judith...Hetty... she I buried in the lake was your mother...
But I'm...not your father...
Judith sensed the old scoundrel spoke the truth as he died.
They'd buried Tom, as well, in the deepest part of the Glimmerglass.
I hope my real father was an honest man, at least.
Later, Hurry asked Judith to come away with him...but she replied she could never love him.
nd then, the grim veries of the five ere interrupted...
Ho, the Ark!
Deerslayer...?
By heaven, it is--and in a canoe!
Did you escape--?
No. I'm out on furlough-- and I must return at noon tomorrow.
What pledge have the Mingos that you'll go back?
I gave my word.
I am sent to tell you they will let you all depart in peace...
...if Hist-oh-Hist returns to wed the Mingo brave that wants her...
...and Judith consents to become the wife of a Mingo who has lost his squaw.
Failing that, I have sworn I will return to the Injuns...
...and to torture and death!

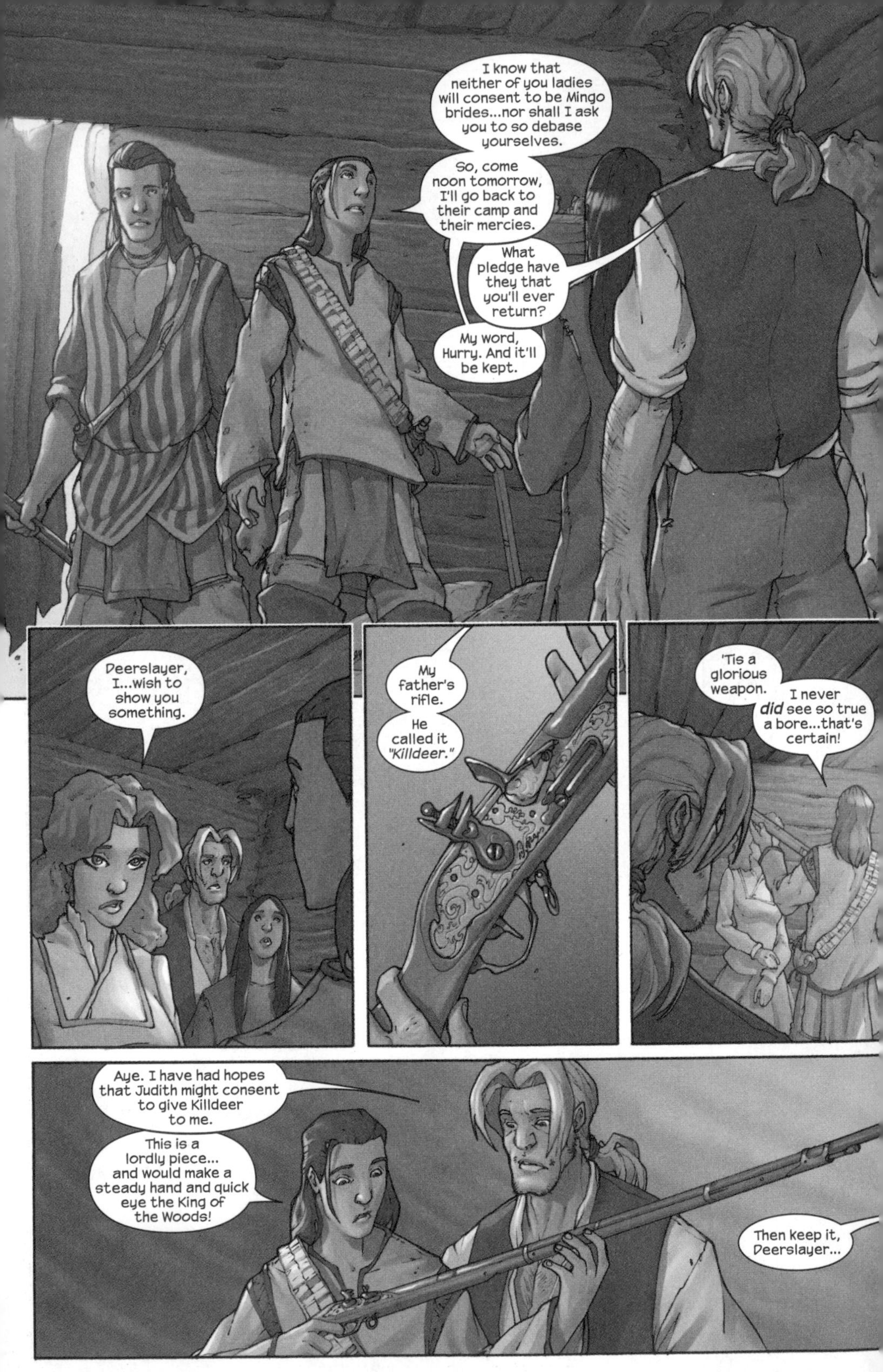
I know that neither of you ladies will consent to be Mingo brides...nor shall I ask you to so debase yourselves.
So, come noon tomorrow, I'll go back to their camp and their mercies.
What pledge have they that you'll ever return?
My word, Hurry. And it'll be kept.
Deerslayer, I...wish to show you something.
My father's rifle.
He called it "Killdeer."
'Tis a glorious weapon.
I never did see so true a bore...that's certain!
Aye. I have had hopes that Judith might consent to give Killdeer to me.
This is a lordly piece... and would make a steady hand and quick eye the King of the Woods!
Then keep it, Deerslayer...

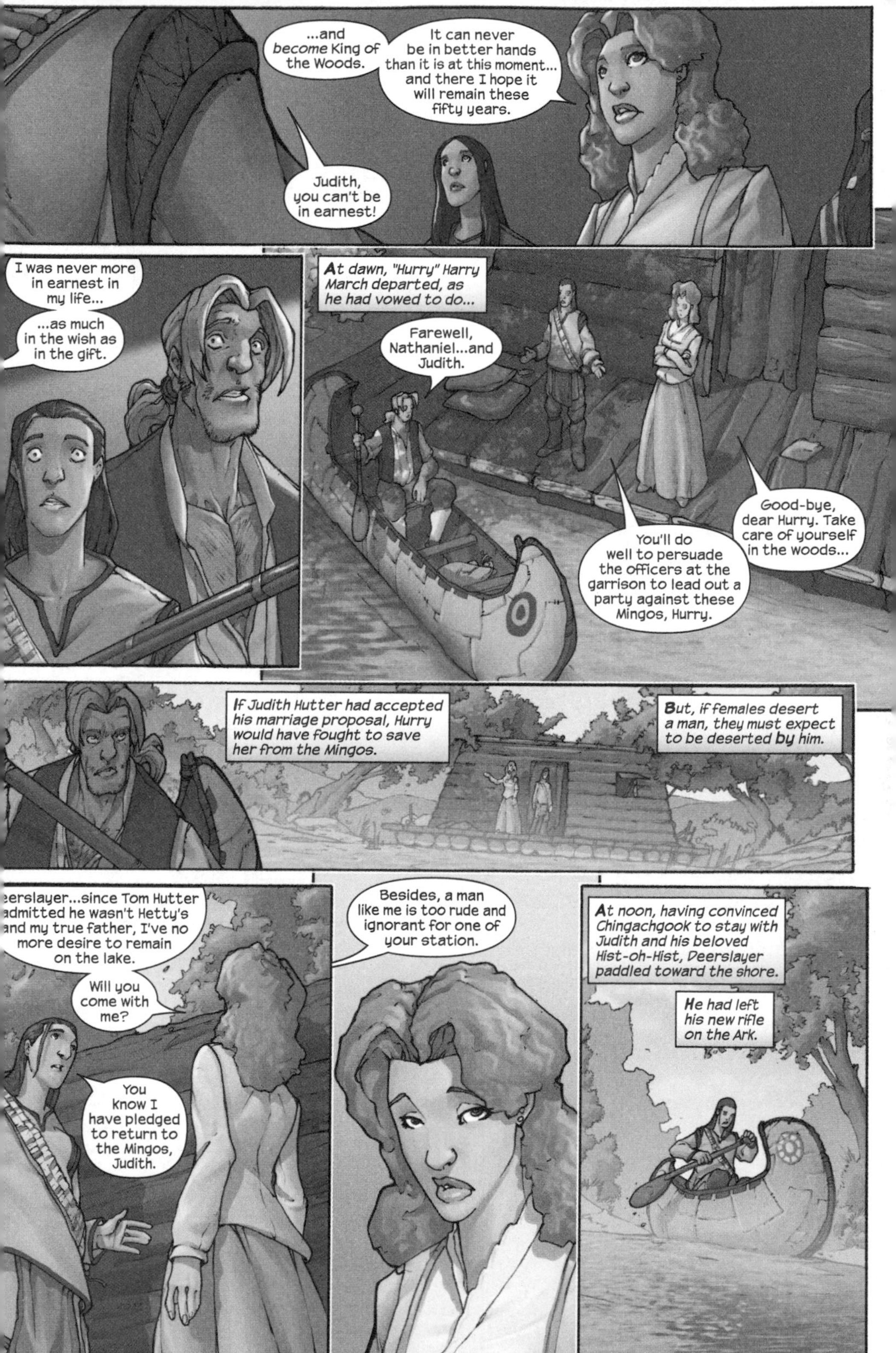

...and become King of the Woods.
It can never be in better hands than it is at this moment... and there I hope it will remain these fifty years.
Judith, you can't be in earnest!
I was never more in earnest in my life...
...as much in the wish as in the gift.
At dawn, "Hurry" Harry March departed, as he had vowed to do...
Farewell, Nathaniel...and Judith.
You'll do well to persuade the officers at the garrison to lead out a party against these Mingos, Hurry.
Good-bye, dear Hurry. Take care of yourself in the woods...
If Judith Hutter had accepted his marriage proposal, Hurry would have fought to save her from the Mingos.
But, if females desert a man, they must expect to be deserted by him.
eerslayer...since Tom Hutter admitted he wasn't Hetty's and my true father, I've no more desire to remain on the lake.
Will you come with me?
You know I have pledged to return to the Mingos, Judith.
Besides, a man like me is too rude and ignorant for one of your station.
At noon, having convinced Chingachgook to stay with Judith and his beloved Hist-oh-Hist, Deerslayer paddled toward the shore.
He had left his new rifle on the Ark.

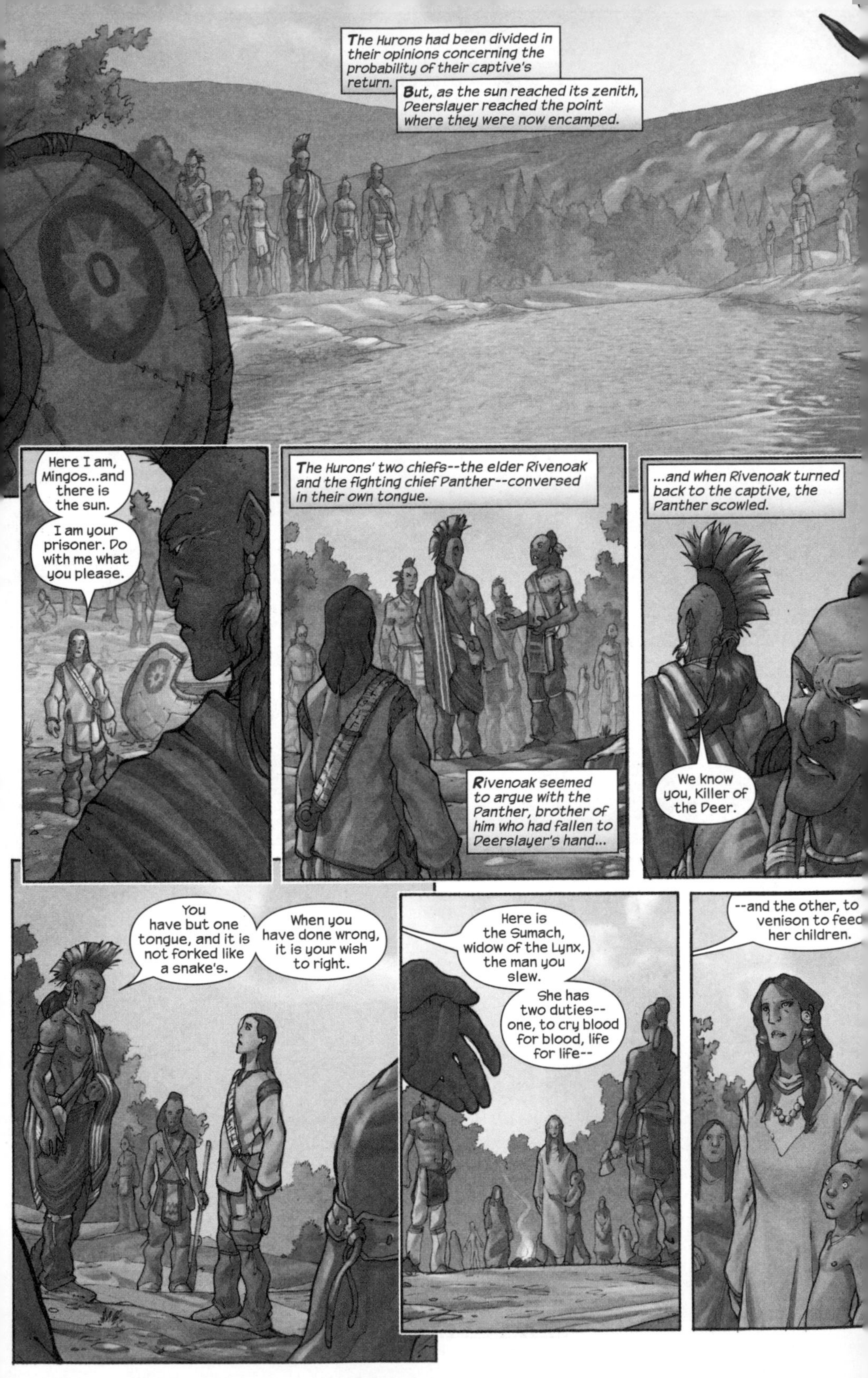
The Hurons had been divided in their opinions concerning the probability of their captive's return.
But, as the sun reached its zenith, Deerslayer reached the point where they were now encamped.
Here I am, Mingos...and there is the sun.
I am your prisoner. Do with me what you please.
The Hurons' two chiefs--the elder Rivenoak and the fighting chief Panther--conversed in their own tongue.
Rivenoak seemed to argue with the Panther, brother of him who had fallen to Deerslayer's hand...
...and when Rivenoak turned back to the captive, the Panther scowled.
We know you, Killer of the Deer.
You have but one tongue, and it is not forked like a snake's.
When you have done wrong, it is your wish to right.
Here is the Sumach, widow of the Lynx, the man you slew.
She has two duties--one, to cry blood for blood, life for life--
--and the other, to venison to feed her children.

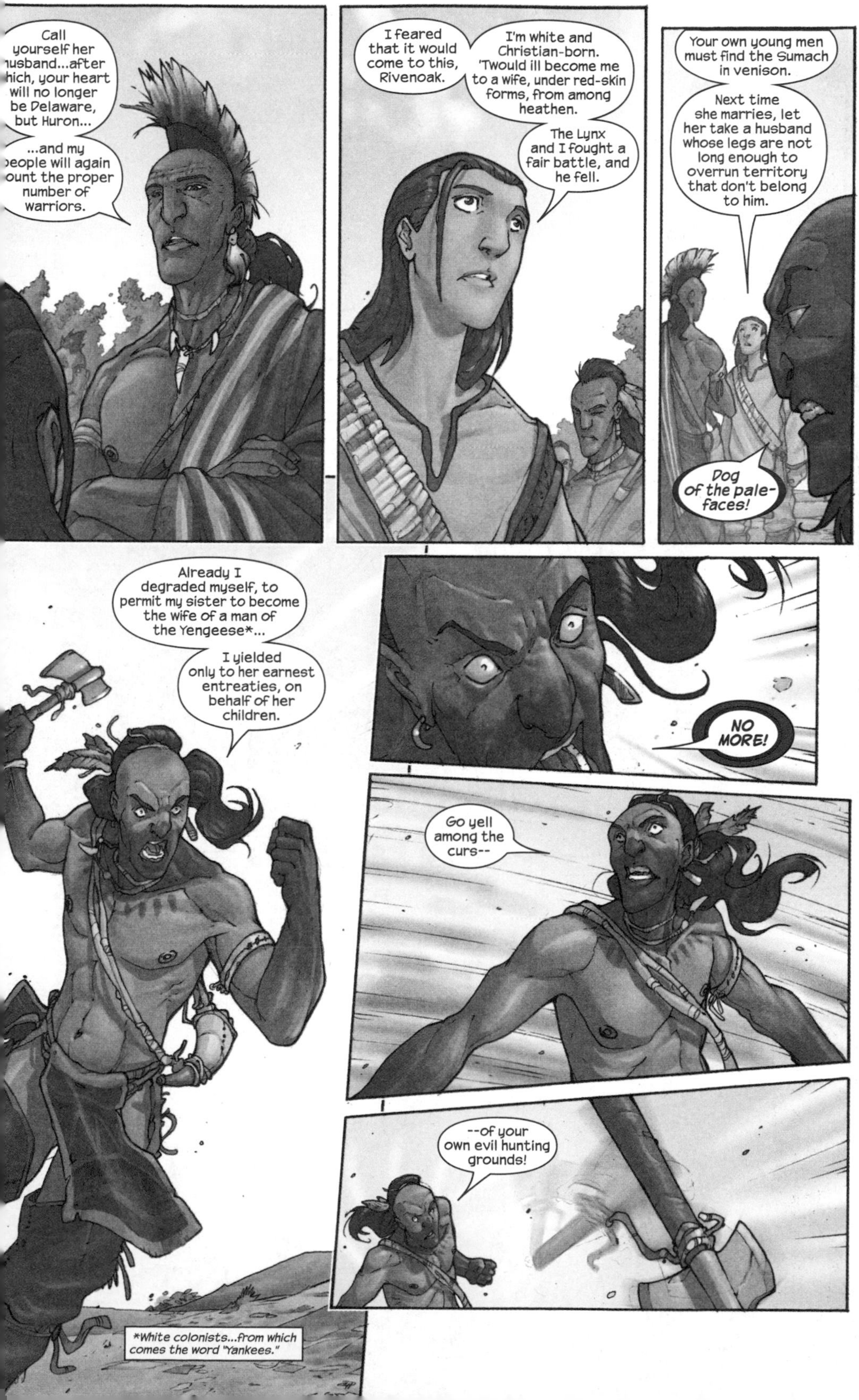
Call yourself her husband...after which, your heart will no longer be Delaware, but Huron...
...and my people will again count the proper number of warriors.
I feared that it would come to this, Rivenoak.
I'm white and Christian-born. 'Twould ill become me to a wife, under red-skin forms, from among heathen.
The Lynx and I fought a fair battle, and he fell.
Your own young men must find the Sumach in venison.
Next time she marries, let her take a husband whose legs are not long enough to overrun territory that don't belong to him.
Dog of the pale-faces!
Already I degraded myself, to permit my sister to become the wife of a man of the Yengeese*...
I yielded only to her earnest entreaties, on behalf of her children.
NO MORE!
Go yell among the curs--
--of your own evil hunting grounds!
*White colonists...from which comes the word "Yankees."

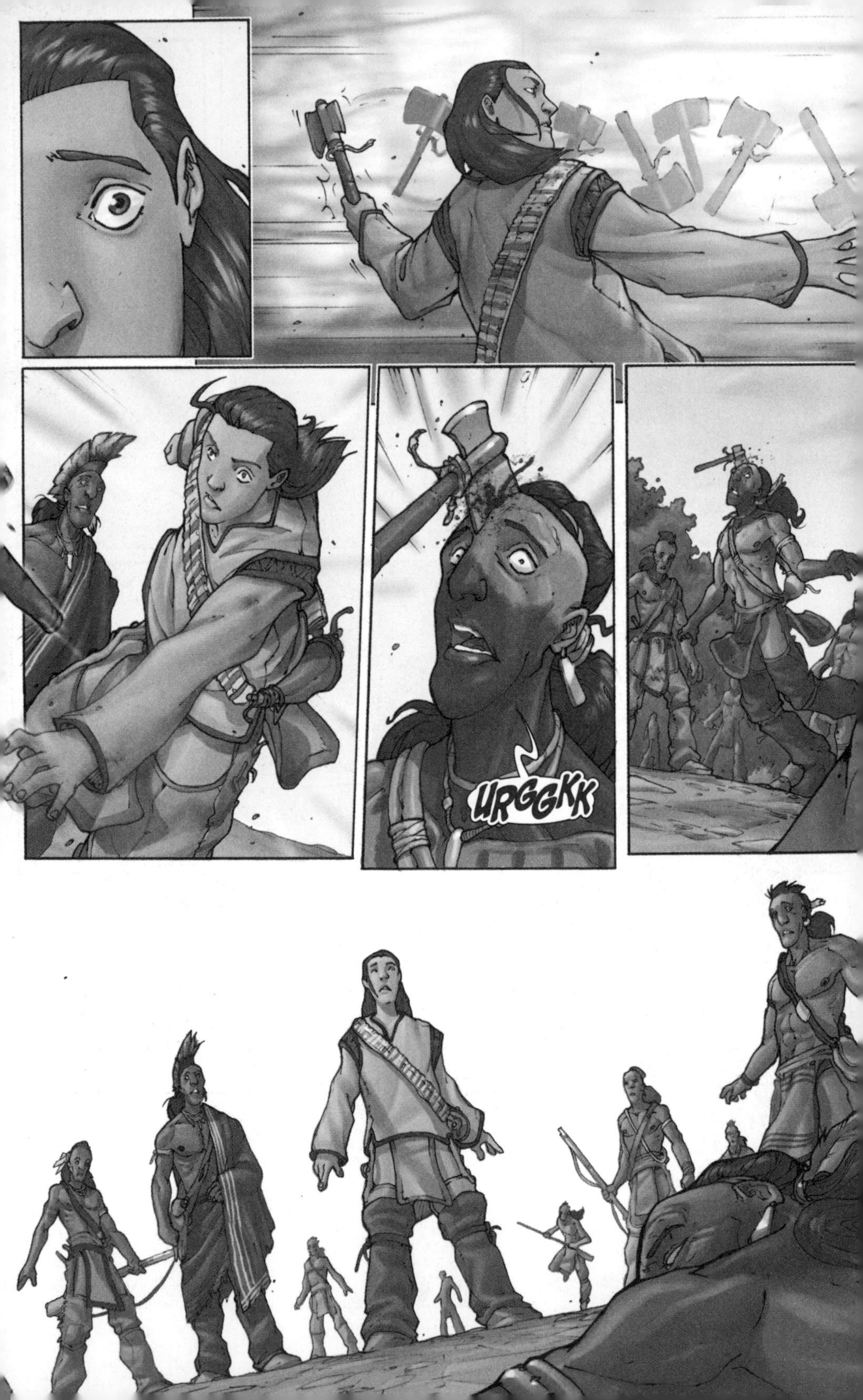
URGGKK

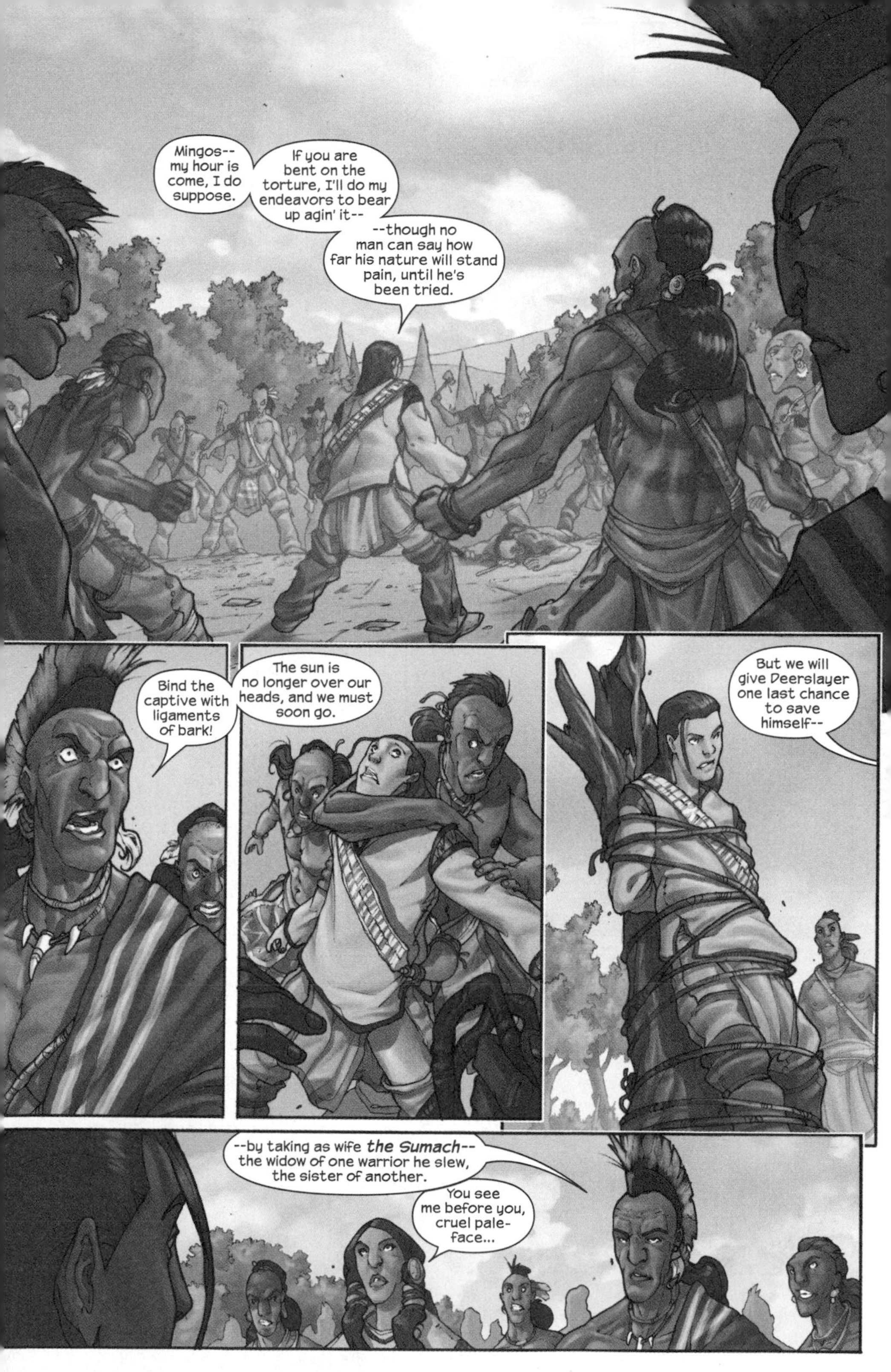
Mingos-- my hour is come, I do suppose.
If you are bent on the torture, I'll do my endeavors to bear up agin' it--
--though no man can say how far his nature will stand pain, until he's been tried.
Bind the captive with ligaments of bark!
The sun is no longer over our heads, and we must soon go.
But we will give Deerslayer one last chance to save himself--
--by taking as wife the Sumach-- the widow of one warrior he slew, the sister of another.
You see me before you, cruel pale-face...

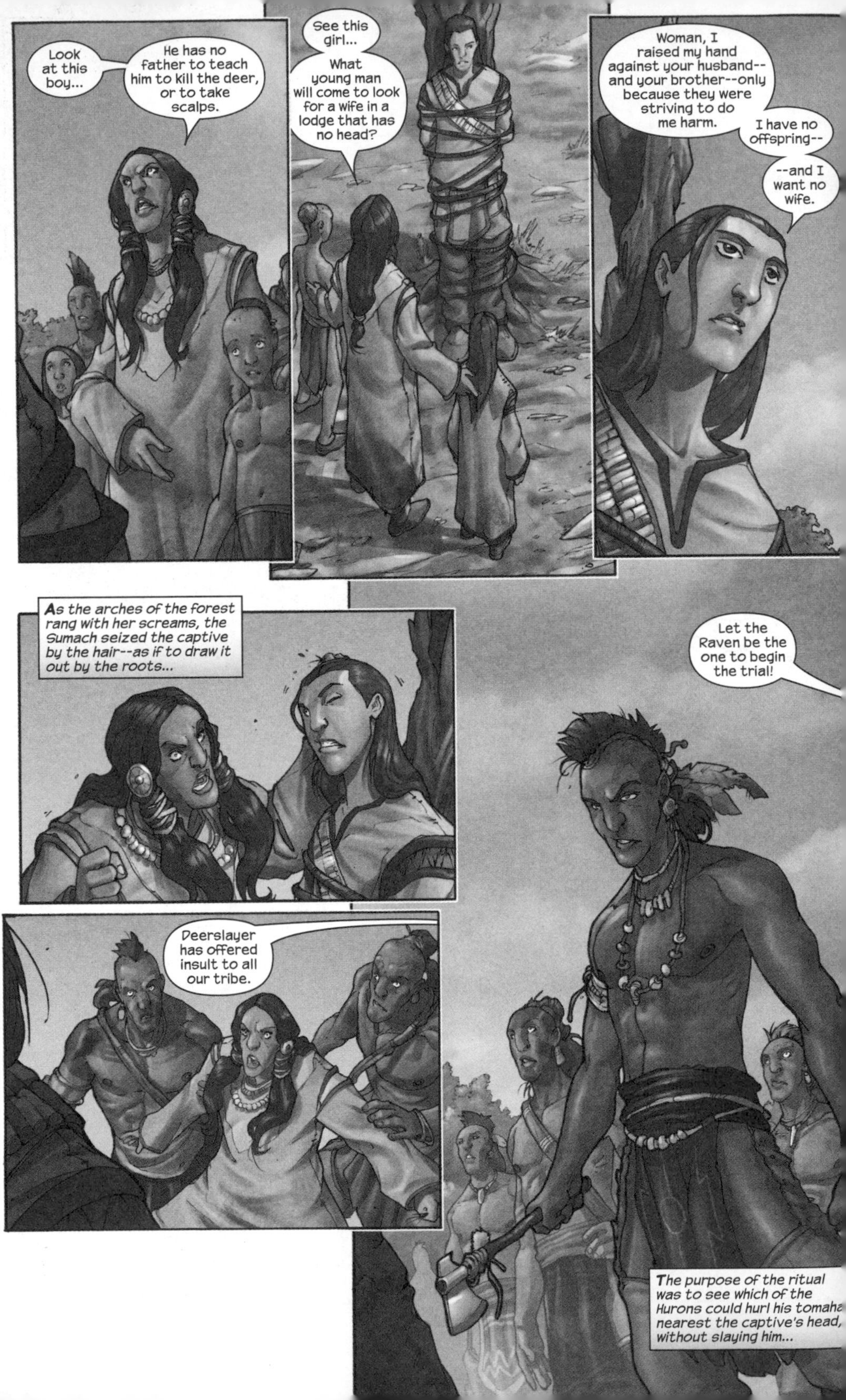
Look at this boy...
He has no father to teach him to kill the deer, or to take scalps.
See this girl...
What young man will come to look for a wife in a lodge that has no head?
Woman, I raised my hand against your husband--and your brother--only because they were striving to do me harm.
I have no offspring--
--and I want no wife.
As the arches of the forest rang with her screams, the Sumach seized the captive by the hair--as if to draw it out by the roots...
Deerslayer has offered insult to all our tribe.
Let the Raven be the one to begin the trial!
The purpose of the ritual was to see which of the Hurons could hurl his tomaha nearest the captive's head, without slaying him...

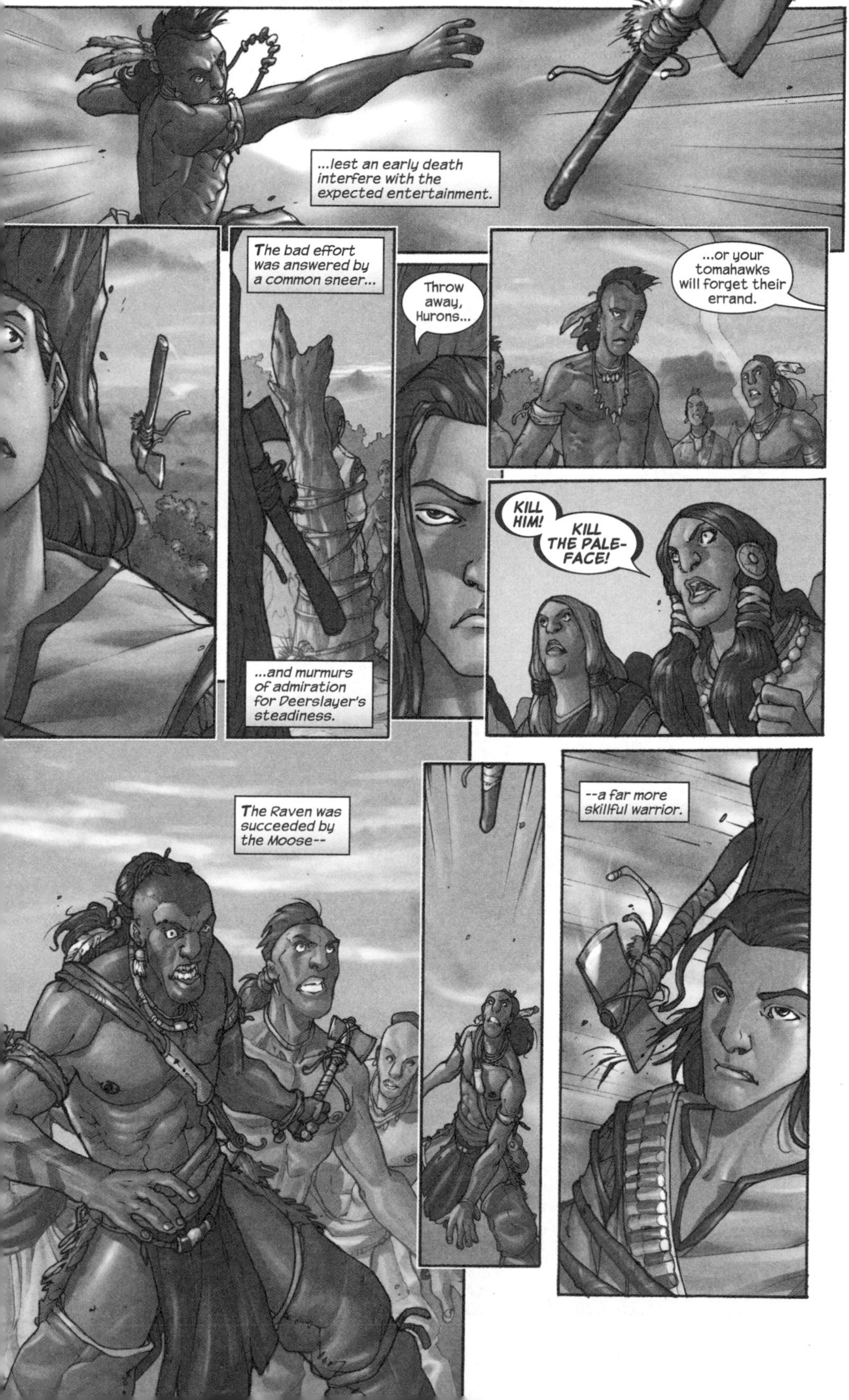
...lest an early death interfere with the expected entertainment.
The bad effort was answered by a common sneer...
...and murmurs of admiration for Deerslayer's steadiness.
Throw away, Hurons...
...or your tomahawks will forget their errand.
KILL HIM!
KILL THE PALE-FACE!
The Raven was succeeded by the Moose--
--a far more skillful warrior.

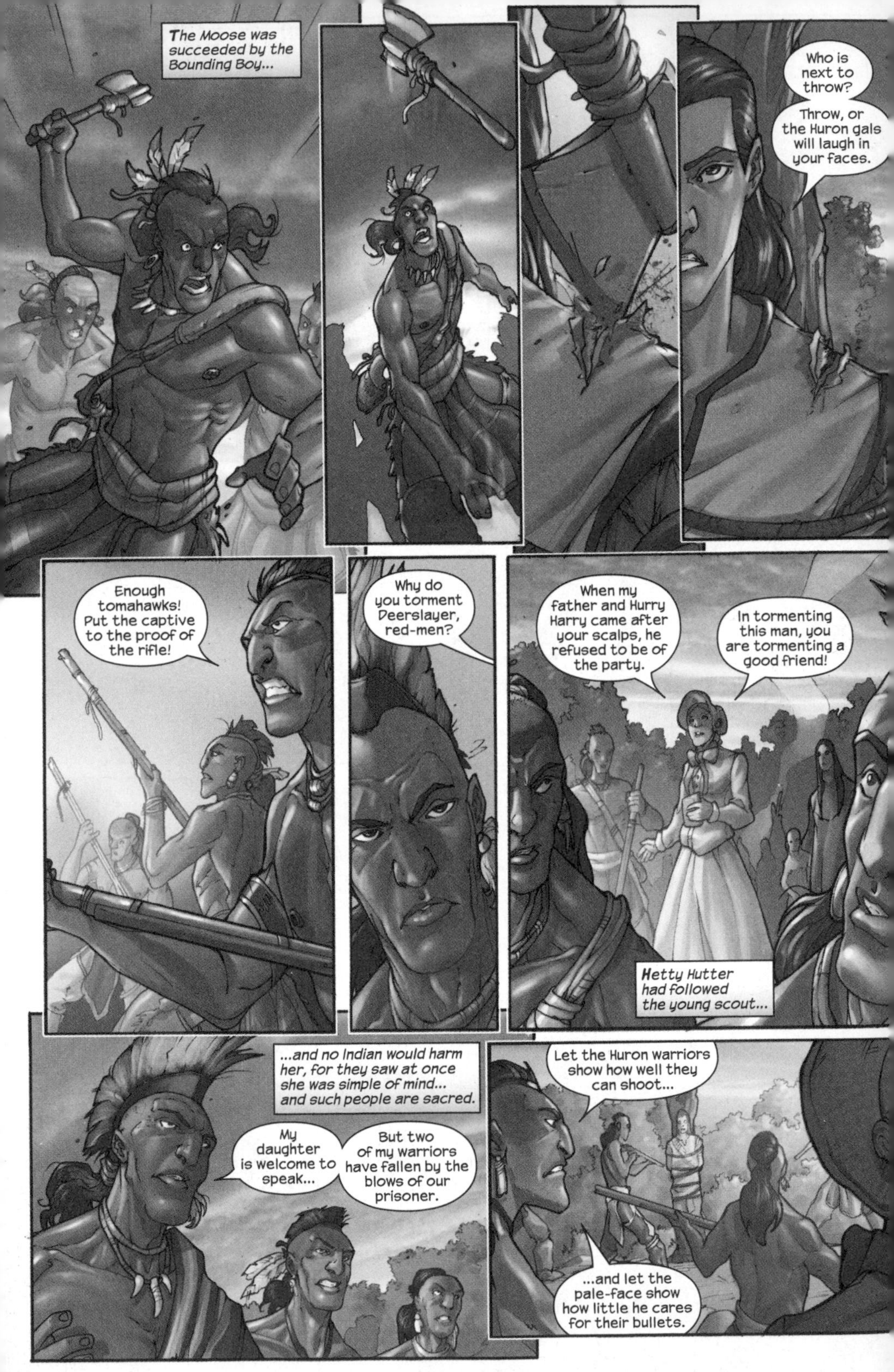
The Moose was succeeded by the Bounding Boy...
Who is next to throw?
Throw, or the Huron gals will laugh in your faces.
Enough tomahawks! Put the captive to the proof of the rifle!
Why do you torment Deerslayer, red-men?
When my father and Hurry Harry came after your scalps, he refused to be of the party.
In tormenting this man, you are tormenting a good friend!
Hetty Hutter had followed the young scout...
...and no Indian would harm her, for they saw at once she was simple of mind... and such people are sacred.
My daughter is welcome to speak...
But two of my warriors have fallen by the blows of our prisoner.
Let the Huron warriors show how well they can shoot...
...and let the pale-face show how little he cares for their bullets.

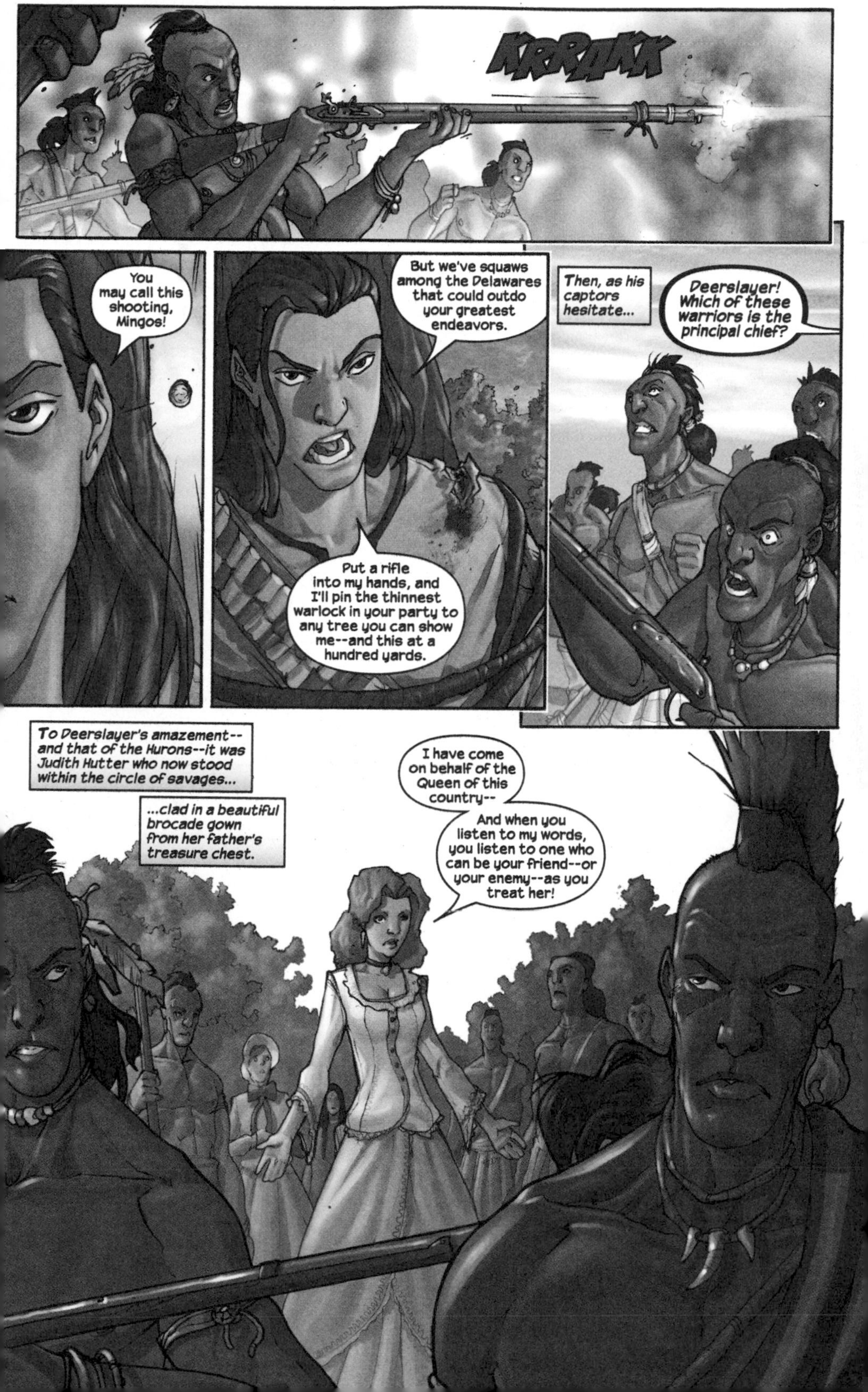
KRRAKK
You may call this shooting, Mingos!
But we've squaws among the Delawares that could outdo your greatest endeavors.
Put a rifle into my hands, and I'll pin the thinnest warlock in your party to any tree you can show me--and this at a hundred yards.
Then, as his captors hesitate...
Deerslayer! Which of these warriors is the principal chief?
To Deerslayer's amazement--and that of the Hurons--it was Judith Hutter who now stood within the circle of savages...
...clad in a beautiful brocade gown from her father's treasure chest.
I have come on behalf of the Queen of this country--
And when you listen to my words, you listen to one who can be your friend--or your enemy--as you treat her!

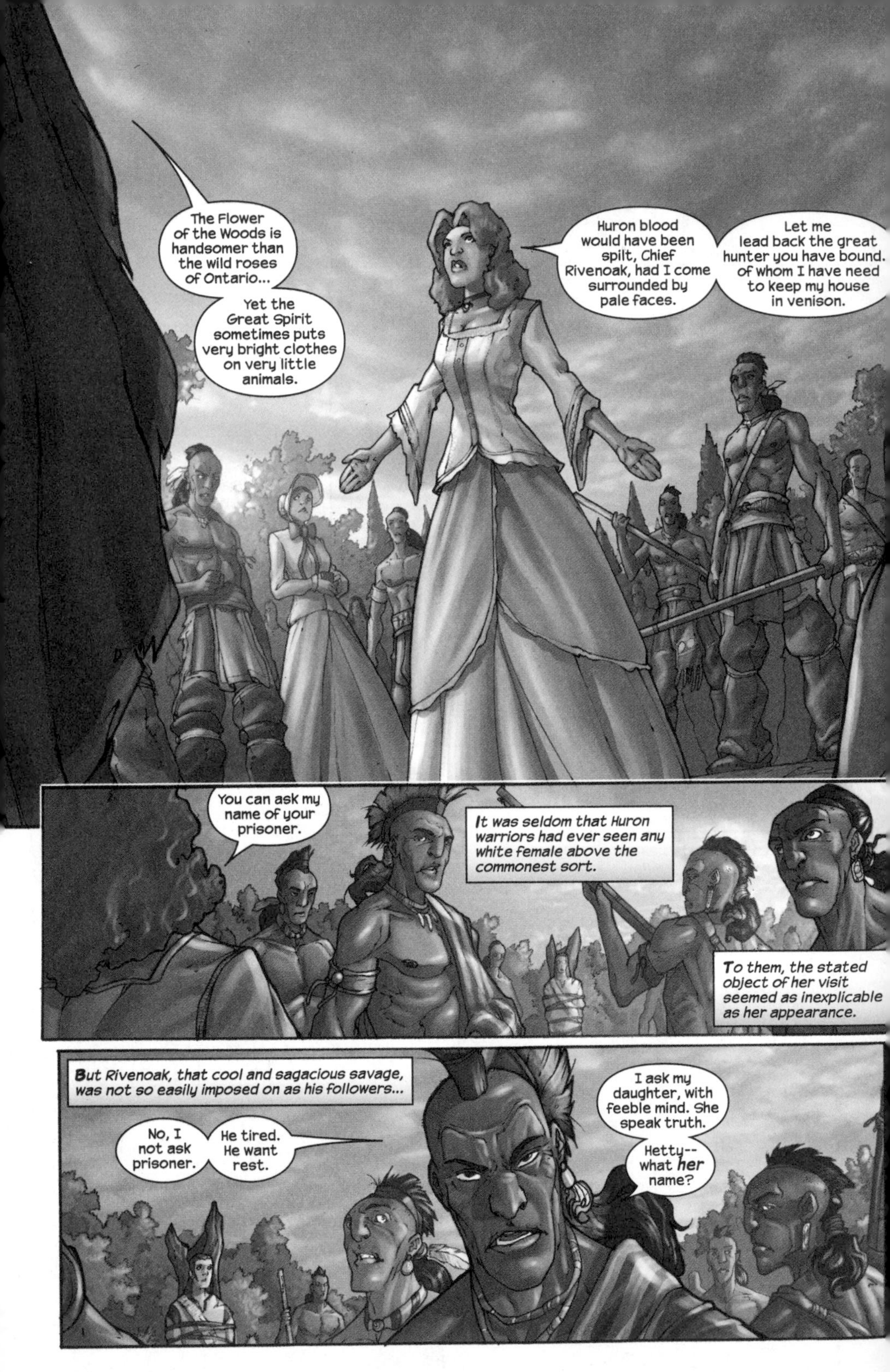
The Flower of the Woods is handsomer than the wild roses of Ontario...
Yet the Great Spirit sometimes puts very bright clothes on very little animals.
Huron blood would have been spilt, Chief Rivenoak, had I come surrounded by pale faces.
Let me lead back the great hunter you have bound. of whom I have need to keep my house in venison.
You can ask my name of your prisoner.
It was seldom that Huron warriors had ever seen any white female above the commonest sort.
To them, the stated object of her visit seemed as inexplicable as her appearance.
But Rivenoak, that cool and sagacious savage, was not so easily imposed on as his followers...
No, I not ask prisoner.
He tired. He want rest.
I ask my daughter, with feeble mind. She speak truth.
Hetty-- what her name?

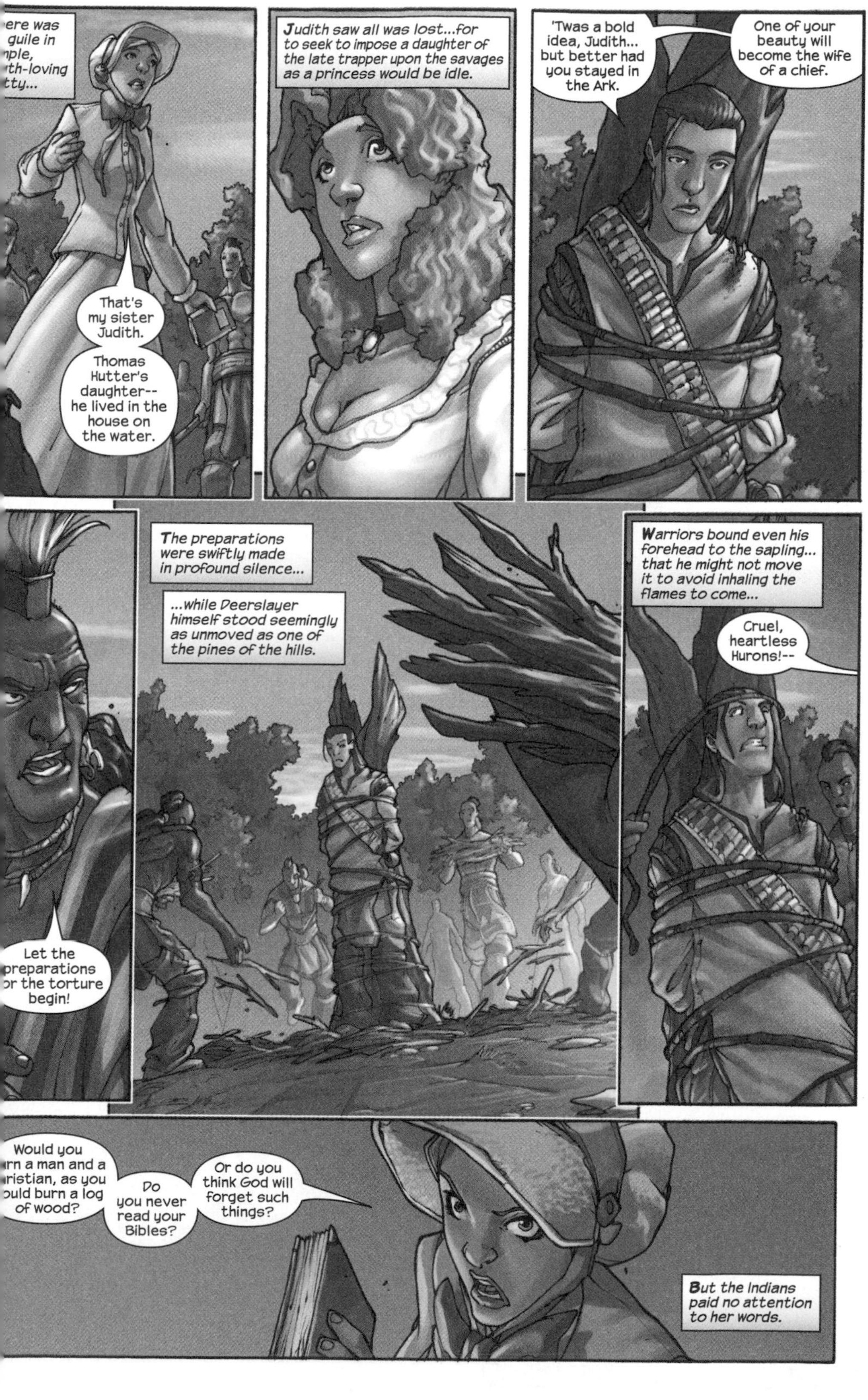

ere was
guile in
nple,
th-loving
tty...
That's my sister Judith.
Thomas Hutter's daughter-- he lived in the house on the water.
Judith saw all was lost...for to seek to impose a daughter of the late trapper upon the savages as a princess would be idle.
'Twas a bold idea, Judith... but better had you stayed in the Ark.
One of your beauty will become the wife of a chief.
Let the preparations or the torture begin!
The preparations were swiftly made in profound silence...
...while Deerslayer himself stood seemingly as unmoved as one of the pines of the hills.
Warriors bound even his forehead to the sapling... that he might not move it to avoid inhaling the flames to come...
Cruel, heartless Hurons!--
Would you rn a man and a ristian, as you ould burn a log of wood?
Do you never read your Bibles?
Or do you think God will forget such things?
But the Indians paid no attention to her words.

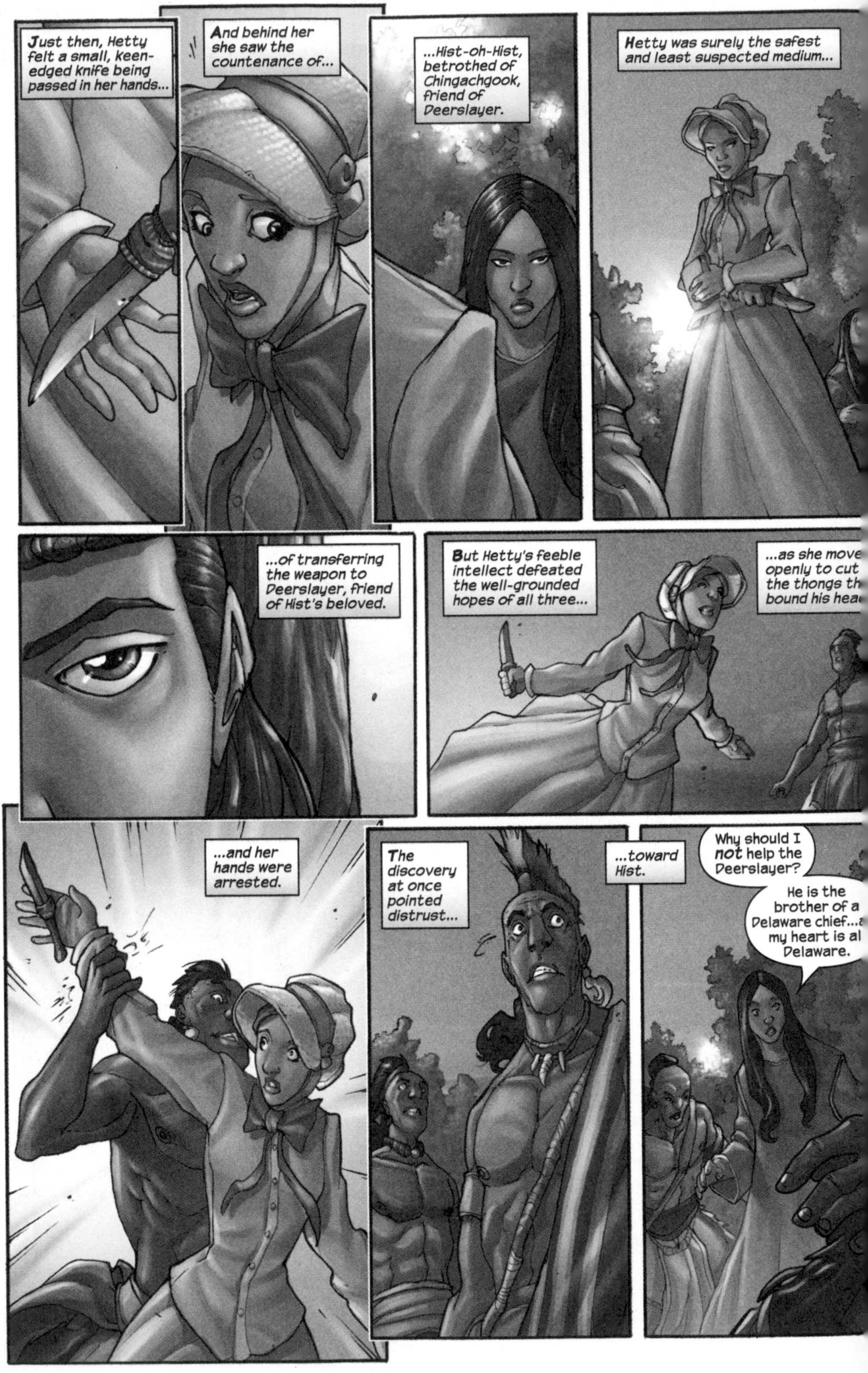
Just then, Hetty felt a small, keen-edged knife being passed in her hands...
And behind her she saw the countenance of...
...Hist-oh-Hist, betrothed of Chingachgook, friend of Deerslayer.
Hetty was surely the safest and least suspected medium...
...of transferring the weapon to Deerslayer, friend of Hist's beloved.
But Hetty's feeble intellect defeated the well-grounded hopes of all three...
...as she move openly to cut the thongs th bound his hea
...and her hands were arrested.
The discovery at once pointed distrust...
...toward Hist.
Why should I not help the Deerslayer?
He is the brother of a Delaware chief...a my heart is al Delaware.

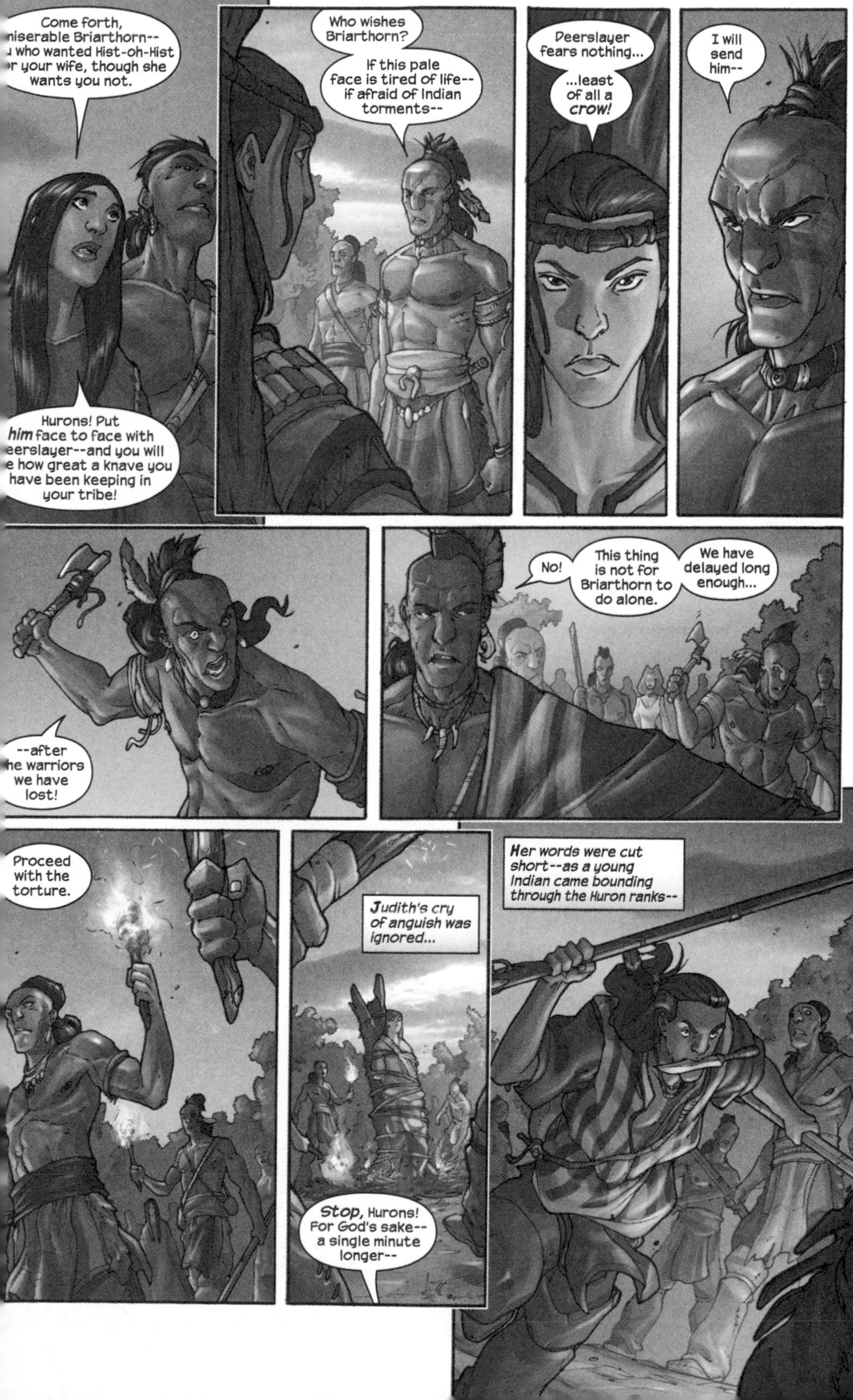
Come forth, niserable Briarthorn-- u who wanted Hist-oh-Hist r your wife, though she wants you not.
Hurons! Put him face to face with eerslayer--and you will e how great a knave you have been keeping in your tribe!
Who wishes Briarthorn?
If this pale face is tired of life--if afraid of Indian torments--
Deerslayer fears nothing...
...least of all a crow!
I will send him--
--after he warriors we have lost!
No!
This thing is not for Briarthorn to do alone.
We have delayed long enough...
Proceed with the torture.
Judith's cry of anguish was ignored...
Stop, Hurons! For God's sake--a single minute longer--
Her words were cut short--as a young Indian came bounding through the Huron ranks--

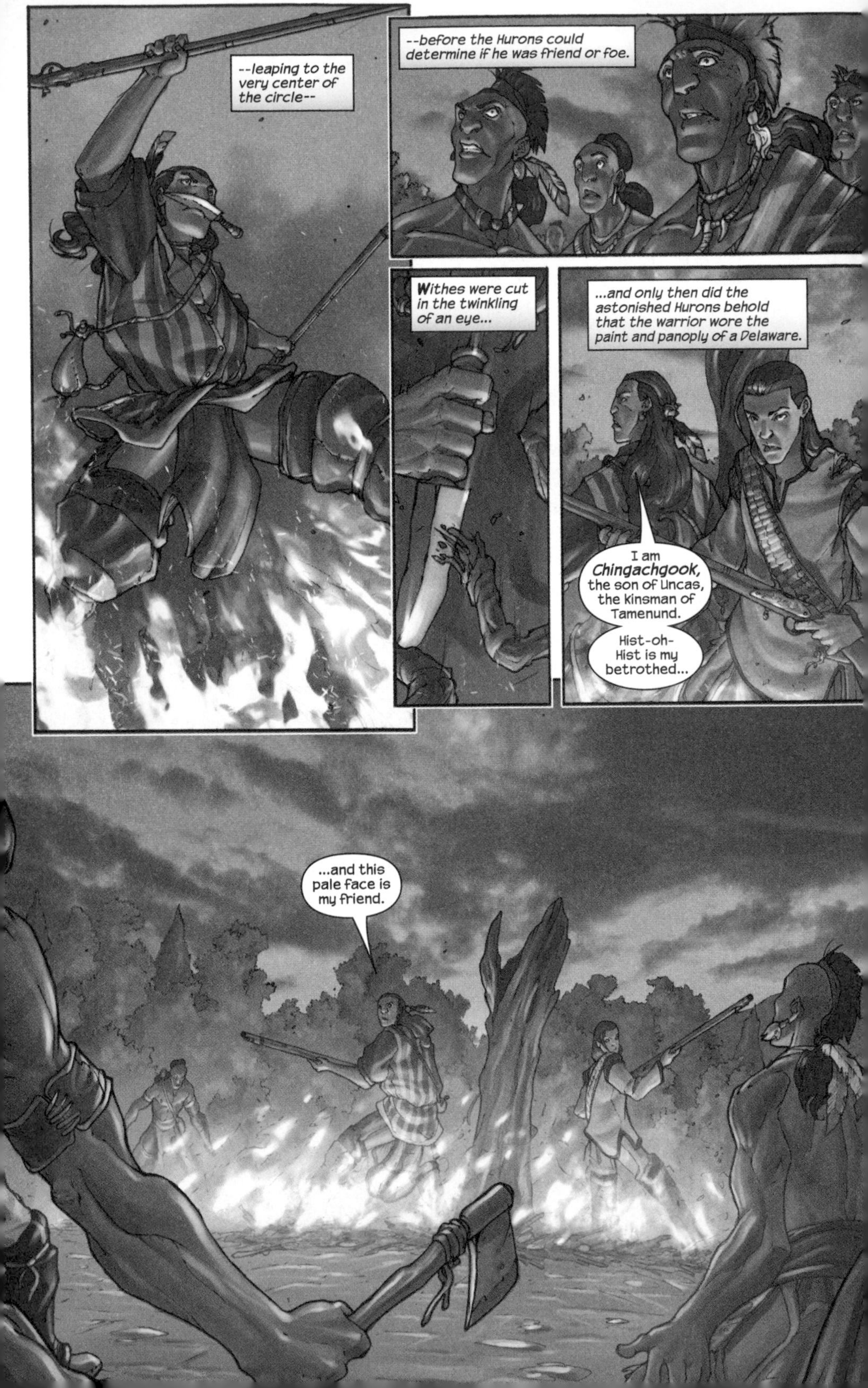
--leaping to the very center of the circle--
--before the Hurons could determine if he was friend or foe.
Withes were cut in the twinkling of an eye...
...and only then did the astonished Hurons behold that the warrior wore the paint and panoply of a Delaware.
I am Chingachgook, the son of Uncas, the kinsman of Tamenund.
Hist-oh-Hist is my betrothed...
...and this pale face is my friend.

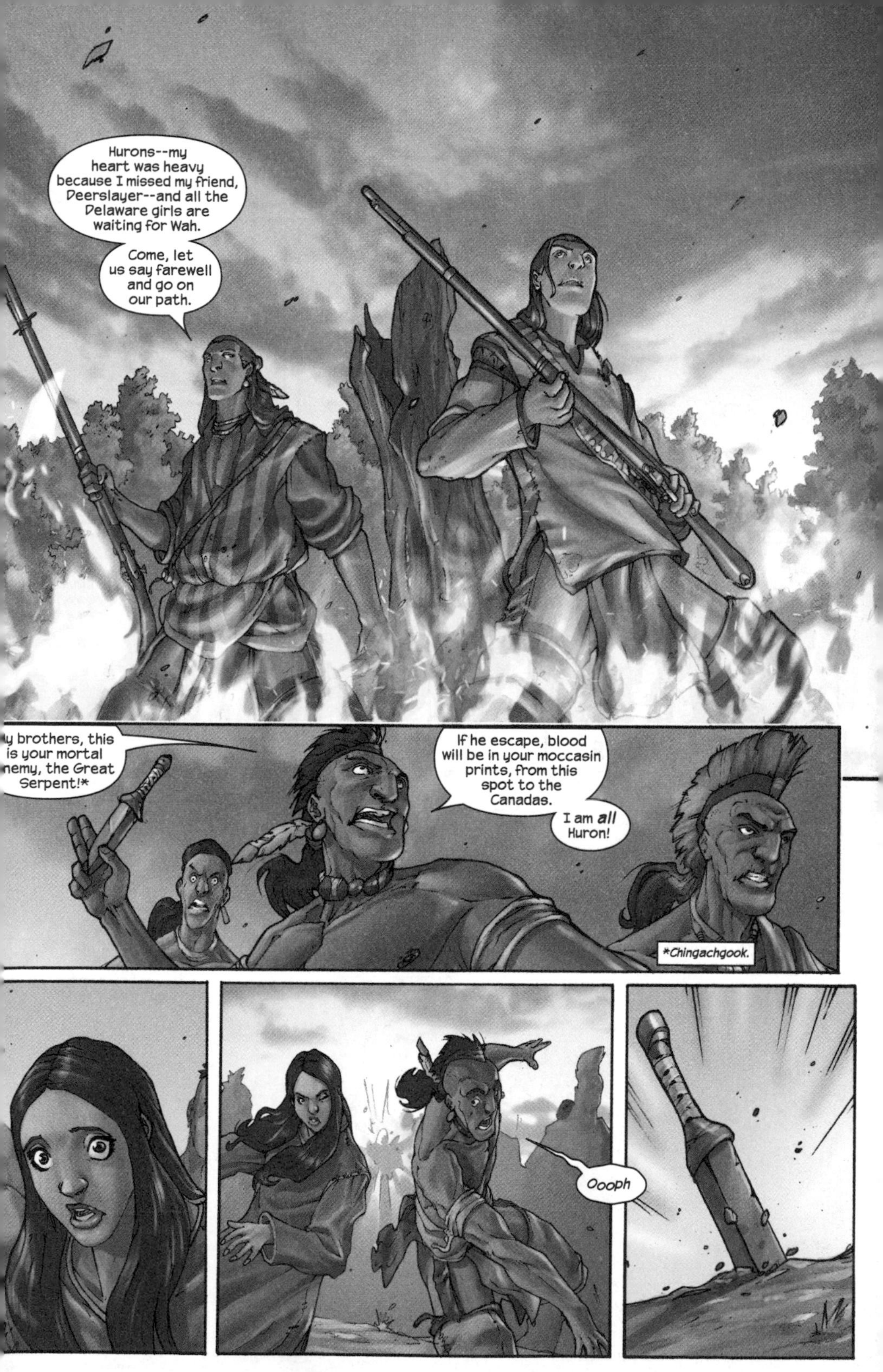

Hurons--my heart was heavy because I missed my friend, Deerslayer--and all the Delaware girls are waiting for Wah.
Come, let us say farewell and go on our path.
y brothers, this is your mortal nemy, the Great Serpent!*
If he escape, blood will be in your moccasin prints, from this spot to the Canadas.
I am all Huron!
*Chingachgook.
Oooph

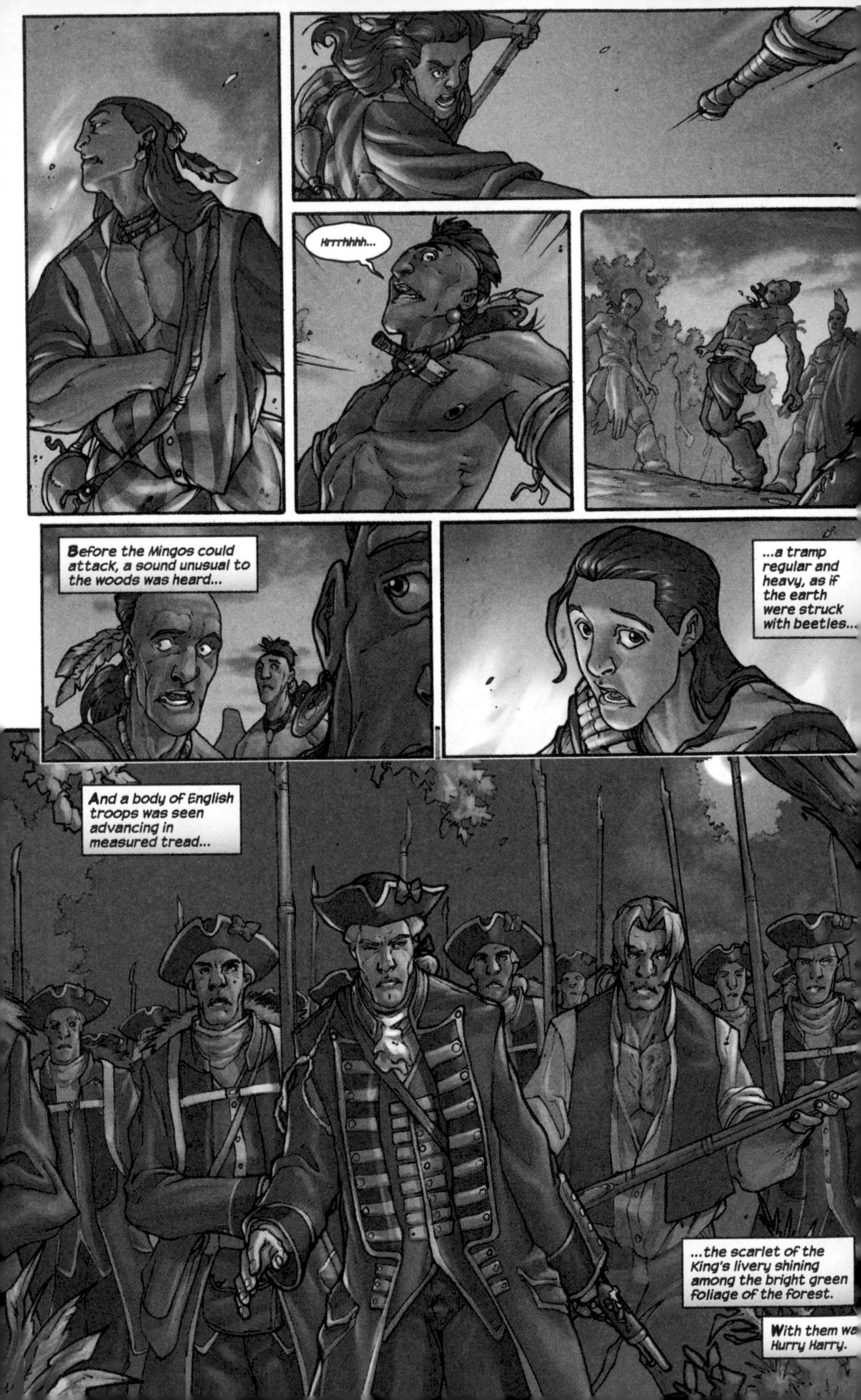
Hrrrhhhh...
Before the Mingos could attack, a sound unusual to the woods was heard...
...a tramp regular and heavy, as if the earth were struck with beetles...
And a body of English troops was seen advancing in measured tread...
...the scarlet of the King's livery shining among the bright green foliage of the forest.
With them wa
Hurry Harry.

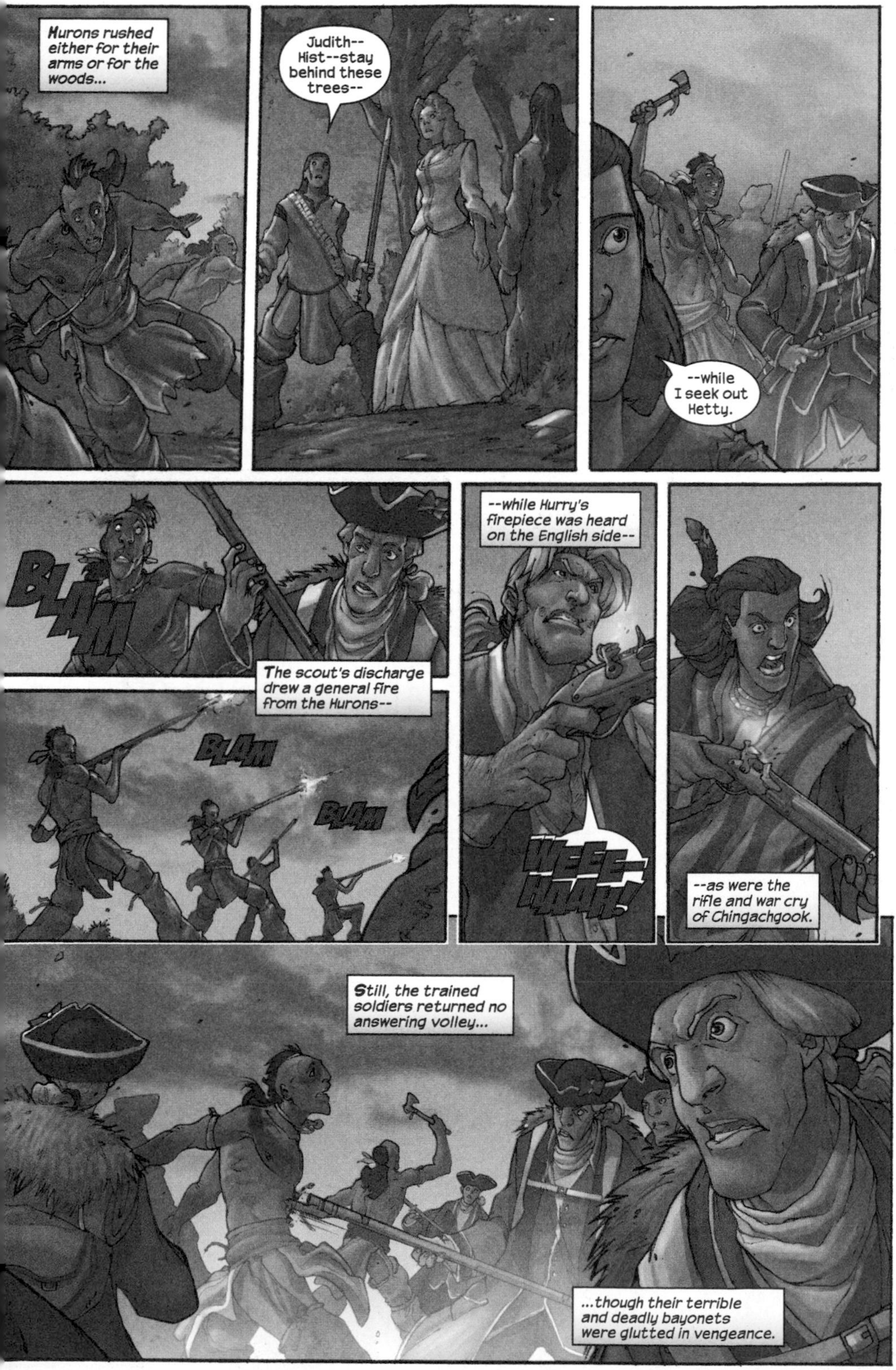

Hurons rushed either for their arms or for the woods...
Judith--Hist--stay behind these trees--
--while I seek out Hetty.
BLAM
The scout's discharge drew a general fire from the Hurons--
BLAM
BLAM
--while Hurry's firepiece was heard on the English side--
WEEE-HAAH!
--as were the rifle and war cry of Chingachgook.
Still, the trained soldiers returned no answering volley...
...though their terrible and deadly bayonets were glutted in vengeance.

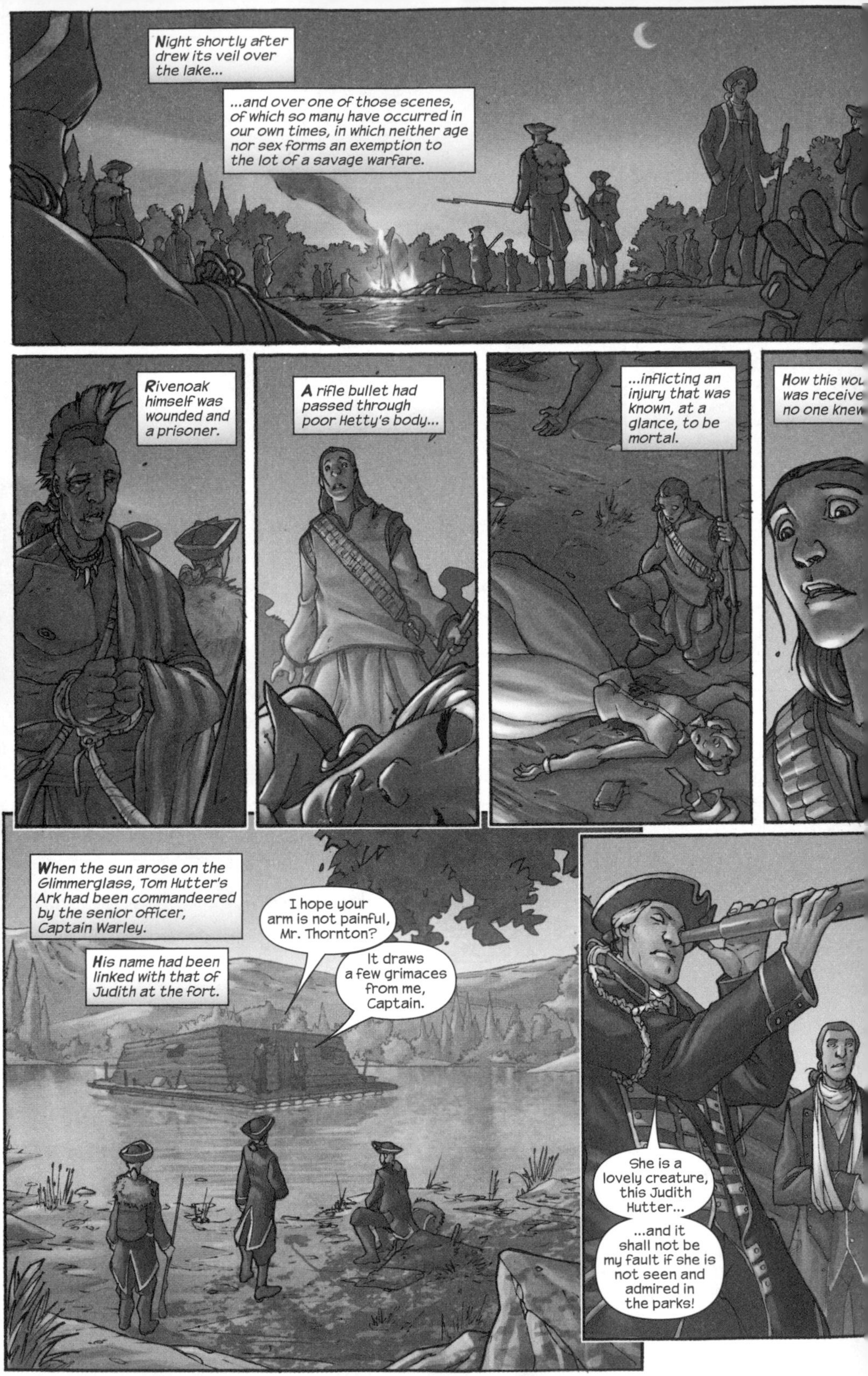
Night shortly after drew its veil over the lake...
...and over one of those scenes, of which so many have occurred in our own times, in which neither age nor sex forms an exemption to the lot of a savage warfare.
Rivenoak himself was wounded and a prisoner.
A rifle bullet had passed through poor Hetty's body...
...inflicting an injury that was known, at a glance, to be mortal.
How this wou was receive no one knew
When the sun arose on the Glimmerglass, Tom Hutter's Ark had been commandeered by the senior officer, Captain Warley.
His name had been linked with that of Judith at the fort.
I hope your arm is not painful, Mr. Thornton?
It draws a few grimaces from me, Captain.
She is a lovely creature, this Judith Hutter...
...and it shall not be my fault if she is not seen and admired in the parks!

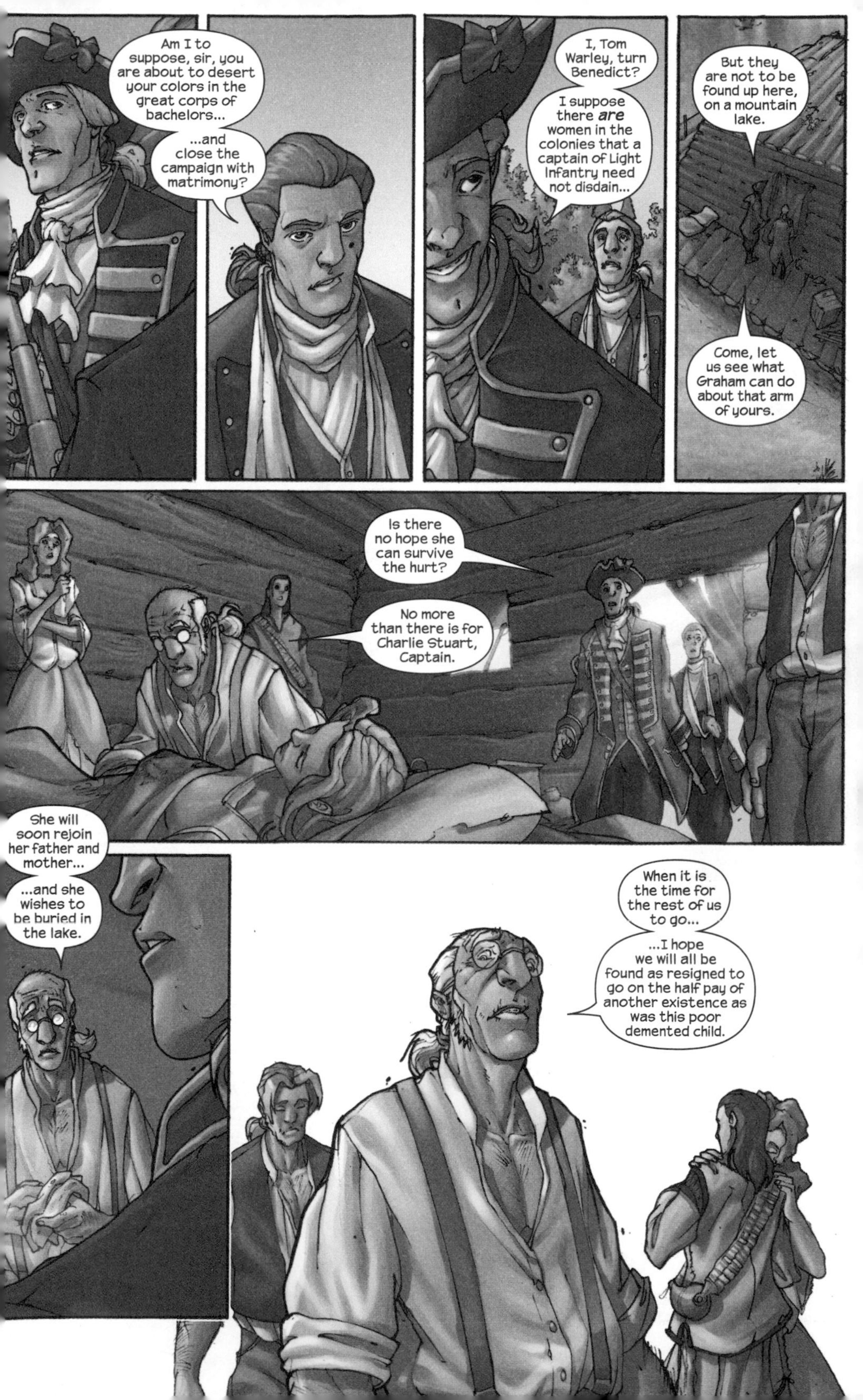
Am I to suppose, sir, you are about to desert your colors in the great corps of bachelors...
...and close the campaign with matrimony?
I, Tom Warley, turn Benedict?
I suppose there *are* women in the colonies that a captain of Light Infantry need not disdain...
But they are not to be found up here, on a mountain lake.
Come, let us see what Graham can do about that arm of yours.
Is there no hope she can survive the hurt?
No more than there is for Charlie Stuart, Captain.
She will soon rejoin her father and mother...
...and she wishes to be buried in the lake.
When it is the time for the rest of us to go...
...I hope we will all be found as resigned to go on the half pay of another existence as was this poor demented child.

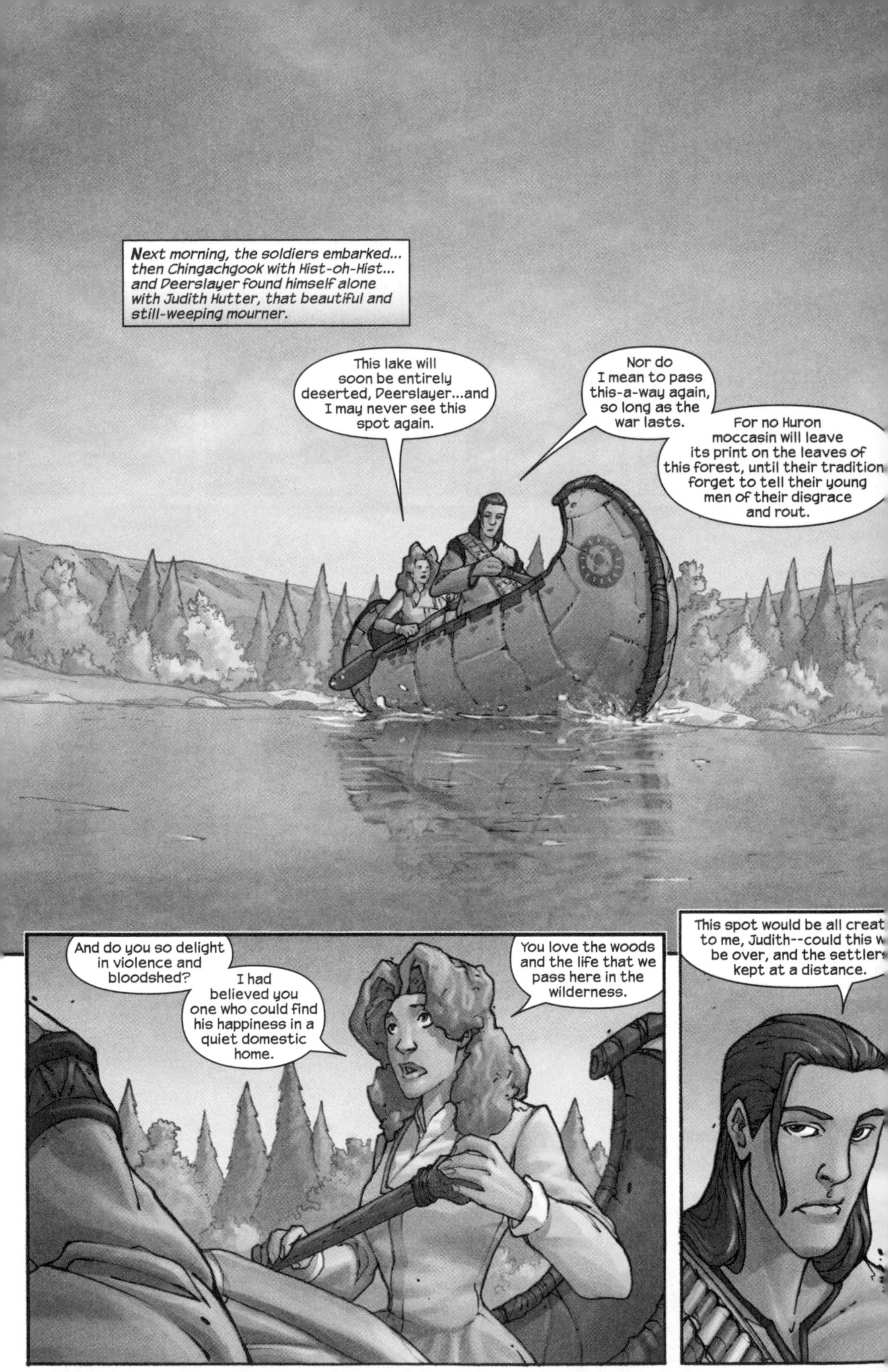

Next morning, the soldiers embarked... then Chingachgook with Hist-oh-Hist... and Deerslayer found himself alone with Judith Hutter, that beautiful and still-weeping mourner.
This lake will soon be entirely deserted, Deerslayer...and I may never see this spot again.
Nor do I mean to pass this-a-way again, so long as the war lasts.
For no Huron moccasin will leave its print on the leaves of this forest, until their tradition forget to tell their young men of their disgrace and rout.
You love the woods and the life that we pass here in the wilderness.
This spot would be all creat to me, Judith--could this be over, and the settler kept at a distance.
And do you so delight in violence and bloodshed?
I had believed you one who could find his happiness in a quiet domestic home.

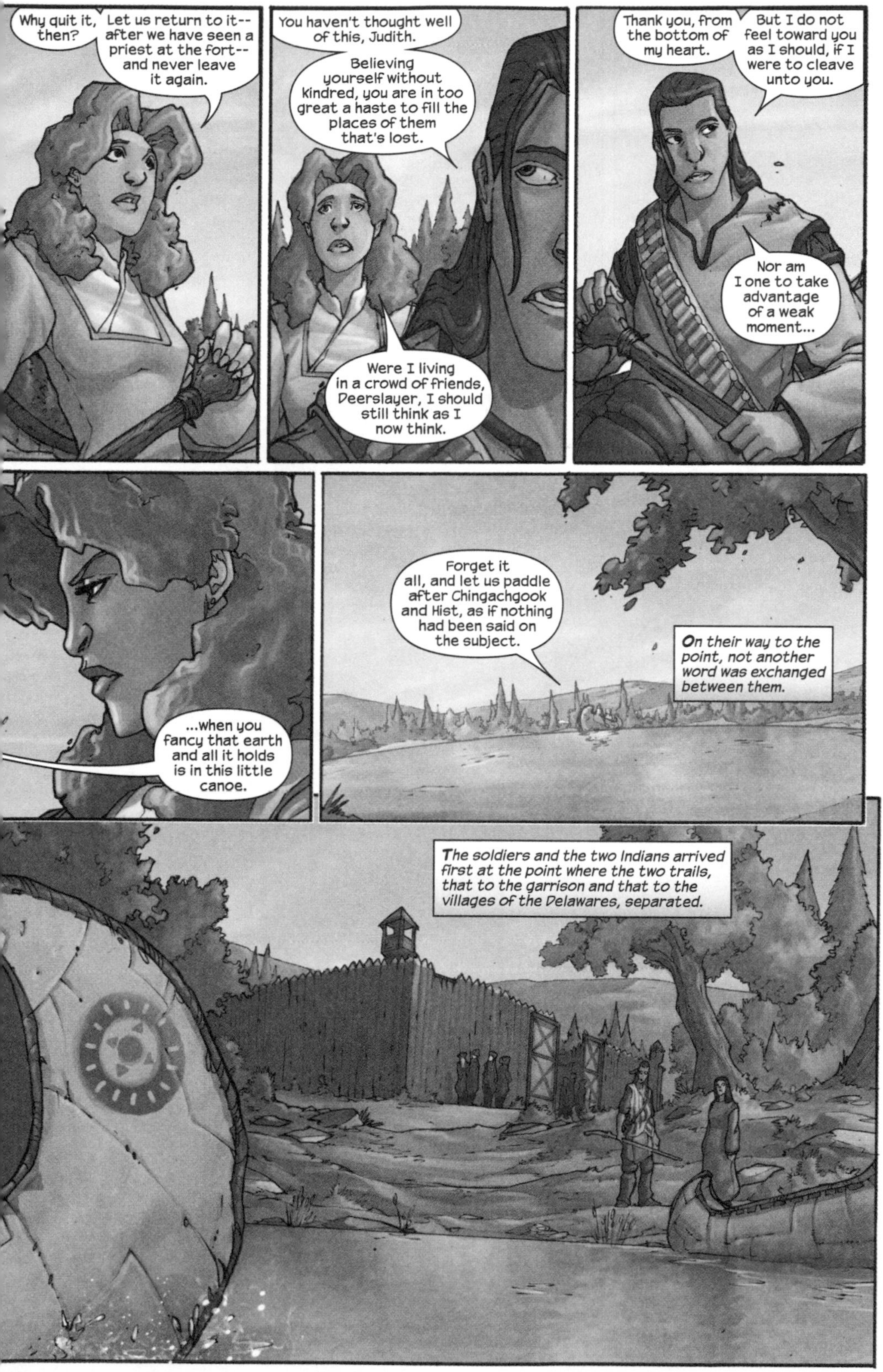

Why quit it, then?
Let us return to it--after we have seen a priest at the fort--and never leave it again.
You haven't thought well of this, Judith.
Believing yourself without kindred, you are in too great a haste to fill the places of them that's lost.
Were I living in a crowd of friends, Deerslayer, I should still think as I now think.
Thank you, from the bottom of my heart.
But I do not feel toward you as I should, if I were to cleave unto you.
Nor am I one to take advantage of a weak moment...
...when you fancy that earth and all it holds is in this little canoe.
Forget it all, and let us paddle after Chingachgook and Hist, as if nothing had been said on the subject.
On their way to the point, not another word was exchanged between them.
The soldiers and the two Indians arrived first at the point where the two trails, that to the garrison and that to the villages of the Delawares, separated.

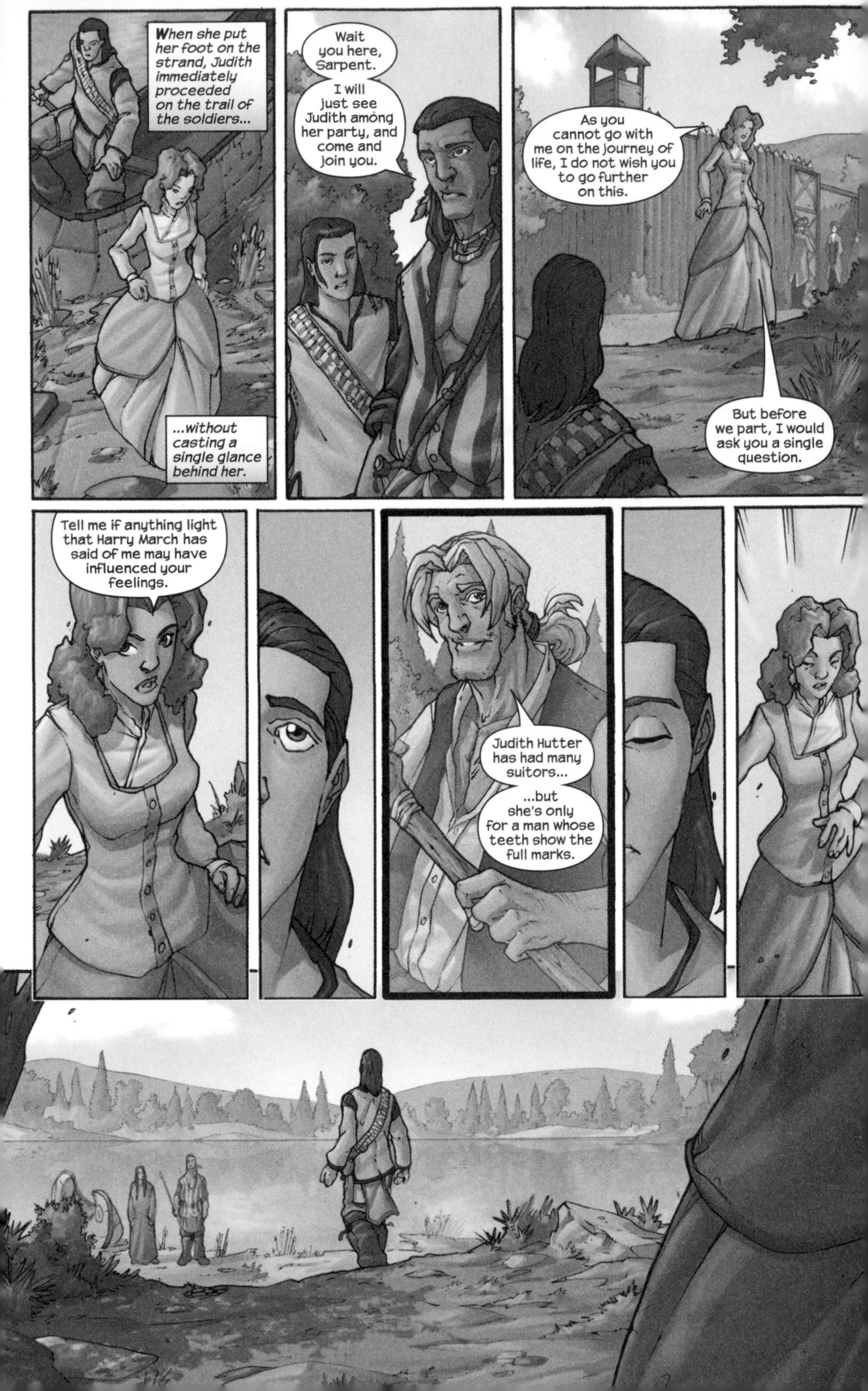
When she put her foot on the strand, Judith immediately proceeded on the trail of the soldiers...
...without casting a single glance behind her.
Wait you here, Sarpent.
I will just see Judith among her party, and come and join you.
As you cannot go with me on the journey of life, I do not wish you to go further on this.
But before we part, I would ask you a single question.
Tell me if anything light that Harry March has said of me may have influenced your feelings.
Judith Hutter has had many suitors...
...but she's only for a man whose teeth show the full marks.

Fifteen years had passed away, ere it was in the power of the Deerslayer--now called Hawkeye-- to revisit the Glimmerglass.

It was on the eve of another, and still more important war, when he and his friend Chingachgook were hastening to the forts to join their allies.

The stripling Uncas accompanied them, for Hist already slumbered beneath the pines of the Delawares, and the three survivors had become inseparable.

They discovered the remains of Tom Hutter's ark, long stranded on the eastern shore.

The scow was filled with water, the cabin unroofed, and the logs were decaying.

And the heart of Hawkeye beat quick...

...as he found an old ribbon of Judith's floating nearby.

It recalled all her beauty...

...and, we may add, all her failings.

He knotted the ribbon to the stock of Killdeer, which had been the gift of the girl herself.

When Hawkeye and his Mohican companions reached the garrison on the Mohawk...

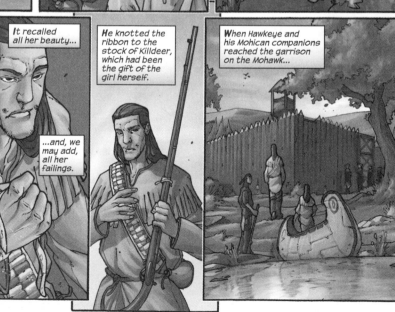

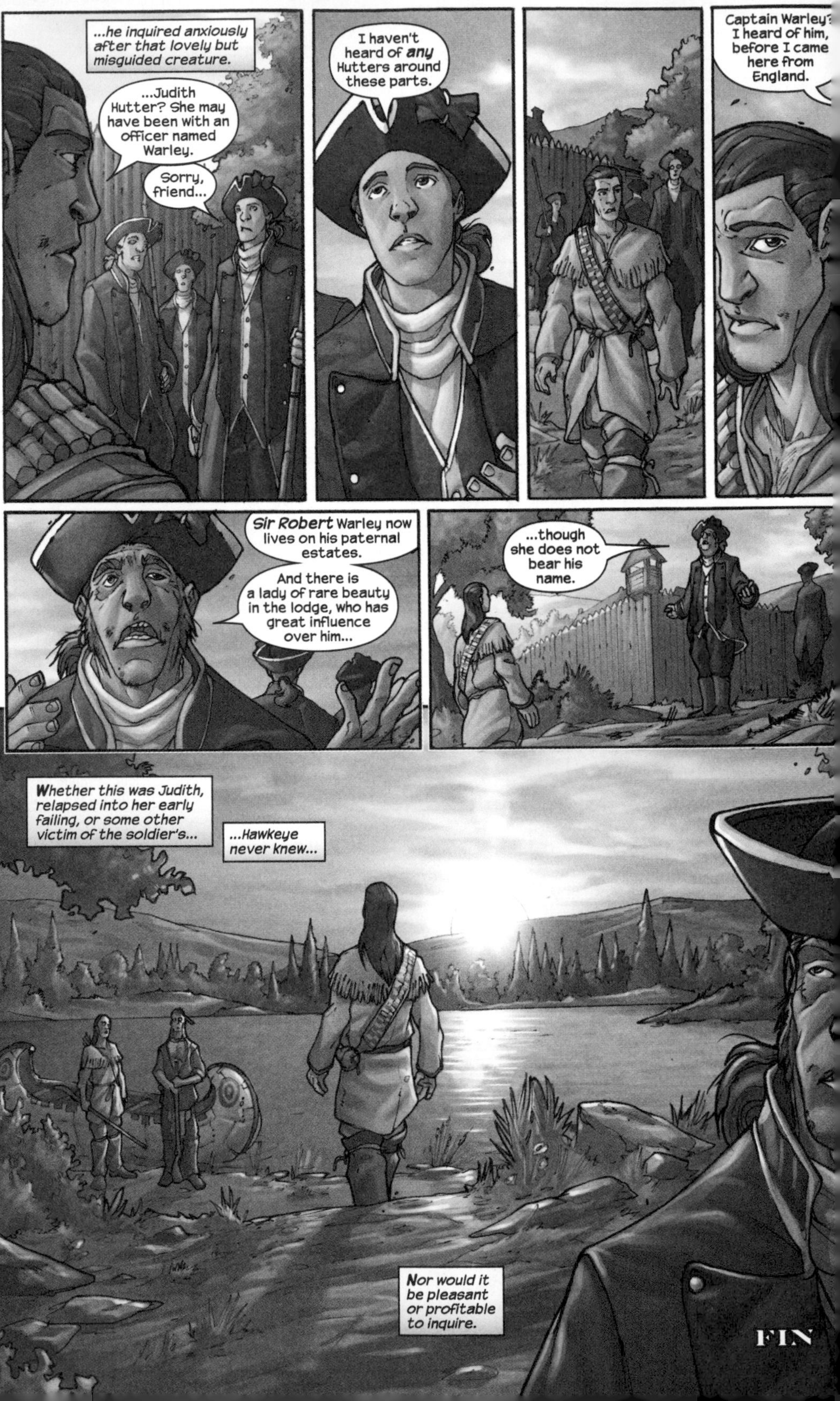

...he inquired anxiously after that lovely but misguided creature.
...Judith Hutter? She may have been with an officer named Warley.
Sorry, friend...
I haven't heard of any Hutters around these parts.
Captain Warley? I heard of him, before I came here from England.
Sir Robert Warley now lives on his paternal estates.
And there is a lady of rare beauty in the lodge, who has great influence over him...
...though she does not bear his name.
Whether this was Judith, relapsed into her early failing, or some other victim of the soldier's...
...Hawkeye never knew...
Nor would it be pleasant or profitable to inquire.
FIN

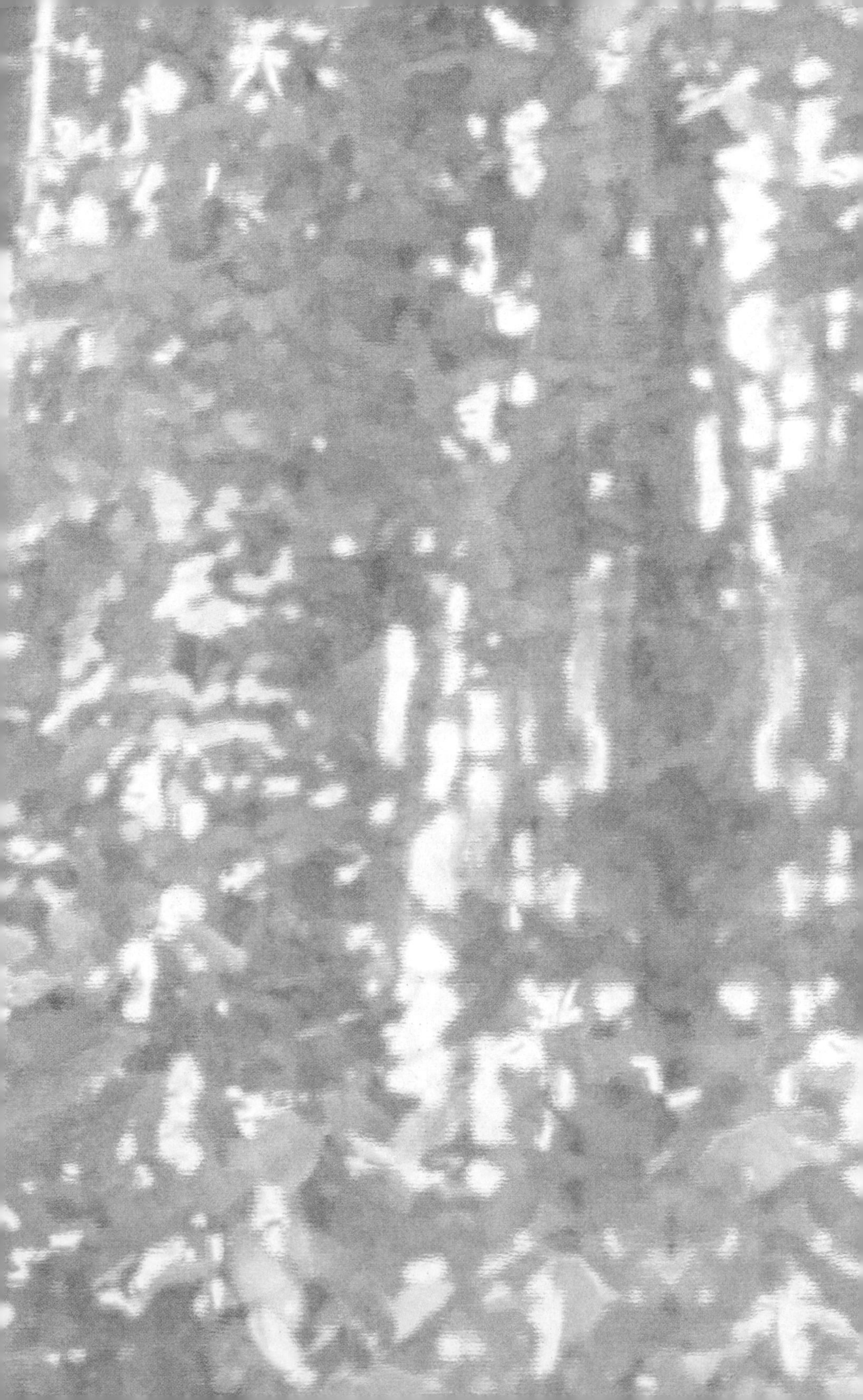

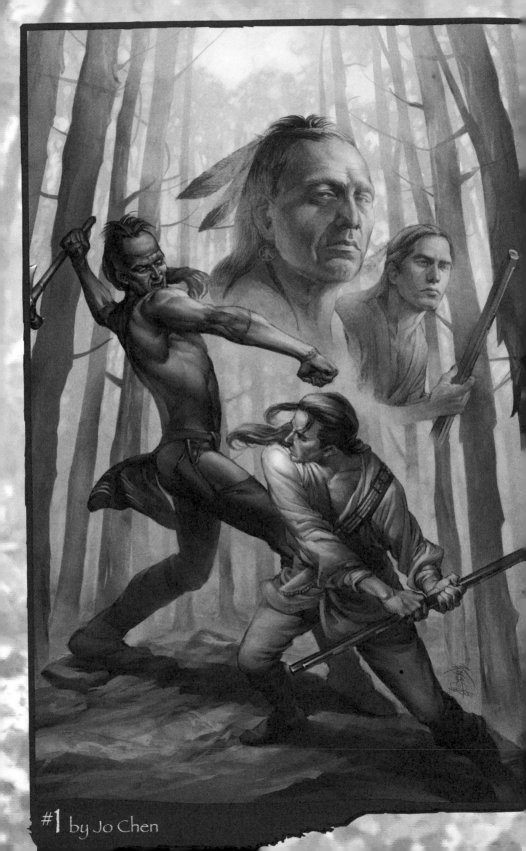

#1 by Jo Chen

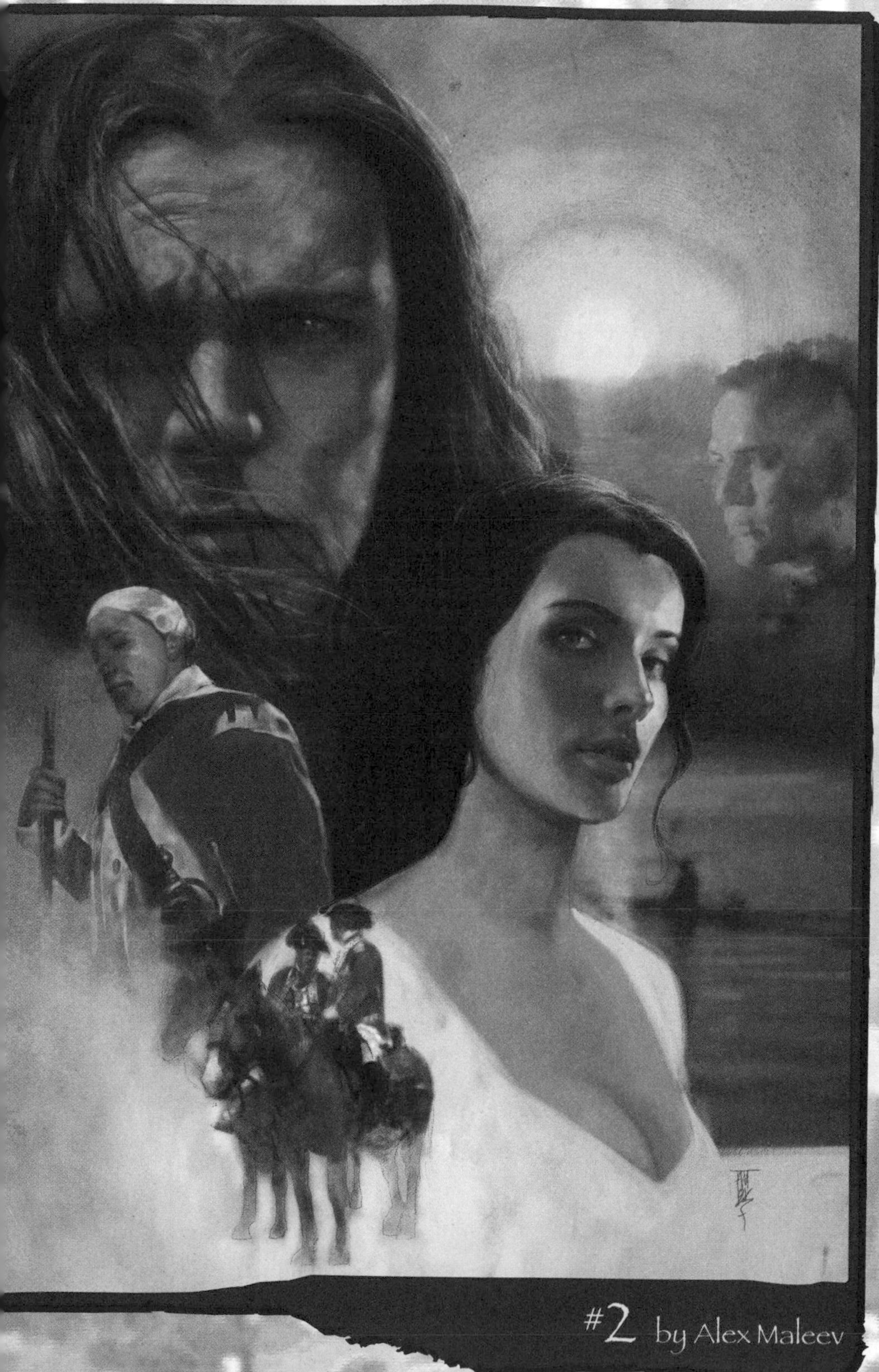

#2 by Alex Maleev

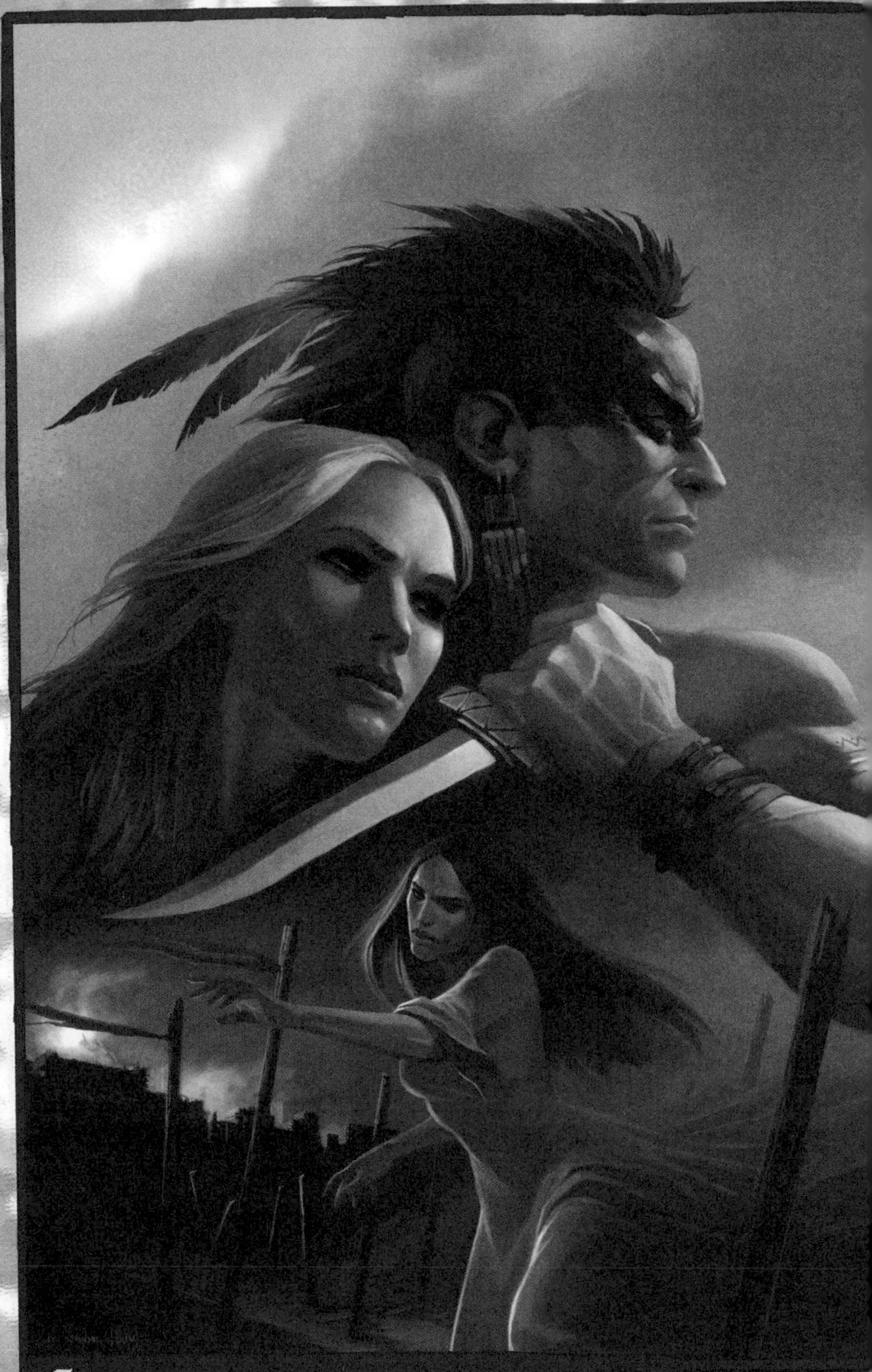

#3 by Jelena Kevic-Djurdjevic

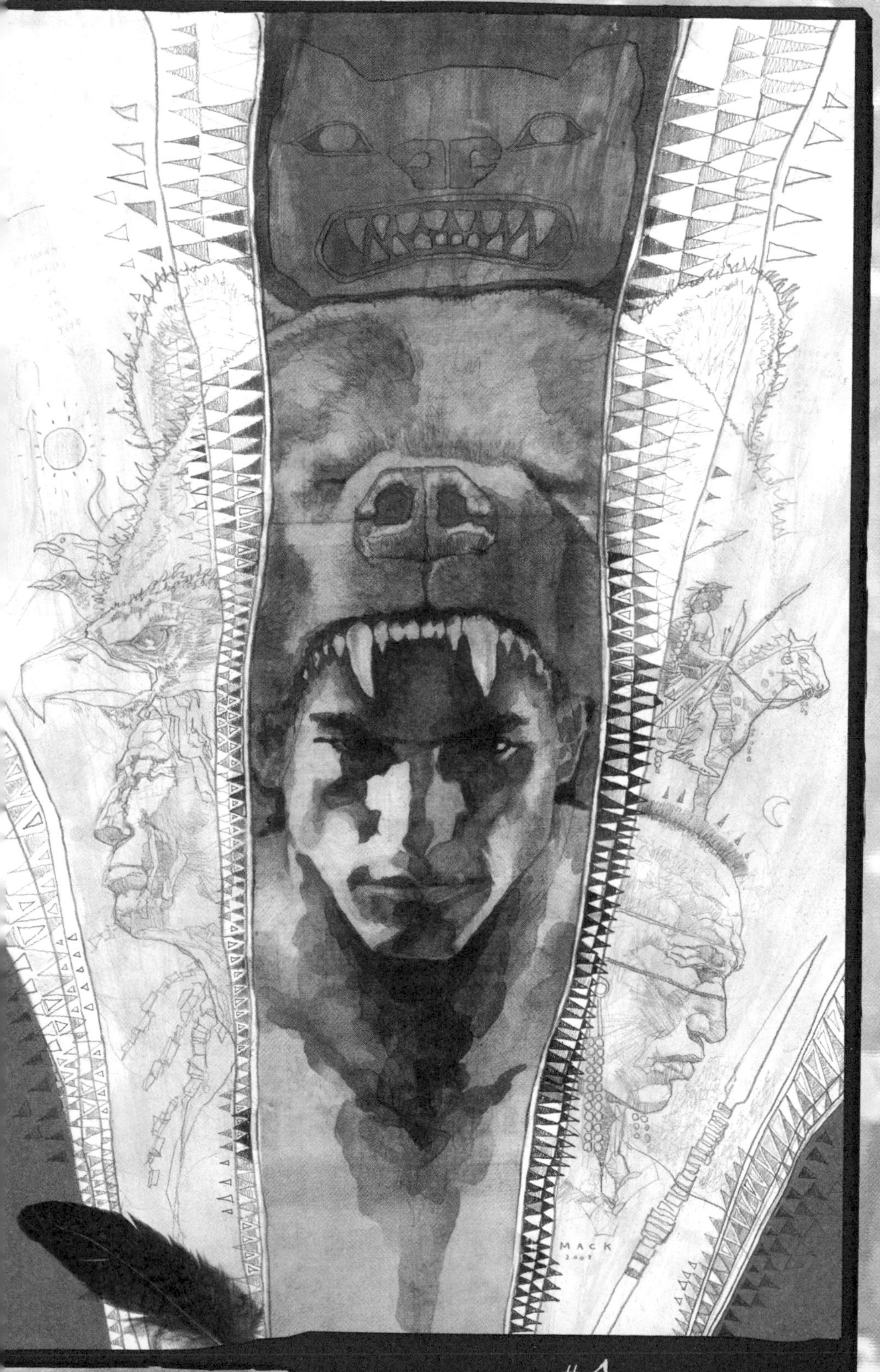
MACK

#4 by David Mack

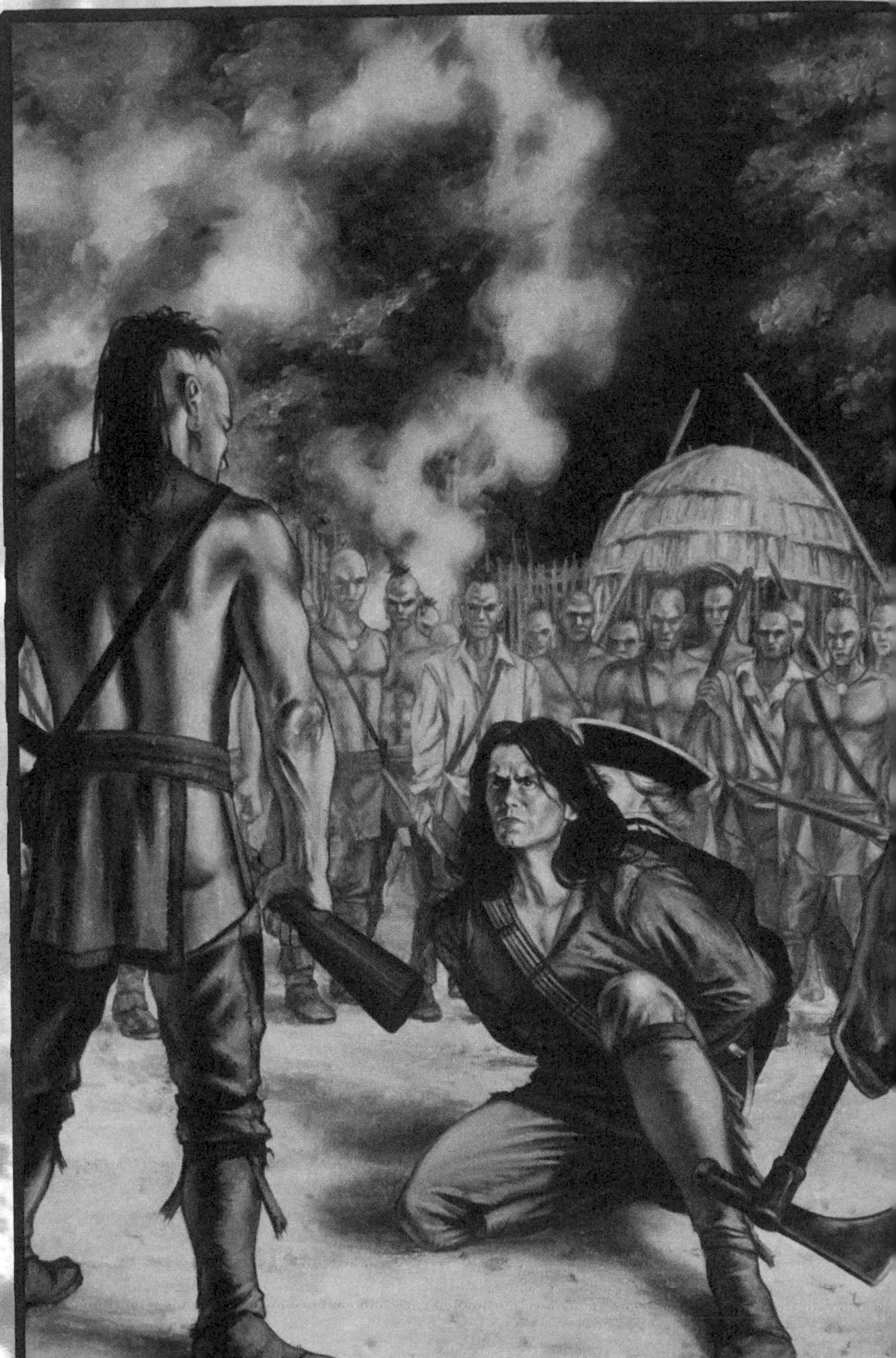

#5 by Gerald Parel

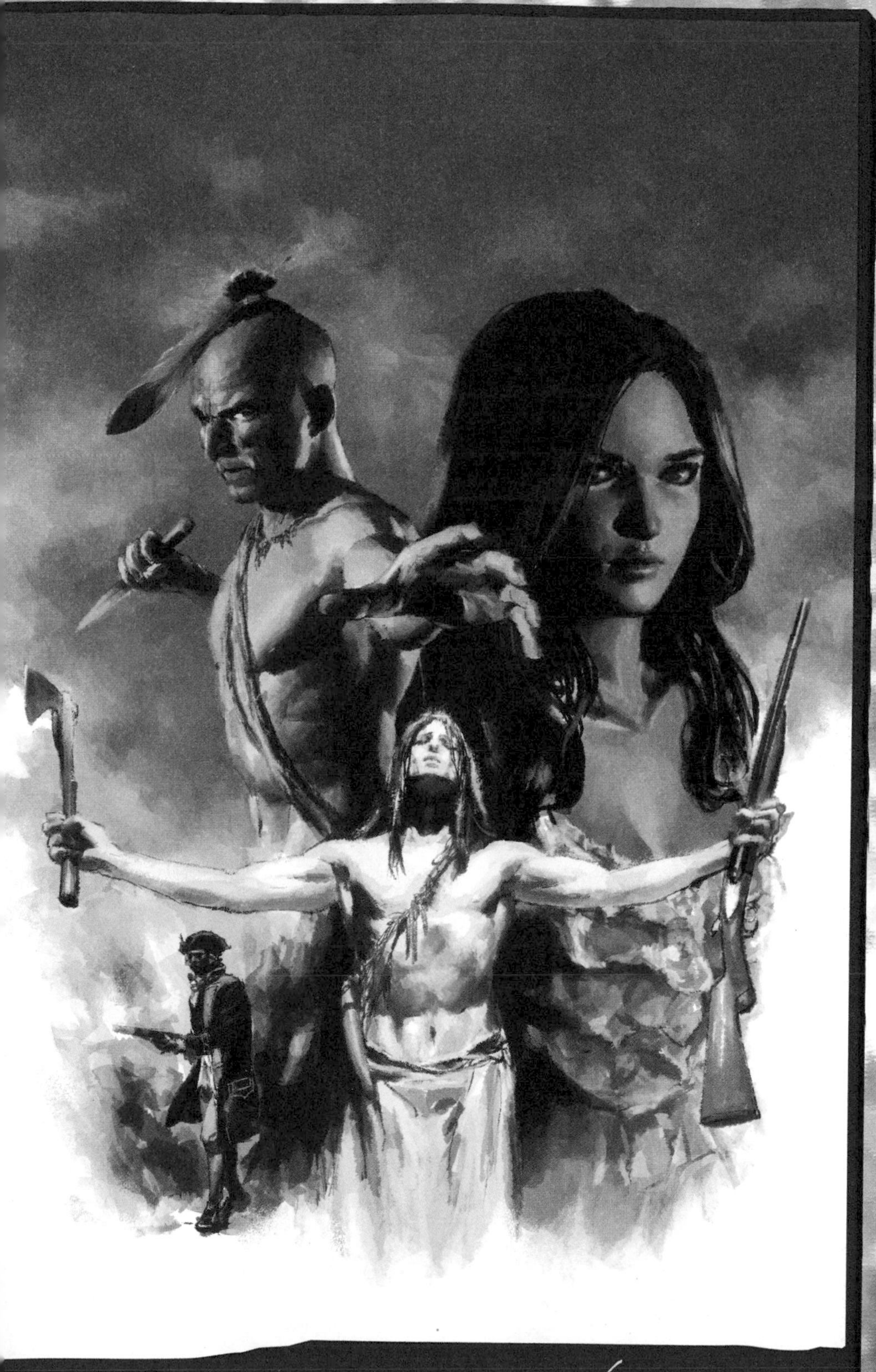

#6 by Gerald Parel

The Last of the Mohicans
Glossary

Appellation - a name, title, or designation

Cataract - any furious rush or downpour of water; waterfall

Churlishly - having a bad disposition; surly

Communion - association; fellowship

Conjurer - a sorcerer or sorceress

Deference - respectful submission or yielding to the judgment of another

Discourse - communication of thought by words

Heathen - an unconverted individual of a people that do not acknowledge God

Imp – person possessing characteristics of a small demon

Impunity - exemption from punishment

Incautious - careless; reckless

Injunction - act or an instance of enjoining; a command, directive, or order

Interminable - having no limits

Invalid – a sickly person

Inviolable - secure from destruction, violence or infringement

Judgmatical - having or exhibiting sound judgment; prudent

Knave - a male servant

Miscreant - an evildoer; a villain

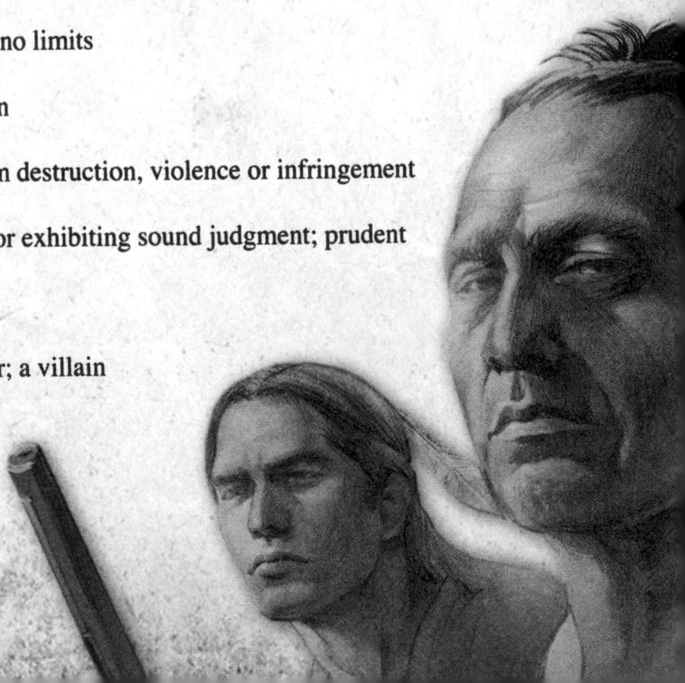

Offal - waste part

Outstrip - to leave behind; outrun

Petticoat - a woman's slip or underskirt that is often full and trimmed with ruffles or lace

Retreat - an upward slope or incline

Sachem - the chief of a tribe

Specter - some object or source of terror or dread

Spruce beer - a fermented beverage made with spruce leaves and twigs

Squaw - a Native American woman, especially a wife

Succoring - giving assistance in time of want

Totem - a natural object or animal assumed as the emblem of a clan, family, or group

Ungainly - not graceful; awkward; unwieldy; clumsy

Urchin - a mischievous boy

Varlet - an attendant or servant

Venerable - commanding respect because of great age or impressive dignity

Venison - the flesh of a deer or similar animal as used for food

Whippoorwill - a nocturnal North American bird

Whoop - a loud cry or shout

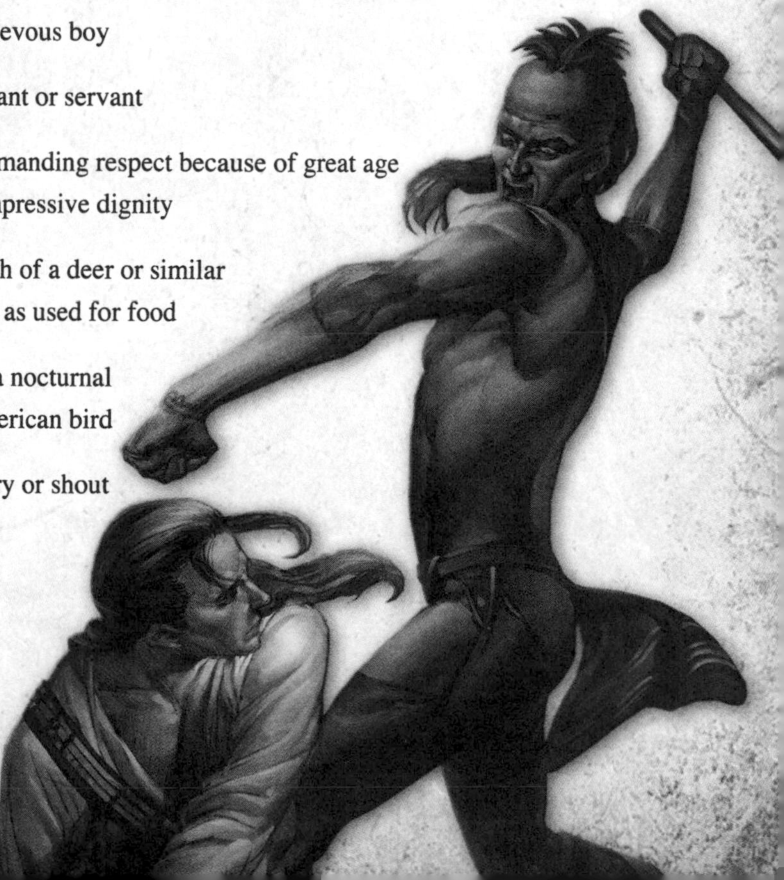

James Fenimore Cooper

(1789 – 1851)

James Fenimore Cooper was born in Burlington, New Jersey, the son of Judge William Cooper. His family helped settle the town of Cooperstown, NY when he was very young. At the age of 13, James was sent to Yale for schooling but was expelled in his third year. Instead of continuing with his schooling, James was sent to sea by his family where he worked part-time in the merchant marines and part time as a member of the U.S. Navy as a midshipman.

After his time at sea, James settled down as a farmer and married Susan DeLancey in 1811. He went on to write over 50 books, despite his first work, *Precaution*, being a failure. He began to find his voice with the *Pioneers*, which was published in 1823, which began his thematic exploration of life on the frontier. Cooper continued writing about the frontier in his series *The Leatherstocking Tales*. His most enduring character, Hawkeye, became the hero in many of his works, specifically *The Leatherstocking Tales*, which include: *The Deerslayer, The Last of the Mohicans, The Pathfinder, The Pioneers,* and *The Prairie*.

Cooper died on September 14, 1851 and was buried in the cemetery of Cooperstown.

James Fenimore Cooper's Must-Reads

Afloat and Ashore: A Sea Tale

Autobiography of a Pocket-Handkerchief

Home as Found

Homeward Bound

Jack Tier

Miles Wallingford

Oak Openings

Precaution

Satanstoe

The Bravo

The Crater

The Deerslayer

The Headsman

The Last of the Mohicans

The Monikins

The Pathfinder

The Pilot

The Pioneers

The Prairie

The Red Rover

The Sea Lions

The Spy

The Water-Witch

The Wept of Wish-Ton-Wish

The Wing and Wing

Wyandotte

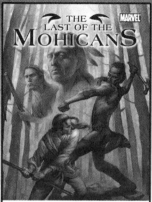

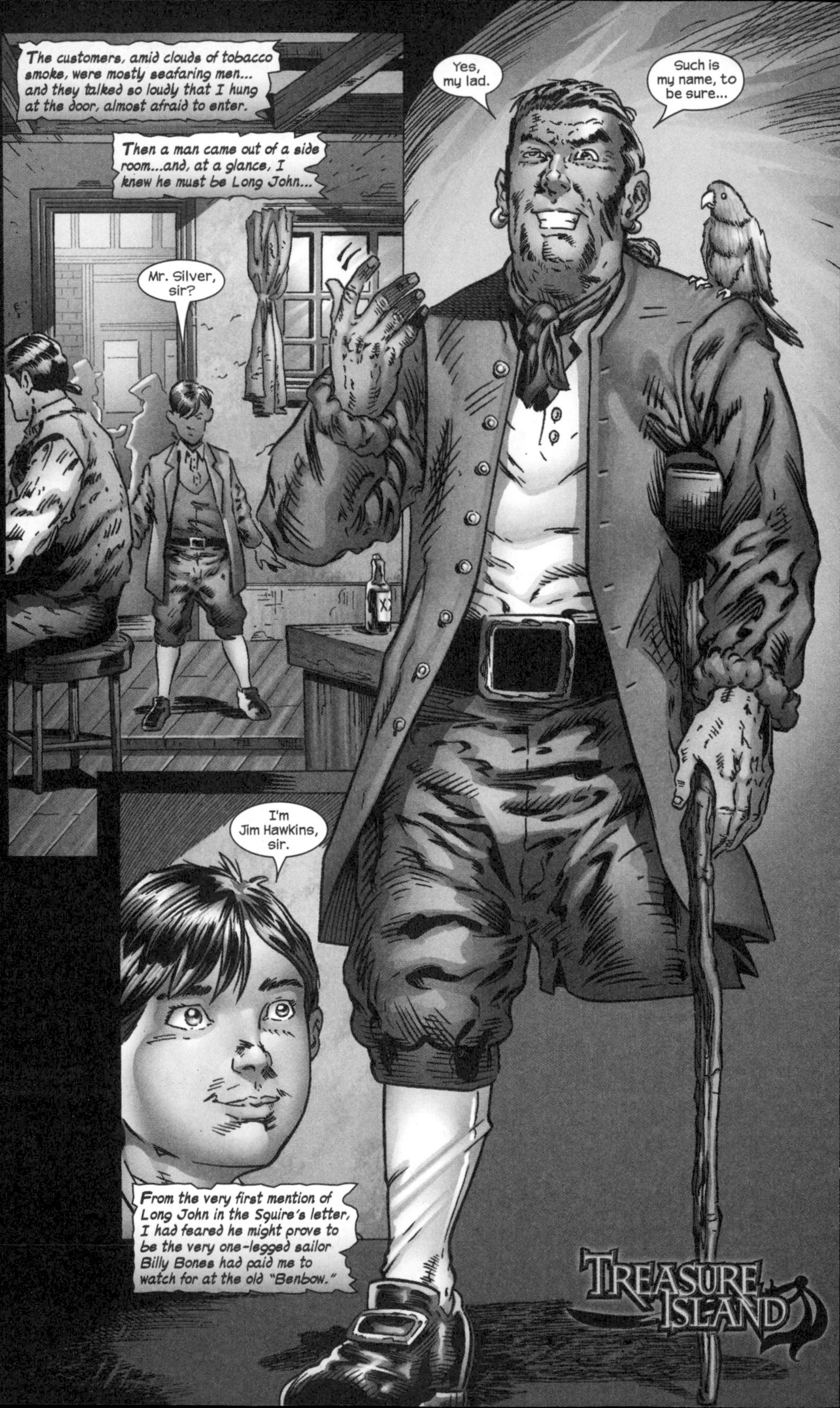
The customers, amid clouds of tobacco smoke, were mostly seafaring men... and they talked so loudly that I hung at the door, almost afraid to enter.
Then a man came out of a side room...and, at a glance, I knew he must be Long John...
Mr. Silver, sir?
Yes, my lad.
Such is my name, to be sure...
I'm Jim Hawkins, sir.
From the very first mention of Long John in the Squire's letter, I had feared he might prove to be the very one-legged sailor Billy Bones had paid me to watch for at the old "Benbow."
TREASURE ISLAND

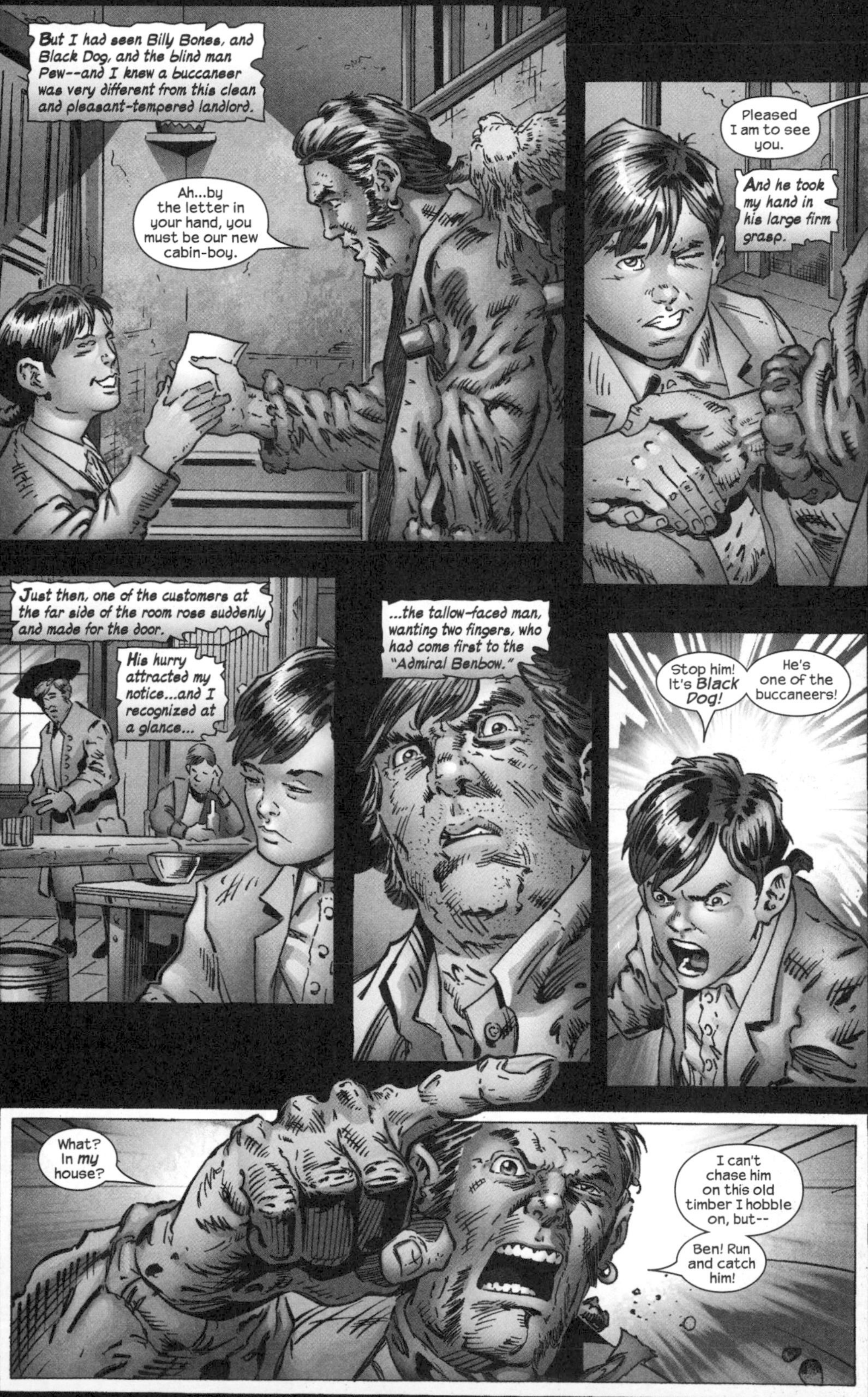
But I had seen Billy Bones, and Black Dog, and the blind man Pew--and I knew a buccaneer was very different from this clean and pleasant-tempered landlord.
Ah...by the letter in your hand, you must be our new cabin-boy.
Pleased I am to see you.
And he took my hand in his large firm grasp.
Just then, one of the customers at the far side of the room rose suddenly and made for the door.
His hurry attracted my notice...and I recognized at a glance...
...the tallow-faced man, wanting two fingers, who had come first to the "Admiral Benbow."
Stop him! It's Black Dog!
He's one of the buccaneers!
What? In my house?
I can't chase him on this old timber I hobble on, but--
Ben! Run and catch him!

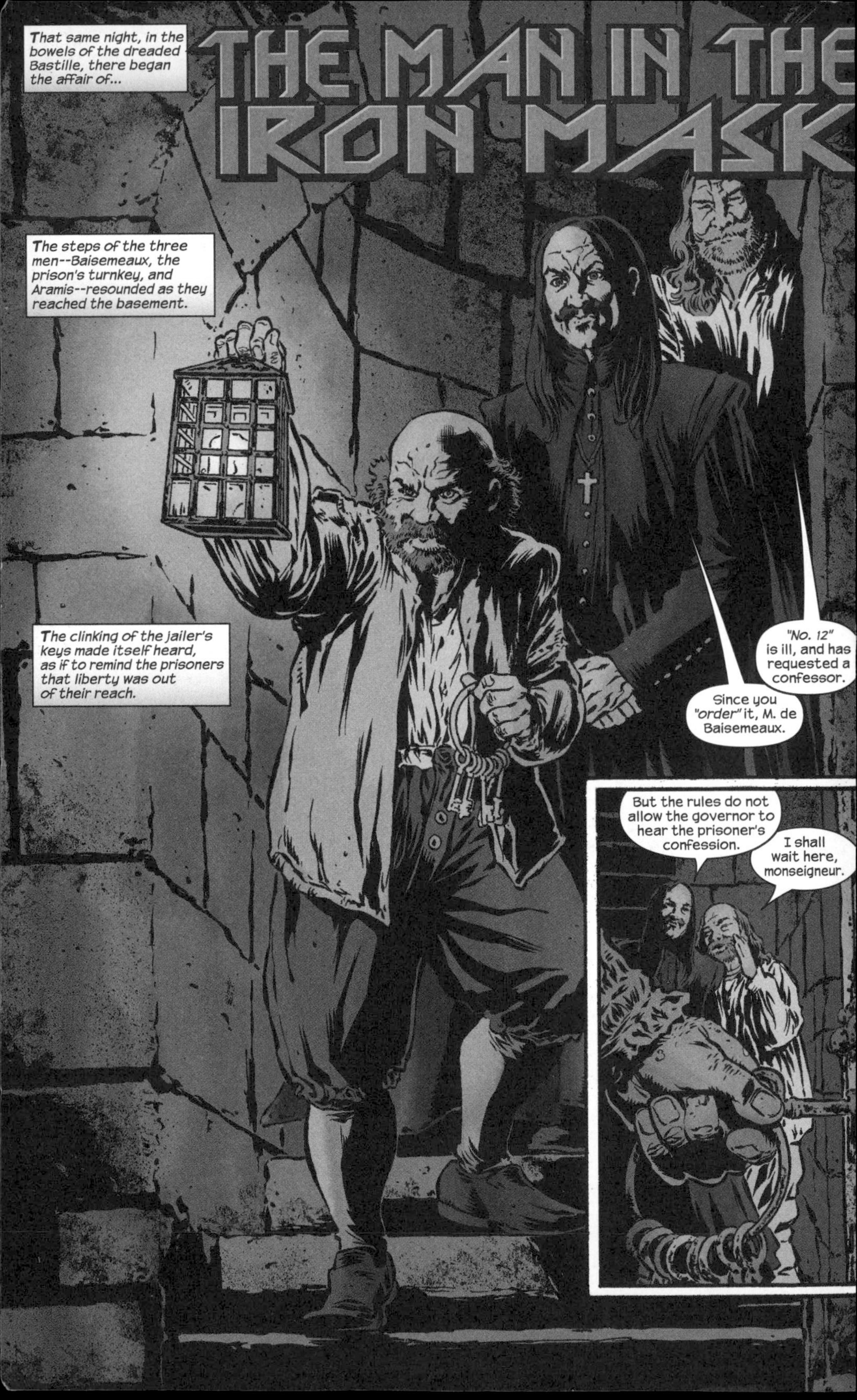
That same night, in the bowels of the dreaded Bastille, there began the affair of...
THE MAN IN THE IRON MASK
The steps of the three men--Baisemeaux, the prison's turnkey, and Aramis--resounded as they reached the basement.
The clinking of the jailer's keys made itself heard, as if to remind the prisoners that liberty was out of their reach.
"No. 12" is ill, and has requested a confessor.
Since you "order" it, M. de Baisemeaux.
But the rules do not allow the governor to hear the prisoner's confession.
I shall wait here, monseigneur.

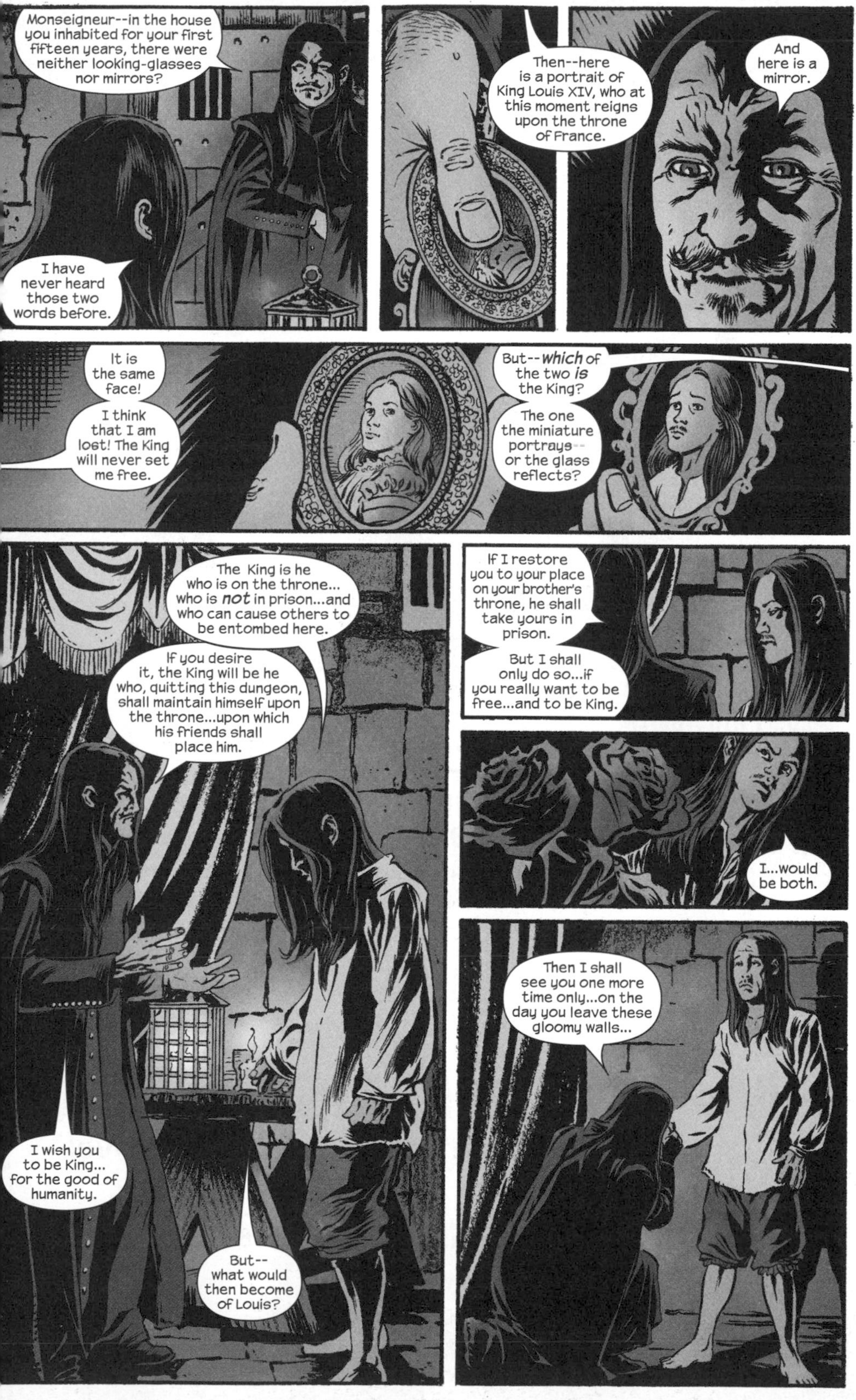
Monseigneur--in the house you inhabited for your first fifteen years, there were neither looking-glasses nor mirrors?
I have never heard those two words before.
Then--here is a portrait of King Louis XIV, who at this moment reigns upon the throne of France.
And here is a mirror.
It is the same face!
I think that I am lost! The King will never set me free.
But--which of the two is the King?
The one the miniature portrays--or the glass reflects?
The King is he who is on the throne... who is not in prison...and who can cause others to be entombed here.
If you desire it, the King will be he who, quitting this dungeon, shall maintain himself upon the throne...upon which his friends shall place him.
I wish you to be King... for the good of humanity.
But--what would then become of Louis?
If I restore you to your place on your brother's throne, he shall take yours in prison.
But I shall only do so...if you really want to be free...and to be King.
I...would be both.
Then I shall see you one more time only...on the day you leave these gloomy walls...

Epic tales that have tested time, like you've never seen before!

Check out these new titles from the Marvel Illustrated line!

**MARVEL ILLUSTRATED:
THE ODYSSEY**

By Homer

8-Issue Comic Series
Rated 13+

**THE WONDERFUL
WIZARD OF OZ**

By L. Frank Baum

8-Issue Comic Series
Rated 9+

**MARVEL ILLUSTRATED:
KIDNAPPED!**

By Robert Louis Stevenso

5-Issue Comic Series
Rated 9+

MARVEL ILLUSTRATED
Putting the "novel" back in Graphic Novel

ON SALE NOW
For a comic store near you, call 1-888-comicbook.